The

Message of Music

Also by PAUL H. APEL:
A Study of the Chicago Federation of Musicians
Music of the Americas, North and South

After a painting by Val. Janschek

WOLFGANG AMADEUS MOZART

The
Message of Music

by

Paul H. Apel, Ph.B., M.A.

VANTAGE PRESS   NEW YORK

WASHINGTON   CHICAGO   HOLLYWOOD   TORONTO

FIRST EDITION

FOREWORD

Why are some musical compositions a success for years, while others are only popular for a year or so?

Music has emotional appeal, but there is more to music. What are the other factors that make music an art?

In preparing this book for publication we wish to show that music has practical use in everyday life,; to help music acquire more intelligent appreciation from listeners as well as performers; to encourage the use of music in various and different ways. Poor music, half-listened to, is tolerated because the need for understanding fine music had never been cultivated in most of the adult population during an early and impressionable age.

Careful study of this book should help the music-lover become an intelligent and enthusiastic appreciator of the fine works already composed and should train him liberally to welcome new compositions. For those who love music no urging will be necessary; but to those whose love is rather lukewarm this book is addressed in the hope that they may grow more ardent. Some good will have been done if interest is stimulated, knowledge increased, and love for music deepened.

Every normal human being is potentially a lover of the best music, provided its possibilities are unfolded to him under helpful guidance. This is the service we wish to perform. That most people have an innate capacity for appreciating the best in music is proved by the fact that they get tired of anything but the best. All good music rests on a foundation of simple tunes and vital rhythms.

In spite of the peculiar characteristics of music, and the difficulty of comprehending logically the sounds and rhythms that float upon us, familiarity usually solves most of the problems of the music-lover. Since the composer is a thinker in tones, our perceptions must be so trained that, as we listen, we make sense out of the material of music. In order to grasp and enjoy its suggestive, rather than its definite, message, we must maintain alertness and concentration, and not be content with mere dreamy apathy. But acquiring musical understanding is not as difficult as it seems. "The person who desires to cultivate a discriminating taste in music may acquire the fundamental knowledge in a few short months. After that, one needs only to live in an atmosphere of good music until the acquired principles become unconsciously the moving factors underlying all attention to the art." Fatigue comes from hearing a swing melody repeated, and every successful popular melody runs that danger. Then it stops being successful. Contrast this with the fact that the more you hear a Symphony by Beethoven or Brahms, the more you like it, and the more you discover in it.

Repetition is the soul of music or enjoyment; he who hears more enjoys more. It is a step-by-step process. A very small proportion of those attending a recital or symphony concert begin to get their money's worth; at least 50 per cent of the musical structure is presented to ears without any capacity for receiving it. To be sure, a musical performance can become important to us only to the degree in which we are able to appreciate it. Even among music-lovers the ability to get the greatest enjoyment out of music is comparatively rare. Like every other art, it has much that lies below the surface and can be gained only through study. There is more to music than merely its emotional appeal.

Many of us have come to the conclusion that we are in need of being re-educated. The failures of the past must become the stimulus for leading us to a better future. Musical re-education aims at making music into a practical study for the average person. What we all need is a close study of the fundamentals of listening and understanding what we hear. Music has been, and still is, taught as something separate from life; yet it has a great deal to do with life.

Indeed, we all sham too much, and musically most of us

put up a bluff. We cannot know much about music merely by attending one or two concerts or operas a season. Music should be studied in the same spirit and from the same point of view as literature.

In order to enter into the essence, or spirit, of music, we must listen and think; as a result, we begin to feel and understand it. Afterwards, we may perform on an instrument if we desire—and if we are capable.

The object of teaching music under our plan is to understand this art and science, to intensify it, and so to enrich our lives. Music must be of practical use to everyone; and to make it that, we must cease pretending knowledge and get down to fundamentals. We must learn to capture a melody with our inner ear, to hear it not only as a melody—i.e., the relation of one tone to another—but as rhythm, and harmony, and tone-color. This requires that we listen, think, feel, and, finally, analyze. Music thus understood from the hearing side, studied and enjoyed through careful listening, thinking, and feeling, brings us closer to truth, to an understanding of life, and to a harmonization of conditions.

Most of us have gone on all these years deluding ourselves that an ability to perform a few easily forgotten "pieces" is knowledge of music. We have looked for the superficial effect rather than for real training. All music has for its end a double object—*self-expression* in terms of music, and the *interpretation* of the music of others. By far the larger part of our musical experience is with the latter. But the essential in all teaching of art is the *formation of correct ideals.*

What good is anything if it is not of practical, everyday use? Music should not be a thing apart from the rest of life. Music, being a language of sound, must be heard and understood in terms of sound. No one should try to sing or play anything until he has listened to, sung, and understood simple tunes. We must hear inwardly and think about, feel, and understand rhythm, melody, harmony, form, and tone-color in order to enter into the realization of music and find harmony and serenity within ourselves. No doubt, many enjoyments and benefits come from understanding.

It is obvious that sensibility, taste, and creative force cannot be acquired. Artistic education must limit itself modestly to the study of technique and the stimulation of latent emotional faculties of the pupil. Books on music and rules of harmony and counterpoint contained in treatises only help by stimulating music study. A deep and consistent study of the great works of all time is indispensable to anyone wishing to have a thorough knowledge of any art, music especially. It is the only way to penetrate the inner sanctuary. To help the public to acquire the means to undertake this study, to teach it to listen, think, feel, analyze, and judge, seems to us the only aim of a sensible musical education.

We are looking forward to the time when every public school will teach the *fundamentals of music from the standpoint of listening* rather than of performance. Rich and poor alike need this education. The main aim should be to develop qualities of appreciation, judgment, and taste.

All this book asks is that you read it and then listen to music with ears open. This book is written for the layman as well as for the professional musician. It tries to show how to get the most out of music by helping the reader to find much he did not suspect was there before. It is addressed to potential listeners rather than to performers. Again, it is written for the layman who is not at all musical as well as for the music-lover. It may prove a source of inspiration and benefit to all these.

It presupposes no knowledge on the part of the reader; neither does it admit a fundamental ignorance. It does not cover the ground in too technical a manner; nor does it try to exhaust its subject, for that would be impossible. It merely hopes to make the subject of music understandable, analyzing the effects of this so-called "mysterious" art upon the listener, whether layman or professional. It tries to find a reason for some of our reactions to a musical performance. Naturally, it assumes a universal instinct for such response, which indeed, we consider the natural capacity of every normal person who has an ear to distinguish one tone from another and prefers order to incoherence.

Some writers on music have insisted on highly technical scholarship, which makes the subject a dull and unpleasant study. Again, others have treated it solely in terms of the imagination, which sometimes makes for maudlin sentimentality.

Surely, music has been given much publicity, especially in the last thirty years, but most people are today still in the dark as to its meaning—"what it is all about." There must be active listening, not passive. Emotional response and sensitory pleasure do not occur spontaneously. In so-called "appreciation courses" (in schools and colleges) it is wrong to associate abstract musical compositions with nonmusical ideas—with stories and literary analogies that really have little or nothing to do with music. The imagination of the listener must be left free to function independently. The listener does not have to be supplied with nonmusical aids. Nothing can take the place of an independent grasp of *musical fundamentals,* those things which enable the composer and the performer to function in their art. These are indispensable to the listener's understanding and enjoyment of music. The listener needs some musical education besides the stimulation of his interest.

The trouble lies partly with music and partly with those who listen. The ignoring of popular taste, the contemptuous dismissal of obvious facts as of slight importance—these are factors in the surprisingly slow development of the public's real appreciation of music. Incidentally, advertising music as if it were a national brand of chewing gum, for instance, will not do, chiefly because music affects people in different ways.

If we succeed in opening to the reader a new world of beauty and joy by calling attention to the things to be listened for most of all, we shall not have written in vain. Books are useful only in so far as they help us to form independent judgments.

There's music in the sighing of a reed;
There's music in the gushing of a rill;
There's music in all things if men had ears—
Their earth is but an echo of the spheres.

—BYRON

Music alone endures as the universal language of Nature, speaking to us in wonderful and mysterious accents. In vain do we strive to arrest and realize them by symbols. But, alas, our artificial system of hieroglyphics hardly enables us even to divine what reaches our ears.

E. T. A. HOFFMANN

If I had to live my life again, I would have made it a rule to read some poetry and listen to some music at least once every week; for perhaps the part of my brain now atrophied would then have been kept active through use. The loss of these tastes is a loss of happiness, and may possibly be injurious to the intellect, and more probably to the moral character, by enfeebling the emotional part of our nature.

C. DARWIN

A thing is completely our own when we understand and enjoy it. . . . The ultimate purpose of music must be to increase human pleasure and understanding and give enjoyment and exaltation through its beauty.

P. H. APEL

For the common things of every day
God gave man speech in the common way.

For the deeper things men think and feel
He gave the poet words to reveal.
But for heights and depths no word could reach
He gave Music, the soul's own speech.

We only get out of anything as much as we bring to it;
this general law of life applies also to music. Music protects
itself by only giving just as much as is demanded of it.

To know is to understand;
To understand is to appreciate;
To appreciate is to enjoy.

The greatest thing a human soul ever does in this world
is to see something and tell what he sees in a plain way.
Therefore: "Make it plain."

CONTENTS

The
Message of Music

WHAT IS MUSIC?

---

1. DISTINCTION BETWEEN MUSIC AND THE OTHER ARTS

MANY books have been written to explain the fine arts. But more often than not, books concerning a "special subject" give us so much technical detail that we do not understand them. We want a clear idea of what "art" means. After all, if rightly presented, no subject is "dry." If rightly presented, "art" is a very fascinating and human subject.

Art and the arts are evolution in other forms, a moving up from the lowest forms of life to higher ones—a spreading out in other ways. When man's mind grew and he began to *think,* to become aware of his feelings, there was no limit to his development. All that is, or happens, in the world is either nature or art. And anything that is not nature, in some way or other, is art. Nature put all the matter into the world. Man combines that matter and uses it. Note the Latin root *ar,* to put or fix things together. Articulated language and the fine arts are the two great means of expression. Words are used for ordinary expressions, and music for the more abstract ones. Man puts things together for use or to please himself and others—for practical reasons or for reasons of pleasure. Thus we have the useful arts (the practical arts) and the fine arts (the arts of beauty). Incidentally, science is "the knowing how" of any art, just as art is the "doing."

The *useful arts* (the art of agriculture, the art of mining, the art of weaving, the art of government, etc.) grew out of man's ambition to improve and perfect the practical ends and aims of life. The *fine arts*, the arts that produce things of pleasure (architecture, sculpture, painting—the arts of form or shape and of space—and music, literature, and dance—the arts of movement and of time) came out of man's search for beauty in various ways and are the means for conveying his emotions and thoughts to others. Works of art are distinguished by the discipline and direction, emotion and idea, which the hand, eyes, and heart of the artist have imposed. Men who follow the useful arts can be trained, although some of them have an instinct for their work, or craft, which often seems innate; but men who pursue the fine arts—the inspired artists—have to possess an inborn genius for their activity. Training will perfect it, but the art instinct has to be born in them.

All the fine arts are related and have certain fundamental principles in common. The fine arts, being related in time, permit us to perceive present objects reflected on the past and shaping the future. Indeed, it is by "listening to music that we understand how every set and thought is reminiscent (and at the same time) prophetic." No one art is separate from the others or developed entirely on its own. In fact, there is a close, intimate connection among them all.

Architecture is a visible and a static art, an art to be seen and examined from any angle or viewpoint. It expresses group, or national feelings as well as individual emotions, and reflects group as well as individual standards of beauty. These standards take solid and permanent shape in stone, cement, steel, glass, aluminum, and marble, in the form of cathedrals and other great edifices. About 2,000 years ago Vitruvius in Rome declared that architecture must fulfill three conditions: *commodity*, or *usefulness; firmness*, or *sound structure;* and *delight*, which grows from a sensitive, poetic, and lucid development of function and structure. Through these the architect expresses the idea and purpose of the building; and in this expression—the handling of space, the clarity of detail, the adjustment of proportion and scale, the revelation of beauty of material, and the relationship of building and site—he arrives at that "delight," that quality of purposeful esthetic beauty which marks the difference between architecture and mere construction.

Sculpture is a visible and plastic art that mainly emphasizes form, or pattern; it makes a record of the beautiful, especially of the human or animal body. It imitates; it holds the beautiful movement of life fast in marble, ivory, bronze, etc., for all time; it also catches the rhythm of life as it passes, and holds and keeps it for us for all time.

Painting, a visible art, mainly emphasizes content or expression through the medium of color; it is free and unlimited in expressing abstract beauty or in imitating things. In a painting there is an object represented as well as the formal beauty with which the artist endows it. The painter can put on canvas anything and everything—man and all his belongings, animals on earth, birds in the air, fishes in the water, seas, skies, landscapes, mountains, deserts, houses, utensils—and makes them seem alive and real.

Music is an audible art and an art of time. Again, music is the most moving, subtle, articulate, swiftly expressive of all the arts man has created. It is the expression by voices or by instruments of melodic, rhythmic, or harmonious tones. "Music is an attempt to reach the ultimate realities through the medium of ordered and beautiful sound" (Vaughan Williams). It became an art through the very slow development of musical notation and forms. It is an invisible art of dynamic, and not static, content; the notes on paper do not alter the fact that music only exists when it is sounded. It can only be experienced in the formal sequence established by the composer. The form of the tonal structure is as essential to its existence and expressiveness as any amount of imagination, emotion, and melodic invention that went into its making. Music is sound that has meaning and beauty; it puts sound together so that our ears recognize combinations regulated by rhythms (the beat, the swing, the time movement). But when we look at music more closely, we find that even musical experience cannot be understood solely in terms of sensuous impressions and feelings. Full understanding and appreciation of the formal relations of sounds in music call upon cognitive powers which often require considerable feats of memory, recognition, and anticipation. No other art requires of its devotees the application of memory to so high a degree. When music sounds, it is absolutely essential that the memory be active and retentive in order to comprehend all of its manifestations. Music goes far beyond the senses, although we perceive it through our ears; it has a magic power no other art possesses. It has something in harmony within us and gives us inspiration; and this something behind the sounds calls up in us all sorts of dream-pictures and visions. That is the mystic side of music.

Literature (*poetry* and *drama*) is an audible art, a verbal art, an art of words which expresses thoughts or ideas in beautiful language or in rhythmical form that reason can understand. Literature is essentially an art to which we listen. The fact that a poem may not be read aloud does not change the fact that it is an audible art, an art of dynamic, and not static, content. The application of memory is not required in so high a degree for the comprehension of a visual art. In literature there is need of associative memory and of the capacity to hold clear in mind the sequence and interrelations of ideas. The rhythm of speech in poetry requires a rather delicate and trained ear. In poetry we have the *epic*, which treats of the deeds of heroes and the fortunes of a people; the *lyric*, in which is expressed joy, love, sorrow, or hope; and the *dramatic*, in which people live and act before us and, by collisions and conflicts, convey the lessons of motive and consequence, cause and result. Thus, the drama (theater) is fundamentally an art, a stirring record of man's inquiry into the meaning of life and of his spiritual aspirations. Prose may express whatever rises or falls in human passion and feeling; or it may delineate the all-inclusive realm of human ideas, work, fate, belief.

The *dance*, the simplest and most concrete form of art, is an extension of bodily rhythm; it is rhythm manifested by bodily movement. The art of the dance (*choreography*) is the art of movement, the art of time and space. The dance catches life as it passes us and holds us for the time being. In the *ballet* and in *pantomime*, the bodily positions and facial expressions communicate the aims of the artist. There is the abstractive, graceful personality of the dancer; there are the figures performed, which correspond to the formal aspect of music—the form or pattern; and there is the spirit of animation which the dancer infuses into the movements.

All the fine arts express life, and the general character of the arts has depended upon physical means for embodiment. Furthermore, all great art transcends the subject matter and provides enjoyment on an artistic level quite apart from what it is saying. All the fine arts have value in proportion to what they express. Expression is the opposite of impression. Impression is made possible by the senses of seeing, hearing, and feeling. We get realistic, objective impressions from the physical, outer world, the experience of our daily life. It is the work of the creative artist to translate these sensual impressions into expressions in order to impress others in turn. The fine arts express human nature, racial nature, the feelings of individuals, and the characteristics of nations. All the arts of every great people in any age or time have something about them—namely, the spirit of the race—which relates them to each other. All of us can understand the arts. All of us can realize the story of art—its edifices, monuments, paintings, etchings, music, poems and plays; its dances, with all their color, human passions, and tragedies; its something *plus*. If we get the meaning, the essence, the gist, the kernel of knowledge out of enjoyable hours spent with the fine arts, our time has been well employed.

The arts of architecture, painting and literature are *definitive;* they record literal experiences; and to create a great work in any of these mediums we must take the subject from life, from nature, the visible, material world. No matter how imaginative the art work may be, it must depict, describe, or interpret something; for "art is simply the bringing into relief of the obscure thought of nature; a simplification of the lines, a falling into place of groups otherwise invisible." The fire of inspiration brings out, as it were, designs traced beforehand in thought. The mysterious grows clear;

the confused becomes plain; what is complicated becomes simple. In short, art reveals nature by interpreting its intentions and formulating its desires. The great artist is the simplifier.

But while *art simplifies and reveals nature,* it *does not explain it;* art itself is inexplicable. It opens the soul to the inexhaustibility of nature. And this is the secret of its power and its joy, this setting free of the soul from all limitations, for limitations make for unhappiness.

The raw material of architecture, painting, sculpture and literature—the building material, marble, colors, or words— is concrete, tangible, and definitive. The raw material of music and the dance—fleeting rhythms and waves of sounds combined into tonal patterns and designs—is in its very nature most incoherent, intangible, and elusive. Music must get its inception not from concrete reality but from the spirit, from ideas, sentiments, and emotions.

Of all the six liberal, or fine, arts, *literature* and the *dance* are nearest to *music,* because they likewise *exist in the element of time;* whereas *architecture, sculpture,* and *painting exist in the element of space.*

In the art of architecture we cannot tolerate a mixed style, bad proportion, nor excessive ornamentation. The architect plans his edifice not only for convenience but also for its fitness and unity with its setting. Architecture is great only when it arouses our feeling by its enduring strength, its good proportion, its simple outlines, its choice materials, and its fine setting.

Sculpture deals at times with designs and forms that are far from representational; and painting has yet more to do with purely idealistic forms and, in addition, often uses color as an esthetic end in itself. The purpose of the figurative arts is not just pure imitation of the aspects of nature. After all, the model is taken merely as a pretext to express a symbol. Differences in interpretation depend upon the artist's point of view about life, his education and training, and the epoch when he was creatively active. Climbing a mountain, the same landscape looks different every few steps.

In the art of painting only those pictures are great which

take the feeling beyond their frames. The use of line and spacing, of form and balance, of design and rhythm, of balance between light and shade, is but a means to a much greater and more important end. In fact, the only end which can justify a great picture is the identification of the human emotions with nature, which the painting simplifies and suggests. Color possesses a psychological value and can impress and express the personality. There are about a thousand distinguishable hues and thousands of tints and shades that the normal eye can grasp. Colors are seen, we know, because light waves of different lengths are reflected from objects about us. Colors may be endlessly combined and varied, much like the tones of music that are combined into harmonious chords. These chords may be repeated in simple melodies or in majestic symphonies. Either consciously or unconsciously, artists strive to do the same in fine paintings.

The strength of a painting lies in its power to arouse unanalyzed emotions. The painter organizes color, line, mass, light and shade to project emotion. *Emotion is the sole source of great pleasure in art*. Thought, again, is limitation, and only the complete surrender of self to the power of a great painting can assure for us what art really has to offer.

But if a great painting brings nature to us simplified, it is more important that it straightway take us to nature. It is a setting free of the human soul, a sudden release from the fetters of mind and the world of the senses into the soundless, limitless spaces of nature and of the emotions. And this sudden, unexpected release is the cause of what we call "ecstasy." Now, at last, we are one with the great mysteries.

In the art of literature only those poems are great which arouse lasting emotions because of their vital rhythms, their unexcelled choice of words, and their deep poetic thought. The poet brings together a group of various images and ideas into a whole, of words whose sound and rhythm arouse a distinctive emotional experience. The dramatist selects certain aspects of character and sequences of events and puts them together into a unified whole whose real purpose is to convey a way of feeling. Poetry comes between prose and music. It has words and thoughts, like prose, and it has rhythm and sound, like music.

Other arts convey an ideal longing connected with a precise message; music alone expresses that longing in an isolated state. Before the painter can stir our aspirations, he must show us an image. The musician expresses the longing we would have had, had we seen the picture, and the aspiration which he arouses is entirely detached; we can connect with it any form of beauty in our personal experience.

The subject matter of music is longing, aspiration, and expectation, in the abstract. This distinction between music and the other arts is fundamental. It is the very nature of music to be absolute. In so far as music adds itself to any program, it must to that extent be practiced. The result may be entirely satisfying to the unmusical, but it never will be music at its best. Music finds its perfection in itself, without relation to other objects, as it does not use symbols of something else. In addition to the literal record, symbols must suggest something over and above, something *plus*. This something *plus* is recognized and appreciated not by the imagination and the emotions. The architect may build only a plain house, a shelter, or he may suggest the abstract desirability of a house in general. Thus, any art, whatever else it accomplishes, expresses in addition that longing, that aspiration, that expectation of the soul. The painter tends to depict something; the poet and dramatist write about something; but music works with a medium that is naturally and immediately nonrepresentational. The composer conveys his emotions, feelings, and thoughts through his music. Music is the art which is characteristically representative; all the other fine arts may be either representative or presentative.

Langhans, with true Teutonic accuracy, says, "Music, by reason of the incorporeity of its material, the quickly passing tone, and the absence of any prototype or corrective in the visible world surrounding us, is justly called the most subjective of the arts." Wagner sought to express through his music dramas the "purely human," by which he seems to mean those deep, underlying affective states that move our lives into their various channels. Evidently, he dimly sensed what Bergson has since made clear, namely, that the modern world is dominated by the rational intellect; and he forsook it as a source of subjects for opera and turned to the world of myth and legend where the characters are free of material complexities and move in obedience to the emotional states that sway the spirit.

Music cannot be translated into other terms, because it is untranslatable; but just the same, it is intelligible to the human mind. True, music cannot express all things, even though it may embody moral ideas. But *its strength lies in depicting emotions* rather than thoughts; in *appealing to the spirit* rather than to the senses; in *promoting intangible moods* rather than concrete forms; and in *depicting ideality* rather than reality. It is the fluent, free, and beautiful form of expression of our deeper feelings and impulses, which cannot be made known by shape, color, gesture, or words. Music is nondefinitive and is what it is in itself alone. Unlike the other arts, it lacks any model in the realm of nature. It has to work out its own laws, and spontaneity and directness are the result. It is not imitative, utilitarian, or bound by arbitrary conventions. Schopenhauer was right when he declared that, while the other arts give us a picture of life, a mere presentation of life, *music is life itself*.

Also, music, unlike the other arts, is largely independent of exterior associations. No matter how imaginative the treatment, in order to convey his meaning, the architect, sculptor, or painter generally use means that are closely associated with the world as we experience it. Even literature, which is closely akin to music in its emotional and imaginative suggestiveness, must use the medium of language, a medium that is part of everyday life.

Why is music such an appealing and dignified kind of human experience? Why does music—pure tonal design—objectify and convey such a universal and powerful appeal and such varied emotional significance?

In its strict sense, art is the presentation of feeling and emotion through a planned pattern. The essential function of all art is to "express and objectify emotion in design."

The art and science of music, in a certain sense, are the products of man's thought and emotion; but back of all are laws independent of all that man can say or do. A study of these laws should be made earnestly so as to reveal to us the origin of the deepest enjoyment and satisfaction that harmonies can afford. The underlying principles discovered will show the sources of inspiration of all art, of all peoples, of all time. A sure method of finding the elements desired is to look deeply into the inner significance of all the music which can be heard—the relationships of all the various types. After all, observation and study serve a useful purpose and are an imperative duty. Observation, consideration, and comprehension result in knowledge; while perception, control, and realization bring power.

An essential characteristic of all art is disinterestedness—the absence of all purposes beyond itself. The disinterested nature of music implies that music is an end for itself. To those to whom music is more than a titillation of the senses, it has absolute value. It is one of the things that makes life worth living.

A work of art, whether it is a wing of the Parthenon, a Rodin figure, a Rembrandt portrait, a Whistler painting, a Frost poem, a performance by Russian ballet dancers, or a Schubert song, represents *a means of communication* among minds—between creator and beholders. It therefore requires at least two parties for its functioning, a giver and a taker, one to give out a message, the other to take it in. Something is passed from one person to another. The fact that this something is intuitive rather than logical, that it must be expressed in an object rather than in ordinary words, does not blunt the point in the least. Incidentally, the dramatist and the composer require an intermediary between themselves and their audience, i.e. the actor and the performer of music—the *creator,* the *interpreter,* and the *listener*.

Art is a product which is inevitably subject to mental and physical conditions, events, and all the other factors of human experiences. Psychologically, all these influences work through the instinct of imitation and the mental faculty of suggestion.

For the creation of an art work, there must first be a person's feeling about some aspect of life or experience and then a recognition of the truth that his feeling may be objectified in a certain arrangement of stones or marble, granite or metal, colors, words, sounds, or movements. These are in addition to the required technique, of course, which permit him to manipulate the necessary materials.

Art is the expression of the feeling for form, or beauty. Beauty is the cause of art and also its effect. A work of art is a product of man by which art material is expressed in an artistic manner, one which is capable of communicating its artistic form to a beholder. The man who creates such a product and so expresses his personality in his work is an artist; anyone capable of responding to it for what it is, is the true lover of art. The artist gives us much help in directing us toward the ideals of peace by creating pleasures of various types as well as universal visions. Needless to say, our appreciation of a work of art depends largely upon the degree of understanding and insight which we ourselves possess.

Art is not beyond the reach of anyone who really cares. Anyone who has learned to share in the consideration of the work of the artist cannot thereafter be indifferent. Thus, learning to discriminate intelligently may in time end in learning how to enjoy and to love art.

When we consider the love of great art, and reflect upon it, we find that it is rather intuitive. The flash of pleasure, the instant lift of the spirit, which comes upon seeing or hearing a beautiful work of art is one of the purest satisfactions of life. No doubt, most of us have this rare experience only by chance. Surely, it needs to be experienced frequently and regularly. It needs to be made an ineradicable part of our lives, especially in children.

To recognize a work of art, we must have the ability to perceive that stones or marble, granite or metal, colors, words, sounds, or movements, *do* embody a way of feeling about some aspect of life or experience. Naturally, if the beholder senses only stones or marble, granite or metal, etc., as such, then the whole thing becomes meaningless and should not be dignified by the words "work of art."

The moment we take from art its warm, intuitive awareness of life, its burden of feeling, it becomes utterly meaningless. Art can justify itself only through its ability to convey intuitive feelings. Art is incapable of dealing with logical meanings. Furthermore, merely decorative art—art which consists of patterned stones, granite, marble, metal; uninspired colors, words, sounds; or movements without genuine feeling underlying them—is trivial in its origins and in its ends. It may serve as a means of titillating the senses but remains completely unimportant so far as the whole of the inner man is concerned.

Appreciation of art is not a mechanical impulse but a spontaneous one. It is a personal expression by the individual, and so we have to be prepared to accept violent differences of opinion. These stark differences of opinion indicate not only the vitality of the art of music, painting, the drama, and the like, but also the intellectual, emotional, and spiritual vitality of listeners and beholders sensitive and independent enough to express themselves.

To understand works of art means to observe not their conformity with reality but rather those spiritual values which the artist makes visible and audible in them. Even science and philosophy make use of images and symbols in order to make clear the real facts which cannot be grasped in the usual sense.

Feeling, then, *is the very essence of art;* and depth of feeling, we all know, is attained only through experience of life. This does not necessarily mean the exhaustive experience of what we call "real" life; but it may consist largely of a sensitive and comprehending living of those vicarious lives which conversation, study and contemplation make possible. A singer or player who is a beginner must make sure that he has a reasonably wide and deep knowledge of life. Without it, he cannot hope to understand and transmit the meaning which informs the music. And here we come to an important point, namely: music is only one of the six liberal, or fine, arts which requires an interpreter to convey the knowledge which the creator has gained. The composer places symbols on a piece of paper which require an artist-musician to make audible to the listener. In fact, a person who is to sing or play something must first find out the intended meaning of the composition, then do his best to convey that meaning to an audience.

What is the significance of music? What does it *really* mean? Extreme formalists declare that it does not mean anything at all. They say that if music has any significance you could state it in plain words; and furthermore, a piece of music may be submitted to the most searching analysis and yet proved to be made up of tones and nothing else—simply differences in pitch, intensity, quality, all combined into various patterns of greater or lesser complexity by means of rhythm, harmony, form, and tone-color. Such extreme formalists also say that music is incapable of expressing even the simplest idea in a manner which will be adequate and intelligible.

Of course, all this is not true. Music *has* meaning. Inability to state that meaning in plain words is no proof that it does not exist. Even scientific analysis cannot find everything there is in an object, for its significant elements are apt to escape from the test tube. There is something in music besides mere tone. Music is quite capable of expressing powerfully not only simple ideas but also amazingly complex ones. Our language is the means of communication between human beings; but is it able to express intuitions, and the like? Just how good is language even in the simple world of the senses? So with musical ideas, which are very real to our emotions and our mind but still not translatable into words. Music is a language by itself and can and does convey its message without the aid of some other language. The acceptance of this cardinal fact is fundamental to any understanding of the art. While music has resemblances to architecture, to sculpture, to painting, to the graceful movements of the dance, it is none of these arts. Often the terms of the sister arts are borrowed to describe music, because their principles, which deal with more concrete subjects, are more definite and therefore more easily understood than the rather arbitrary terms that serve to describe music. Sometimes music tells a story almost with the force of words, yet the music is neither the story nor the words. It is music— and nothing else. To be sure, music may be expressed in scientific terms, just as a cow may be summed up as so many pounds of matter combined according to well-understood chemical formulas and acting on the basis of perfectly comprehensible physical laws; but we are not justified for that reason in saying that music, or the cow, is nothing but what is indicated by chemical and physical formulas. Let us remember that the job of science is not to tell what the *whole* of reality is like but merely to deal with that part of reality which corresponds to man's cognitive faculties and to bring it into a system of controllable cause-and-effect sequences wherever possible. There is more than one "method of knowing," and the known object cannot be summed up by one means alone. What escapes from the test tube may be, and often is, far more important than what remains for inspection and analysis.

To repeat, *music embodies all the fundamental principles of all the arts*—namely, an endless variety of group spirit, form, content, and of ideas—no matter what medium is used for its presentation. Of all the arts, music is the most deeply a living art. Architecture and sculpture are static. Painting, by means of color, line, and space, only suggests rhythm and atmosphere. Literature is limited to the use of words, which carry only the meaning that has been given them by custom, and, by the way, suffer by translation and transposition. Dancing is limited to rhythm and movement. Again, the arts of architecture, sculpture, painting and literature may convey practical knowledge, but it is not so with music. We accept and admire things in music we do not find in literature. Music can sustain an emotional intensity impossible by any other art. In music there is no possible comparison with everyday reality. No wonder Romanticism attains an expression in music which it does not achieve in literature, painting, or sculpture.

All arts make their appeal to the higher nature of man, but music does this in a greater degree than any other art.

Music is free from many limitations of a material kind. Music is beauty in dynamic form; it is the truest expression of the Eternal Intelligence, the freest and subtlest manifestation of beauty. As its medium is plastic, invisible, and capable of endless variety, so is its appeal to man's spiritual nature. Music, in its fullest degree, is an expression of life. Is it not obvious, then, that music might well be called the greatest of all the arts?

Music is the special art of the modern world. It has its roots in the folk songs of European peoples and services of the medieval church. The backbone of musical art is the orchestra, including, of course, the human voice as one type of instrument. As the orchestra is inseparably bound up with mechanical invention, the invention of a musical instrument or enlargement of the range and quality of an existing one means an enlargement of musical thought. Each enlarged musical thought in turn calls for enlarged musical technique; thus, music has become the most progressive of the fine arts. It is music which has placed the modern world artistically on a par with the great ages of the past. A Bach, a Beethoven, a Brahms, a Wagner symphony or opera, rendered by one of our best orchestras or singers of our day, is as marvelous an artistic achievement as a painting by Raphael or a Gothic cathedral.

2. THE FUNCTION OF ART

A. MUSIC CREATES FOR US THE SPIRITUAL WORLD— THE WORLD OF THE BEAUTIFUL

Music has great virtues, and it has always occupied a prominent place among human activities. Music has been used among all peoples of all times, being associated with dancing, magic rites, religious cults, poetry and the drama, war, and as a means of expressing sentiments and emotions. Our sense of the beautiful should be cultivated to give us an antidote against the ravages and depredations of the machine and to obtain gracefulness and a true sense of proportion of life. *Beauty* is essential. Of all the artistic forms, music is the most vital. The senses of smell, taste, and hearing touch life most intensely. Painting, sculpture, architecture, and dancing are the "beholder" arts; they are the ones that are contemplated esthetically. But in the arts of music and literature, the listener, reader, or onlooker relive the art work whenever they are esthetically experienced. Through its rhythmic pulse, music animates life and evokes a physical response. Through its melody, harmony, form, and tone-color it stimulates an intellectual and emotional response which recreates moods and emotions. Music represents artistic perfection. The greatest virtue of art, in general—and music, in particular—lies in the power of this artistic perfection to create a world not based on the outward and the visible but on that invisible realm of thought, feeling, and emotion which is our real world—the world of the *True,* the *Beautiful,* and the *Good.* Since earliest times *man has continually sought some escape from reality.*

In the matchless tales of the *Arabian Nights,* the source of modern fiction, as well as in the tales of the *Decameron,* as told by Boccaccio, which mark the beginning of the modern love story, and, also, in the simple folk tunes, which form the beginning of the suite, the sonata, the symphony, and the tone poem—in all these we may note the dreams of the common people. We realize then what an important part dreams have in the spiritual economy of life. We all must hope, and we all must escape from the drudgery of our lot. To attempt to describe minutely these feelings and tendencies is, obviously, impossible. Indeed, the deepest feelings of all are just those which, because they are remote from the material things of life, cannot be analyzed. Surely, art takes us out of ourselves and makes us free. Thus, art is one of the greatest blessings of life. Indeed, the very fact that the printed page of a book or a simple, beautiful tune well rendered can do this today shows the great advancement of the average intelligence in modern times.

The fine arts—music, dancing, painting, literature, sculpture, and architecture—all have this in common. In common with ethical inspiration, knowledge, and faith, they have the capacity to *lift us completely out of ourselves, to escape* from self-love, *from ordinary reality,* and to provide a relief from the forces of science and commercialism, a place of refuge from materialism. All arts express exaltation and intelligence. They are supreme expressions of the human spirit.

Now, do the fine arts simply entertain us? Are they a mere escape mechanism? Or have the arts a fundamental role in the social life of our time? *Art serves as a means of recreation. It provides escape; it communicates; it provides revelation of form and content; it evokes ideal beauty; it provides a means of self-expression;* and it *serves religious, ornamental, commercial, and other ends.* But to emphasize only these functions (as many recent writers have done) ignores those purely esthetic values which make art great. And art is a terminal value which enriches directly the life of any society. Instead of turning their backs upon society, as did some practitioners of modern art at the turn of the century, artists must realize that their materials, their opportunities for creating art, the sources of their inspiration, and their very reasons for being, originate in their environment. Indeed, artists, more than any other members of society, can further the values of art and create objects for enriched esthetic experience.

Man has built for himself a perfect world of ideal beauty to which he should give a direct and involuntary response, an ideal beauty which should satisfy his eternal longing and make him forget the imperfections, inconsistencies, and injustices of his own life. Very naturally, his make-up has caused him to seek perfection somewhere, and so the development of the liberal, or fine, arts was the outcome of this ever active striving.

It is this direct and involuntary response to ideal beauty that places man above the higher animals (who, by the way, possess some of the "virtues" that we treasure as our own: loyalty, self-sacrifice, ambition—another word for "self-preservation," or "survival of the fittest"—and even love).

The thrill of a direct response to all ideal beauty is indescribable. It is one of the joys of life that cannot be denied to the poorest of us. That is why artists throughout the ages have set themselves the task of expressing the abstract in concrete art forms, for thus do we realize beauty most directly and inevitably. But in no case have they been so successful as the composer of absolute music. An architect, a sculptor, a painter, a writer must deal with tangible, definite things. He may give his works an abstract title, such as boldness, courage, calmness, despair, ecstasy, agitation, joy, sorrow, love, hate. But we see only a concrete figure or group of figures endowed with such qualities. The composer has a wider range; he deals with intangible, elusive things. Through the medium of absolute music he comes closest to the ideal of abstract expression. He can make us *feel* courage or despair, calmness or ecstasy, joy or sorrow, by the direct transfer of his own moods or emotions. (And if he is a genius, he needs no program to tell us of his intentions.) Human emotion and character can be, and often are, affected by music. All the truly great music (certain pieces by great composers, as well as certain folk music) has this capacity. To this extent, therefore great music really expresses the abstract in terms of the concrete. It is obvious that the esthetic thrill comes most easily through music, for the stimulus is more direct and unmistakable than in any other kind of art. Yet we do not know how much this response to great art may be due to tradition and to the association of ideas.

Psychologists tell us that music affects people in different ways:

1. As a sensory, emotional attitude (hope and despair, etc.). Very little discrimination is needed for this kind of listening, and no complete satisfaction results from it.

2. As a personal, associative experience. Music can arouse all sorts of associations, many of which have little or nothing to do with the music itself. (A melody or rhythm may remind listeners of a day spent at a certain place and so awaken some very personal associations.)

3. As an intellectual, enjoyable experience. Some consider music as such—ie., without reference to anything else—just a matter of beauty of melody, of form and structure, and of the technique of its performance.

However, music as an art has suffered because to many

it is a harmless amusement or a gentle emotional stimulant, not something to be studied and lived with until the trained ear and awakened mind perceive its real beauty.

Music creates for us a spiritual, or immaterial, world, one not made up of actual objects, theories, dogmas, or philosophies. It provides a means of forgetting the cares of the day, a way to rise above the sordid limitations, the various imperfections, inconsistencies, and injustices which we experience right along.

It is one of the main functions of art to give expression to the feeling-tendencies (not a specific emotion brought about by some external happenings, but rather an emotional disposition that is common to all mankind) which otherwise would be frustrated. If our feeling for beauty could find no outlet, it would die. It is easy to understand that our feeling-tendencies may deteriorate by disuse or be cultivated in a proper environment. The feeling-tendencies of our nature crave suitable expression; hence we turn to the fine arts. *Music, the art of feeling, is the most basic and universal of the arts.* All over the universe, feeling is the most basic to life. Wherever there is life, there is feeling. Of all creatures, man, no doubt, is the most alive and feels most widely and intensely. Hence his desire for the esthetic. It is in music that he finds great satisfaction for his craving. Music provides the most complete expression of feelings as pure feeling. *Music plays an important role in all our activities and interests*—in our work, our recreation, our play, our joys, our sorrows, and our worship. Needless to say, these countless feeling-tendencies are hidden away in the subconscious, and we are hardly aware of them until they are elicited by some stimulus. It is the indefinable element in any art that constitutes its strength. There is always a suggestion of something that we cannot express in words, something that eludes and yet impresses us. To express adequately in words the emotions that appear in the flow of the great musical compositions would tax the wit of man.

B. ESTHETICS OF MUSIC

Esthetics is the theory of the beautiful and artistic. It

seeks to find the laws which determine the criterion for art. Esthetic theory considers the relation of art to life, nature, truth, ethics. Esthetic theories have been formulated by Plato, Aristotle, Kant, Hegel, Schopenhauer, Bosanquet, Santayana. Hegel's *Lectures on Esthetics* is perhaps the greatest work on the subject.

The esthetics of music has to determine the criterion of the beautiful in music. There are two questions: Does the beautiful in music arise from the creation of feeling (emotion)? Or, does the beautiful in music lie entirely in the tones and their artistic connection? In spite of the fact that E. Hanslick, in his tract *The Beautiful in Music,* answered the questions with much erudition, stating that music could not express feelings, for it presents only moving forms in sound, we agree with the modern esthetics of music which take the opposite view.

The esthetics of music, in particular, concerns itself with the question: What is the beautiful? It also tries to formulate some of the fundamental laws of musical beauty.

The Greeks identified beauty with what was good or with what was useful. They realized that an alertness to beauty affected their daily lives. There have been other ideas as to the nature of beauty, for example, that beauty is an orderly arrangement of shapes, colors, or sounds which elicit in us a sort of natural expression of feeling. Very likely, the concept of beauty lies somewhere between the personality and the object. It is not wholly subjective, not wholly objective, but an emotional and an intellectual activity not dependent entirely on the value of the object, the person who experiences it, nor upon that which is experienced.

Kant (1724–1804), the great German philosopher, says that the beautiful is that which, through the harmony of its form with the faculties of human knowledge, awakens a "disinterested, universal, and necessary satisfaction."

Kant further distinguishes between "free" and "adherent" beauty. "Free beauty presupposes no conception of that which the object ought to be; merely adherent beauty implies both such a conception and also the perfection of the object as determined by comparison with the conception." Now, is it not perfectly obvious that music, beyond all the other arts, supplies us with both free and adherent beauty? The musical thought, or melodic idea, which is the absolute musical concept, does not, and in the very nature of its existence, cannot, presuppose any conception of what it ought to be. That is to say, not one person could have determined beforehand what kind of theme any composer should conceive (or invent) as the principal subject of a symphony; yet the moment it is heard, that theme surely does awaken "a disinterested, universal, and necessary satisfaction."

"Free beauty in music, then, is that which belongs to its germinal conception. The adherent beauty is that which belongs to its expression and must be sought in the sensuous and the intellectual. The emotional content of music is not merely a part of its beauty, it is also a cause of it; for it is that which the art symbolizes." And, by the way, all art is symbolical.

Kant, in his *Critique of Judgment*, correlates design and beauty. According to him, the beautiful is that which shows symmetry and beauty of structure "as if it had been designed by intelligence." In short, the intangible quality of beauty in an object lies in the skillful arrangements of its parts by means of order, symmetry, or balance, in repetition, and contrast of design, plus climax—in other words, in its form.

1. From what has been said above, we find that the first law of the esthetics of music is the *law of beauty—a composition must contain beauty.* The melodic ideas must in and of themselves be beautiful. Beauty lies in perfection of harmony, in exquisiteness of outline, in loveliness of color, and in words and sentences of choice selection—all the characteristics of the gifted workman—while wisdom and power underlie it. The artist is the revealer of the great beauty in form. Really to know an objective, we must begin with an emotional response. But such a response is only the beginning. We can learn to recognize those ideas which are

lasting and universal in art only by grouping and analyzing the art creations of the past.

2. But free beauty is not enough. The second law of the esthetics of music is the *law of judgment*—it demands that *a work of art must appeal to the judgment*. The duty of criticism—judgment—is to recognize the power of imagination independently of any contribution from society and of any sympathy or dictate of an intellectual, moral, or practical kind. This is an intellectual process. As a matter of fact, the very word "art" indicates something in which skill, effort, thought, and taste are exercised; and to perceive the results of such an exercise is the labor of reason. *Appreciation of art is a matter of spiritual development and enfoldment.* Consequently, a musical composition must also have inherent beauty, and that beauty is surely to be found chiefly in those qualities which have been described as intellectual. In the art of music the inherent beauty of the intellectual development of a composition has a singular quality of its own. It satisfies us by an immediate conviction that it could not have been other than what it is; it at once betrays that element of inevitableness. This inevitableness is an intellectual quality because it is produced by perfection of form, by absolute logic of development. In music every tone has a rational relation to the tonic and tends to move in specified, predetermined direction within a musically logical standard, whereas in poetry the movement of the vowel sounds is controlled by any tendencies that inhere in them by virtue of their positions on a scale.

3. A third law of the esthetics of music is the *law of fitness*. There are two phases to this law—the intellectual appeal and the esthetic. The intellectual appeal is based upon the significance of the subject, the story of the painting, statue, or composition, which may in itself evoke emotions and affect the spirit. The esthetic appeal is based upon the disposition of the object with reference to abstract form to give pleasure on the basis of formal expression (design). *The law of fitness demands that the manner shall be suitable to the matter;* and it is almost wholly concerned with suitability of style, which, of course, includes form or design.

Untrained persons generally recognize only the intellectual appeal; but both, the intellectual and the esthetic appeal, are of equal importance and should be recognized. The law of fitness not only forbids the development of a secular style in sacred music, but it prohibits the juxtaposition of incongruous styles in any work of art. Applied to vocal music, the law of fitness demands that the musical ideas shall be appropriate to the text—that is to say, the music shall be as complete and lifelike an embodiment as possible of the emotions set forth by the poet. "It is the principle which lies at the basis of opera, and adherence to it is the only excuse which operatic writing has for its existence. Opera music which does not voice the emotions of the text is empty jingle."

4. Concerning the emotional content of a composition, with reference to the esthetics of music, the fourth law of the esthetics of music is the *law of proper emotional expression—that the emotional schedule must not include anything incapable of being expressed in music.* The older range of elementary emotions is open to the composer as long as he treats them in the abstract. In other words, he must not try to tell the cause of the emotion; he needs a text in order to do that. Perhaps it is needless to add that great emotions should be found in great compositions.

As Kant points out, the conception of beauty belongs to man alone. Animals do not share it with him. Music is wholly the creation of the human intellect and feeling. It is the one art which has no counterpart in nature, in contrast to painting, architecture, sculpture, and literature. The materials out of which music is "fashioned," so to speak, are the products of man's thoughts and feelings. Music is the highest product of the imagination; and for this very reason it is closer to "free" beauty than any other fine art. It proceeds out of the elements of human nature—sensation, reason, and emotion—and consequently it appeals to us with irresistible force.

The noted philosopher Spinoza (1632–1677) holds "beautiful" and "ugly" to be two subjective terms. "Only in relation to our imagination can things be called beautiful or ugly, well ordered or confused." Spinoza and his followers hold that the beauty of a thing lies in the reactions which it arouses in the mind of the beholder or listener. In short, beauty is not intrinsic in the object itself; but rather it is an esthetic experience by the beholder or listener.

Now, it is not necessary to hear much music in order to realize that our ideas of beauty can hardly ever coincide with those of others. To some Mozart's music is completely satisfying in its natural beauties; others are not so taken by it and are enthusiastic about Debussy's or Verdi's music. In order to discuss intelligently and reasonably what we hear, we must assume that whatever beauty there is in music lies in the relationship between the audience and the work of the composer.

As we have seen, *symmetry, proportion, balance, and logical development are essential to the perfection of an art work*. These factors are the result of design, and no composition can be truly great unless it is built according to the fundamental laws of form and content. In short, a truly great composition is one in which there is both *sensuous beauty* and *emotional content*, governed by the satisfying but wholly inexplicable and undefinable feeling of beauty. There is one test which we may apply to all music we hear, namely: Does it convey to us the spirit of life? Does it have that feeling of creative energy? Does it have that sense of freshness? All the great masterpieces that have survived the time in which they were produced certainly do possess this vigor, this spirit of ageless beauty. What this beauty is nobody knows. All we know is that it is the most satisfying experience in human life; and it must, we feel instinctively, represent some great truth of higher consciousness.

Longevity is the supreme testimony to the value of a work of art. There is no other equal criterion. As to the duration of the art work, it seems to rest fundamentally upon two things—*the truthfulness of its emotional expression*, and *the strength and beauty of its form and content*. In order to endure, the work of art must possess these two qualities.

The motive of art is to reveal beauty, to provide communication, revelation of form—to serve as a medium of self-

expression. Beauty is perfection of creation; it is the synthesis of form and quality blended in a perfect equilibrium, and it manifests itself in freedom of movement in symmetry and harmony. Beauty captivates and inspires the beholder and listener and awakens joy which is the essence of life. That which does not captivate and inspire is not real art—it is a body without life. Artists, as a rule, stand on a higher step of the spiritual ladder of development than those having no understanding of art.

As to decorative art, it, too, has its code of esthetic laws:

1. Decoration is subsidiary to utility.

2. The basic form of the article decorated must not be so modified by the decoration as to hide its identity and purpose.

3. While the purpose of decoration is often to break the monotony of a blank surface, "overloading" of the surface must be avoided.

2

FURTHER DISTINCTIONS OF MUSIC

1. PECULIAR CHARACTERISTICS OF MUSIC

MUSIC began when human beings found that certain successions of tones have an effect on the emotions and that there is some vague connection between the hearing apparatus and that mysterious something that is known as "feeling." The nature of the connection has never been understood. In fact, any approach to what might be called a standard of good or bad melody has always been blocked. Our methods are purely empirical. One succession of tones leaves a man cold, another causes intense emotions. Even to this day we cannot say exactly why the themes of Beethoven's symphonies are better than those of "Hearts and Flowers."

Music is the most intangible of all the arts and perhaps the most suggestive. Music demonstrates its importance not only because it is a better interpreter of nature than any other form of art, but also by the fact that it has distinct utility. According to the ancient philosophers, music was a great educational factor in the formation of character. Pythagoras (540–500 B.C.) considered music, mathematics, and astronomy to be the three cornerstones of knowledge. Music is also essentially subjective, and it is rare to find two or more people for whom the same piece of music produces an identical effect.

Our existing musical system is the product of several

thousand years of work by innumerable patient and mostly unknown musicians who slowly felt their way by trial and error, retaining what was valuable and discarding what was not. Their discoveries have been extended and stabilized by the great composers.

In the days when music began, a succession of tones was good if it satisfied man's inexplicable instincts; it was poor if it did not. This simple truth still holds good today. In thousands of years of development, music has been able to codify its empirically obtained knowledge of harmony (the simultaneous use of two or more sounds), and rhythm (the arrangement of sounds in a time scheme). But music has never even established as fact the existence of any law of melody. The qualities that give a tune its permanence, its power to grow on one, are as mysterious and as irreducible to scientific measurement as those that make it attractive on first hearing. It is extremely difficult to think up good melodies. Obviously, it is a gift that composers have or have not. In the latter case, little can be done to acquire it.

The effect of music upon a given individual is determined by the psychic disposition; it depends not primarily upon the ear but upon "an intricate selective activity carried on by the mind." Knowledge, culture, experience come into activity only as auxiliaries to the primary sensuous impression. Of course, they will add to the sum total of the effect produced and, most likely influence the quality of the esthetic enjoyment. To understand a painting or work of literature, the spectator or reader must possess a certain amount of knowledge and culture and know some facts about the subject matter with which the artist or writer is dealing. But in absolute music the subject matter is nil; form and content are one, and the medium, *sound,* is intangible. Because of the intangible medium in which he works, the composer can only indirectly exert his power to suggest, to evoke, and to arouse emotions. Music must always speak, whether subtly or not, of human associations, ideas, emotional and sensuous experiences. No doubt, emotion is the prime requisite of art, though it must be tempered by intelligence and practical knowledge. Music is the art whose function it is to express the inexpressible.

1. A peculiar characteristic of music is that *it can prevent us from becoming emotionally stagnant* amid the million harassing details of everyday life. It is intimately connected (nobody knows just how) with that mysterious something which we call "beauty."

Our response to music is based on the recognition of beauty. Beauty is intimately related to those immensely powerful and mysteriously significant emotions which lie beneath the surface of man's conscious, articulate, everyday self. When the origin and the true character of time, motion, and life shall have been satisfactorily explained, then the savant will take over the comparatively simple job of learning why the beautiful sounds of a violin have always had such an unearthly effect on human beings. These powerful emotions have no name and no existence in the three-dimensional world. They cannot be expressed nor communicated by means of music, the other fine arts, and whatever else is capable of vividly revealing beauty.

Music is the most complex of the arts; it only lives by motion, and we have to catch it as it passes by. Complexity in music is more obvious than in the other arts and, of course, more difficult to grasp. This is due to the fleeting character of music and its appeal to the least trained of our senses. A composer tries to catch something of this essence of life and experience, embody it in his music, and thus play upon the hidden, worldless emotions of his listener. Of course, the composer cannot be bothered with descriptions of ordinary "soul" states such as anxiety and cheerfulness, as these are not the kind of emotions which concern art. Neither can he be bothered with descriptions of street scenes or waterfalls, for words are better for such lowly tasks. A cheap snapshot will shame a great canvas if accuracy of reproduction be made the test. Indeed, great art always goes beyond the obvious message.

A composer must be able to conceive sequences of tones (repetitions of a melodic pattern) that will be satisfying emotionally on repeated hearings. Further, he must be able to clothe them in satisfying rhythmic and harmonic dress if his music is to have any genuine appeal. A mass of technical accomplishment will not relieve him from this necessity. Of course, he is at liberty to make whatever use he can of the accumulated knowledge of the centuries about rhythm and harmony.

Notice how often great art—art with no *obvious* message —can raise a wave of emotion in a man by this simple process of revealing beauty. Notice, too, that the person experiencing the wave of emotion is as powerless to describe his feelings in words as the artist would be to communicate in any such everyday medium what he has to say. For a century and a half now, the first theme of Mozart's G minor Symphony has been stirring human emotions. What is the secret? It does not seem to convey any obvious message. It is neither gay nor sad, neither assured nor anxious. The reason for its tremendous effect lies in the simple fact that it is . . . beautiful. Here Mozart has sought and fixed forever in these amazing measures an aspect of that ideal beauty which is the privilege of great art to reveal. No matter how mighty an emotional upheaval the music may produce, we must not make the mistake of trying to tell about it in words. Mozart has told all there is to tell.

The essence of beauty informs all the universe and manifests itself in a thousand ways frequently and powerfully through music. This is not intended as a reflection upon the potency of quick laughter in round young eyes, or upon full fall moons wanly lighting a world that smells coldly of decay. These things, too, can prevent emotional stagnation, but music often retains its peculiar power long after we have become too busy and too distracted to notice other phenomena.

2. Another peculiar characteristic of music is that *it is both the most natural and direct of the fine arts, as well as the most complicated and subtle.*

It is the most natural and direct because the materials of which it is constituted—*rhythm, melody, harmony, form and tone-color*—make an imaginative appeal to every normal human being. Everyone likes to listen to beautiful sounds merely for their sensuous effect. Likewise, the rhythm, akin to the ceaseless change and motion which is the basic fact of all life, appeals at once to everyone's own physical vitality. Notice the many people wagging their heads or beating time with their hands at a concert.

Indeed, complexity has little to do with the value of music. We have today a perverted idea that complex rhythm and harmony may have some direct bearing on the value of the music, that it may make the work "interesting." More often than not, a complex musical work lacks the spontaneity, the solemnity, the beauty, the grandeur, or the simplicity it otherwise might have. Above all, *great music contains ideas.* Too many composers hide mediocrity behind scholarship. There were *Kapellmeisters* who probably knew more about counterpoint than Handel, and there were learned men of music who had a better grasp of the sonata form than Beethoven. But these people could not write a good melody, and their music did not amount to much. Unable to think up good melodies, they reverted instead to a scholarly study of the possibilities of rhythm and dissonance.

Every so often music displays the tendency to depart from its reason for being, namely, *the ability to give pleasure and to communicate a state of feeling by means of sound.* It then becomes a dull and dry mass of tones. Music should be thought of in terms of pleasure rather than in terms of science and scholarship. Great compositions are really simple, after all. Many of the finest symphonies and operas abound in good melodic ideas, and the composer's technical skill is used to project these ideas in vivid style. Often the "development" section of a work in the sonata form is more interesting and emotionally exciting than the first statement of the themes. There is less mechanical working over the themes by well-recognized methods than a genuine development of new ideas from the old. Even the Bach fugues are comparatively simple, for in the best of them counterpoint is used only to display the beauty of the original ideas but never for its own sake.

Music is also the most complicated and subtle of the arts. First, because of the nature of its component parts—*an in-*

tangible and evanescent world of sound, yet indestructible; second, because of its subtle method of structure—*form or pattern;* and third, because of its presentation, by which its parts are used for personal communication—*content or expression.* Behind the materials of rhythm, melody, harmony, form, and tone-color, lies always the personal message of the composer; and if we are to grasp this and make it our own, we must listen closely so that the music actually lives again in our imaginations. In fact, everyone can derive much genuine pleasure and even spiritual exaltation merely by opening his ears and listening to the simple sounds and rhythms in their marvelous variety. The all-important reason for the lack of appreciation of music is that so many people stop at this point; i.e., for them music is nothing but a sensuous art. But music is more than that. Its outer form is merely a symbol of the inner feelings, ideals, or ideas of the composer, performer, and listener. Thus, music can give a single life a certain unity and even the momentary illusion of some sort of meaning through its uncanny power to evoke a time, a mood, a person, even a lost set of values. Music can open windows into the infinite and allow finite man a glimpse of the void. Music partakes of the mystery which surrounds the universe. Because it provides a universal, or at least widely current, language, music is quite capable of uniting most of the nations of the world—provided, of course, that they care about being united. Even if they do not, the music of one nation percolating through the barriers of another should be enough to convince the warlike citizens of both that some of their more important aspirations are shared. Why does it not work out that way? Simply because the men and women most sensitive to music do not govern.

3.   A third peculiar characteristic of music is that *it is a language used as a means of personal expression*—a means of communication between the mind and soul of the composer and that of the listener. Music is a language in and of itself. The notes that are written on the staves are not the language; they are the letters of music—the symbols by means of which that language is made available. They came into existence long after the language of music was being

hummed, moaned, spoken, or shouted. Surely, we delude ourselves if we think that we understand the message expressed in this language just because we happen to like beautiful sounds and stimulating rhythms. We must study this language in order to understand it. In other words, we must learn something of the material of which it is composed and, above all, the fundamental principles of its structure.

Comprehension of music really resolves itself into a grasp of its combinations of sounds, its succession of sounds, and the patterns (melody, rhythm, harmony, time values, and form) into which these combinations and successions are woven. It is by the use of these that whatever meaning the music may have is evoked or conveyed. This meaning is the *idea* the language has been used to express, but it is *not* the language. The sounds, the motion, the design (or musical form) constitute the language of music, just as words, phrases, and sentences constitute our spoken language.

4. A fourth peculiar characteristic of music is that *the language of music,* "in distinction from the static, concrete, and imitative arts, *is always in motion.*" There is a living quality in music. Only music can present in vibrant tones an art work to all intents and purposes fresh from the mind of the composer. However, *to follow music, "requires an intensity of concentration and accuracy of memory* which can be acquired, but for which, like most good things, we have to work." Any work of art must be re-created in the imagination of the beholders or listeners. This process of re-creation, as applied to music, has to be done without any help from nature. It exerts a tonic effect upon the pride of faltering, uncertain man; for did he not create this marvel himself out of nothing, with hardly more than a hint or two from nature? It is easy to understand, in a simple way at least, a work of architecture; it must have doors and windows and should conform to practical ideas of good structure. In like manner, a painting or a work of sculpture must show some resemblance to nature herself; and so we have definite standards—a sort of model—to help our imagination. But

music, an art work created out of man's pure fancy, having little to do with other forms of thought—nor having any sort of model in nature—causes us to be simply lost, "drowned in a sea of sound," unless we know something of its principles of construction. Music *is* itself. To equip ourselves so as to feel at home in this language, to receive the message as plainly as possible, and with perfect ease and satisfaction, demands a *strong, accurate memory,* a *keen power of discrimination,* and a *sympathetic, open mind.*

A new work of music should be judged by the following standards: *Has it melody? Are its ideas good? Is it capable of producing pleasure and evoking or heightening significant emotional states?* If the piece of music cannot pass such tests, the public ought not to be made to listen to it—not even if it contains polyphonic devices and is structurally perfect. Good music is an interesting fabric of tones made from a few simple materials that are used with masterly economy and imagination.

2. THE ELEMENTS OF MUSIC

The study of music from prehistoric times to the present day is a record of human feelings expressed in rhythm, melody, harmony, form, and tone-color through the vehicle of voice, instrument, or both. *Rhythm, melody, harmony, form, and tone-color* are the so-called "elements," or materials, of all music. They can be found in every composition, from a popular song to a sonata or symphony. Rhythm is the most primitive of these; harmony the least understood; melody the most obvious, as it is the primary and most characteristic element of musical expression and everything in music turns upon it; tone-color indicates the quality of sound; and form binds all the materials of sound into a complete work of art. In short, rhythm, melody, harmony, form, and tone-color all combine in an infinite number of ways to produce music. Each is at its highest when they are all in complete equilibrium, when one does not predominate over the other. We find in the music of the greatest masters this perfect balance and equipoise, a fine blend of all elements. We cannot readily isolate melody from rhythm, harmony from counterpoint, tonality from the sonata form, although for purposes of analysis we are compelled to abstract one component from the other or from the whole. Rhythm is immeasurable, mysterious. When formal design and rhythm cease to be representative, they automatically become geometrical patterns, as in a carpet or strip of wallpaper. Thus, musical rhythm separated from melody and harmony becomes merely metrical, mechanical, lifeless.

A. RHYTHM

Rhythm is the first and primal element in the arrangement of sound into music. Its elements are the systematic grouping of units, repetition, stress, and pause (or point of repose). Rhythm depends upon the organization of sensory material into cognizable patterns determined by accentuation, duration, and pause. These three factors work together to produce a grouping that we perceive. The word "rhythm" literally means "flow." Taken separately, neither tone nor rhythm can make music. The primal difference between music and noise consists in the intensity of vibration and in the grouping of the sounds into a regular series by means of accents. Just as no succession of unrelated words makes intelligible language, so no succession of unrelated tones, not grouped rhythmically, makes music. There can be no music without musical sounds grouped into rhythmic divisions.

Rhythmical form is universal. We have the course of each world about the sun, of each satellite about its world, and the rotation of the various worlds upon their axes, making the rhythms of the year, month, and day. Scientists have pointed out that the monthly rhythm seems to be especially connected with the reproduction system and the nervous system. The period of gestation in various species of animals is usually a month, or a number of days which is seven or a multiple of seven. Primitive man had to show an instinct for rhythm in order to preserve the species. He was forced to contend with a hostile nature and with animals of great strength. It was necessary for several men to work together in rhythmic movement to pull down a tree or to move a stone. Thus, throughout the ages, man has worked rhythmically in groups and thereby has accomplished more by such concerted action. In time, this instinct has developed until it now is a means for the expression of our emotions.

Again, there are various bodily rhythms, such as the pulse, walking, respiration, and speech. Every cell seems to have its own rhythm of alternate activity and rest. Fatigue is also rhythmical—a period of exhaustion alternating with one of recovery.

Man's earliest experiences were performed rhythmically. Rhythm of a crude sort even exists in the surf rolling on a beach, slow rain dripping from a tree, etc., although it had little or no meaning to man until he had produced or reproduced it himself. The first human who discovered that it was fun to beat rat-a-tat-tat with a dry branch on a tree trunk was the "inventor" of rhythm. This probably consisted at first in beating a log with a stick, clapping the hands, or stamping the feet so as to make a regularly recurring noise in order to keep dancers together. Historians agree that the earliest manifestations of what we call "music" may be traced to the rhythm of primitive dancing. Later on, log or stick were replaced by drums or other percussion instruments. Most of the musical instruments of the savage tribes today are still drums of different kinds; and many savages even prefer music in which drums, rattles, cymbals, banjos, etc., are much used. Without understanding consciously what he was up to, man, through the method of trial and error, extended the expressive range of rhythm. He made various metrical combinations of sound that meant something to him. He found that such emotional states as valor, fear, and awe could be produced or intensified by various kinds of rhythm.

Mental processes likewise are rhythmical. If we try to hold one idea unchanged, we will be able to see clearly the rhythm of our attention. Almost any state can be produced in susceptible persons by appropriate rhythms, from putting them to sleep to rousing them to a state of frenzy closely akin to madness.

We reflect to a greater or less extent in our own personalities the rhythm and harmony which pervade all nature. This rhythm relieves the monotony of existence and is the agency through which we are able to bring ourselves into harmony with the forces of nature and the thoughts and emotions of our fellow beings.

The human mind cannot give attention to any passing phenomenon except for the shortest period, unless there is some co-ordination or design in what is being seen or heard. There is a reason for the rhythmic grouping of sounds. To enable us to apperceive anything, it is necessary that it enter into, and fit in with, associations already stored in the mind. It is difficult—in fact, almost impossible—to retain any image of what has been experienced unless there are such associations. A succession of sounds that are not rhythmically grouped or made to stand in a certain order with each other have no symmetry or design, and it is practically impossible to give any prolonged attention to such sounds. But the grouping of such sounds into divisions produces a feeling of symmetry, and the mind can apperceive the relationship of one group to another group.

In short, rhythm is a fundamental occurrence in nature. Human ingenuity and sense of order have formed sound waves into patterns of beauty. These sound waves are motion, and they exist in time, not in space. Music is motion always in perfection. Of course, this rhythm is fundamental also in all the other arts.

But rhythm in music means more than it does in the other arts. The difference between music and poetry is that in music a sense of both *meter and rhythm* may be more obviously present at the same time. It is necessary to make clear the distinction between meter and rhythm. There is seldom in art and music a rhythmic scheme that is not made up of these two factors, meter and rhythm. When we scan a line of poetry (a verse) we are merely measuring its metrical units, just as we do when we divide the notes into evenly distributed note values. Thus, if we recite the following line, stressing the regular beats of the metrical line, we get: We dánce todáy, but nót untíl/The sún has góne awáy.

Also, it is impossible for poetry, for instance, to present

three or four different rhythms simultaneously, as music often does. Rhythm in music has diversity, flexibility, and a physical vigor far superior to that of any other art. These are some types of rhythms (unit groups) which exist in poetry:

Iamb   trochee   dactyl   anapest   amphibrach

Rhythmic unit groups; rhythmic lines made up of sequences of unit groups; rhythmic patterns of two or more lines occurring simultaneously—these are the basic patterns created by accentuation, duration, and pause, in which we perceive the rhythm.

From the standpoint of performance, good rhythm involves:

1. Proper tempo, steadily obtained. The speed varied only when demanded by changes in the nature of the music.

2. Correct accentuation.

3. Accurate performance of the various rhythmic figures.

4. Correct phrasing—division of the music into its phrases, sections, etc.

Rhythm is the group of tones into indivisible units; it is regularity of pulsation, as well as forward movement; it implies the periodical recurrence of accents, or strong beats, and a corresponding regularity of nonaccented beats; and variety in tone length.

There are three characteristics or aspects of rhythm in music:

1. *Pulsation*—regularity of gait in forward movement.

2. *Accentuation*—strong and weak beats (the periodical recurrence of accent).

3. *Variety* in tone length—long and short tones.

Pulsation is the obvious thing in music, and it is found even in primitive dances and songs. It forms the basis of musical rhythm, beats or pulses occurring continuously in regular alternation. As an example, take band music, with its strongly marked rhythm and simple melodious structure. When we hear it, we all beat time to it.

Accentuation is the grouping of sounds with reference to their duration and accent. It is represented by notes and bar-lines.

Fundamentally, *all music is based on two schemes of pulsation*:

1. Strong beat followed by one weak beat: $1_2 1_2$.
2. Strong beat followed by two weak beats: $1_{23} 1_{23}$.

All other pulses are made up of these two schemes: 4/4 time: $1_2 3_4$; 9/8: $1_{23} 4_{56} 7_{89}$; etc. In 3/4 time we have three quarter notes in a measure, with the principal accent normally on the first beat. In 4/4 time we have four quarter notes in a measure, with the principal accent on the first and a secondary accent on the third beat. Rhythm and meter in music are distributed in a similar way as in poetry. Rhythm is especially noticeable in poetry and music, and similar technical terms are used in both; viz. foot, line, stanza, canto; measure, phrase, sentence (period), double period (division), and division, or movement. Meter is the rhythmical arrangement of syllables into feet.

(Note: In medieval plain song (Gregorian chant) the rhythm was free, and the repetition of beats followed the accents of the Latin text. For this reason, plain song is not divided into measures and has no regular repetition of strong and weak beats. To some extent this freedom of accent has been preserved in the recitatives of opera and oratorio.)

Variety in tone length secures freedom from monotony. If musical tones were always of the same length, the effect would not be pleasing, even if some of them were accented. Indeed, the very life and character of melody depend upon its rhythm.

The student of classical music will hardly ever find the primitive, monotonous, accented tapping that is found in popular music. The rhythm of almost all popular music is absurdly simple. It does not follow, however, that good music must necessarily have a complex rhythm. The music of a good composer shows that he is a careful worker, that his music has variety of rhythm as well as a large unity enclosing the whole. Here and there, little changes add to variety while leaving enough regularity to make his theme very "swingy." In fact, there is no lack of rhythm in classical music or other great music. All the listener has to do is free himself from the too simple and monotonous effects of commonplace music. Many examples of the music of the great composers might be cited to prove that it too is rhythmical.

In summary, the general pulsation scheme gives unity and firmness. Variety and interest are furnished by the combination of long and short tones into musical figures. Finally, these figures repeated, contrasted, varied, and woven into the larger rhythmic units are what give us form or pattern. Every piece of music that is at all coherent has been constructed out of such a combination and orderly arrangement of rhythmic units.

Rhythm is fundamental in all art. Without rhythm there could be no art of music. Rhythm is a measured succession of tones of a composition in respect to time; the measured beat which marks the character of expression of the music. This distribution of tones easily creates a definite form or pattern which may be repeated again and again in a piece of music, just as it would be in a carpet or a section of wallpaper. The rhythm of a composition, in the larger sense, is governed by such patterns, rather than by the fundamental time beats; and this naturally permits an infinite variety of effects. A good singer or player expresses this feeling for rhythm in phrasing, which is the logical division of the music into rhythmic and melodic patterns. A skillful dancer feels this larger rhythm, rather than the mere count of 1,2; 1,2,3; or 1,2,3,4; etc. Again, anyone reading a poem does the same thing instinctively, helped by the division of the lines and the various punctuation marks. Interest in rhythm marks the beginning of musical interest and, therefore, of appreciation.

Time applies *only* to the number of beats in a measure. As we listen to a march, we notice the regular succession of a strong beat or pulse (accent) and a weaker one, every alternate tone receiving an accent, which is the stress given to certain tones at intervals to bring out the rhythm. It is pulsation that forms the basis for marching and for all rhythmic movements that call for concerted action, whether singing or playing together. To repeat, the general pulsation scheme gives fundamental unity and firmness. The music, therefore, falls into little groups of tones, one strongly accented, the other weak. Each of these little groups is called a *bar*, or *measure of music*. The measure gives simplicity, definiteness of structure, and regularity; it corresponds in a general way to the *foot* in verse. The measure units are themselves combined into distinct groups known as *phrases*, and into *sections*, or *periods* (separated by cadences). Each of the equal parts into which the measure, or bar (vertical divisions), is divided is called a *beat*. Each measure, or bar, contains the same sum of beats: 2, 3, 4, etc.; and each of the beats is expressed by either 1/8, 1/4, 1/2, etc. All music is based on only a few schemes of pulsation. Fundamentally (as mentioned before), there are only two such schemes: 1) *duple;* and 2) *triple.* As in a march, there are only two or four beats to each group of beats in a measure; this piece is said to be in "duple time" (when beats run in 2's, or in multiples thereof, as in common time). On the other hand, when listening to a minuet or a waltz we notice that there is a regular succession of a strong accent and two weaker ones—three beats in a measure; this piece is said to be in "triple time" (when beats run in 3's, or in multiples thereof, as in compound time).

Time is designated by two numbers; one describes the number of beats to the measure, and the other the duration of each normal beat. The longest note (or rest) commonly used is called a "whole note" (or rest); a note (or rest) held for half that length of time is called a "half note" (or rest); and so on. Thus, when we say that a certain piece of music is in 3/4 time, we mean that there are three beats to the measure, and each beat is equivalent to a note (or rest) held a quarter of the length of time of the whole note (or rest). In such a piece we might have a measure consisting of a quarter note (or rest) and four eighth notes (or rests); or one half note (or rest) and four sixteenth notes (or rests), or any other combination which would leave us with three quarter notes (or rests) to a measure.

Tempo applies to the rate of speed at which the music is sung or played. Compositions differ in respect to the quickness of the beat. Some are slow; some are moderately fast; and some are fast or very fast. Tempo, like rhythm, also affects the character of music.

Syncopation is a peculiar quality of uneven rhythm; instead of falling regularly on the first beat of the measure, the strong beat shifts to the later beat of the measure—a displacement of the accent.

All jazz, ragtime, and swing music, with its varying accent and emphasis, is founded on the cornerstone of a steady, unchanging rhythm in the bass. The basic rhythm of marchtime—1_234—was made more interesting and exciting in jazz by displacing the accents so that the basic rhythm became $1_23$4. The melodic line, giving it its characteristic quality, is a syncopation.

One reason why many feel a dislike for certain dance tunes is the monotony of the reiteration of strong beats. All they hear is this fundamental rhythm, a perception of regularity that is agreeable at first and then becomes annoying to us, because our nerve centers are soon wearied by the persistent attack. However, over and above these strong beats are other rhythms, and it is the combination of the two that gives jazz whatever rhythmic vitality it has. Usually a chief defect of so-called "popular music," in comparison with classical or with program music, is its extreme simplicity. The rhythm of almost all popular music is absurdly simple. Of course, this does not mean that good music must necessarily have a complex rhythm; but the simplicity of the popular songs shows a poverty of ideas not characteristic of true art. Good music abounds in a variety of rhythmic effects and also has a large unity embracing the whole; it does not show that obvious seesaw of popular music. Good music is rhythmic enough. Indeed, there is no lack of rhythm in the music of the great composers; when once the listener has freed himself from the too simple and monotonous effects of commonplace music, he will be able to enjoy it greatly.

If we listen carefully to the performance of a great conductor, we will find that "following the instructions" of the composer is much more complex than bouncing along *à la swing time*. Herein lies the fundamental rhythmic difference between the two types of music: jazz is based on the beat; serious music (classical and program music) varies the beat occasionally to conform with the flow of the music and the musical phrase, which is the basis of the beat.

The trained music-lover who wishes to keep pace with the progress of the art and recognize the beauties in the works of the best composers should strengthen his ability to understand complex rhythmic patterns. As music becomes more highly organized, the simple, rudimentary tone patterns that are uniform in their regularity and very obvious in their reiteration of a few simple figures give way to freer forms. Naturally, the listener whose rhythmic reactions are narrowly limited finds himself utterly confused by complex tone patterns. Such complexity consists in displacement of accents, avoidance of cadence, interweaving of melodic lines and harmonic masses, etc. Every semblance of order and system seems to be avoided. But it is only a question of degree. Unity and plan are noticeable in the great works as well as in the simple folk songs or dance tunes. We must learn the method by which these combinations resolve into coherence and symmetry.

Rhythm is apparent only when we understand it. Likewise, in music we perceive only the meter when we stress the down-beat: 1 2 3 4, etc. We perceive the real rhythm only when we stress the tones according to the musical sense of the phrase. Incidentally, even the most complex rhythms are meant for our ears. They need not be analyzed in order to be enjoyed. Let us relax and allow the rhythms to come and go. By listening more intently, and not resisting the rhythmic pull in any way, we may enjoy music from a new angle also when we hear the greater complexities of modern rhythms and their subtle interplay.

It is practically impossible to describe in detail all the

potential patterns of rhythm. Once we get the habit of hearing rhythmic similarities, we will have no difficulty in picking out the rhythmic patterns in any piece of music.

Rhythm moves in measured time, by patterns of strong and weak beats:

6-part measure Very quick; count 2.

Examples of rhythmic patterns:

Schubert March Militaire

Schubert Moment Musicale, F minor

Author Unknown Long, Long Ago

Author Unknown America
(God Save the King)

Author Unknown
Volga Boat Song

Questions: What kind of movement is suggested by joy, by sadness, by a cradle song, by a tarantella? Is the rhythmic movement of the piece you are listening to light or strong; lively or slow; even or uneven; gay or sad; delicate or vigorous; strong or weak?

Tempo is of great importance, as performing a composition faster or slower than the composer intended may entirely change the effect he wanted to produce. Certain words have, therefore, been adopted to indicate the tempo at which each work, or part of it, is to be performed. Words such as *adagio, andante, largo, moderato, allegro, presto,* etc., are also often used as titles for compositions. Variation in tempo is indicated by such words as *ritardando* (getting gradually slower) and *accelerando* (getting gradually faster).

In music the first tone in every measure invariably carries the strongest accent. If there are two beats to the measure, the first is a down-beat and the second is the up-beat. That is the way a conductor of an orchestra would actually beat time with his baton—down for the accented, and up for the unaccented tones.

Music requires a system of notation whereby every tone has an absolute indication of its pitch and duration in beats or fractions of a beat. The important thing is to be able to hear the fundamental beats of time in all kinds of music. In architecture the profusion of ornament upon capitals, architraves, friezes, and cornices rests upon columns or arches standing at equal distances from one another. In music, likewise, the many varieties of rhythmic figuration are united by the throb of steady pulses within.

A change of rhythm conveys about the same expressiveness as a change of key or modulation from major to minor scale. Recitative and chanting abandon strict time and assume the irregular rhythms of speech, thus taking on a new meaning. Syncopation and its modern development, "swing," are an expression of youthful exuberance. Slow rhythms add stateliness and dignity when needed; fast rhythms add impetuosity, exhilaration. Coloratura and bravura singing electrify when marked by a strong accent. Repetition, when made rhythmic by means of grouping and accents, becomes decorative. Some rhythms are racial and national; others are characteristic of various occupations; and still others portray states of mind. Note the characteristic gliding rhythm of the barcarolle and the waltz; the dignity of the polonaise and minuet; the impetuosity of the tarantella and the czardas, etc.; note also the dignified Walhalla motive; the hammering motive of the dwarf Mime; the elemental force of the nature motive in Rheingold; the funeral motive in Siegfried; and so on.

To repeat, *rhythm* means movement, or flow of music, which varies according to its *tempo* (speed), its *measure* (time), and the arrangement of tones of different length of which the music is composed.

In *regular rhythm* the longer tones come on the principal beats; in *irregular rhythm* the contrary is the case—it is jerky or varied.

Every tone, played or sung, is affected by *pitch* (frequency of vibration), *time* (duration), *intensity* (loudness), and *quality* (timbre).

Pitch of a tone is either high or low; it is determined by the rapidity (frequency) of vibration.

Time of a tone is of either long or short duration.

Intensity of a tone refers to its softness or loudness.

Degree of intensity to be observed in a piece of music is indicated by such terms as: *piano, pianissimo, forte, fortissimo,* etc.

Variation in intensity is indicated by such terms as: *crescendo* (becoming gradually louder); *decrescendo,* or *diminuendo* (becoming gradually softer); etc.

B. MELODY

Melody is an agreeable combination of successive tones into a coherent whole; a sequence of single sounds arranged in some line of beauty; a pleasing succession of tones at various levels of pitch following one another in time. In other words, a melody is a sequence of tones that may be perceived and understood; it is a movement from lower tones to higher, and vice versa; it implies a succession of tones rhythmically arranged; and it also implies some sense of form or design as well as a clearly defined structure which carries the mind from one point to another. It expresses a motive, or idea. Melody depends upon how tones are put together. The question is: Do the sounds seem to belong together? Does the succession of tones make sense?

The repetition of a phrase in another octave is always expressive of a new meaning. As a rule, the higher octaves express the fanciful; they suggest joy, lightness, delicacy, while lower octaves indicate solemnity, awe, fear, and the like. An ascending passage may indicate exhilaration and buoyancy, while a descending one may show depression, discouragement. All these are but generalities and subject to endless variation.

Frequency is the rapidity of vibrations which causes a difference in pitch—high or low tones. Intensity is the amplitude of the sound waves, the volume or degree of loudness of the tone. *Intensity, amplitude, volume, and loudness* are different aspects of the same thing.

Obviously, a tone becomes musical material only by association with another tone. Tones used in music are selected for their expressiveness, their beauty, and their availability. Tones, as such, are a forceful and stimulating agency which can arouse deep bodily responses and intensify conscious processes. A tone can never become music so long as it remains isolated—although we might hear it alone, study its quality (timbre), and determine its pitch. But there is power in tones. Mere tones by themselves, or with simple combinations, exert an important influence on our sensibility. Apparently, this influence baffles analysis. It evidently can be explained only as a direct nervous reaction. The expressiveness of a simple song is not due solely to the particular tone or group of tones that express emotion but also to the particular place in which it occurs. If it were put in a different place, it would lose its significance. Each part of a musical composition is related to its other parts and to the whole—it is more than a series of pleasant sounds.

It is difficult to trace the development of melody. All we know is that music of some kind existed very early in human history. Long before man learned to talk, a mother making low, crooning sounds to her infant may have allowed herself, almost instinctively, to fall into some rude form of melody. Without rhythm, melody is almost inconceivable. Possibly, that prehistoric mother was rocking her child to and fro as she crooned to him, and the sounds which she emitted had a rhythmic pattern even before they became musical sounds of varying pitch and, therefore, melody. Then, too, nature gives a real suggestion of melody in the songs of birds. The two bird calls which have the most definite pitch are those of the cuckoo and the bob-white (quail).

One type of primitive melody came from the natural

accentuation of the words. The Greeks sang their epic poetry and their drama. In another type of primitive melody—the dance type—the form was determined by the rhythmic structure of the dance. It was probably a monotonous melody at first. In time, variation and contrast were added. Still later, the primitive dance melody grew into the folk song, with its well-defined rhythmic structure and usually rather regular length of phrases. In the folk song we also find *repetition* and *contrast*—two principles of very great importance in the construction of music.

The rise of the early Christian Church brought with it a conflict between secular and sacred music. This conflict concerned the rhythmic or measured style of melody arising from the connection of melody with the folk dance and folk song versus the nonmeasured, or recitative, style associated with Church music. Thus, there developed two types of melody: one with a clearly defined scheme of pulsation, definitely measured tone lengths, and regularity of phrase construction; the other with no definite scheme of pulsation and very little regularity of phrase construction. The first type was the *folk dance* and the *folk song;* the second was the *Gregorian chant* or *plain song. Church music developed the great art of counterpoint, whereas folk-dance tunes and folk songs gave rise to instrumental music.* From then on, secular music was in the lead and developed into various forms.

With the development of harmony, rhythm and melody became much more complex. This greater rhythmic elaboration in turn brought with it not only greater expansion and irregularity of form and design but also a much more expressive melody. Now melody changed its structure and became itself a vehicle for expressing a greater variety of moods and emotions.

☞ A good melody has unity and coherence as well as originality and variety. It has grace and strength, and it expresses something. It has satisfying proportion, gives us a sense of completion and of inevitability, has its low and high points of interest and a climax, usually near the end. A melody may be pleasant for its own sake, or it may, in addition, express a mood or idea. A melody must be sincere and spontaneous as well as show a sensitivity to rhythmic flow. It must have enough repetition to seem unified and must not overemphasize any one element, such as cloying sweetness, or syncopation, for example. From a purely technical standpoint, every melody must exist within the limits of some scale system —Oriental, Greek, Ecclesiastical, or Modern. A melody of this type makes a universal appeal to the affections and emotions of the great mass of people. *Music without melody will not last.*

It is not hard to answer the question: "What is a good melody?" Before our judgment as to whether the quality of any art work is worth something, we must have maturity of thought as well as considerable experience. Why a good melody has the power to move us has so far defied analysis. Evidently, the idea of melody is associated with the mind and the emotions. Melody is practically the direct messenger of emotion in music. But it takes a very great composer to give us such a message directly, without the help of words, title, program suggestion, or other previous association. Indeed, the creation of an outstanding melody requires inspiration and a true inventive power.

If we do not recognize a melody at a first hearing, it does not mean that it is not there. Some compositions may require several hearings before we become aware of the essential tunes.

Melody is one of the most valuable assets of a composer. Of course, it is clear nonsense to imagine that great music exists which is absolutely without melody. Some of our modernists think that they can put together a lot of notes without any logical connection, and somehow, the results will be pleasing, as well as make sense. In simple so-called "popular music," melody is divided into exact phrases to suit the rhythm of the piece. While this division is often useful, it should not be the only one, any more than a succession of "long-meter" lines in hymns (eight-syllabled lines in iambic tetrameter) should be the only kind of poetry. Good music is tuneful and melodic, but it should not be forced to fit a commonplace rhythm. Instead of being restricted to specified lengths, it ought to be presented to us in a pleasing variety. Many passages in classical music show a marked melodic character, in addition to a clear rhythm.

The good composer uses melody in a different way. A short, lovely melody or theme may be balanced against another of different type, or it may be contrasted by heavy, somber chords. Schubert and Wagner, two of the greatest writers of melody, can paint a picture for the listener, making the melody of their music gay, sad, pathetic, stormy, or tragic. Beethoven, too, is a master at changing his melodies or themes so that they are never monotonous. Tschaikowsky and Sibelius are perhaps the two composers whose melodies can evoke great tragedy and utter gloom. Strauss uses the oddest theme, or melody, to describe the character Till Eulenspiegel, a gay and reckless fellow. In certain types of great music a large part of the composition is taken up with this sort of whimsical, fantastic, or logical working out of the various possibilities of the melody, theme, or subject.

When a composer has worked out a good tune, no matter how beautiful, he can not simply go on repeating it until the end of the piece. If it were done that way, the composer could either stop at once or go on indefinitely—it would not matter. He therefore varies it, adds to it, or takes from it, making little changes each time the tune is repeated. Finally, when he does get back to the melody, it is with a sense of both novelty and familiarity at once, which makes a lovely tune still more charming. So the composer does not often follow one simple style of melody, but tries to use more than one style so as to bring out in his works the beauty that comes from variety and the solidity of structure that depends upon artistic contrast and balance. Besides the mere creating and repeating of a melody or theme, the good composer may use the material of melody in a new way, namely for design-like imitation, which may be strict or free. This process is known as *"development."*

The simplest kind of musical pleasure comes from following the rhythm and enjoying the beautiful melodies. However, the greater and more lasting delight comes from observing what the composer does with his melodies, or bits of melodies, from the beginning to the end of a piece. It is important, on first hearing the piece, to *listen closely and remember the melody or theme in its original form*. Among the tricks the composer plays with the theme are: *Expansion,* the intervals of figures or motives are increased more than would result from any altered scale position; *contraction,* i.e., a reverse of expansion, by which the intervals may be made smaller; *repetition,* i.e., repeating certain tones of the figures or motives in the necessary number of smaller tones; *elaboration,* making a figure more intricate by the addition of new tones; *simplification,* making a figure simpler by taking away tones; *rhythmic imitation,* or imitating the rhythm of a figure on a single tone, or by a bass drum, triangle, etc.; *diminution,* or shortening the time value of tones; *augmentation,* or repeating a theme while lengthening the time, i.e., playing it in longer tones; *inverting* the theme, or playing it upside down; *omission,* or *cutting off* part of a theme; *transposing* the theme or playing it in different keys; turning it over to *different instruments; changing* a few notes; and the like. A melody repeated an octave higher or lower suggests a change of expression as the speaker repeats a remark more excitedly or quietly, more sarcastically or solemnly, etc.

The composer does not only repeat his melody, making little changes and variations to give the melody a wide range of expression, he may also *add embellishments*—that is, small groups of notes which accompany the melody and ornament it, thus enriching the theme.

The melody that gains the quickest and easiest popularity is the one that follows well-established formulas. No doubt, the human ear can develop its appreciation and enjoyment of more and more subtle and unusual melodic progressions, but whether such development is potentially unlimited is hard to tell. It is very difficult for the average human ear to distinguish clearly intervals of less than half a tone. The average listener cannot recognize quarter tones, but he can hear whether a tone is somewhat sharp or flat. Nevertheless, he is not able to tell definitely if any interval has been sounded.

The *scale* (mode) is the foundation upon which rests any melody, as used by all composers from J. S. Bach to the present day; in fact, it is the organized basis of all musical systems. The function of the scale in music not only means the use and "belonging together" of a specific collection of tones, but the *way* these tones are used in definite relation to each other.

The beginner should first analyze the appeal of melody in its traditional forms. Later on he may study the less obvious melodies. The melody should be followed like a continuous thread which guides the listener through a piece of music from the beginning to the end. The melody may disappear momentarily, but soon it will reappear and then be felt more strongly. Do not let the melody become lost by the accompanying voices; you must be able to hear it.

A melody is made up of phrases. *A phrase is a short musical thought,* or, more particularly, a small group of tones, one following another. The ability of the performer is shown in his *phrasing,* that is, his expressiveness in bringing out the musical meaning of the phrases and their relation to the piece as a whole. Phrasing is simply making the rhythmic structure apparent to the ear. Phrasing is one of the merits of good singing or playing—piano, violin, cello, or orchestra.

Here are some patterns of melody: Starting with the middle C on the piano, we note, first of all, its *octave* (a tone eight tones away). The octave is one of the universal facts of music, and yet it is also one of the great mysteries. The interval of the octave has a scientific background which is well illustrated by the piccolo. The piccolo is exactly half the length of the flute and sounds an octave higher. In short, a string or a tube cut or stopped at half its length sounds exactly an octave higher.

The *diatonic scale* (major and minor) is made up of seven whole and half tones, plus the repetition of the first tone, or twelve different half tones, plus the repetition of the first tone, one octave higher.

These twelve different tones of the *chromatic scale* are actually the entire materials of melody. Anything above or below them is merely a duplication in another octave. The major mode (scale) has half-steps between the third and fourth and the seventh and eighth tone, and whole steps between all other tones; it has a major third.

The so-called "diatonic" and "chromatic" scales, with no interval smaller than half a tone, are basic for all the great melodies known to us. A diatonic and a chromatic scale can be started at any point in the keyboard, and yet the relationship of the tones will be the same.

Now, if we can think of the scale as an absolute entity from the outset, regardless of pitch, we will find the whole subject of melody (and later that of harmony) greatly simplified.

The smallest pattern of melody consists of only *2-tones*. Notice the cuckoo call—5-3; listen also to the German song Bier Her; and Beethoven's Turkish March; I. Berlin's Pack up Your Sins; Daquin's Le Coucou; etc. The reverse of the cuckoo call are the 2-tones 3-5. Notice Brahm's Wiegenlied; MacDowell's To a Wild Rose; etc.

The commonest pattern or *3-tones* is the bugle call: 1-3-5 (Reveille, Taps, etc.). Notice: Holy, Holy, Holy; The Watch on the Rhine; Wachet Auf; the Russian National Anthem; the beginning of the Tannhäuser March and the Pilgrim's Chorus; etc.

The *4-tone* pattern usually goes: 5-below, 1-2-3. Notice: Lead Kindly Light; How Dry I Am; Merry Widow Waltz; Sweet Adeline; etc.

The *5-tone* pattern is usually: 1-2-3-5-6, or 5-6-below, 1-2-3. It is used much in folk music. Notice: Harris, After the Ball; Linke, Glowworm (1-2-3-5-6).

The *8-tone* pattern usually follows this outline: 8-7-6-5-4-3-2-1. Notice: Joy to the World; etc.

Chromatic scale tones are almost as common as the diatonic variety. Notice: Saint-Saens, My Heart at Thy Sweet Voice; Rimski-Korsakov, Song of India and Hymn to the Sun; also Ciribiribi, etc.

There is great beauty in the *minor mode*. It has delicacy, grace and can show sadness and even tragedy. Without question, training in appreciation of this mode is a necessary part of every listener's education. Notice: Mendelssohn, Ov.

Hebrides (opening theme) and Scotch Symphony (first and last movements); Tartini, Violin Sonata (Devil's Trill); De-Beriot, Violin Concerto #7 (second movement); F. Veracini, Largo in F♯ minor (V & P); etc.

The *Hungarian minor scale* is the same as the harmonic minor with the fourth tone raised: a b c d♯ e f g♯ a. This eight-tone pattern can be written in all keys.

A melody may start on any step or even half-step of the scale, but there are very few tunes that start anywhere except on the first, third, fifth, or eighth tone of the scale.

Beginning on 1: America; Hail Columbia; Men of Harlech; Doxology; Holy, Holy, Holy; All Through the Night; Integer Vitae; Blue Danube Waltz.

Beginning on 3: My Old Kentucky Home; Turkey in the Straw; Annie Laurie; Hail, Hail the Gang; Sweet and Low; Abide With Me; Till We Meet Again; Salut D'Amour; Meditation from Thais.

Beginning on 5: Blue Bells of Scotland; Auld Lang Syne; Old Oaken Bucket; Santa Lucia; How Dry I Am; O Tannenbaum; London Bridge; Good Old Summer Time; Ach Du Lieber Augustin; Lead, Kindly Light; Rock of Ages; La Marseillaise; Handel's Largo.

Beginning on 8: Joy to the World; Ein Feste Burg; The Girl I Left Behind Me; Tschaikowsky's Song Without Words.

C. HARMONY

Harmony is the distribution of sounds with reference to their union, i.e., the science of arranging the effect of tones which are to be heard simultaneously. It also governs the proper scientific sequence, or progression, of the groups, or "chords," as they are called. Harmony is the use of two or more related tones or chords sounded simultaneously and producing a pleasant, or satisfying, or even an interesting effect. Harmony deals in masses; they strike simultaneously and produce an immediate sensation. In music harmony is comparable to color in painting.

Melody came out of rhythm; harmony came out of melody.

Music is an art which exists in the element of time. This

implies that the nature of sound is volatile. For this reason various ways of arranging musical material have been evolved so as to give it a degree of permanence and greater cumulative and co-ordinating expression. No one series of sounds arranged into a melody can long survive the substitution of another series unless it is restated entirely or, at least, in part. This means that music must be expressed according to some *form or pattern*. This involves symmetry. In folk songs, for instance, the form is a repetition of a first phrase after a second contrasting one, etc. (The subject of form will be discussed in detail under the heading of *Form*.)

Historically, harmony and tone-color were the last of the elements, or materials, of music to be developed. The old Greeks speculated on the possibility of harmony. However, they did not go beyond speculation, although they devised a scale capable of supporting the structure of modern harmony and let their women and children sing an octave above the men. The idea of the octave led Aristotle to wonder why the voices could not move along together at distances less than an octave; but his speculation, so far as we know, was never acted upon. Medieval musicians, led by the Flemish monk Hucbald, decided late in the ninth century that the slow melodies of the church services lacked richness of texture. They added a second voice, a fourth or fifth away from the original. This was harmony at last. Now music boasted three basic elements—rhythm, melody, harmony.

Once this new factor had been added, there began a series of experiments of exactly the same type as those which followed the discoveries of the earlier elements. Efforts were made to make the meaning of music richer and more varied. These efforts were hugely successful. The present power of music to produce or intensify significant emotional states is one of the wonders of the world. Its shades of meaning have been multiplied a thousandfold. The experiments, of course, are still going on, and there is no reason to believe that the limit of the expressiveness of music has been reached or even approached.

As mentioned earlier, for many centuries tones were not combined. It is only about a thousand years ago that the practice arose of sounding simultaneously several voices of different pitch. The definite influences responsible for the development of harmony were, first, *folk music,* and second, the *invention of opera.* Chords and other parts of harmony were especially suitable for folk music, as the latter was primarily rhythmic in character and, therefore, regular in form (as compared with church counterpoint, which was almost nonrhythmic, and also intricate and indefinite in construction). It thus helped to develop harmony. The invention of opera, the result of a search for a more dramatic form of musical expression, involved different principles of construction. It brought about the creation of a new kind of tone combination. This also helped to develop harmony.

Chords were formerly regarded as the result of the progressions of different melodies in counterpoint. It was not until then that Rameau wrote a treatise on chords as entities by themselves. But his method contained errors, one of the chief of which was the effort to derive the progressions of chords from nature. Catel, a Frenchman, in 1790 published a more practical method, but it was not until 1817 that a clear and definite system of harmony was given to the world, a system which included the present method of marking chords. This new musical science was devised by *Gottfried Weber* (a Ph.D. in law and philosophy), a Hessian procurator of state living in Mannheim. Weber was an able lawyer who had become a musical amateur and a composer of note. He had attained most of his musical knowledge by self-instruction (although his friendship with C. M. von Weber also helped him), and the difficulties which he found in the methods of Kirnberger, Marpurg, Vogler, and others led his logical mind to invent a better system. We surely owe him gratitude.

We have seen that the earliest harmony was really a combination of melodies. By singing or playing the same melody simultaneously at two different levels of pitch, a new effect was created. Later on it was discovered that the sounds were more pleasing if the different melodies were joined together; and this led gradually to polyphonic, or many-voiced, music. By singing simultaneously the tunes of Swanee River and Dvorak's Humoresque, we can obtain a good illustration of the principle.

No single chord in itself conveys any meaning whatsoever. All it does is to give a vague impression. Not chords so much as their progressions make harmony good or bad, and their potency is affected by their place in the rhythmic scheme. Thought in music can be transmitted only by a succession of chords, each chord depending on the one immediately preceding and following it. In other words, music is a vital organic whole, a sort of "chord melting into chord— a flow of harmonic change." Melody represents the rise and fall of the flow—the horizontal view. Harmony (at any given point) represents the simultaneous flow of sounds—the vertical cross-section of it. Any intelligible sentence in any language emphasizes certain words and syllables more than others. Likewise, any musically significant group of tones has certain definite accents. And if we can read any simple metrical line of verse, we cannot help giving it the proper accents and quantities. In language we need at least two or three words to convey our simplest meaning—"Please call me," or, "I am hungry," etc. In music, as well, we need also two or three chords to convey the simplest musical thought.

The addition of harmony (chords) to folk tunes made them more interesting without increasing their difficulty for singing or dancing. Harmony also influenced form or pattern by making it easier to indicate the subdivisions of the tune through *cadences.*

The comparative monotony of harmony in so-called "popular music" is evident. Much of it consists simply of the few elementary chords. Naturally, the good composer will show his ability by using even those simple chords in a more tasteful and artistic way than is usual in popular songs. Incidentally, not all popular music is worthless; but some of it is, and the general public often does not know the difference. Brahms, in the opening theme of the finale of his First Symphony, uses simple chords; Beethoven's Seventh Symphony contains simple chords in the first theme. The listener must learn the difference between artistic and inartistic harmony. He must be able to judge whether or not chords in a composition follow each other in a pleasing succession or are merely put down carelessly without design. Of course, it requires labor to learn to appreciate the different styles of harmony. We do not know as yet why certain harmonies produce certain effects upon us. Obviously, association will help us to judge music better; but it does not explain everything. We know, for instance, that high tones are cheerful; very low ones are gloomy; rapid rhythms are gay; and the slow ones are somber. In harmony, however, no such clear distinctions are noticeable. The appreciation of harmony demands a perception of the relationships among successive chords. The relationship may be simple or abrupt; or it may be made by a delicate adjustment. In simple harmony the changes of chords are slight, nearly all the tones of one chord being held for the next. In current harmony the changes of chords are sudden, and there is very little connection between them. As long as the listener is able to perceive the relationship, whether simple or delicately adjusted, he will continue to appreciate the music to a certain degree. But whenever the progression of chords is not easily perceived by the listener, the music becomes a meaningless discord, a mess of unrelated sounds.

Very naturally, at first, some of the more complex masterpieces of music seem discordant to the listener who has not trained his sense of harmony. But after continual and intelligent listening to good works, he begins to find harmonic order emerging from seeming chaos. Obviously, there is only one way of learning to develop our taste for good harmony, and that is *listening diligently to good music* with the will to succeed. Growth in the appreciation of good music is something that follows frequent hearing, provided the listener knows what to listen for.

Harmony is really not a mystery; nor is it the intricate study that we have been led to believe. It is the law of order as applied to music. It is something that should appeal more to the ear than to the eye. Just as the baby should be taught first to talk before it is taught to spell, read, and write, so in music we should first hear chords and be able to sing them before writing them or calling them by their names. Most people imagine that the study of harmony implies long years of dry plodding. This is not so. Anyone *can* be taught by listening to recognize the simple harmonies of a tune, and everyone *should* be taught. Given a tune, the object is to be able to hear its harmonic setting. Many unsophisticated children can hear naturally the underlying harmonies of a melody.

No matter what the harmonic style of the music may be, the underlying structure of the chords must have its own logic; otherwise a composition lacks a sense of movement. A well-constructed harmonic framework will provide a steady foundation that is always there, even though there be all sorts of embellishments or decorative complexities. It will not make the work too static or too elaborate.

Great composers are readily identified as much by their harmony as their melody. The harmony of Handel is different from that of J. S. Bach, Schubert, Rossini, Liszt, Berlioz, Chopin, Wagner, Debussy, Brahms, Bartok, Stravinsky, Hindemith, Schönberg, Milhaud—all of whom have contributed to the seemingly limitless possibilities of combination and sequences. Rules have become established, but never to the final exclusion of new contributions. After Wagner and his *chromaticism*, the new pathfinders in creating our modern system of harmony are Debussy, with his complete *harmonic freedom*, Schönberg, with his *atonality*, and Milhaud, with his *polytonality*.

Even a little theoretical knowledge puts the listener on the watch. As we become familiar with some of the sounds of harmony, our powers of observation and co-ordination increase with each new experience in listening, and we hear what we never heard before. The first step is to hear the keynote; in this way the inner realm of harmony is consciously penetrated.

There are some who declare that listening to, and recognizing, harmony is a pleasure greater and even more lasting than the pleasure of listening to, and recognizing, melody and rhythm. Harmony gives a satisfaction that no amount of repetition can diminish. It is always possible, at least, to recognize interesting harmonies while listening to music. How curious it is that we have gone on all these years fooling ourselves into thinking that performing a few easily forgotten "pieces" is knowing music! If anything in life is not of practical use, what good is it?

The definite harmonizing of one melody with another is called *counterpoint—puntus contra puntus*—note against note. Counterpoint is the art of writing two or more melodies so that they produce agreeable harmonies when sung or played together.

The round, canon, and fugue are the three forms of composition based on the musical service known as *imitation,* which means the repetition of a phrase by a voice or instrument other than the one which originally gave it out.

In the *round,* imitation usually begins on the same tone or its octave (above or below) and one or two measures later.

Whenever we are singing or playing a round, we are making a melody harmonic within itself. Sumer Is Icumen In is an old English round written in the 13th century, the oldest round we know today. It is composed for six voices.

Rounds (North Country Fisks) were known as "country dances" in England.

Examples of Rounds:

Row, Row, Row your Boat.   Three Blind Mice.
Hear the Songster of the Grove.
O Wie Wohl Ist Mir Am Abend (Lovely Eve—Old German).

In the *canon,* imitation begins before the original phrase is completed, so that the two phrases overlap, so to speak.
Examples:

C. Franck—Finale of the Sonata for Violin & Piano.

In the *fugue,* imitation generally begins on a fifth higher or a fourth lower at an interval of four measures—i.e., the *subject* is given out first, which is followed by the *answer.* The fugue is the most elaborate and complicated development of canonic imitation. It is subject to very rigid rules of construction and probably the most difficult form for the composer to write.

In time counterpoint became too controlled and dominated by rules. It seemed too rigid and too much of an intellectual exercise, losing its feeling. Now, when any medium of expression becomes inadequate to convey all that needs to be expressed, then that medium must either be modified or displaced by something else. Thus, a reform came in the adoption of harmony—the *vertical style* of construction as opposed to the *horizontal style*. Music exists for its beauty, its capacity to give esthetic enjoyment. Harmony gave the needed flexibility and originality.

Music which consists of a single melody and is accompanied by chords is called "homophonic," or single-voiced, music.

When two or more voices or instruments sound at the same time, it is called "unison." This is the most complete harmony possible. Next comes the *octave,* then the *perfect 4th,* the *perfect 5th,* and last, the *major 3rd.*

The major chords or common chords (*triads*)—octave, 3rd, 4th, 5th, and 6th (1 3 5; 1 4 6)—are considered "concords." *Concords* are two tones heard together which sound agreeable; *discords* are two tones heard together which grate upon the ear. The intervals of the 2nd and 7th (1 3 5 7) are still considered discords, although modern composers use them for novel effects. *Consonant chords* are those which seem to be final or at rest; *dissonant chords* are those which seem to require some further chord to satisfy an anticipation aroused in the listener. *Chord progression* is the logical succession among chords. *Resolution* is the movement from a dissonant chord into what follows.

Music is a form of discourse. It is expression in motion that goes by *question* (dissonance—a chord which must move on to another chord), and *answer* (consonance—a chord which demands nothing after it and satisfies by itself), from what we have heard to what we expect to hear.

(Note: Sounds are lettered and have the label of "sharp" and "flat" only in books. To the ear they are merely sounds.)

A chord may be built on any tone. All chords are built

from the bottom up. The base-note, or "root," of a chord is considered the most important part.

There are three systems of *modes*:

1. *Greek,* in which seven different modes were reckoned on descending scales, the Lydian mode being equivalent to our modern major scale.

2. *Ecclesiastical, or Gregorian, mode,* in which two main modes, the authentic and plagal, are reckoned on ascending scales, a system still used in the Roman Catholic Church.

3. *Modern, major, and minor modes* were developed in the 17th century. The ascending major modes resemble the Greek Lydian; and the descending minor, the Greek Hypodorian. (There are three kinds of minor scales: *harmonic,* 1½ steps between 6–7; *melodic,* like major after minor 3rd; *normal,* like A minor, all white keys, ascending and descending.)

The best way to become acquainted with harmony or, in particular, with scales, chords, and keys, is to sit in front of a piano, even if one cannot play a note. The keyboard consists of white and black keys, the white ones running in a uniform row, the black keys in between them in groups of two blacks, then none, then three, then none, again two, again space, etc.

Locate a white key just to the left of one of the groups of two black keys. Strike this key and play the white keys, working up the keyboard to the right, counting your starting key as number one. You will find that number eight is also a white key to the left of a pair of two black keys and with no black key to the left. Strike number one and number eight together at the same time. You will notice that the tones blend perfectly and that you will get a similar blending from striking number one with the eighth key below it in the opposite direction to the left. The space between the two notes is called an "interval," and this kind of interval, eight steps apart, is the simplest. It is called an "octave."

Now, the key with which we started (just to the left of one of the groups of two black keys) is known as C. If we play through a regular succession of whole and half tones to its number eight, or octave, we get a scale. Naturally, the scale can be extended as far as the keyboard will go, i.e., for more than an octave. The usual piano contains seven or seven and one-half octaves. The number one of any of these scales is called its "keynote," and the key denotes the relationship of the series of notes.

After gaining some idea of scales and keys as the relations of the tones played successively, let us consider chords, which are the relations of tones played simultaneously. Taking number one, or C, and striking at the same time the corresponding number eight, we obtain an octave chord, which has the peculiar property of blending more perfectly than any other combination of two tones. Number one and number three also blend very well, as also do number one and number five, or even 1 3 5 and 8 together. Such chords, as just played, are called "major" chords; they have a solid, blending sound.

The *1 3 5 major chord, or triad,* is the commonest and most useful pattern of harmony. It should be recognized not only in its original form, 1 3 5, in all keys, but also in either of its inversions: 3 1 5, or 5 1 3.

The next important chord is the *dominant 7th*: g b d f and its inversions—1 3 5 7; 3 5 7 1; 5 7 1 3; 7 1 3 5. It, too, should be recognized not only in its original form but also in any of its inversions.

Next in importance comes the *subdominant chord*: f a c —1 3 5.

(Note: A single chord gives only a vague impression; it conveys no meaning. Only a succession of chords in a forward movement may transmit thought in music. However, chords have an individual quality that give them significance. But music is a living organic whole, not a series of detached chords strung together; and the place and function of any chord is largely dependent on what immediately precedes and follows it.)

Listen to the major chords of these famous tunes:

Aloha Oe.	Annie Laurie.
Sweet and Low.	Carry Me Back to Old Virginia.
Home Sweet Home.	Massa's in the cold, cold Ground.
Old Black Joe.	Comin' thro' the Rye.
Santa Lucia.	My Old Kentucky Home.
Swanee River.	The Quilting Party.
Ein Ton	Now the Day Is Over.

(Monotone by P. Cornelius).

Minor harmony is difficult to explain. Actually, the difference between the *major* and *minor chord* is simply that the interval of the 3rd is sounded half a tone lower in the minor than in the major. The major chord is a bright, cheerful, happy, gay, joyous sound; whereas the minor chord is by comparison rather dull, dreamy, thoughtful, melancholy, sad. However, this distinction is not an absolute one. Many a composer has successfully expressed melancholy in the major key and cheerfulness in the minor key. Generally, of course, this distinction is a good one; and in the long run the ear can tell quickly whether the music is in a major or a minor key.

We should now become acquainted with minor chords.

The *1 3 5—c eb g minor chord, or triad,* should be recognized not only in its original form in all keys but in either of its inversions: 3 1 5, or 5 1 3.

Chords built on the various degrees of the scale are:

g	a	b	c	d	e	f
e	f	g	a	b	c	d
C	D	E	F	G	A	B
1	2	3	4	5	6	7
Maj.	min.	min.	Maj.	Maj.	min.	dim.

The original Greek modes, or scales, were all in minor keys, corresponding roughly to the white keys of our modern piano, without sharps or flats. The scales were initiated by the later ecclesiastical modes and used in early Church music and sung in unison, without harmony. The distinction between major and minor is basically a distinction of mode or mood rather than that of key or melody.

The *chromatic scale* consists of 13 half-steps:

C	c♯	d	d♯	e	f	f♯	g	g♯	a	a♯	b	c
1	2	3	4	5	6	7	8	9	10	11	12	13
C	d♭	d	e♭	e	f	g♭	g	a♭	a	b♭	b	c

The modern *whole-tone scale* goes up and down in steps of a whole tone (without any of the half-tone intervals used in the diatonic scale). Eight tones of the whole-tone scale go up to the 6th. This explains why chords of the 9th are so common in modern music, especially that of Debussy and of those composers who have imitated him. These chords take the place of the perfect major chord when the whole-tone scale is used.

The *chord of the 9th* should be recognized not only in its original form: c e g b d—1 3 5 7 9—but also in either of its inversions: e g b c d; g b c d e; b c d e g; c d e g b.

An interesting interval is the *augmented* one, i.e., an interval to which half a tone has been added: c e g♯.

Another interesting interval is the *diminished* one, i.e., an interval from which a half a tone has been substracted: c♯ e g; c e♭ g♭.

A very popular chord is the *diminished 7th*: C♯ e g b; its inversions are: e g b c♯; g b c♯ e; b c♯ e g.

The notorious *"blue" chords* make liberal use of minor 7ths and diminished 7ths. Minor 7th: c e g b; diminished 7th: C♯ e g b.

The minor 7th is the regular interval in the dominant 7th chord, and it is only when this appears as a primary and not as a secondary that the *blue effect* is produced. That is, when we put a minor 7th into the final tonic chord, we at once have a blue harmony.

The blue endings of modern popular music are considered conventional, and almost all the ultramodern serious music is totally unorthodox.

The addition of harmony to folk tunes made them more interesting without increasing the difficulty of singing, dancing, or understanding them. Also, harmony influenced form, or pattern, by making it easier to indicate the subdivisions of the tune through cadences.

The ending of any composition (or any strain of it) is called a "cadence." Cadences are chord progressions at the end of a composition and at other places not the end itself which give a sense of finality or of punctuation. Cadences are the point of repose (a point of rest in the music) where the phrases naturally end. Certain cadences give a very strong effect of finality, while others arouse a feeling of something more to follow.

(Note: When the ending falls upon the unaccented part (beat) of a measure, we have a *feminine ending*.)

When the cadence ends in a tonic chord following a dominant chord, it is called an "authentic," "perfect," "full," or "complete" cadence. It gives us a definite effect of close in both melody and harmony:

V to I

When the cadence ends in a dominent chord following a tonic chord, it is called an "imperfect," "half," or "incomplete" cadence. It partially suggests a conclusion and makes us feel that there is something more coming:

I to V

When the cadence ends in a tonic chord following a subdominant chord, it is called a "plagal" cadence. This cadence is used very often in the Amen progression of hymns:

IV to I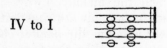

When the cadence ends in some other chord than I after V, it is called a "deceptive," or "interrupted" cadence. The ear, expecting to resolve it to I, is surprised when it fails to do so: V to ?

Other cadences are classed as *irregular*.

So-called *"barber-shop chords"* are chords in which the voices move around a 4th, which remains stationary. These chords actually originated in barber shops where Negro quartets first flourished. Note the following examples:

Changing from one key to another by logical harmonic sequences is called "modulating." The simplest one is from a given key to one nearly related to it—i.e., the 5th (dominant) or 4th (subdominant), its relative minor, or the relative minor of its 5th. Its purpose is to please the ear with a fresh procession of chords. A good rule to apply in modulation is to have at least one tone in common between two adjoining chords.

(Note: A change of representation without a change of pitch is called an "enharmonic" change (e♭–d♯; c♭–b).)

The theorist must thoroughly comprehend, compare, and select while working with chord progressions and combinations of moving parts; the trained listener, on the other hand, will be content with just enough to enable him to sift the masses of sound that enter his brain and to recognize in them a certain reason and order. He should know the fundamental distinction of major and minor, of consequence and dissonance, of tonality and atonality, etc.

In a piece of music the centralization about one chord is called "tonality," or "key." Tonality means the feeling that a certain tone is the central one of a group—the resting point, or home-tone, to which the melody always has a tendency to return, and which almost always constitutes its final tone. A composer chooses a key as the painter chooses a color. The primary colors are few, like the tones of the scale, but every color has a variety of shades. Key, or tonality, is a matter of harmony; it is the most subtle of all the means at the disposal of the composer for giving his work that variety in unity which is beauty.

The increasing freedom of tonality in music corresponds

to similar developments in color and form in painting by Picasso, Cezanne, and others. Colors formerly considered unsuitable are now used on the same canvas in relatively close relationship and give much pleasure to many by their bold and vivid contrast. Everyone must decide for himself what contrasts in tone and tonality and color have significance. Everyone's sincere reaction is his own, even if such contrasts are meaningless or painfully disagreeable to others.

(Note: A discord is stronger if it occurs on a strong beat than if it is merely taken "in passing" and falls on an unaccented part of the measure.)

Atonality discards any recognizable key in a piece of music.

Polytonality juxtaposes alien tonalities in a composition.

D. FORM

Musical form, or pattern, is the next subject. After learning to recognize the various rhythms, melodies, harmony, and tone-color, a little knowledge of how musical patterns or designs are made will greatly increase the pleasure of listening to music.

In almost all the arts—except music—our first impression is of the whole, then of the parts. In music it is necessary to remember the parts as they flash before the mind, and then, by way of memory, to combine these parts into a whole. Because of this so-called "difficulty," many inexperienced listeners feel that they "do not understand music." Thus, because they do not understand it, they conclude that it has no form, no plan of construction. They assume that music consists simply of a series of pleasing tones put together by a clever composer. The fact is that a piece of music of value is just as carefully planned as any other work of art.

Form or pattern is the first manifestation of law. Ideas must be repeated in order to become definitely fixed in our minds. We must know something about the structural plan in order to form an idea about a work of art. The beauty of structure can be one of the greatest delights to the music-lover. There is no fine piece of music in existence that does not obey the general laws of form.

In nature, form is a predominant law. We find form in leaves, flowers, fruit, snowflakes, frost, all types of crystallization, seeds, etc. In art, form is essential. All art expresses itself through the vehicle of form, in which the parts are pieced together in such relations of proportion and symmetry as to make a unified whole. Form is simply the means of securing the greatest effect with a minimum waste of energy. The same principles of organization and system are found in business. Form in music is the constructive principle of artistic design, the method of development of musical thought, the logic of sound. From the study of form we learn to perceive the structure, the artistic design, of every composition we may listen to or perform.

Order is the first law in art as in nature, and the recognition of the orderly arrangement of sounds is the first requirement for understanding music. The search for orderly relations among audible phenomena must be cultivated. *Order, system, proportion is noticeable in the simplest folk song or tune.*

Form is not only an indispensable means for the artist to make clear to himself and to others the impulse that stirred him to utterance, but it is in itself a thing to be enjoyed, because of the beauty that lies in proportion, order, and unified variety.

However, an art occasionally enters upon a stage of deterioration whenever it ceases to be vivified by a new element. To keep constantly to the forms sanctioned by time and custom is to surrender the free development of music. In fact, it may even prevent the return of old forms, which still possess vigor and sudden important for living generations. For everything begins over and over again; a current of intense life links the present to the future, which itself is often but a resurrection of the past.

In order for the listener to gather distinct and lasting impressions, the composer must so plan his music that the important ideas stand out conspicuously and are readily distinguishable; and the leading musical thoughts must be repeated often enough to become fixed in the memory of the listener.

The principles of form co-ordinate the various elements of music—rhythm, melody, harmony, and tone-color—into a complete work of art. Form in music is an orderly arrangement of a musical idea or ideas. It is a specific arrangement of the various parts of a composition. Indeed, music is formally patterned sound. Form refers to the particular pattern (rondo, variation, sonata, etc.) which the composer uses; it is the actual arrangement of melodies, rhythms, and harmonies. As a result, we have a characteristic structure—a unified whole—that is easily recognized by the ear. This unified whole, which gives the impression of completeness to the listener, takes in unity of tonality or key and unity of general rhythmic effect, as well as unity in the grouping of the various parts of the work (phrases, periods, movements).

We might have a long composition unified—as, for example, a conventional border design—but it would be, at the same time, very monotonous as music. The repetition of a small motive or unit of design builds up the border to any length desired in an unvaried rhythm. However, such mechanical, unvaried repetition of a motive or a unit of design in music would be tiresome. It is necessary to find some method of grouping certain smaller divisions together into a still larger unit—the work as a whole.

After a composer has created a melody in a certain rhythmic pattern, he harmonizes it and applies form as his organizing factor, for only through form can he arrive at a complete and logical conclusion of a work of art. He then also gives his musical material to certain instruments or voices for effective tone-coloring.

It is possible for a painter, writer, sculptor, architect, or musician to be a master of form without possessing the creative inspiration to give it real importance. On the other hand, it is also possible for a man with vast creative instincts to fail in the achievement of true art because he neglects the mastery of form. *Form* and *content* in music are inseparable and interchangeable. This can hardly be proven logically, it would be splitting hairs to differentiate between form and content in music as we do between the metrical structure and the idea of a poem. Some sort of starting point, some part of human experience, is a necessary ingredient in the purest and most formal piece of instrumental music. Where music is mere pattern-making or note-spinning, it is without warmth and without life. Now, if this content of music can be said to be its meaning, it is valuable to us because of the fact that: 1) *Some sort of human experience is expressed in music;* and 2) This music affords us an insight into the mind of its composer. It is what the mind of the artist makes of the subject matter that constitutes a work of art.

Form cannot be omitted in any art. Architecture, sculpture, painting, literature—all exemplify the same fundamental principles of good form as music; namely, a central idea which, through repetition, contrast, and unity, is emphasized in proportion to its importance to the secondary or subsidiary idea. The subject matter is not the same as the material. The subject matter, or content, is the emotional experience which is finally embodied in the material (stone, granite, marble, bronze, wood, color, words, sounds). In looking at a great edifice, we usually notice first the large divisions of the building as a whole. If it is a church or a capitol, the thing that strikes us most are the two towers or wings with the immense dome which, from the distance, seems to separate, and contrast with, the towers. The two towers or wings are similar in design and are evidently meant to balance one another. Examining the three main divisions individually, we find that each one has a definite plan of construction all its own. The other parts of the edifice have their own well-developed plan of construction also; and everywhere we find repetition used to give unity, while constrast is used to avoid monotony. Any musical idea, no matter how good it is, will become tiresome with ceaseless repetition. It should be stated once or twice, followed by something different; then it may be repeated in the original version toward the end. Really, musical form is simple if the idea of contrast or variety be kept in mind. Notes are combined into phrases; phrases into melodies; melodies into whole compositions—always with the need for contrast molding the form.

In every good painting the artist selects, rejects, and arranges. He never gives a literal photographic reproduction of his subject. Straight lines and curves echo or balance one another. Various objects relieve one another. Masses, colors, lights, and shades are arranged for the purpose of variety, reinforcement, and concentration. The eye of the trained observer is directed by several subtle devices to the central point of interest. Whether in a picture, an edifice, or in a composition, the various parts must be welded together into a unified whole that will be effective as an entity and not merely in its parts.

Rhythm, melody, harmony, and tone-color are all, to a certain extent, instinctive, although their command may be developed by training and experience. Form, also, may be instinctive to some extent; but as a rule, it is acquired only through study and practice.

Every type of music has its own possibilities of form. Great inspiration, plus a good command of form, will inevitably produce a highly significant composition in whatever style the composer may have selected.

The necessity for form in music or in the other arts is practical as well as artistic. A melody, even an inspired one, soon becomes monotonous if repeated over and over again without a change. This monotony is avoided usually by the combination of several tunes with interludes and changes of key or orchestration. Now, the larger the form, the more elaborately and logically the melodic material is worked out by the composer.

The simplest musical form is the song, or tune. Songs are composed of melodies which, in turn, consist of phrases; these may be made up of similar units called "periods." If one is writing a song, he cannot simply sing a melody and then stop. As a rule, the melody would not be long enough; and besides, it would be rather dull. Songs are, therefore, made up of either a melody repeated or else two or more melodies or phrases.

There are two methods of writing a song, or tune. One is to arrange melodies in two sections, the second contrasting with the first. This is called "binary" form, which we may indicate as *A-B*. The other method is an arrangement of melody, then a contrasting melody, and then a return to the original melody. This is called "ternary" form, which we may indicate as *A-B-C*. Both methods satisfy the ear; and both have been the basis of the intricate and more developed art forms of the great composers.

The structure of a melody is only a small part of form in the larger sense. A folk song or piece of popular music may consist of only a single tune or two which is obvious and easily remembered. A work of greater dimensions, however, has several tunes or themes combined; these themes are broken up into their component parts, with the rhythm, the harmony, the key, and the instrumental tone-coloring changed.

Music begins with feeling or imagination. A theme or musical idea is the first thing needed to express feeling. A good theme divides itself into two or more phrases.

The fundamental principles active in all the fine arts are:

  1.) *Repetition or imitation* (due to the fleeting nature of music).
  2.) *Contrast or variety.*
    a) imitation.
    b) transposition.
    c) restatement (with shift in accent).
  3.) *Symmetry or unity* (i.e., the effect of coherence and completeness every work of art should give).

These three principles make for *balance, or proportion.* Themes must balance each other if the song or tune is to be beautiful.

Of course, in addition to these fundamental principles there must be present such qualities as *originality, sincerity,* and *workmanship.* Otherwise the art work will not live.

Repetition or imitation is the basic form in every art. Any art work must provide sufficient repetition to establish the feeling of unity; that is, the parts must obviously belong together as one unified whole.

In poetry it is meter, verse length, and construction of

stanza that are repeated; and these give the feeling of definite structure.

In architecture it is the grouping of large units, such as towers, wings, and arches, together with the repetition of smaller units, windows, doors, columns, details of ornamentation, etc., that make up the fundamentals of design.

In music it is the grouping of large sections with characteristic repetition of parts, the balancing of phrases of similar construction, and the repetition of rhythmic patterns and harmonic progressions that provide the basis of form.

Contrast, or variety, as an art principle, is as necessary as it is interesting. The best way to avoid monotony in any art work is to present contrasting material. When man tired of monotonously repeating a little figure and varied it, he became a master of form. Variety in unity is the foundation of form. So the pattern, or form, emerges by *exposition, contrast* (development) and *recapitulation.*

For example, let us consider this principle applied to a novel or a play. The author presents his characters and states the dramatic situation. Next, he introduces some problem, some contrasting or hostile force that will create suspense and enlist the interest and sympathy of the audience. This is the plot of the novel or play, corresponding to the development of musical thought. However, if the author fails to solve his problem and does not arrive at a logical ending, he has disappointed his audience. In order to adhere to the principles of form, he must have a final recapitulation, a reminder that everything is as it should be. Similarly, the composer ends with recapitulation or reminder of his most important melodies or themes, thereby creating satisfaction in the minds of his listeners.

Reduced to its simplest terms, this common pattern of form may be called *A-B-A.* It is the most important and widely used of all musical forms—the A-B-A form, or *statement, contrast, restatement.* Many folk songs or tunes are constructed after the A-B-A pattern or after a pattern very similar.

Symmetry, or unity, of form is achieved through repetition and variety. This is a well-established axiom in all art.

The principles of unity and the relationship of parts exist in all great art. The different parts must have some resemblance to each other, or else the piece will sound nonsensical. Therefore, most musical compositions end in the same key in which they began; and we often find that the last phrase is more or less like one of the phrases in the first part. When an artist has combined contrasting elements and arrived at a recognizable unity, in spite of their seemingly antagonistic qualities, he has put the stamp of individuality on his work, regardless of whether or not he has used original material as his themes.

No one knows how folk music attained its lovely forms. The beauty and vitality of the world's best music rests on the pattern discovered in folk music. A folk song is a perfect, though simple, example of musical design or form.

Folk music is a natural art—it reveals national feeling.

Silcher, the German, Foster, the American, as well as other fine song-writers had a good command of form. The permanence of their folk songs in the hearts of men should be sufficient proof of their unique qualities of inspiration. A Silcher or a Foster song may be considered more significant than an uninspired symphony.

All folk songs having more than one stanza use the same tune for each stanza, no matter how varied the words are. This is called the "strophic" style of song-writing. All popular music (which is really an artificial sort of folk music) follows this style.

The art song, or "through-composed" song, usually has its music follow the words closely throughout, striving to fit their spirit as well as their meter.

All comparatively simple music is constructed of short groups called "phrases." One or two measures may constitute a *phrase*, similar to a few words in poetry. In language, for instance, the meaning would not be clear if it consisted simply of a succession of words with no accent and no division into phrases. The form of poetry is much more obvious than that of prose, because the phrases are of more regular length. Phrases in simple music correspond closely with the lines of poetry.

When an answering phrase is added to the first phrase, we get a musical "sentence." Again, as it takes two lines of poetry to establish regularity of meter, together with size and style of design, so in music two phrases are combined into a sentence. If this sentence ends in a perfect cadence, it is called a "period," just as a complete sentence in English ends with a punctuation mark, the period. The first phrase of a period is often referred to as the "thesis," and the second phrase as the "antithesis."

At first, rhythm in music was very regular. Practically all phrases were four or eight measures long. The four- or eight-measure period is the easiest to recognize and to remember, like a group of four words which the eye discerns quickly in reading.

Very naturally, all melodies of folk songs, hymns, minuets, gavottes, marches, waltzes, etc., are usually written in the binary form, which consists of two units, mostly eight-measure periods or *sixteen-measure periods* (*double period*).

Some of these songs, minuets, gavottes, etc., are also written in the *ternary or three-part form,* which consists of three larger units, the first and third being very much alike, but the middle much different. The middle part usually is in contrasting mood. Often this middle part is in a different key, and practically always it has a different rhythm. Composers early realized the importance of making the end of a piece resemble the beginning. They found that it is sometimes a good idea to repeat the entire first part after the second part. This gives the listener a strong impression of unity; and, at the same time, it enables the composer to introduce still greater variety or contrast in the second part. The ternary is probably the most common type of musical construction, especially in the smaller forms. It is represented by the symbols *A-B-C*.

As soon as the song had been developed in either of the simple binary, or two-part, and ternary, or three-part, form, restless and enterprising musicians began to devise ways to make it richer and more effective. As time went on, many varied musical forms were invented. Thus, form enters into every step of construction in every composition, from a simple pattern of only a few tunes to the complex structure of a symphony or a tone-poem.

To repeat, in order to recognize the three fundamental principles of art—*repetition, contrast, symmetry*:

1. Concentrate intensely on the music while you are listening. Do not allow yourself to think of other things. Try hard to memorize the main theme, or themes, so that you may be able to recall at least the outlines of the parts that have gone before.

2. Hear and rehear a good composition, small or large, so that by becoming familiar with its parts as the result of repeated listenings (memory), you may ultimately come to understand the plan of construction, the form of each work as a whole.

Listen to folk songs and folk dances, and recognize: Rhythm; key—major or minor; form—binary or ternary, etc.; nationality.

Examples of binary form:

BAYLEY
    Long, Long Ago.

MACDOWELL
    To a Wild Rose.

NEAPOLITAN
    Santa Lucia.

RUSSIAN MONJIK TUNE
    Volga Boat Song (a-a-b-a).

GRUBER
    Silent Night (a-b-c; four measures each; 6/8 time).

GERMAN FOLKSONG
    Du Lieber Augustin (a-a-b-a). (comp. 1799)

?
    For He's a Jolly Good Fellow (a-b-a).

?
    Gaudeamus Igitur (a-a-b-c).

SCOTCH
    Auld Lang Syne (a-b-b-c).

H. CAREY
    America (a-b; only fourteen measures long; a is six measures long).

GIARDINI
    Come Thou Almighty King (a-b; sixteen measures long).

HADYN
  Deutschland über Alles (a-a-b-c; old Croation folk tune).

A. S. SULLIVAN
  Onward Christian Soldiers (a-b-c-d-e-f, each four measures; an interesting, though irregular structure of twenty-four measures).

PORTUGUESE HYMN
  Adeste Fidelis—O Come, All Ye Faithful (a-b-c-d-e; four measures each; irregular in structure).
  America the Beautiful (O Mother Dear Jerusalem; a-a-b-c; four measures each).

SPANISH
  Juanita (a-a-b-b-c-c; each section shows a decided variation in its repetition to reach a different cadence).

H. BISHOP
  Home Sweet Home (a-a-b-b-c-b; it is quite elaborate in form; by English composer).

J. S. BACH
  Air for G String (a good example of two-part form on a larger scale; the second part is longer than the first; both are repeated).

ST. C. FOSTER
  My Old Kentucky Home (a-a-a-a-b-a; the first part consists of eight measures and is repeated; the second part, or "chorus," also consists of eight measures, the first four of which are composed of new material [introducing variety], while the last four measures are exactly the same as the last four measures of the first part—which makes us feel the unity of the song as a whole).

NEGRO SPIRITUAL
  Swing Low, Sweet Chariot (repeats its first idea only after the middle section, "I looked over Jordan," has provided the necessary variety).

OLD ENGLISH
  Drink to Me Only with Thine Eyes (the nameless composer states his melody twice; then he introduces new material at the words, "The thirst that from the soul doth rise"; this, and the following line, provide the needed contrast; then he goes back to the original idea at the words, "But might I of Jove's nectar sip.")

  Smoke Gets in Your Eyes (notice the formal reason for the short section in sharps, "So I chaffed them and I gayly laughed").

St. C. Foster

Swanee River—Old Folks at Home (a-a-a-a-b-a; each four measures. *1 a* ends in an incomplete cadence on the dominant chord; *2 a* ends on a complete cadence; *3 a* repeat; *4 a* repeat; *5 b* harmony swings from tonic to dominant and then to subdominant; *6 a* is like *2 a*. The entire melody of this beautiful, simple song consists of rhythmic phrases, the first two balancing each other and forming a period, the third and fourth similarly constituting a second period; while in a still larger way, the entire first period balances the entire second. It is this arrangement of phrases into periods and larger groups that gives definite form to music and enables the listener to grasp its structure easily).

Examples of ternary form:

Ghys Amaryllis.	Beethoven Minuet in G.
Gossec Tamborin.	Schubert Military March in D.

(Notes: 1) Songs are chosen only because it is so easy to indicate, by means of their words, the formal scheme of the music. The A-B-A structure (or some obvious variant of it, such as, A-A-B-A; A-B-A-B-A; A-B-A-C-A) occurs in folk tunes, dances, overtures, symphony movements, etc. There is something in it which satisfies a basic human sense of balance and design. This, in addition to its great value for purposes of contrast, accounts for its wide popularity.

2) Formalism, which values form for its own sake, is not the same as form. The technical virtuosity of a composition sometimes stresses poetic form at the expense of content.

3) When musical forms grow according to the nature of their themes and rhythms, and not according to some preconceived idea, the form is organic. When new kinds of music are put into old, traditional forms, there can hardly be unity. The real nature of the new music and the traditional nature of the old forms are antagonistic to one another. In the future, new music very likely will create new forms which will grow naturally from the themes, rhythms, and inner feeling of the music. Only then does music have unity. Form and content must be truly one. In the future, musical ideas themselves will create their own forms.

E. TONE-COLOR

The matter of tone-color in music is not such a poor subject, after all. It has to do with a tone's actual timbre, or quality of sound, produced by a particular voice or instrument, and it touches the fascinating science of instrumentation.

Tone-color is the quality, or timbre, of a tone; it gives a tone its vocal or instrumental individuality and is determined chiefly by *overtones.* It is very important in modern music because the resources of rhythm, melody, and harmony have been quite exhausted, whereas the possibilities of instrumentation and the invention and discovery of new effects of tone-color seem to be infinite. It is very difficult, indeed, to be original in rhythm, melody, or harmony unless one goes in for absurdly illogical progressions and combinations; but tone-color provides opportunities for new effects. The differences in tone-quality of each instrument are the product of their *size, shape, and construction.*

Music without color of some sort is inconceivable. Even before music itself was born, the primitive men who experimented with rhythmic patterns certainly came to recognize differences of color in their sounds. A bludgeon pounded on a hollow log produces one sort of sensation; a dry stick struck against the trunk of a standing tree is something else again. This holds good even if the rhythmic pattern is the same. The difference is one of quality, or timbre. When man found that a slow, steady beat suggested awe or terror, he was not long in discovering that the hollow-log idea strengthened the suggestion immensely. The ominous coloring certainly produced much more awe and terror than the dry stick and the live tree ever could, even though pace and spacing were identical in the two cases.

But tone-color did not really come into its own until melody started. First, there were the differences of timbre in the singing, as in the speaking, voice. Then more subtle differences came to be noted. A man could use his singing voice to suggest or identify such emotions as color, love of wandering, hatred of the nearby tribe, etc. Women could express tenderness, love, merriment, etc. The patterns of rhythm and melody for these two general classifications were radically different, of course, but the contrast in tone-colorings also had an important bearing on the emotional response of anyone lucky enough to have heard those forgotten singers. Here were plenty of opportunities for color —the varying timbre of the human voice, and the different kinds of crude percussion instruments that could be evolved from the hollow log. But many more were coming. Somebody tried blowing through a reed—and so started the wind instruments' long process of development. Somebody else plucked the sun-dried tendons stretched across the opening of a tortoise shell—and thus started the development of stringed instruments.

Then followed long ages of development during which new instruments and improvements on old ones constantly appeared. Each new instrument and each important variation on an old instrument added new colors to music. Human voices of various types were combined with one another and with instruments. Man discovered so many different kinds of timbre that the resulting richness of resource came to have an immensely important effect on the expressive power of music.

We are the heirs of all the knowledge of color possibilities laboriously gathered by the trial-and-error method through several thousand years. The number of colorings at our command is almost infinite, for each voice or instrument boasts many hues, and the process of combining them in differing proportions can still go on.

It is essential for the enjoyment of music not only to recognize various patterns of rhythms, melody, and harmony but also to distinguish the tone-colors of different instruments and various types of human voices. In time we can perceive their effects in combination.

On the whole, it is rather easy to recognize tone-color, for most musical instruments have quite a definite quality of tone; while the differences between male and female voices—and even between tenor and bass, or soprano and alto—are quite obvious. In addition, there are boys' choruses and girls' choruses. All of these voices have their own individual timbre as well as their peculiar tone-color when considered as a group. The human singing voice surpasses all instruments in its ability to express nuance and in its definiteness. The more we listen, the keener our ear becomes.

The intelligent listener should have two objectives in regard to tone-color: 1) to become unfailingly aware of different instruments and voices and their separate tonal characteristics ;and 2) to gain a deeper appreciation of the expressive purpose of a composer in using any instrument, voice, or combination of instruments or voices. Naturally, the expressive meaning or value of any specific instrument or voice determines its choice by the composer. And this is true not only in the case of a single instrument or voice but also in combinations of instruments or voices. The choice of any specific instrument or voice depends entirely upon the emotional feeling that a composer wishes to convey. There is definitely a characteristic way of writing for each instrument. The various tone-colors that an instrument can produce and which are truly its own are the ones sought after by the composer. The percussion instruments are used generally either to heighten rhythmic effects, to increase the sense of climax, or to add color to the other instruments. Naturally, the more they are saved for important moments, the more effective they will be.

A great variety of tone-color is possible not only because there are many different instruments of various kinds, but also because each instrument has a certain individuality of tone, such as the human voice; and, finally, each instrument and each voice present a wide variety of colors within their own range. The tones in the upper range of the piano have an absolutely different quality from those in the lower range. Likewise, the tones played on an E string of a violin have an entirely different quality from those on a G string; and even the human voice shows a wide range of tone both in speaking and in singing.

Tone-color depends on the friction at the point where the vibrations of the air, which produce a musical sound, are started, as well as on the nature of the resources amplifying the tone. Every musical tone consists of a fundamental tone (which determines the recognizable pitch) and a series of overtones in harmony with the fundamental tone but not audible.

In order to make the air vibrate, some tone-producing surface must first be set in vibration.

A musical tone is generated either by: striking (drum), *blowing* (horn), or *rubbing* (violin).

Feeling is often conveyed through the *quality* of the human voice. But much of our reading and singing fails to arouse an appropriate response because the quality of the voice does not fit the ideas that are presented. In vocal music the composer has practically no way of indicating appropriate tone quality. For this reason, therefore, much depends upon the performer.

The human voice is a wind instrument, and the vocal cords are like the vibrating reeds that are placed in the mouthpiece of some woodwind instrument. The tone-color resulting depends partly on the vocal cords themselves and partly on the resonators that amplify the tone. Thus, we know that people who sing or speak badly try to make their vocal cords do all the work. Their voices sound "in the throat," and they obviously strain to create more volume.

The resonators are very important for tone-color; and their quality makes all the difference between good and bad instruments. Purity of tone is attained through lack of interference; and if a singer produces a harsh, rasping sound, it is a sure sign that something is interfering with the free passage of the vibrating air. A good singer makes use of the resonating chambers in the mouth (including the lips), nose, the cavities in the forehead, the chest, and to some extent, the entire body. In addition, a good singer stands upon a board surface, instead of a carpet, to secure still more resonance. He also removes any heavy curtains in the background.

To repeat, a pure and beautiful singing or speaking tone requires, first, absence of interference; second, a quiet and steady command of air pressure. If a voice is harsh, insipid, or uncertain, the trouble usually may be traced to a lack of one or more of these three requirements.

A piano would have little tone without its wooden sounding board. Wind instruments depend upon the size and shape of their tubes and the formation of the opening from which the tone emerges. The development of the various wind instruments rests upon the scientific fact that a tone-producing tube, tuned at any pitch, will give out at least five natural tones by mere variation in the force of breath. These tones are: the fundamental, the octave above, the fifth above, the next octave, and the third above that. Here is the law of nature that created the bugle tones and the 1-3-5 combination so significant in music. As with the stopping of strings, so also with the air in a tube—the process of shortening produces higher tones. Thus, a complete scale can be obtained by the various ways of controlling the length of the tube. Drums have their volume and quality affected by the size and shape of their resonating chambers, as do also the violin, viola, cello, bass, harp, etc. The very first drums had no definite pitch and were probably nothing but hollow logs. Later on, a skin was stretched across the end of a hollow log, and the tone then had a sort of pitch. A definite step toward melody was reached when it was found that a more tightly stretched drumhead produced a tone of higher pitch. From the drums of different pitches were developed the various kinds of string instruments, such as the lyre, harp, dulcimer, zither, clavichord, harpsichord, viols, etc.

(Note: When a sounding body vibrates, it also divides into segments which produce higher tones. The laws governing the vibration of stretched strings were formulated by Pythagoras in about 600 B.C. He found that, all other things being equal, the number of vibrations varies inversely according to the length of a string. Now, when a string vibrates, it does not merely swing as a whole but subdivides into fractional parts which form shorter vibrations superimposed upon the main one. These fractional parts, as they are shorter than the whole string, give higher tones; they are called "overtones" (natural harmonics) and blend with the fundamental, or main, tone whenever it is sounded. The series of overtones, starting from any C, will be ascending: CCGC E G B♭ C D E F♯ G A B♭ B C. The F♯, high A, and the first B will be somewhat off-pitch from our scale. The first ten overtones are enough for all practical uses. It is the presence of these overtones in various amounts which causes the differences in tone-color among various instruments or voices. The acoustic principles governing air-volumes in tubes (organ, pipes, flute, oboe, clarinet, trumpet, etc.) are somewhat similar.

In addition to the diversity of individual timbres, there are many possibilities of multiplying musical instruments and human voices by combining them. Ten violins in unison produce a tone that is absolutely unlike the tone of a solo violin, quite apart from the difference in volume. A hundred male voices singing softly together produce a completely new tone, entirely different from the ordinary solo singing voice or small chorus. Much variety and subtlety are possible when the responsibility is concentrated, as in a solo quartet.

The natural qualities of many of the musical instruments have been impressed by such devices as muting, the playing of harmonics (overtones), plucking the strings with the fingers, etc.

In orchestra music, the appropriate tone quality forms a very valuable means of conveying ideas. The trumpet is associated with the martial; the oboe with the plaintive; the bassoon with the comic; the trombone with the majestic; etc. Thus, a theme given to a certain instrument arouses a certain mood or idea when the listener hears its particular tone quality.

Any instrument in the orchestra is apt to be combined with one or more of the others in order to produce the desired tone-color or effect. In a musical composition the different instruments, played at the same time, create a blend of sounds which expresses to a great extent the meaning of the piece.

The mixed quartet of human voices consists of: *soprano, alto, tenor, bass.*

The string quartet (the parallel in instrumental music) consists of: *first violin* (soprano), *second violin* (alto), *viola* (tenor), and *cello* (bass).

When the string quartet is duplicated many times, it becomes the major portion of a symphony orchestra with the addition of a fifth part—the double basses. The basses double the bass part of the cello an octave lower and supply the groundwork for the harmony of the entire orchestra, leaving the cellos free to play the melody when desired.

The four French horns of the symphony orchestra are a complete quartet in themselves, but they also combine admirably with the various wood-wind instruments, as well as the strings.

In addition to the strings and the wood-wind instruments, we have the brasses and the percussion instruments, making up the four great divisions of the symphony orchestra.

One thing is sure: there are a great many more varieties of tone-color than most of us realize. All we need is long and persistent training. As a result of listening more intently, we may not only become surer of our understanding of the message of a particular piece of music but may increase many times our appreciation and enjoyment of it.

It is *the power of music which arouses in us infinite shades of feeling;* and it is because *feelings are the incentives of action in human beings* that music is so powerful an influence in our lives.

3. THE SIGNIFICANCE, OR CONTENT, OF MUSIC

A. THE PHYSICAL, OR SENSUOUS

Even the most passive listener cannot help noticing that there is something more in the art of music than the form in which it is molded. The question at once arises: How can we judge the excellence of a composition—i.e., what are the qualities that serve as a basis for critical judgment?

Surely, no rule can be laid down for recognizing the excellence of a musical idea. The ability to recognize the elevation of a fine musical thought must come to the mind which has lived much with music, thought intensely about it, and absorbed its inner spirit. However, there is a substantial basis for musical understanding and criticism. It is necessary only to get at the fundamental qualities and from them to deduce certain principles of artistry.

Let us briefly examine these qualities, one of which includes—or rather produces—*form*, and all of which are a part of the *content*. These fundamental qualities inherent in music are: the *physical or sensuous*, the *intellectual*, and the *emotional*. It is by the presence and degree of influence of these qualities that the artistic value of a composition must be estimated. Every great composer has shown in his masterpieces the ability to command a physical, intellectual, and emotional response. These three are also the great classifications of human activity—the physical, the intellectual, and the emotional. Whenever we touch or see a thing, a physical relation is set up; whenever we know a thing, an intellectual relation is set up; whenever we desire or love a thing, an emotional relation is set up.

The *physical basis* of the art of music is, roughly speaking: 1) vibrations; 2) air; and 3) the auditory organs of human beings. The *physical, or sensuous*, embraces that part of music which *appeals solely to the sense of hearing*—namely, *rhythm, melody, harmony*, and *tone-color*. In and of themselves, these factors are simply sensuous.

It was the creatively active physical ideal out of which music has grown: 1) The *sense of rhythm*, which obviously is a physical matter, a response to a physical stimulus. We cannot help humming, whistling, or keeping time to a tune to which we dance. It inserts itself most easily into our consciousness. When the band goes by, or when the orchestra plays a teasing foxtrot, our feet are ready to respond to the rhythm. We are stirred by sonorous, harmonious sound and are disturbed by discords. 2) A *desire of beauty in tone itself*, as a pure sound, the sensuous pleasure of the different colors and qualities of tones and their artistic intermingling or contrast. The physical ideal may be termed the pleasurable in sensation; it depends upon the acoustical incidents mechanically reported by the ear to the brain with very little necessary co-operation of the mind.

Unorganized, without design, without form, but employed simply to fascinate the sense of hearing, the rhythm, melody, and harmony are nothing but mere pleasant sounds. But organized, with design, they are the materials of musical form, whether it be simple or highly developed. In short, they cease to be mere sensuous things when they work together in a composition. Even tone-color, the most absolutely sensuous factor of all and, therefore, the most easily dazzling, ceases to be simply that when it is employed with an intellectual or emotional purpose.

The sensuous is the part of music which makes its appeal to the indolent, unintelligent listener—the passive listener. He refuses to trouble his mind sufficiently to detect evidence of design in a piece of music. He abhors its intellectual attributes; consequently, its true emotion never reaches him. As a matter of fact, there is even less credit in having this universal response to rhythm than in responding to beauty of tone itself. Even savages are strong on rhythm. Again, notice the great number of different kinds of dances among civilized people. Thousands never go beyond a response to this sensuous ideal; all they need to make them happy is a good, lively trap-drummer.

The laws which govern the employment of the sensuous in music belong partly to the intellectual and partly to the emotional. The sensuous must obey their commands. It is a means, not an end.

B. THE INTELLECTUAL

A little reflection makes it obvious that there are fundamental intellectual qualities in all music, whether it be classic or romantic. All art, whether creative or interpretative, has emotion; and this emotion must be under the dominance of reason, or else there is no method. And art without method is inconceivable.

The intellectual ideal creatively active in music is that of producing by means of a tonal succession an impression of logical coherence, dependence, and completeness; and not only the completion of the particular succession but also a suitable resolution of the musical idea dominating that particular succession. Every completed melody becomes, in a way, a tonal personality not only complete in itself but also complete in character; so that in any large collection of tone poems we have an individuality, or rather a collection of individualities. In short, *the intellectual in music embraces first of all the principles of design, the laws of form and development.* In a work of art the requirement of organic unity demands that no accessory shall be foreign to the general design. "In music it especially demands that the form shall be perfect, that the whole shall be equal to the sum of all its parts, that nothing can be subtracted without causing imperfection, and that nothing can be added to what is already complete. It calls for an absolutely reasonable development of each movement from its germinal melodic ideas. It demands that no extraneous matter shall obtrude itself upon the attention, and that if new thought is introduced it shall clearly grow out of the ideas first propounded. It demands that the several movements of a work shall be organically related to one another in melodic character, emotional mood, and in style."

To be sure, the conception of musical ideas may be, and in great music generally is, the result of some emotional state; but the construction of a composition and all that belongs to that task is a purely intellectual accomplishment. In music the intellectual element issues in form, because form is the *method* of expression. Harmony, form, tone-color, technique (repetition, variety, contrast, balance, climax) add further emotional qualities but also make certain demands on the intellect. The intellect is the designing power, and the design must be based upon a full and sympathetic perception of the form and the emotional content of the work in hand. "The emotion of a musician contributes the sympathetic element, without which no amount of intellectual application will be sufficient to reveal the content of a composition. The player (or singer) must be able to feel the composer's emotion, or he cannot reproduce it for the hearer."

The intellect, therefore, has a twofold duty: first, the acquisition of information as to the general character and purpose of the period to which a composition belongs and the individual theories of the composer; second, to make a keen and exhaustive analysis of the work to be performed so that, in the reading, the artistic proportions designed by the composer may be faithfully preserved. From these two operations of the intellect we get a synthetic result known as a "reading." The technical manifestations of this reading are in the general tempo; the observation of crescendo and diminuendo; of forte and piano; of staccato and legato; and so forth. It is only when all these various elements of musical expression are correctly placed that the composition glows before us in its original power, convincing us and swaying our emotions.

As pointed out earlier, hardly any good music has been written to appeal to pure reason. No composition is of lasting value that has not also a physical or an emotional appeal. J. S. Bach wrote much intellectual music, but his popularity depends upon his ability to write wonderful melodies and upon his dramatic sense. Even finger exercises may contain beautiful melodies; Heller, Liszt and Chopin put much inspiration into their pieces known as *études,* or studies. Brahms gave some of his piano pieces such titles as "Capriccio," "Intermezzo," "Rhapsody," etc., and he established in each a definite, unmistakable mood.

C. THE EMOTIONAL

Music conveys emotional states and sentiments of some kind, and it arouses feeling in the listener. *Music is a language;* some understand it better than others, but everyone is more or less emotionally affected by it.

Without question, most normal people (i.e., those who are not physically or psychically tone-deaf) have vague and unsettled ideas as to the expressive powers of music. This usually is due to foolish and sentimental criticism which pretends to see definite poetic imagery in music; ignorance of the true nature of musical expressiveness; and ignorance of musical history, which leads them to look for effects not sought by composers of a certain time or school. The matter to be discussed, then, is: What constitutes the emotional content of music?

The idea that music could directly affect human emotions and human character has persisted since the days of ancient Greece or even before. The history of the world bears this out. Of course, it is impossible to state definitely, until further scientific researches have been made, how much of this direct influence is due to the pure beauty of music itself and how much to the association of ideas, habits, and traditions. Certain pieces by the greatest composers, as well as certain folk tunes and folk songs, have created in many hearts a direct and involuntary response that is practically identical. Thus, to this extent, composers have actually expressed the abstract in terms of concrete art forms. They have expressed themselves in universal terms and then found receptive spirits sufficiently aware of those terms to accept them as their own. Musically, this is achieved whenever the composer, the performer, and the listener reach a common level of understanding.

The emotional ideal creatively active in music is that of *expressing in these purely musical elements* (rhythm, melody, harmony, tone-color, and form combined) *our feelings, aspirations, our noblest ideality*, especially before they have become quite definite enough to be put into words; *also, to express all those complications of moods, contests, and strifes of the inner nature*, in which contradictory tendencies struggle with each other, with an outcome either comic, optimistic, or tragic. After all, though they defy our analysis, it is the melodies which seem to exert the strongest, surest, and most consistent emotional appeal, even when no program has been announced or no title suggested.

Most of the better folk songs have a distinct emotional interest. They appeal by a moving melody which often fits several sets of words equally well. The Star Spangled Banner originally was the tune of a bold tavern song, To Anacreon in Heaven. The old Russian national anthem is used both as a hymn and as a student song of the University of Pennsylvania. God Save the King serves equally well as the song America, and it is used also by various other nations.

Then there are such songs as Auld Lang Syne, Annie Laurie, Comin' Through the Rye, Old Black Joe, My Old Kentucky Home, etc., which would be almost unthinkable with other words.

Grand opera is splendid emotional music. Note how the plot, the words, the action, the costumes, the scenery, the lighting, and the social glamour create a very strong illusion. This makes an emotional response almost inevitable. Note, also, that the music itself may have very little to do with it. Wagner's opera music consistently holds its own. That is why we hear excerpts from his works played in the concert halls.

Just as *there can be no really great art without passion*, so we cannot imagine music without all the emotions of mankind—our loves, hatreds, hopes, excitements, joys, sorrows, despair, patriotism, and ideals. In fact, music is a presentation of emotional experience fashioned and controlled by an overruling intellectual power.

In studying form, we learn that the song was originally a free expression of fancy or feeling, and that the melodic intervals were based on the inflections of the voice in speech. In other words, music imitated speech. This primary law of musical expression lies at the base of the greatest songs, symphonies, and tone poems. For instance, the minor key is used to express grief. Why? Because the inflections of the human voice in expressing grief usually ascend through intervals closely resembling those of the minor scale. Stronger grief, that which has a note of tragic passion in it, is expressed by chromatic tones. Why? Because the human voice in such a situation actually moves through the chromatic scale. In an agitated mood our speech does not flow but is spasmodic and irregular; hence, music which is to convey such a mood imitates speech, with complex rhythms, with staccato chords, rinforzando, and syncopations. Again, in calm, conversational speech the voice flows smoothly and equably; therefore, such a mood would call for steadily maintained rhythm and a moderate tempo. And so on.

It can readily be seen from the above that the means of musical expression are not altogether arbitrary but are founded on natural law. *Music is not only a combination of sounds arranged in a certain order but also an art able to express by its own inherent power (or quality) the most diverse ideas or feelings.* But because music has more complex machinery than the human voice, it can express itself in a more complex manner. It has wider compass; it has higher dynamic force, it has larger number of rhythms; it has a greater variety of tone-color; and, finally, it has harmony which the voice has not. By way of parenthesis, we may note that by "the powerful projection through song of a singer's personality, we are often misled into supposing that the human voice is the most expressive of all instruments; but pure musical expressiveness exists in its highest degree in the orchestra, when the influence is not personal, but absolutely musical."

Because music has no particular speech, it is compelled to express emotions in the abstract. The materials of musical expression do not admit of such a delicate statement as, "The hero is slain—let us grieve." The composer cannot tell the story; he can only voice its feelings. While music can express sadness more intense than words, it is the privilege of poetry to tell the cause of sadness. *Music, then, is an art which expresses moods,* and it expresses them with definiteness, tremendous eloquence, and influence. The mistake of those who are ignorant of the true nature of musical expressiveness is that they try to discern in music the *cause* of the moods; and this, as we pointed out above, is just what music cannot tell us.

"With the classical writers, pure musical beauty was the chief end of the art, and the emotional scheme had to remain subservient to the laws of form. It was Beethoven who first definitely arrived at making emotional utterance the purpose of music, and from his time dates the development of the knowledge of the full resources of the tone-art as the wordless poetry of the soul."

Of course, emotion is not a separate or isolated part of our being. It may be guided by mind and transfused by the imagination so as to become intellectual and imaginative. When the qualities known as insight, feeling, and imagination must find for themselves expression through music—a more plastic medium of expression than language—and when music has those qualities of coherence, continuity, and form which are essential to all intellectual expression, we are justified in calling it intellectual.

The response to the combined *rhythmic, or physical,* the *form-technique, or intellectual,* and the *melody, or emotional ideal,* is known as the *esthetic response. Esthetic appreciation* is a simultaneous response to the sum total of all three factors. It has no independent existence. Every really great composer shows in his masterpieces the ability to command a physical, an emotional, and an intellectual response. Correspondingly, any really appreciative listener in time succeeds in becoming aware of the music's physical, intellectual, and emotional content, even though he may never sound it to its uttermost depths. After we have responded physically and emotionally to the rhythmic and melodic inspirations of a great composer, we must use our reasoning power. Then we recognize the piece of music not only as a beautiful but also as a skillful work.

Great music emanates from the mind of a great man who has subjected emotion to the control of the will and has exercised the highest function of the mind, that which we call "imagination." Are we not justified in saying that music is a means of expressing the deepest wisdom, one which defies categorical expression? May we not agree with Schopenhauer, who says: "Music is an image of the will"?

3

THE VALUE OF MUSIC

1. THE GENERAL VALUE OF MUSIC

THE love of good music is universal. It appeals to more people than any other art. Almost every family has one or more members interested in music. The craving for music is apparent on all sides. Notice the crowds flocking to hear a park concert or a band passing down the street; observe the children dancing to the tune of a grind organ. Music, like the other liberal, or fine, arts, such as architecture, sculpture, painting, literature, and the dance, is indissolubly linked with the *True*, the *Beautiful*, and the *Good*. From the song of the babe to the wedding of yesterday and the funeral dirge of today, music touches life.

The value of music in the economy of human life is still neither widely nor fully understood or appreciated. Clearly, general musical training as well as appreciation courses are justified on the grounds that music makes life more liveable. Its values are :

    1)   Individualistic—each student studying music is creatively active.

    2)   Social—there are great possibilities and values in group music.

    3)   Intellectual—hard work and discipline are needed for creating and re-creating anything of lasting merit.

4) Emotional—it gives pleasure and provides a sociably acceptable means for emotional expression.

5) Cultural—it decidedly develops distinctions of taste and refinement; and its cultural values, individual and social, are beyond computation.

In short, every true thinker of the present age is agreed that music is recreational, educational, inspirational, as well as cultural. Music constitutes one of the most pleasing forms of expression, through which actions, thoughts, and emotions find utterance. It is the avocation which provides restfulness from the strain of daily pursuits and comes as a solace to the weary brain and as a stimulus to the depressed spirits.

It is rather difficult to explain the importance and the scope of music to the uninformed or the uninterested. Agriculture and commerce, for instance, deal with increasing the output of the land, improving business methods and transportation. Law and medicine bend their energies toward combating the frailties and diseases of mankind. To be sure, it is a mistake to consider art entirely as an escape from life, because its true effect is to increase our pleasure in living. We become blind and dulled to those objects and that part of our environment which are not directly entangled with our immediate actions or economic future. The stockbroker does not often admire the beauty of cloud formations; and French painting leaves the cowpuncher cold. But the chief function of art is to cure these human blindnesses, to awaken us from apathy, to increase sensitivity, to clarify, intensify, and interpret experience, and thus to widen immeasurably the gamut of our enjoyment.

In philosophy, architecture, sculpture, painting, literature, and music, men of all times have looked at the facts of the world and endeavored to find the meaning which controls them and the aid they offer to an understanding of the enduring values and purposes of life. By classifying and unifying the facts discovered by science and through history, the philosophers seek to interpret life either as it is at its best or as it could be at its best. By means of the various fine arts the artists express—also in orderly form—the most valuable and permanent emotional discoveries of mankind. Without philosophy and the fine arts, the world remains a chaos of infinitely varied scientific facts. Without philosophy and the arts, the world would be a place without understandable unity and without the ennobling investiture of lofty emotions.

Art is a reflection of humanity. The *love of beauty is latent in all human beings.* It is one of the few constant things in life. Complete expression of beauty is a necessity to man's nature. Of course, like all things, love of beauty is subject to change; but the change is one of growth and development. Man thinks and feels, he combines his thought and emotion, and art results. It is just as impossible for humanity to be without art as it is for a material object to be without its shadow. Man may receive impressions, study them, classify and develop them, and thus acquire the ability to recognize and use this beneficent gift. The awakening of the appreciation of beauty brings joy; and its further development brings a realization of man's noble aspirations.

Music, in its higher aspects, is concerned with enriching and ennobling life. It is so elastic and comprehensive that it ministers alike to the rich and the poor, the cultured and the ignorant, the just and the unjust. It is so simple that children become enthusiastic over it. It is so complex that its depths are sounded only by those especially endowed. It is a social, religious, and esthetic necessity. It comforts in sorrow and intensifies in joy. It can lend increased eloquence to words; it can enhance the emotional value of drama; furnish "motive power" and mood to the dancer; add excitement to the expression of human passion; create various moods and induce a martial spirit. It dignifies any occasion or function, no matter how important or imposing. Its use puts a stamp of culture on any community.

Music gives a feeling of devotion to religion and solemnity to funeral rites. Music is the greatest consoler in times of anguish after the loss of a relative or friend. If music were a "nonessential," why is it introduced at nearly all funerals? Everywhere this is done, and has been done at all times of which there are records. Even savages and barbarians invariably express their grief in songs of mourning or in instrumental dirges.

Music gives joy at the marriage festival and varying thrills of delight to all forms of human gatherings and experiences. We serenade our sweethearts; we dance to the measures of gay music; we go to war stirred by martial strains; as infants, the crooning of lullabies hushes us to sleep; when in trouble, we are soothed; and when weary, we are refreshed by music. The world would be poor indeed without the simple folk songs that reach our hearts, without the great choral works, cantatas, and songs, as well as wonderful concertos, symphonies, and tone-poems. It is hard to realize how life could be the same without music. Every orchestral instrument made by man is merely a means of musical expression, the visible indication of man's determination to express those deeper feelings and impulses which cannot be made known by words, colors, shapes, or gestures.

A factor of highest value in the consideration of music is the encouragement it affords us in our progress toward a realization of the harmony which may exist in the world. And the blending of voices in harmonious strains in accordance with the unerring laws of vibration should, in the life of each individual, symbolize the larger possibilities and attainments of the entire human family and forecast the time when all eventually may react in harmonious response to that which is best in the world.

We are to decide the use of music—destructive or constructive. Nothing is wholly bad or destructive—it is the use we make of it which determines its value. Music touches life so intimately that it may well challenge the attention of the educator, the philosopher, and the philanthropist.

2. THE PHYSICAL VALUE OF MUSIC

Among the general physical benefits which result from the properly conducted study of music in public or private schools, we must not overlook the well-known fact that vocal music is an exercise contributing to health. It is, to a large degree, a safeguard against those diseases which affect the breathing organs. Singing calls into action the most powerful breathing muscles and helps to tone up the circulatory and nervous systems. Besides, its favorable influence on the voice itself is another item worthy of recognition.

Participation in music-making tends to *develop skill;* furthermore, it leads the individual to subordinate himself habitually to the purpose of the group, and this *results in teamwork.* The playing of an instrument, such as the piano, violin, cello, or clarinet, demands the finest possible *co-ordination between mind and hand.* President Eliot, in his monograph, "The Concrete in Education," has pointed out that the mastery of the pipe organ demands of the performer the utmost skill imaginable; that it presents the finest illustration known of complete co-ordination of body, mind, and soul. Without question, the educative ends of manual training are found in musical performance. Indeed, music in a more complete way harmonizes and relates muscular co-ordination with the inner intelligence. Besides, would not proficiency in the mastery of a musical instrument help the home life of many more students than the ability to use tools? This is no argument against manual training. It merely raises the question whether or not the mastery of a musical instrument should be substituted for other forms of manual training, especially in the case of a student who is musically talented. Lastly, music affords those who practice it beneficent *relaxation* from their vocations. There are great possibilities for music to serve as recreation. The indirect enrichment of life through contact with music is, after all, the primary purpose of music study, not the acquirement of a skill or knowledge by which a livelihood may be earned.

3. THE EDUCATIONAL VALUE OF MUSIC

In determining the educational value of music, we endeavor to establish the proper relation of music, considered as an art and as a science, with that of other subjects taught privately or publicly in our various institutions of learning.

Music has held an important place in both ancient and modern education. It has been ranked with the first group of essential educational subjects by noted philosophers and leaders in education. Aristotle justified its place in the curriculum of a public school by the argument that the scholar should be fitted to employ his leisure profitably while he was being trained in those practical things which would make leisure possible. An equally strong argument is to be found in the child's natural love of song. Children begin to sing about as soon as they begin to talk. And they go on singing, imitating any tune that they happen to hear, if it be sufficiently simple. The child blindly follows his imitative faculty, whether in acquiring a vocabulary or a repertory of tunes. He puts a word or a tune into his mouth just as a few years before, he put other things there quite indiscriminately. *Musical virtues, like other moral attributes, are the result of habit,* hence the importance of early musical influences. Therefore, we favor the inclusion of music in the curriculum on an equal basis with the other subjects. We believe that, with the growing complexity of civilization, more attention must be given to the fine arts. Music offers possibilities, as yet but partially realized, for developing an appreciation of the finer things of life.

Music as an educational activity, if properly conducted, is of far-reaching influence. The study of singing or of an instrument demands fine discrimination in tone, in shading, and in quality. It requires perseverance, patience, and the constant exercise of thought and common sense. It demands an adequate memory, often exercised on a complex and involved whole. It requires correct analysis, logical conception, keen judgment, quick decision, poetic imagination, fine interpretation, refined taste, and a good sense of proportion and observation (perception). Again, it demands self-control and accuracy in performance to a degree that no other fine art can approach. Breathing, enunciation, tone control, tone gradation, etc., must constantly be brought under a degree of centralization in order for immediate and perfect response to be realized. The intellect is constantly employed in the solving of problems presented by rhythm, melody, harmony, form, and content. To be sure, the pursuit of vocal or instrumental music, taken together with a fair knowledge of their history and of the principles on which they are based, is of great value. Such study implies mental discipline, an indispensable element in general culture. Such study also opens up new meanings; it admits of an appreciation distinct from that which is connected with the senses alone.

With the growth of a just and comprehensive idea of education, the claim of music to an equal place with other leading subjects in secondary schools and colleges is becoming more general—and for the same reasons on which the introduction and retention of other leading subjects are based. Educators everywhere are encouraging the extension of the study of music not only in the vocal field but, to an equal and growing extent where competent teachers are available, in the instrumental field as well. Without question, music is a great mind-trainer. H. T. Finck, the noted former music critic, quotes the experience of a famous English university: "Positive proof that music is the best mind-trainer has come from Magdalen College, where all the musical instruction at Oxford University is given. There are many prizes and scholarships. Only 10% of the students at Magdalen take music; yet this 10% take 75% of all those prizes and scholarships, leaving only 25% for the other 90% of students. This is not the record of one year, but the average of thirty successive years" (*The Golden Age of Music*).

Music, when properly taught, fosters as much mental development as any other subject in the curricula of schools and colleges. Except for literature, no other subject is so highly cultural when opportunity is given to use it in a really significant way.

We have long held the erroneous idea that to be musical implies considerable ability in performance; and we have thereby relegated this most expressive of all languages to the *few* who, through some unusual gift or favored circumstance of birth or wealth, had the opportunity of cultivating the eye, voice, or hand to the point of virtuosity. Intelligent study (without special voice or instrumental training) helps to create understanding and so to increase the scope of our appreciation of music. Listening with understanding increases our enjoyment of music. Systematic training in listening also is an important activity in education. *Every normal individual is born with sufficient musical capacity to succeed in music if the capacity is cultivated.* His chances of success rise or fall according to the amount of training he has had at any age.

Music study helps further by inducing the student to do more attentive listening than if he were not studying. *Man is,* generally speaking, *notoriously lazy mentally,* and he usually rests on what he has already done or knows rather than make the effort to push ahead. This requires time and trouble. A course of study is, in effect, a compulsory undertaking which, of course, will prove to be profitable. Types of music which would otherwise remain uninteresting and unknown appear, on closer examination, to have much to recommend them. Composers who at first seemed uninteresting are revealed, in the course of forced attentive listening, as men who have something to say and who say it, necessarily, in a different way. Thus, the wider scope of comprehension and taste which careful music study can promote are assets that prove valuable throughout life.

The *aim of education* now most generally accepted *is* that it is *to train the faculties inborn in each and every individual* so that they may be developed to their fullest, making a well-rounded whole. Thus, the student is enabled to make the most of the place in society which he chooses or is called upon to occupy. This encourages the full enjoyment of life. It is doubtful if any subject contributes more to the fulfillment of this aim than the understanding and appreciation of music, together with the power of self-expression in the art.

4. THE EMOTIONAL VALUE OF MUSIC

It is in the realm of imagination, both emotional and spiritual, that music exercises its greatest power. *Music is particularly adapted to the excitation and expression of the deepest and strongest emotions of human experience.* Sound is the normal medium for the expression of the emotional experience; it is both the natural stimulus and the natural outlet for feeling. The peculiar claim of music lies in its almost unparalleled power of producing emotions and its responsiveness to our need for self-expression. Thus, in both its impressive and expressive aspects, music is closely interwoven with the feeling side of our natures, the side which influences so large a part of our conduct. *Practically everybody has the capacity to love music.* A few are gifted to compose, but many are gifted with the talent to sing or play. This is the reason why the world is so full of music.

The emotions and sentiments are not only worthy of development, but they are in need of refining. *The emotional nature of man,* in its close relation to the will, overpowering the latter too often with the force of its activity, *is as much in need of rational development as the intellect.* For the emotions no discipline can be more effective than submission to the fascination of music. Emotions are as much entitled to expression as thoughts, especially as music can stir us more deeply than any thought. Music aids powerfully in reaching and developing the emotions of the child. Perhaps no aspect of education has been so much neglected, none so little understood, and none is now being so vigorously studied. We have seen the fallacy of the idea that mere knowledge of a thing is sufficient to make us care for it enough to be our guide to action. We realize that most of our actions are dependent upon our feelings. It is only *when the experiences of life touch our emotional nature* that *will is aroused and activity results.* It is a well-known fact that emotion, to be useful, must express itself in action. This is the basis of all the fine arts. On a higher level all the fine arts have an emotional significance. This is true of architecture, sculpture, painting, music, dancing, as well as of literature. But it is practically impossible to isolate all the elements that combined produce these emotional effects. A chemist can analyze a drug down to its most minute ingredients and even construct a pattern of the way they are put together. We do not possess such unerring ability to determine the origin of a laugh, a sigh, an outburst of ecstasy, or an expression of indignation in a literary phrase. All we can do is point out a few of the means used to bring about the emotional effect desired by the writer. These means are:

vocabulary, figures of speech and other rhetorical devices, knowledge of the meaning of words, and, above all, style. The product of any art activity arises from a feeling for perfection of form; it is an expression of a significant experience; it is a reflection of a personality.

The problem, then, is how we may best develop the high emotional tension which shall lead to the right action. We may safely assign this large task mainly to music. To be sure, the primary end of musical education is to train the sentiments, to make the children *feel* nature, reverence, devotion, religion, tranquility, death, fear, sorrow, home, country, duty, love, joy, sympathy, anger, and all the rest.

Sir C. Parry, in his excellent book, *The Evolution of the Art of Music*, says, "If the art [of music] is worthy of the dignity of human devotion, it is worth considering a little seriously, without depreciating in the least the lighter pleasures to which it may minister. If it is to be a mere toy and trifle, it would be better to have no more to do with it. But what the spirit of man has labored at for so many centuries cannot be only a mere plaything. The marvelous concentration of faculties towards the achievement of such ends as actually exist must of itself be enough to give the product human interest. Moreover, though a man's life may not be prolonged, it may be widened and deepened by what he puts into it; and any possibility of getting into touch with those highest moments in art in which great ideals are realized, in which the noble aspirations and noble sentiments have been successfully embodied, is a chance of enriching human experiences in the noblest manner; and through such sympathies and interests the humanizing influences which mankind will hereafter have at its disposal may be infinitely enlarged."

The greatest significance of music lies in its relation to life itself. Music unquestionably is the most human of all the fine arts, the one that enters most into everyday experience. Music *does* something to us. Just feel your pulse when listening to the stirring and gay melodies of a military march, or notice your heart beat when, in a more quiet mood, you relax under the influence of a string trio, quartet, or restful hymn. *Music has an ethical, an emotional,* and, indeed, *often a physical effect on human beings.* The importance of music cannot be ignored even by those who would like to think of it merely as a luxury or an idle pastime. Courage, love, patriotism, and all other human virtues are not only expressed but greatly stimulated by music. Imagine a church, a theater, a festivity, a public ceremony without music.

School music should be one of the main agencies for training in the appreciation of beauty. We find that the tonal art is the most universal and immediate of the fine arts in its appeal to the sense of the beautiful; although let us remember, it yields its rarer delights only after years of patient study.

Music, as well as poetry and the other fine arts, is an instrument in the moral training of men. It is akin to them in its underlying principles. *Music is a character-builder.* It has been definitely observed in certain penal institutions that "as better taste in music is developed, a general improvement in personal appearance, courtesy, and morals takes place." Time after time a complete change in both manner of conduct and purpose in life is evinced, proving beyond a doubt the therapeutic value of music in adult personality adjustment. Real music does not lend itself to ignoble expression, so the masterpieces of music—i.e., the symphonic works, as well as the fine songs of home, friendship, religion, and of group feeling—give an appropriate outlet to human aspiration, sentiment, and thought. We need music when we rest and when we play, because it satisfies the deepest feelings of joy or sadness that stir us. Music, thus, is another great mode of expression, voicing and affecting the higher life of man; and in all ages these uses of the art of tones are illustrated. Music vitalizes as hardly anything else can; and under its influence the hearts of people are sometimes stirred by one mighty bond of brotherhood. Music comforts us in sorrow, sustains us in grief, and enhances our joy. We forget pain and perplexity in our musical utterance, and we express our highest aspirations in noble strains. "A Mighty Fortress Is Our God" has inspired many to heroic endurance; and "Praise God from Whom All Blessings Flow" has filled many with courage and renewed hope. The power of music can be utilized for the betterment of mankind; and for this reason alone, if for no other, should every school in the land be filled with song. Singing has practical values. The morning song wafts many worries away from countless little hearts and tends strongly to harmonize and unify the group; likewise, the parting song has its value.

Music has an ethical value. If school music can be shown to have a distinct and moral force, its universality and its permanency are established beyond question. What is morality? There are two different views on this subject. One is that "by their fruits ye shall know them." Everyone is moral until you catch him in some immoral act. The other view takes into account the tendencies of life and thought; education has to do with the latter phase of the subject. It is no part of a teacher's concern to engage, directly or indirectly, in a campaign against vice; but rather his duty is to start children off right. Whatever the school does for morale, it must have in mind the broadest possible view and deal with the trend of thought and action.

Education is starting children in the right direction. The ethical mission of the school is to establish hope as a habit of mind. That is a good thing. "The kingdom of heaven is within you." Fear, as a habit of mind, is not a good thing. Music is the sunlight of hope, the purifying ripple of the water of life, the vigor of pure air in us and over us and about us. But there is music *and* music. Morally, the jazz and swing of the street, the voluptuous music of the dance hall and night club, is from the lower world. Jazz and swing are not music in its sweetness and purity, its nobility and vitality, any more than a smirk is a smile or giggling is laughing. The mission of the school is to bestow upon every child in school all that is best, purest, and noblest in music. Those who are past the school age may also get out of music something that will give them strength to fight the battle of life. The whole nation can be benefited by the power of song. We may not understand other peoples' languages, but we can understand their music, whatever their race or speech.

Indeed, we have not yet realized completely the power of music. This realization often comes in a flash. Those who hear it are lifted up by its power, because a tune is essentially a spiritual thing. We can neither see nor touch it; but listening inwardly and learning step by step how to remember a tune so that we may recall it in time of stress protects us from destructive feelings and thoughts. If we are really musically conscious, music brings us a feeling of harmony without and within which at once promotes spiritual mindedness. A few take away with them the strength and joy that music gives, and it is from these few that we get an inkling of its power.

We need not enter into the vexed questions of the relationship of morals and esthetics, but we can all agree that one who has been trained to *a sense of law and order, proportion and grace*—in other words, to *a love of the beautiful* —will at least have a strong tendency to make his life reflect these characteristics.

5. THE SOCIAL VALUE OF MUSIC

Music, indeed, *is* the most *unifying,* the most *humanizing,* the most *socializing* of all the expressions of mankind. It forms the basis of the most effective correlation and concentration of the energies and purposes of the social body. Wherever people are gathered together with a single purpose, there music comes naturally into expression. Music is a wide avenue of social development; it leads to a common center of human consciousness and sensitivity by the appeal of beauty in its myriad forms. Music is unquestionably the greatest single force in giving unity and fellowship to a group of individuals, even those of widely different ages, interests, beliefs, and nationalities.

Music is a universal language. It speaks through tones that any normal person can hear, and in symbols that anyone can understand. In addition, it has a vast advantage over spoken language because, even when imperfectly understood, it gives the listener joy that no one can take away from him and for which there is no substitute.

The Church has long recognized the power of music. In fact, religion has never been able to get along without it. The Church utilizes music in blending the emotions of its worshipers into a harmonious and unified whole. There is a psychological value in the song or anthem that precedes the discourse or sermon. It corresponds to the preparation of the seed by the farmer in order to encourage germination and growth.

Commercially, music has many advantages. It brings added business to tradespeople, especially at times of concerts; taxies, streetcars, buses and railroads, restaurants, drugstores, various other stores, program- and ticket-printing and music publishers. The city or town in which the concert is held also gets publicity.

Psychologically considered, military music of a rhythmic nature promotes co-operation; but its main function, no doubt, is that of stimulating the individual to greater energy and effort. On the battlefield the aggressive or defensive forces are brought into concerted action by the strains of a military band. The spirit of courage in soldiers is intensified and co-ordinated by the rhythmic expressions and the sentiments of folk songs and the strains of familiar airs. Clearly, it behooves all musical organizations throughout the country to join in a comprehensive program for putting the morale-building value of music squarely behind the effort of the nation during war.

Activities for maintaining the civilian morale and increasing industrial production should include:

1. The promotion of noon-hour and other concerts in industrial plants, and the devising of other musical activities, such as glee clubs, choruses, bands, and mass singing for workers and their families in factories.

2. The presentation of free concerts for the public in libraries, museums, schools, and other places.

3. The stimulation of musical organizations, the encouragement of continued performances, and the fur-

therance of musical composition and musical study so that skills may not be lost.

4.   The encouragement of the increased use of music in churches and assemblies.

Music makes everything go. It benefits all of us by a welcome change from the pressures of business and work, the bondage of worry and fear, the load of suffering and pain. It makes a peace-meeting more peaceful. At family gatherings of various kinds deep-felt emotions must be expressed, and music expresses these moods and feelings wherever and whenever mere speech fails. It uplifts, it stimulates, it soothes, it heals, and it cheers. Music expresses all of the deeper emotions and manifestations of the subjective life more satisfactorily than words, colors, shapes, or gestures. As for present-day family life, it is well for us to remember that "there are influences at work tending to dissolve the family, and along with these influences are movements tending to give the individual greater freedom and opportunity. At the same time, the necessity for careful thought for an adequate family life is more urgent now than ever; and I know of nothing so effective in cultivating this life as the ability to produce and listen to music together as a family group."

To be more specific, music is so simple that the humblest peasant as well as the young child can grasp and retain a plain melody; yet it is so complex that it is worthy of study by the greatest intellects. The field of music compares well in size to that of literature. Music is as comprehensive as mathematics, for it is built upon an exact science, with its beginning in simple melody and its culmination in the oratorio, the opera, or the symphony. To solve the intricate problems of counterpoint requires as much concentration as correspondingly difficult problems in any of the exact sciences. The great architect, lawyer, or constructive engineer cannot be more perplexed than the creator of great orchestral works when facing his various problems, such as the development of ideas, the balancing of form, the knowledge and application of orchestral instruments, the blending of tone-colors, and the like. "The music dramas of R. Wagner rank in the sublimity of their conception and execution with the greatest thought or expression that the human mind has produced in any form and in any age."

Music is not only an art but an exact science; and in its highest form it is absolutely logical and unrelentingly mathematical. Its mastery requires years of patient study and continuous application. The imagination does not have a free flight but is bounded by the limits of form or pattern. "The mere possession of the poetical imagination and the capacity to receive music in its fullest emotional power will not lead one to the highest achievements in musical art. With these subjective qualities must be combined the mastery of the theoretical intricacies, the logical sequences, and the mathematical problems which are the foundation principles of music. It has every technical detail that characterizes absolute science in its most rigid forms," writes Upton. In short, *music is not only a mere matter of the emotions and imagination*. It is the art of *expressing joy, grief, and exaltation*.

Music study develops not only the intellect—the so-called "power for accurate and rapid thinking"—but it also brings out the emotional side of one's nature. Temperament is just as definitely a factor in success as is intellect. We do not merely need to have our intellects educated and controlled, but our emotions must also be disciplined.

Music is a strong answer to juvenile delinquency. It is vitally important in the prevention of crime because it induces moods and states of mind that are incompatible with wrong doing. In the years of existence of the Music School Settlement in New York's East Side (founded in 1903), not one of over 30,000 children enrolled ever came before a juvenile court for delinquency. According to Olga Samaroff, out of eleven penal institutions, only four had any musically trained inmates at all. Of these four institutions, with 12,401 convicts, Sing Sing had the highest number of musically trained—nineteen out of 2,408, or less than 1%; the Joliet (Illinois) State Penitentiary had not one among its 4,787 charges.

Surely, there is some correlation between music and character. "Trained musicians do not commit crimes—and men who receive musical training in penal institutions stay out when released." There is nothing new in the concept of musical therapy. In ancient Greece its importance in the development of character was recognized by Plato, who said in his *Republic*: "Musical training is a more potent instrument than any other, because rhythm and harmony find their way into the inward places of the soul, on which they mightily fasten, imparting grace, and making the soul of him who is educated, graceful, or of him who is ill educated, ungraceful." Unfortunately, music is still regarded only as a special skill or as a diversion. Of course, the physically exciting rhythms of popular music are not beneficial. In fact, an overdose of this type of stimulation may play a large part in contributing to delinquency, but great music exerts an influence for good. But *to perform acceptably* or *to listen intelligently, adequate musical guidance is necessary.* Parents as well as teachers of music share the responsibility of providing inspiring musical experiences, for they are character-building influences and remain through life as a force for good.

In business we have given much thought and study to intelligence tests, and we have employed trained experts to help us in our problems. Our tests have shown that, in many instances, there is high intelligence joined with weak emotional control; and applicants for employment who have proven themselves very "smart" are often, by reason of temperament (personality, sensitiveness, emotionalism, etc), undesirable for business careers.

It is the prospective employee's emotional fitness more than anything else which determines how well he will work with the organization and with those around him. It is for this reason that we should have such high regard for musical training. Music is disciplined emotion. In order to play beautifully and effectively, one's entire being must be under perfect control. For this reason, if for no other, a musical training is a valuable asset to any boy or girl. Many a brilliant man has become impossible in a business organization because of an uncontrolled temperament. He refuses to fit in and feels that all others must bow to him and depend upon his judgment. He declines assistance, fails to consult sufficiently with his superiors, and is irritated by the slightest criticism. Because he is unable to control his temperament, he is often more harmful than helpful to the business.

However, overindulgence in music sometimes may produce conditions which result in temperamental excesses; and this, unfortunately, has given some practical people an entirely wrong idea as to the value of music. They see here and there some musical freak, with all sorts of conceits and eccentricities, and come to the conclusion that this is normal, and therefore, that music is of little consequence in the world. Such freaks are the product of over self-indulgence and deserve no more consideration than the glutton or the inebriate.

The chief advantage of music in the formation of character is really the *discipline of the emotions,* which goes to round out a well-balanced life. Emotional discipline in music is constant; and for this reason it becomes a great factor in the encouragement of human success. More than this, music gives the man deeply engrossed in business, or other matters, a natural, simple, and direct outlet, *a means of self-expression* of almost priceless value.

6. THE VOCATIONAL VALUE OF MUSIC

Popular education, or the training of the masses, tends to a recognition of every subject of instruction at its due valuation. Without doubt, it moves strongly in democratic lines both in securing opportunities for every member of society and, also, in securing adequate treatment of hitherto neglected subjects. Every normal person in the world is born with some degree of musical potentiality. This endowment is a common inheritance. The pulse and breathing are rhythmic; the consciousness responds to tone and pitch and is exhilarated in varying degrees by their combinations. Thus, it is the inherent right of everyone, and not the special privilege of a few, for this gift to be developed and allowed expression in musical study. For this reason the study of music has come to be considered part of our general education.

Moreover, music carries over in later life as a hobby, recreation, or vocation more readily perhaps than any other subject taught in the schools. Also, music furnishes a vocation for greater numbers of people than any of the other fine arts. In fact, there is no other art in which so many participate. It is a well-known fact that every advanced civilization has its music teachers, composers, and performers and recognizes their work as an indispensable factor in the development of individual, social, and national life. From our doctrine of democracy we derive this declaration of equality: "Treat all alike." The educator takes his cue from this educational maxim: "Make all alike." But surely the musical pupil has a right to expect that instruction and training shall be adapted to his nature and needs. Other things being equal, a musically talented person should have courses proportional to his talent. *Why not*—and this refers mainly to the high-school student—*afford our children the means of acquiring the working principles of the art and science of music by recognizing its study as an integral part of the educational system?* Besides the cultural value of music we know that, after the beginnings of reading, writing, arithmetic, and geography, music has greater practical value than any other subject taught in the schools. In the higher institutions we must provide a course of study to the future musician of equal vocational value as the one we give our future lawyers, physicians, preachers, teachers, engineers, scientists, merchants, etc.

The playing of an instrument involves three senses— *sight, hearing,* and *touch.* It calls the intellect into play for rhythm, time, and muscular response, faculties no other study demands. Every student should select some instrument and learn to play it well enough to join the school orchestra or band. What practical value has this in later life, in comparison to other studies? No matter what work the student will pursue, his progress depends much on his ability to get along with other people, on his human relationships. The destiny of our democracy as well as the growth of a business can best be realized by all members pulling together for a common goal. *This teamwork is absolutely necessary in an orchestra.* Harmony is the prime essential, and every member must look to the leader. There is always a leader in every business or in government. This discipline is much easier learned in early life than later on. The musician will not lose his individuality; but by playing well, he will attract attention to his skill. So there is not only the social incentive of working together but an individual incentive, too. Musical training develops *concentration, alertness,* and *memory,* things so much needed later in life and business.

7. THE HEALING VALUE OF MUSIC

Since the dawn of human intelligence, music has been associated in some manner with the idea of healing. The name "Apollo," mythological god of music and of healing, is taken from an obsolete Greek verb meaning "to heal" or "to lead out of discord." Aesculapius, the mythical son of Apollo, is still the traditional patron of medicine. The hieroglyphs of ancient Egypt contain many references to the use of music in the treatment of diseases, and there is abundant evidence to show that the physicians of that age used music and heliotherapy as the principal agents of their healing art. The ancient Greeks, masters of beauty in all its forms, amplified the technique of the Egyptians; and, with the discovery of the diatonic scale by Pythagoras, the use and scope of music were immeasurably widened. In the Middle Ages groups of singers soothed the ill during epidemics. Some fifty years ago William James was using music in a mental hospital in Boston. Some forty years ago Van de Wall began to study the effect of music on human beings and came to the conclusion that music was potentially the most powerful of mood-conditioners.

Through the centuries in which there is a record of music, its power to affect people both physically and mentally has been observed. When the music is functioning properly, and we are attuned to it, we are in various ways benefited, solaced, or stimulated. When we are not attuned to music, for some reason or other, it is possibly an exasperating experience. The question is: What method should be adopted for this sensory experience to heal and integrate body and soul through the intelligent use of the curative forces of music? Again and again, where all other methods were apparently fruitless, the use of music has aided in the restoration of mental and moral resources and opened new ways of self-discovery and affirmation.

Modern science, being concerned with facts, wants to discover specifically the reactions experienced by human beings on listening to various types of music; it wants to know what this or that composition does to the healthy and the ill; it wants to gather data on these reactions so that general conclusions may be reached.

Two different experiments have been conducted, one by U. Couchman, research worker at the Psychopathic Hospital of the State University of Iowa, and the other by R. L. Cardinell of the Stevens Institute of Technology. They made a study of music in war plants. Each report was illuminating not only in proving that music in general exerts a salutary effect but also in pointing out the wide divergence in emotions aroused by different types of music. Other scientists who studied the influence of music on work and fatigue found that it has a powerful effect on muscular activity, which increases or decreases according to the character of the music used. When the music is sad, or of a slow rhythm, and in a minor key, the capacity for muscular work decreases to the point of cessation if the muscle had been fatigued from previous work. Men working at building roads, etc., do better work, are in better humor, and are less fatigued on days when they sing.

The very elementary forms of music—lullabies, marches, work songs in countless varieties which induce moods, lighten toil, or soothe or excite the sensibilities—are proof of the power of the tonal art. It affects both the conscious and subconscious mind.

Most realistic is the finding that all bodily functions—respiration, circulation, metabolism—respond positively to music. Physical exercises are carried out most successfully when accompanied by music. Certain selections of music and certain musical instruments and qualities of vocal sounds exert a favorable reflex action on the cardiac-vascular system, and very likely they have a favorable influence upon muscle tone, working power, digestion, secretion, and other functions of the body. Such music as: Invitation to the Dance, selections from Madame Butterfly, the Intermezzo from Cavaleria Rusticana, etc., lower the blood pressure and pulse rate. Whereas Dvorak's Overture Carneval; Gershwin's Rhapsody in Blue, and Sousa's march, Stars and Stripes Forever, raise both the blood pressure and the pulse rate. Most people are rather unfavorably affected psychologically and physiologically by mournful, tragic music, and favorably affected by music that is gay and rich in harmony. Individual differences in native endowment and training are revealed by different reactions to certain compositions. Some types of music slow people down. Among soothers and pacifiers are Ave Maria, largos, lullabies, nocturnes, serenades, Invitation to the Dance, Chopin waltzes. Others speed people up; such as marches, spirited overtures, Hungarian rhapsodies, Rhapsody in Blue, etc. For nervous debility Burleigh's Song of the Brook, Raff's Cavatina, Melody in F, Brahms' Hungarian Dances, etc., may be used. Selections most likely to dispel a depressed mood are Schubert's Ave Maria, Meditation from Thais, Moonlight Sonata, old familiar hymns and songs, To a Wild Rose, Barcarolle from Tales of Hoffman, etc. Whatever its effect, however, music allows the patient in the hospital to rid himself to some degree of his inhibitions and his tensions; and it lets him shed the defensive armor he has assumed as a protection against real or fancied ills. It has been noticed, for instance, through experiments at the Iowa Psychopathic Hospital, that when a Mozart symphony, a Strauss waltz, or the gay Nutcracker Suite have been used to awaken patients in the morning, they climb cheerfully out of bed and go about their duties with alacrity. But Debussy's Nuages, Tschaikowsky's Symphony Pathetique, or a "blues" will slow up their morning routine by at least fifteen minutes and cause some of the patients to weep. Stravinsky's Fire Bird Suite will sometimes induce almost hysterical activity.

Music harmonizes conflicting moods which depress the nervous system, and that is why it uplifts us. Music apparently has some effect upon the ductless glands, thus affecting our emotions. We cannot think in circles and, at the same time, concentrate on a piece of music we like. Pleasant associations arise to replace unpleasant ones; new strength is gained; in spite of ourselves, we yield to the ministrations of music.

Music recalls forgotten associations more quickly than any other means; and for this reason it has been found valuable in the treatment of amnesia. When we hear a tune familiar to us long ago, we evoke memories associated with that period of our life. A pianist in this therapy plays for each patient individually, beginning with nursery pieces and continuing through adolescent and adult stages until some tune establishes a chain of associations with the world of actuality. Recommended are such tunes as Brahms' Lullaby, Holy Night, O Solo Mio, Silver Threads Among the Gold, etc.

Dr. I. M. Altschuler of the Eloise Hospital (Eloise, Michigan) reported some successes in the treatment of mental patients, including "insanes." The use of music produced a reflex, an automatic activity, in the thelamic region, the lower brain, which is believed to have much to do with the emotions of fear and anger. The activities of the thelamic region in turn stimulate the higher brain centers, and thus the stuffiness of the man's brain is relieved. Music is 35% more effective in quieting disturbed patients than the wet-pack method. Music also increases the patient's span of attention, diverts those inclined to brooding, provides at least temporary relief for those in the clutches of obsessions, and "replaces illusions with realities, also soothes, relaxes, and balances."

Recognizing the value of music in general as a therapeutic agent, physicians in various countries have begun to apply it. The medical staff of the Veterans Administration Hospital, Lyons, New Jersey, decided to organize a method susceptible to clinical analysis and rational explanation after adequate experimentation. To this end, Dr. E. Sharp, at that time the reconstruction officer at the hospital, was designated in March, 1934, to initiate the project. Since then the music therapy project has demonstrated with constantly increasing success its value in the treatment of mental and nervous disorders. The visitor may be deeply impressed by the results obtained thus far at Lyons. There is no doubt that, after further research, the idea will spread to other hospitals.

In the Walter Reed Hospital, Washington, D. C., music has been used as a curative agent for arthritis, spastic paralysis, and heart trouble. The psychiatric clinic of the Johns Hopkins Hospital, Baltimore, Maryland, has tested music as a cure for insanity in its various phases with encouraging results. It has been found to subdue the fury of the most violent, to awaken the sleeping memory in certain cases of amnesia, and to be an effective and harmless soporific.

Music as a medicine has been applied for various types of illness as well as for emotional disturbances. The mentally ill are quite receptive to music. There is power in music to revive the patient's interest in life; but musical programs must be adjusted to their needs, which run from low to high. In cases of manic depression, when patients are "high" musical therapists begin to play music of a lively character, gradually decreasing the melodic stimulation. In cases of melancholia, when the patients are "low" the melodic progression is reversed. Beginning with an Ave Maria or Schubert's Serenade, i.e., a slow, soft melody, the musician builds the program upward to a more lilting number in order to provoke a quiet, happy mood.

The hospital in Huntington, West Virginia, reports that progress has been made in the use of music in neuropsychiatry. "Music is an important adjunct to medicine and surgery at this hospital. . . . The work in this field has been going on for some time, and the results to date are such as entirely to justify its use, and the value attained establishes music . . . as part of the treatment here." A number of hospitals have played recorded music in operating rooms. The Roanoke, Virginia, Veterans Administration Hospital, for example, plays a patient's favorite selections during frontal-lobotomy operations. Music helps to calm the patient, doctors tell us.

Music promotes digestion. The main nerve of the tympanum ends in the center of the tongue and thus reacts both to taste and sound sensations. Music stimulates animation; a lively march or a sprightly waltz will refresh fatigued bodies. The right kind of music, properly applied, energizes the blood, nerves, and mind. A brass band is an effective stimulant; and a lullaby is a good sedative. Stringed instruments (violin, cello, autoharp, etc.) have proved most effective in therapeutic treatments. Patients seldom ask for jazz; and so boogie-woogie as well as jazz are eliminated.

As reported in 1948 by doctors I. M. Pallin and A. E. Chiron of the Jewish Hospital, Brooklyn, New York, babies are ushered into this world to the strains of soft music, such as Debussy's Claire de Lune, Kubisch's Poems, or a Beethoven Sonata.

To reduce muscular tension, music is used in operations with spinal and local anasthesia in which the patient feels no pain but is uncomfortably nervous. Here music diverts the patient, who then will not disturb the surgeon. Dentists use music effectively. It calms nerves and quiets the human spirit.

At the Billings Hospital (University of Chicago) all patients who undergo local anesthesia—spinal, reginal, or local—are asked the night before to select the music they prefer to hear. The hospital has a constantly growing library of classical, semiclassical, and popular music; and children are offered choices from Cinderella, Peter and the Wolf, Pinocchio, and current favorites. Since 1947, the various clinics have been experimenting with the use of music to alleviate the tensions of patients undergoing surgery. Concerts are now standard practice in all six operating rooms and five preparation rooms. Music is wired through lightweight stethoscope-type earphones and comes from tape recordings. It is audible to the patient but not to the surgeon. Occasionally, the anesthetist tunes in to make sure the music is not too raucous or exciting.

Music with anesthesia has proved especially helpful for peptic-ulcer patients who are already so tense and nervous that routine medical sedatives are not very effective. It is comforting and calming, too, in cases where the patient is too old or ill to receive sedatives.

Mrs. H. A. Seymour, founder of the National Foundation of Musical Therapy, was a pioneer. Active as a concert pianist, settlement worker, teacher, and radio commentator, she began her therapeutic treatments by playing the piano for the wounded of World War I. Through experience in various hospitals she observed how certain illnesses affected the sufferers mentally. Her treatments already have revealed results of unquestionable value, as for instance, those accruing from the use of music in the healing of difficult cases which could not be reached, mentally or physically, by any other method in our hospitals, for veterans of World War II. Mrs. Seymour applied different types of melodies to suit various ailments. Music was classified as either stimulating or soothing, and the whole method of musical therapy was considered as an adjunct rather than as a "cure." We understand that graduates of the foundation are now working in public hospitals of 43 states, and the curative powers of music are being supplied to every type of illness.

Much care must be exercised in selecting the rhythms and instruments best suited to specific cases. As lively music stimulates inactive muscles, jigs, marches, dances, and action songs are played in orthopedic, polio, and amputee wards. In some hospitals heart ailments are treated half an hour daily with music in 2/4 or 3/4 time. Slow, soothing strains are prescribed to modify pulse, respiration, and blood pressure, thus bringing the patient back into a more even rhythm. Some mental patients are put into a quiet frame of mind by listening to serene music played in the evening.

Other things being equal, those pieces of music are most enjoyed which are highly emotional; and those which show several emotional effects are considered more enjoyable than those which show only one. *Emotions* may conveniently be *classified into* two kinds—*active and passive*. Active emotions include gaiety, happiness, joy, fun, playful humor, teasing, frivolity, the fantastic, flirting, the whimsical, the exhilarating, the stimulating, the confidential, courage, certainty, force, triumph, dignity, majesty, hurry, unrest, confusion, bewilderment, etc. Passive emotions include calm, peace, the soothing, reminiscence, contemplation, thoughtfulness, sentimentality, sadness, melancholy, suspense, doubt, uncertainty, longing, anxiety, wistfulness.

Music possesses direct advantages over other agencies as a co-ordinating force. It animates the faculties, arouses dormant sentiments, and may be used to rectify mental derangements arising from physical ills. Exposure to fine music in hospital wards is primarily an interlude of pleasure and beauty to adults; it helps to alleviate the mental and emotional strain of hospitalization. Musical therapy at the Rancho Los Amigas (Los Angeles) has been developing slowly but steadily. There are classes in music appreciation and community singing for ambulatory patients, and active participation by the patients is encouraged. For some time a social hour of community singing has been given in the male psychopathic wards, and the response, in some instances, has been more marked than in the mentally normal wards.

According to *Time* magazine (January 4, 1954), "Music has been used for centuries to calm patients in many kinds of hospitals; only recently has it been used to break through the icy calm of schizophrenics. At Central Oklahoma State Hospital, at Norman, Dr. Witten has introduced one of the most vigorous programs of music therapy in the U. S. He tries to match the music to the patients. For the elderly and conservative, there are Gay Nineties tunes; for the young, hops. Except for deliberately sedative programs, strong rhythm is essential to get attention. After contact with the patient has been regained, the doctors can go to work with occupational and recreational therapy. Music itself is no cure, but it has helped so many patients that Dr. Witten says: 'We don't talk in terms of hopeless cases; we don't believe there are any.'"*

Very effective work has been done with children. Working on the theory that a handicapped child is held back only to the extent that his affliction has impoverished him mentally, emotionally, and spiritually, the music therapist carries on an intensive musical program to offset these tendencies.

Adjustments to illness are quite difficult for children. Consequently, doctors had to combat the resentment which the children felt at being not only bedridden but away from home. Also, there was apathy and boredom, plus the disciplinary problems which resulted from too much undirected leisure time. Clearly, children in hospitals need joyful, creative activity. So they began their contact with music by learning to sing folk songs. Next came the introduction of motion with music. Little girls rocked their dolls slowly and rhythmically as they sang Brahms' Lullaby. To Tschaikowsky's Waltz of the Flowers, they swayed their arms in graceful motion as they made believe they were the dancing flowers. To the Russian Trepak they clapped their hands faster and faster as the music gained in speed and wildness. The next activity was that of forming a rhythm band. In addition, piano lessons are a part of the schedule, as well as instruction in drum-playing and on the mouth organ, if the children show a desire to study. Such activity has helped to regain the use of a hand badly affected by infantile paralysis. Musical therapy has given these children a feeling of belonging, as well as of self-confidence. Hence, they no longer are resentful, lonely, and frustrated; they become happy, busy, and eager to do things.

So far as we are able to learn, only the State College of East Lansing, Michigan, gives a four-year course in musical therapy. An increasing interest is being taken in the subject, but there is a big handicap in getting trained workers in the field of psychology and music who can teach the

---

* From the story entitled "Jingle Bells." Courtesy TIME; copyright Time Inc. 1954.

course and supervise the work of students without going into the hospital to do internship. For the time being, several institutions doing research in musical therapy are building up case records; but so far they have been reluctant to release any experiments or data until they have further proof.

Therefore, we are especially interested in recent reports of the extension of the Music Research Foundation. This is a nonprofit organization dedicated to the development of music to be used as therapy in fields of medicine and psychiatry. Francis Paperte is the founder, and the chairman of the research committee is Dr. R. C. Williams. Bruno Walter is one of the musicians who serve the organization. The Music Research Foundation will engage in scientific research on the effect of music on normal and suffering people, whether they suffer from mental or physical ailments. They will collect information about the efforts of those using music as an addition to medicine. They will apply music as a therapeutic tool as much as possible and train technicians for more extensive development of this field in the future. The work has been progressing in the eight years since it has been established by experimental work at the Walter Reed Hospital, under the supervision of the surgeon-general of the U. S. army.

The objectives of the foundation's research are broad and simple, and the procedure is to make a careful examination of each individual case; to study the physical and psychological condition of the patients and whether they are susceptible to music; what kind of music treatment they need; and how it is to be administered. Some persons react very strongly and others only passably to musical stimulants. Ways will be found, and even now much has been accomplished to indicate a great future for musical therapy.

8. THE USE AND VALUE OF MUSIC IN INDUSTRY

Very likely, folk music began after the sense of rhythm had been fairly well established. Centuries ago it was found that manual labor was made easier when done to a rhythmic accompaniment. The Greeks had special work songs for harvesting, threshing, grinding grain, spinning, and weaving.

The primitive peasant sang his rhythmic accompaniment while his flail pounded the rye or wheat on the threshing floor. To prevent exhaustion from pulling a heavy barge along the river bank, weary toilers droned the famous Song of the Volga Boatmen. Sailors will sing rhythmically while pulling on a rope; their "Yo heave ho!" gave rise to a colorful collection of songs of the sea. Many a modern workman prefers to swing his sledge hammer to a rhythmic accompaniment. Note how soldiers march better to music; and if there is no band, the rhythmic beat of the drum is sufficient. Singing on the march surely helps reduce the miles. Rhythm is the first thing we discover, or should discover, in music. Rhythm is the physical response to a primitive stimulus. Rhythmic tunes are direct aids to the performance of labor, for the timing of effort helps to conserve energy and therefore makes more of it available.

The value of music as a help in industry is just beginning to be realized. It lightens the task of labor by refreshing nerves and spirit. No wonder, for workers accomplish more with music than without it. Interesting experiments have been conducted using music in shops and offices. It was found that *music reduces fatigue and tension and thus sustains production* over those hours, 11 A.M. to 4 P.M., when accidents and spoiled work usually mount. Noise is definitely an unfavorable environmental influence; it causes fatigue, increases tension, generally works against efficiency, and lowers the levels of performance in almost all types of physical and mental work.

But the effects of tone are the opposite. Tone possesses certain psychological characteristics. It stimulates most organic processes and, in many cases, makes possible an increased output of work while reducing fatigue. Music relieves boredom, a cause of fatigue. Mind-wandering and consequent carelessness in the inspection- and packing-room, which cause mistakes, are considerably reduced by music. We are told that music is used in very noisy factories to bring relief from the din; machines are stilled in the morning at 10 o'clock and in the afternoon at 3 while the employees listen to music. This loss of time is offset by increased production and a material reduction of imperfect work. In addition, *listening to music boosts morale.* In Newark, New Jersey, the Westinghouse Electric Company provided loudspeakers throughout the factory to bring music to its workers. Before long it was observed that production and morale were higher whenever the music was broadcast. Some factories confine concerts to lunchtime and breaks between shifts. At any rate, no less than one hour of music a day nor more than two hours is the rule, as continual music loses its effect. It was noted that, with music, 55 clerks in a Minneapolis post office made 13% fewer errors in handling the heavy Christmas mail. In more than 1,200 factories all over the country (according to the Stevens Institute of Technology) music is being provided for workers. Incidentally, once a music-amplifying system is installed in a factory, it may also be used for broadcasting important announcements, which usually is more effective than posting bulletins.

Some factories start off the morning with some military marches, fox trots, polkas, or college march songs (On Wisconsin, Boola Boola, etc.). It wipes the gloom off the faces of the incoming employees and instills a little *esprit de corps* into the whole group. Certain selections calling for a physical response, like the Indian War Dance, etc., are not suitable for every type of shop. They make the workers stamp and whoop it up, up and down the aisles. The stimulating effect may be good for production, but it certainly is no help in protecting those workers who have to remain at their machines. Therefore, the use of the right kind of music is very important. A plain, simple melody, undisguised by heavy instrumentation or figuration, is the best. Naturally, music that slows up the job is anathema. The age, sex, nationality, and intellect of the plant personnel help to determine the type of music to be presented. A high percentage of Polish and Czech employees calls for mazurkas and polkas. Bagpipes will do marvels for the Scotch but are detrimental to practically everyone else. Italian employees in the Acme Steel Works, Chicago, go in for excerpts from operas; and those of the Cystoscope Makers, Inc., of the

Bronx, prefer the classic suites of J. S. Bach. Interestingly enough, mental workers like the classics; marches are considered as strictly masculine music; and current popular tunes go rarely with routine work.

But variety is the spice of life; it is well not to slip into too much of a groove or routine. A full period of only one type of music, such as Strauss waltzes or Latin-American music, is inadvisable. The selections should be mixed up in each period and played in a different order some other day. In work involving mental, rather than physical, effort, music of the "salon" type brings most satisfactory results. Stimulating or distracting types of music should here be avoided, and so-called "dinner music" chosen instead. As far as we know, the music presented at all times should be melodious but not dressed up in fancy orchestrations. During fatigue hours, stimulating music should be used; while relaxing music should be given during rest periods. According to psychologists, music does something to us, whether we like it or not. A fast tempo invariably raises our pulse, respiration, and blood pressure; slow music lowers them. And some people find that music stimulates thought.

4

MUSICAL UNDERSTANDING

---

1. INTRODUCTION

ACCORDING to Leon Barzin (conductor of the training orchestra of the National Orchestra Association), "the 'musical trouble' in this country is not with artists but with audiences. Too small a percentage of them are adequately prepared, and their ideas about music are often superficial and notional. In fact, the only difference between appreciating a simple tune and Beethoven's Fifth Symphony is a matter of practice in listening, requiring simply different degrees of musical memory. We have neglected the very nerve center of cultural education—the classroom."

The most important mission of highly educated professional musicians, performers, or teachers today is to teach the rest of the people how to listen to music. "There is a greater need for piano-teachers and singing-teachers, and that is a numerous company of writers and speakers, who shall teach the people how to listen to music so that it shall not pass through their heads like a vast tonal phantasmagoria, but provide the varied and noble delight contemplated by the composers." *Surely, we do not want more music teachers, nor more performers;* the world is full of them—good, bad, and indifferent; *but we do want more intelligent listeners.* Listening is just a habit—an intelligent habit. Early in life children should acquire the habit and learn that music is something to think about, something more than an entertainment. In turn, listening should bring a delight that is physical, intellectual, and emotional.

"Of all art, music is practiced most and thought about least." A great mystery still enshrouds music. The material part is subtle and elusive. *To master it on its technical side alone costs a vast expenditure of time, labor, patience, and money.* Generally, it is the absence of a standard of judgment employed in the criticism of music which makes intelligent and significant talk about the art so difficult. We cannot have a sound opinion of anything until we understand it—know the truth about it. We cannot criticize an address given in a language of which we are ignorant.

It is not a rare and special privilege to possess the power of enjoying and loving the best music. A taste for good music comes largely from listening to it; the layman should be patient with good music and not condemn all of it at once. Time will teach him that it is not so bad as it sounds.

The element entering into musical perception and enjoyment is, first of all, a *perception of pitch*. The capacity for the enjoyment of music is inherent in practically all normal human beings who have ear enough to distinguish one tone from another and to prefer order to incoherence. All people may achieve success when placed in a favorable environment and if they couple their desires with intense application. Everyone has the capacity for learning music. This is not an exclusive gift of the favored few. Being musical does not necessarily lie in performing music. It is rather *a state of being* which every individual is entitled to by nature and which he can attain, to a greater or lesser degree, provided he is normal physically and has no serious auditory defects. The art and science of music rests on the same psychological basis as everything else that may be learned. Practically no healthy body and mind lacks the musical faculty entirely. Music appeals to our various moods and emotions. The greatest cause of almost all misjudgment in music lies in want of observation—in the failure to hear what the composer is saying and to interpret it in reference to our own needs and emotions. That is why so much of the best music gains by repeated hearings. It is practically impossible to "get it all" at first presentation. A piece of music is *not* like a picture, a statue, or an edifice, which we can look at all at once; but it is more like a train passing by. We get an impression of only a few cars at a time. Music goes out of existence with every performance and must be recreated at every hearing. We can hardly ever be too closely acquainted with the greatest music. Its meaning is as infinite and unfathomable as the works of Homer, Plato, Aristotle, Euripides, Shakespeare, or Goethe; but at each repetition we may understand more of it, if we will. *Admiration grows as knowledge grows;* and the keener the perception of a person, and the more sympathetic his judgment, the fuller and more enduring will his pleasure become.

Of course, whether any given person is tone-deaf, has no perception of pitch at all, or simply lacks training, can be discovered only by scientific tests or experiments; and, even if not up to the average, many a person's ability can be much improved by systematic practice. It is surprising how few of the thousands of people who consider themselves lovers of music have any real understanding of it. The average audience, whether it be made up of children or adults, understands little or nothing of music to gain adequate appreciation. Therefore, the art of teaching musical understanding and enjoyment is mainly this: we must persist in giving to people what they do not understand, but be ready to stand by and help in all possible ways until understanding and appreciation awaken. We must do everything we can to make the inherent beauty of all music a clear and convincing reality. *The ear must be trained to the beauties of the music by a great deal of listening.* Those who have not listened much are not likely to enjoy much, just as the person who has never read anything but the cheap novel of the day is not likely to care for works of genuine literary value. *Those who know music best enjoy it most.* An accurate and thorough knowledge of music does not reduce our pleasure. The more definitely our intelligence is employed, the more quickly we come to sense the artistic and emotional qualities of any work of art.

But listening to music is essentially a selective response

and is not substantially the same thing for all persons. There are various types of listening, and music may be listened to and enjoyed in many ways. Different individuals tend to respond to different elements of musical content at different times. Psychology has proven that in listening it is important "not to try to hear everything, but to select the right things." Good listening is a selective response to one or another of music's characteristic or structural elements. The difference between good and bad listening does not depend upon the grasp of every detail but rather upon the elements singled out as the controlling points of attention. We may listen to music for various purposes.

The response to music is rather complex and varied; it involves kinesthetic and emotional factors. That is why music has been of such great importance in human life and why it is capable of sustaining and objectifying emotional meanings. Good music, well performed, usually is capable of bringing to the fore a mood or a succession of moods.

The presence of emotion (general mood—a prepared and appropriate affective attitude) is the most important single extrinsic factor in the active listening necessary for full musical enjoyment. Naturally, oral comments, program notes, and the general presentation of music are important, because they concentrate and re-enforce the emotional response. In the teaching of "appreciation and understanding of music," literary comments should serve as factors to set the mood in its proper direction.

Millions of people fail to participate in our amazing musical civilization. Clearly, the rightful place of music in modern life can be assured only if it becomes an important part of general culture. Music will become a living part of culture only if children as well as adults are made aware of the deep and inspiring experiences that await those who possess a developed musical consciousness. Music, as a living part of general culture, must be placed within reach of all.

The capacity to listen properly to music is a better proof in many cases of musical appreciation than the ability to sing or to perform upon an instrument. Indeed, it is just as necessary to train our ears as it is to train our fingers or our

voices. Writers and instructors have stressed the necessity
and importance of systematic training of the musical ear.
Their advice has been little heeded, and most music teaching has been for performance. Why not open the student's
ears to the beauty of music which is for everyone to enjoy?
No on can listen for us. Intelligent listening enriches our
inner life. *Recognition of beauty is a matter of education
and of culture.* No doubt, *we see beauty and truth only in
proportion to our intelligence.* Others must show us the
things which they have discovered. Quite often, we do not
interpret correctly the meaning of music without this assistance.

THE LISTENING HABIT

Let us learn the principles: first *listening;* then *thinking;*
then *acting.* In order to enter into the spirit of music, we
must go back to this principle. If this method were adopted
in all branches of education, we should become thoroughly
schooled in a practical way. As it is, we are slaves to name
and form.

Music makes three appeals: 1. *Physical,* or sense appeal;
2. *Intellectual,* or mind appeal; and 3. *Emotional,* or spiritual
appeal.

1. *Sense appeal:* By it we mean *the joy that comes
through the mere tone qualities of sound we hear.* The simplest way is to listen for the sheer pleasure of the musical
sound itself. It is the appeal in which we hear without thinking, without considering it in any way. It is the appeal that
uses music as a consolation or an escape. Here music lets
our mind wander and then go off to a place of dreaming.
The sense appeal is an important one, but it does not tell
the whole story. The highest value in a musical masterpiece
lies beyond mere tones, just as the highest value in literature lies beyond mere words. We can only get at the highest
values in all the arts when we are conscious of the medium
employed. So we must boldly approach technicalities and
logically begin with the science of musical tone. The sound
element varies with each composer, and his usage of tones
is an integral part of his style; for this reason it is an es-

sential factor in listening to music. The rich, clear tone of a
bell gives us a definite feeling of pleasure. We study the
various tone qualities of different voices or instruments. In
listening to rich harmonies, we find further expression of
this pleasure. We also mean by sense appeal the response
to music predominantly rhythmic in character. (See Chapter on "The Physical or Sensuous.") It is true, we ought not
to be ashamed if our feet respond to mere rhythm; but we
should not be satisfied with this purely sense appeal, for it
is only a beginning. In fact, for many people the actual
sound of music—its depth, splendor, or variety of tone—becomes a sort of intoxication. They are content to let the
sound waves surround them passively, extracting a genuine
and entirely legitimate sensuous pleasure from the act, but
missing, in this too relaxed state, a great many things it were
better not to miss. Unfortunately, too much of so-called
"musical understanding and appreciation" is mere sensuous
enjoyment of pleasing sounds, alternating with dislike for
unpleasant combinations or bewilderment. Surely, losing
oneself in a mass of tonal effects is not understanding and
appreciation but, as said before, a sort of intoxication.

2. *Intellectual appeal:* The art of listening to music is
to approach tones in such a way as to "make sense" of them,
to get the meaning *behind the tones.* The meaning behind
the tones constitutes what the piece is saying. Ordinarily,
when we listen to the "sounds themselves" with some effort,
we first recognize the melody, which we consider pretty or
not. Usually, that is the end. If the rhythm seems exciting,
it is likely to get our attention next. But harmony and tone-
color are generally taken for granted, if they are noticed
at all. As to form—the fact that music has a definite form of
some kind—this idea hardly ever occurs to us. The composer
creates and develops a theme in just the same way as a
playwright creates and develops a character. The theme and
its development, structure, and form are the equivalent of
the plot and the plot's development. It is important to all of
us to become more alive to this aspect of music. The intelligent listener must be prepared to become more and
more aware of the musical material and how it is used.

We must hear the rhythm, melodies, harmonies, tone-colors, as well as the various forms. Listening to all these is listening to music for its intellectual appeal.

The first step in making sense out of any unfamiliar thing is to *get clearly in mind its central subject or subjects*—as, for example, the fundamental idea of a poem. Without a background of general education, the understanding and enjoyment of great literary works is apt to be limited, if not actually lacking. However, in concentrating our attention exclusively on the "sense and emotional response," we forget that consciousness must precede emotion in listening to music. In music, the *intellectual appeal is developed by the consideration of the structural element* and *by a study of motifs, phrases, sentences, and the succession and relation of part to part* established through the faculty of memory, without which there would be no recognition of connection, relation, dependence, proportion, and thought or imagination as exhibited in thematic development. Furthermore, it involves knowledge of musical history, conditions under which compositions originated, distinctions of style between one period and another, something of the lives of the composers, and the plots of oratorios and operas. Thus, listening is as much an analytical act as the examination of architecture, sculpture, painting, or literature. After all, *real appreciation can come only through the act of thinking.*

3. *Emotional-spiritual appeal:* To love the Beautiful requires something more than pleasurable sound—the sensuous appeal—or the inherent expressive feeling—the intellectual appeal. It requires something which feels intensely and sees impressions and aspects rather than thoughts—the purely musical, the emotional-spiritual appeal—*something which arouses in us a feeling of love, devotion, joy, grief, pathos, longing, sympathy, hatred, and subtle fancies.* Music is tonal discourse; and to understand and appreciate its message completely involves physical and mental processes as well as emotional and spiritual response. Of all the fine arts music is the most emotional. Music that does not convey emotion has repudiated its most essential quality and so has

abandoned its great advantage. In comparison with literature, it compensates for a lesser ability to deal with specific detail by a deeper eloquence in the presentation of underlying moods and attitudes. Its reaching the profoundest levels of our consciousness is much like that of philosophy; but it expresses emotionally what philosophy only formulates intellectually. Schopenhauer recognized this more fully than most philosophers. We can deepen our understanding of music only by being a more conscious and aware listener— by not just merely listening, but by *listening for something*. Now, while there is an expressive meaning to music, it is next to impossible to say in so many words what that meaning is. And herein lies the difficulty. But we can readily see that music expresses at different moments excitement or serenity, regret or triumph, gaiety or sadness, fury or satisfaction. It expresses each of these moods, and some others, in a numberless variety of subtle shadings and differences. In fact, music may even express a state of meaning for which we have no adequate words in any language. The more beautiful a theme seems to us, the harder it is to find any words that will describe it to our complete satisfaction. Or, if we are able to describe to our own satisfaction in so many words the exact meaning of our chosen theme, we do not know whether or not others are satisfied with this description. They may not accept our meaning. It is important that each person feels for himself the particular expressive quality of a theme or an entire piece of music. Furthermore, if this should be a great work of art, do not expect it to mean exactly the same thing every time you hear it again. "While the psychological effect of music remains a considerable mystery, and the appreciation of great music must be a personal and individual act involving a certain receptivity and sensitiveness to musical impressions, yet the perception of the logic or sense of a piece of music is a long step toward understanding it, and one of the best means of cultivating that receptivity and sensitiveness."

So, by emotional-spiritual appeal, we do not mean merely a naïvely emotional response to music. Many there are who seem to think that the joy of listening to music is destroyed if one knows too much about it. This kind of listening—succumbing to the emotions and nothing more—is greatly affected by much that is outside of the music itself. Note that most of so-called "heart-songs" make their appeal not only through the melody but also through the words, the title, and the inevitable association of ideas, traditions, and habits brought up by them. Any "Dream of Love," or "Revery," will call up sentimental images from childhood to the grave. Much of grand opera also belongs to this type of music. The story, words, actions, costumes, scenery, lighting effects, as well as the fashionable society attending—all blend and create an illusion so strong that an emotional response is inevitable; and yet it is almost impossible to tell how much credit is due to the music itself, and how much should go elsewhere.

The purpose of discussing the understanding and enjoyment of music is to assist in the acquisition of intelligent listening habits so as to understand clearly, feel intensely, and to enjoy fully the message of the composer. It seeks to refine the individual faculties. It is a sort of development, somewhat laborious, from the simplest to the most advanced, from the folk tune to the symphony. As different people vary widely in their faculties, it follows that *each student must listen, analyze, compare, discriminate, and judge for himself*. Even at that, results are obtained only gradually. Each person is limited because of his individual make-up—his ability; and it is no discredit to him to stop at this point because of an honest opinion. All artistic taste is something very individual. One is esthetically better off by expressing an honest preference, based on his own impressions, however crude they may be, than to be a highbrow who slavishly follows fashion or the dictate of someone else. We must refine our own impressions—climb only by our own activity—and results will come. Our own senses and our own intelligence must be the final authorities. *Musical understanding is not general information about music and musicians*. We appreciate art and life not from the stimulation of general information but from our individual knowledge and experience.

Appreciation is a more comprehensive term than taste, susceptibility, impressionableness, or even admiration. It takes in all these, and it implies also judgment founded on knowledge. Appreciation is the action of eliminating inessential qualities or things . . . a delicate judgment . . . perception, recognition, intelligent notice, especially perception of nuances or distinctions.

Generally speaking, the enjoyment of a painting depends upon:

1. Ability to see its beauties of line and form.
2. Ability to see its beauties of coloring.
3. Ability to understand its subject (where it has a subject requiring understanding); and, in any case, to be moved by the emotions that moved the artist as he selected his subject or worked it out.

Likewise, the enjoyment or esthetic appreciation of a piece of music depends upon:

1. *Ability to realize its beauties of melody, rhythm, harmony, and form.*
2. *Ability to grasp its beauties of tone-color*—of one or more instruments.
3. *Ability to understand its subject*—to enter into the mood of the composer and to be moved by it (emotion).

Of the three parties to the musical experience—composer, performer, listener—the listener is as important as the other two. Certainly, the emotional depth, intuitive power, imagination, skill, and integrity of the composer and performer fail to achieve their proper end if the listener is ignorant or indifferent to the qualities of music. If composing and performing are a species of communication, then the listener is the person who receives the communication; and, to some extent, he must be able to enter into the feelings of the composer. The listener's feeling tendencies will be aroused in proportion to his esthetic make-up. The music not only creates a general emotional state but also carries in itself—in its particular patterns and in its particular tone-colorings—indications as to its specific emotional meaning. The way of feeling which the composer objectified in his music, and which the performer grasped and conveyed, now suffuse the listener. Needless to say, these final processes are as unconscious as those which preceded them.

The good listener is a person who is reasonably sensitive to the power of music to embody emotional meanings, and who is willing to listen alertly, undistracted by irrelevancies. The excellent listener will take the trouble to learn enough about musical theory to be able to understand and appreciate the superlative workmanship which so much first-rate music reveals. He will read musical history and biography in order to become better acquainted with the art itself, with numerous fine composers, teachers, performers, and musicologists, and with the social and national environments which have always affected music in one way or another. All of this helps to create musical delight of the highest type, as well as to stimulate further interest.

The power of discriminative listening is of supreme importance. Perhaps it is strange that we must learn to listen, and it is regrettable that so few have acquired the habit. At any rate, *no concert can rise in excellence above the capacity of its audience;* and understanding and enjoyment of music grows with increased discrimination in listening.

Good or excellent listening cannot be acquired in a day or so. Usually, it is only the music-lover, one sufficiently eager to be willing to search patiently and to listen persistently to the best, who will finally be rewarded and thus grow to understand the real message of music. Good music, like good literature, fine paintings, or great architecture, takes maturity of thought and breadth of experience for its comprehension and appreciation. This understanding of the masterpieces cannot come about through an occasional thoughtless trip to a concert hall to hear some widely advertised artist or orchestra, any more than appreciation of fine pictures can result from passing through a famous gallery or two, or even from reading a book on "How to Look at Pictures."

Musical understanding and appreciation is not a study

exclusively for high-school and college students. It properly begins with the teaching of the first *rote song*. Every song that children study should have in it the features of the listening lesson. A complete study of the song should involve consideration of technical, interpretative, historic, and esthetic points. The experience of children through the grades should be *singing or playing, writing music, and listening*—the three factors of music-making. *We evaluate art and life* not from the stimulation of general information, but *from our individual knowledge and experience.*

In order to train intelligent listeners, we must state here that *there is a difference between listening and hearing. In hearing, we have a passive mentality*—we do not think of what we hear. But there is something more in listening to music than merely hearing the sounds. We might say that bad listeners divide neatly into two groups—those who hear passively and those who insist on listening for irrelevant things. If a person claims that he likes music, yet proves himself unable to recognize a composition after several hearings or even to give the roughest idea of its general character, the chances are that he has been giving it only a part of his attention and hearing only a corresponding fraction of the music. *In listening we have an active mentality* —we *think* of what we hear. We must understand music just as we understand a language. However, it does not necessarily follow that we must like what we understand. Yet, if it is good music, we are likely to appreciate it.

Listening demands: 1. Sympathetic mental activity on the part of the listener; doing something; concentration; discrimination; association; imagination; 2. Information as to title, type of music, and composer; 3. Exercise of feeling; and 4. Memory.

I. *Concentration*—The *sine qua non* in the art of listening, is merely sustained observation, and this means self-control.

Discrimination—To make a distinction; to differentiate; to separate by discerning differences; to learn by experience to discriminate certain qualities of music.

Association of ideas—Music arouses pleasurable associations of great experiences more or less familiar. A feeling may be associated with an idea. The sound of a bell awakens certain sentiments. A poem or a painting may recall an interesting experience. Music likewise owes some of its charm to association. Songs we sang in our youth, or at a certain special occasion, are reminders of previous experiences. Music yields a compound interest of satisfaction, the enjoyment once experienced tends to renew itself on later occasions.

Imagination—Music is an art that appeals to the imagination. The composer gives his personal message to the world through his creative imagination. But whether that message shall be transmitted faithfully and be received effectively depends upon the possession of a rich imagination on the part of the performer, or performers, and listener. Hence, unless our imagination is very active when listening, we miss the spirit of the music. In music there is variety, suspense, realization, contrast, climax, and identity.

II.　Listening requires knowledge about what we are to hear—an intellectual activity.

1.　*Information*—a)Title: indicates composer's intention; also, purpose and origin of composition. b) Words, if any; music is an expressive art. When it is employed in conjunction with poetry, the words must be understood in order to get the meaning of the music.

2.　*Type of music*—Knowledge of form or structure (pattern) of the composition. Music is an art of design. Beautiful forms are woven together, for the recognition of which it is essential that we know what we hear. Knowledge of form will enable us to detect the musical subject matter of the piece. What was formerly a puzzling web of sound now becomes a clear, logical arrangement of definite tunes (themes). We can recognize the relation of parts to one another and to the whole.

3.　Acquaintance with the leading theme of composition. The most effective aid in grasping the formal side of music is to memorize the leading themes upon which the work is constructed. Indeed, the most subtle and pervasive influence in music, one that affects the taste and judgment of everybody, comes from the music we daily hear and make our own.

4. Ability to recognize tone-color—Knowledge of the instruments used in the performance of a piece will provide new interest in listening. The ability to recognize tone qualities of the various instruments, singly or in combination, makes it possible to observe tonal contrasts which formerly were missed. The tone-color of a piece is now clearer.

5. Composer—When and where he lived; his characteristics (individuality); influence of his time that affected his way of writing (style and manner); nationality and environment; period in which the piece was composed, and the stage of musical development it represents; also, the school to which his works belong. All this makes the composition no longer a mere piece with a pretty melody, or one of technical achievement, but a human document—a medium of human expression.

III. Listening requires control over, as well as the exercise of, our feelings or emotional make-up. Of course, all knowledge is of some value; but the ordinary listener, engaged day after day in building, driving a truck, baking, banking, tailoring, teaching, practicing law, buying or selling, etc., needs to have a thorough elementary knowledge of these three—concentration, knowledge, and control over feelings. His time will not allow more than that. It is encouraging, indeed, to know that these three can be quite easily acquired through mere general reading, gradually and pleasantly pursued as the days go by.

IV. Listening requires effort—We need to *cultivate a musical memory*. We have to listen to what is passing, remember what has gone, and, to some extent, anticipate what may be coming. And we have to relate these things to each other.

2. A FEW POINTERS

Actual musical experience is essential. It is very important to become thoroughly familiar with the suggested musical examples or similar ones. *Recognition of a tune is the first step toward musical understanding and enjoyment.*

The reason why most people derive the greatest enjoyment from the music they know is that sound can only be interpreted in the light of past experience. We like the things we recognize. Thus, the greater the experience, the wider will be the field of enjoyment. "Popular music is familiar music." Indeed, the problem of making good music popular is simply that of making it familiar. *Music is made to be heard;* use your opportunities to hear music, and record the results of your musical experiences (notebook record of music heard; name of composition; name of composer; name of performer; voice or voices; instrument, etc.).

After the intelligent listener has learned to know a musical work, he can enjoy without any conscious effort an imaginative, emotional, as well as purely musical experience which will be entirely different from that of the untutored layman.

If you do not recognize a melody at first, do not conclude that it is not there. Even a fairly obvious composition may require several hearings.

Listen to all music in the same spirit. Give all music an equal chance.

If you like a tune, do not be ashamed to say so. On the other hand, do not express an insincere opinion merely for the sake of agreeing with someone considered as an authority. Form your own opinion, and use your own ears.

Do not worry about your musical taste. It will develop normally if you listen carefully to good and bad music. Soon you will find that some pieces grow tiresome very quickly, whereas others become more likeable every time you listen to them. It is possible to appreciate music without knowing a great deal about it. As a matter of fact, there are some who know it well from a theoretical standpoint who, nevertheless, fail to appreciate it properly. Remember, the love of a good tune is the surest road to musical appreciation.

If we can progress from baby talk to an intelligent reading of literary masterpieces, why can we not, with equal ease, advance from the crude response to rhythm to an understanding of the fine works of the great composers?

Of course, merely reading this book will not make a performer out of you, nor even an intelligent listener. You will have to be quite active while listening and studying. If you expose yourself consistently to music in a mentally active attitude, you will be amazed at your progress. In listening to qualities inherent in the tonal-rhythmic pattern, remember that none of these ever operate in entire isolation from the rest. Most assuredly, you will follow the line of least resistance at first, listening only to the most obvious tones and rhythms; but gradually you will discover for yourself more and more of the music that has lasting value, and in time you will even add the more complex works to the list of those thoroughly enjoyed.

Do not try to do all this at once; and, above all, be honest with yourself. If you do not like a piece of music at first, drop it and come back to it later. It may be that you need further education along that line or that you are not in the mood for it. Listen sincerely, enthusiastically, and intelligently. Do not allow yourself to think of other things while listening.

Important: characteristic and appropriate mood responses to music do not depend upon intelligence or upon musical training—i.e., we may be stirred emotionally without being clearly aware of the tonal or rhythmic patterns, nor may we be aware necessarily of imagery, associations, or any other musical elements.

Ear-training is the most important part of musical study, whether for the music-lover or the professional musician, for the goal is the ability to listen and discriminate clearly.

Listening can be successfully conducted only by alert, active curiosity, guided by constant application in the formation of habits of perception. We learn to listen well only by much listening. Listening is an active process. As we see what we are *prepared* to see, so we hear what we are *prepared* to hear—what we have put there by much intelligent practice. We hear good music in order to have something for which to listen. This is very important, as it not only forms our tastes but also establishes our habits of listening. If our capacity for appreciation has been injured by hearing nothing but trashy music, we are esthetically ill and need attention and care in order to develop a wholesome taste. "Music in this respect is like literature. If we constantly read poor works, depending for interest on sensationalism and excitement rather than on truth and beauty, we not only form a taste for poor literature, but we also form bad habits of reading and listening." The necessities of daily life require us to use language; thus, we are able at least to understand what is said in good literature, even if we do not like it. But because we have so little musical experience, after we have heard poor music for a while—especially in early childhood—we are unable even to listen intelligently. Under such conditions good music sounds dull instead of interesting.

Indeed, the need for good guidance and help has become more urgent than ever with the great increase in the quantity of music in the house as a result of the phonograph, radio, and TV. In addition, we have the systematic concertising of artists, orchestras, singing societies, choruses, etc.

Methods of study: The several plans of teaching or studying the understanding and enjoyment (appreciation) of music are:

1. The historical or chronological.

2. By schools of composition—such as the classic, romantic, impressionist, the national, the recent modern.

3. By musical forms—the old suite, modern suite, rondo, gavotte, theme and variation, sonata, sinfonietta, etc.

4. By types—a) vocal; b) instrumental.

5. By composers—J. S. Bach, Palestrina, Handel, Beethoven, Wagner, etc.

6. By instruments—string, wood wind, brass, piano, violin, etc.

7. By nations—German, French, Italian, Russian, American, etc.

Beginners should study only compositions with definite musical content. After all, the cultivation of the musical memory is absolutely essential to anybody who hopes to listen to music intelligently. Practice in listening and remembering makes it possible for us to listen and remember more. *The more we listen and remember, the more we get out of music.* If the ear is trained, the memory will store away the beauties of music after they have been heard. Be sure to grasp the opening theme, as well as other themes, in order to follow them and to enjoy their subsequent growth in the complete work. Be able to recognize at least the main theme whenever you hear a musical composition more than once. We should be able to distinguish the character of simple pieces having definite outlines, marked rhythm, and well-balanced phrases.

As to structural design, most people hardly understand a composition as *an organized, unified, inwardly evolving whole* but, rather, hear it either "as a shifting mass of tonal content or a melodic flow and recurrence with rhythmic and harmonic elements reinforcing the tonal effect and occasionally rising to a position of predominating interest." Because there are various types of listening, one can hardly be aware of every aspect of a complex musical composition.

Folk songs provide admirable and simple material for exercises. If we listen to many of them, we will find ourselves making surprisingly rapid progress in hearing clearly and definitely.

(See *German Folk Songs,* edited by J. Brahms; *100 Folk Songs of All Nations,* edited by Gr. Bantock; *Folk Songs of Many Peoples,* edited by Fl. H. Botsford; *International Folk Song Book,* edited by H. Riemann.)

Pieces containing the *element of suggestion or refined description:*

a) Songs based upon familiar poems—Sweet and Low; Last Rose of Summer; Annie Laurie; Lorelei; Little Rosebud; The Cuckoo Clock; Narcissus; etc. Also, noted hymns—A Mighty Fortress Is Our God; Now the Day Is Over; Holy, Holy, Holy; Old Hundred; etc.

b) Dances—minuet; gavotte; saraband; gigue; rigadoon; march; waltz; gallopade; mazurka; polka; tango; fox trot; two-step; etc.

Preliminary questions: How is sound produced? What is the difference between noise and tone? What are the properties of tone? How is duration of tone measured? What is rhythm? What is time? What is tempo? What is pitch? What is melody? What is intensity? What is dynamics? What is tone quality? What are scales—major, minor, chromatic? What is harmony? Can you hear the keynote? Can you follow a tune? Can you recognize a motive, a phrase, a sentence, a section? What is form, or pattern? What is timbre, or tone-color?

What kind of music are you listening to? Is it for home, or street, or church, or hall? Is it stirring or sad? Is it quick or slow, grave or gay, active or contemplative, songful or dancelike? Do you feel like marching or dancing? Does it sound like a lullaby or a hymn? Does it sound delicate or tender, happy or grand? What is a theme? What is a cadence?

Listen to: Old Black Joe; Home, Sweet Home; Blue Bells of Scotland; etc.

Determine 1. The *meter*—does the song begin on an upbeat or down-beat? 2. Is it in the *major or minor mode?* 3. *Cadences*—what kind? 4. *Motive*—and how is it used, in sequence or repetition?

After a short time spent in systematic and careful listening, these results should follow:

1. An enlarged and enriched musical experience and listening repertory.

2. Improved standards of judgment and musical taste.

3. A tendency to prefer good music.

4. A feeling for rhythm, meter, and note-values.

5. Ability to recognize a melody and the accompaniment.

6. Ability to detect recurring themes and simple patterns.

7. Increased ability to sense different moods.

8. Ability to recognize by tone-color and appear-

ance the various orchestral instruments; also, various types of voices.

9. Ability to recognize different types of marches and dances and, to some extent, pure and descriptive (program) music.

10. Familiarity with several composers through their music and biographical data and ability to recognize some twenty to thirty tunes or more.

Listening for *rhythm:* Certain of these rhythmic patterns ᵭave us calm; some are exciting; some suggest solemnity; ᵭthers invite us to dance. In some striking passages, rhythm ᵭay become the chief determining factor. Some listeners ᵭe more susceptible to it than others. Tell in what time 2/4; 4/4; 3/4; 6/8) and tempo (slow, quick, moderate, ᵭc.) the following pieces are written. Cultivate your rhythᵭic sense. Persistent practice along this line will soon quickᵭn your recognition of rhythm.

Examples:

Turkey in the Straw (American folk dance).

BEETHOVEN
  Minuet in G; Turkish March.

  BISHOP
    Home, Sweet Home.

  BRAHMS
    Hungarian Dance #5.

CHOPIN
  Mazurka, A minor; Polonaise Militaire, Opus 40, #1.

DELIBES
  Valse from Copelia.

DVORAK
  Humoresque.

ELGAR
  The Tame Bear.

GERMAN
  Shepherd Dance.

GHIS
  Amaryllis Gavotte (Air Louis XIII).

GOUNOD
  Waltz from Faust; March and Soldiers' Chorus from Faust.

BARNBY
  Sweet and Low.

BOCCHERINI
  Minuet Antique.

CAREY
  America.

Yankee Doodle.

DE LISLE
  The Marseillaise.

D. EMMET
  Dixie.

GOSSEC
  Gavotte.

GRAINGER
   Shepherd's Hey (English folk dance).
GRIEG
   Peer Gynt Suite (Anitra's Dance; In the Hall).

V. HERBERT
   Dagger Dance from Natoma.

NEVIN
   The Rosary.

KREISLER
   Toy Soldiers' March.

OFFENBACH
   Barcarolle.

PADEREWSKI
   Minuet in G.

SAINT-SAENS
   Dance Macabre.

SCHUBERT
   March Militaire; Moment Musicale, F minor.

SCHUMANN
   Soldiers March; Knight of the Hobby Horse; Happy
   Farmer.

SOUSA
   The Black Man; Volunteer March.

J. STRAUSS
   Waltz Blue Danube; Morning Papers; Tales from
   Vienna Woods.

THOMAS
   Gavotte from Mignon.

WAGNER
   The Ride of the Valkyries.

WALDTEUFEL
   Any waltz (The Skaters, Loved Ones, etc.)

WEBER
   Invitation to the Dance.

VERDI
   Aida, Triumphal March; Rigoletto, La Donna e Mobile.

Listening for *melody:* Certain melodies are like songs;
others are gay; some are sad; some invite dancing; other
are rather hard to follow. Melody is a fundamental and
common center of interest and pleasure. Try to memorize
the theme—memory is of great importance in learning to
appreciate music.
   Examples:

J. S. BACH
   Air on the G String (D major Suite).

BACH-GOUNOD
   Ave Maria

BEETHOVEN
   Andante, 5th Symphony.

BIZET
   Intermezzo.

BRAHMS
   Lullaby.

DVORAK
   Largo (New World Symphony).

GLUCK
  Musette; Ballet Music (Orpheus).

SCHUMANN
  Träumerei.

GRIEG
  An den Frühling; I Love You; Solweg's Song; Peer Gynt Suite.

HAYDN
  With Verdure Clad.

MACDOWELL
  To a Wild Rose.

MASSENET
  Elegie; Meditation (Thais).

GODARD
  Berceuse (Jocelyn).

HAUSER
  Cradle Song.

JARNEFELT
  Berceuse.

MENDELSSOHN
  Spring Song; On Wings of Song; Intermezzo (Midsummer Night's Dream).

MOZART
  Voi che Sepate.

RAFF
  Cavatina.

RUBINSTEIN
  Melody in F; Romance.

SAINT-SAENS
  The Swan.

SCHUBERT
  Ave Maria; Serenade; The Linden Tree; Unfinished Symphony (first movement); etc.

R. WAGNER
  Walter's Preislied; Pilgrim Chorus and, Oh, Thou my Beautiful Evening Star (Tannhäuser).

  Londonderry Air; Believe Me If All Those Enduring Young Charms; etc.

Examples of *minor*-key melodies:

DEBERIOT
  Andante, Violin Concerto #7.

GLUCK
  Largo for Violin & Piano (Mittell Edition).

GOLTERMANN
  Notturno, for Violin & Piano.

LOCATELLI
  Sonata for Violin & Piano.

RODE
  Adagio, Violin Concerto.

TARTINI
  Larghetto G minor, Violin Sonata (Devil's Trill).

VERACINI
  Largo F♯ minor, for Violin & Piano; Sonata, for Violin & Piano.

VIEUXTEMPS
  Andante, 2nd Violin Concerto.

Listening for *harmony:* It is of considerable importance, but usually less so than rhythm.

Examples:

BARNBY
Sweet and Low; Now the Day Is Over.

J. S. BACH
Bouree.

BEETHOVEN
Sonata (first movement) Opus 27, #2.

DEBUSSY
Afternoon of a Faun; Reflets dans l'Eau.

V. DITTERSDORF
Andante, Quartet in G Major.

FOSTER
Swanee River.

GRIEG
Asa's Death (Peer Gynt Suite).

RACHMANINOFF
Prelude C♯ minor.

HAYDN
Adagio (String Quartet in D).

HANDEL
Largo.

MacDOWELL
Sonata Tragica, Opus 45.

MOZART
Sonata #9, A major.

LISZT
Liebestraum.

RAVEL
The Fountain.

SCHUBERT
Ballet Music (Rosamunde); Erlking.

WAGNER
Prelude and Love Death from Tristan and Isolde; Parcifal, March of the Grail Knights; Ride of the Valkyries; Pilgrims' Chorus from Tannhäuser; etc.

Listening for *tone-color* (timbre): Tone-volume and its timbre are important; pay close attention to instrumentation i.e., the various instruments used and their effects.

Examples:

BIZET
Farandole (strings & wood winds); Soldiers Changing Guard (wood winds & brasses).

GRIEG
Anitra's Dance (strings); In the Hall of the Mountain King (wood winds).

LIADOW
Music Box (wood winds).

BARTLETT
A Dream.

PIERNE
March of the Little Lead Soldiers (wood winds & brass).

TSCHAIKOWSKY
Nutcracker Suite (harp, brasses, wood winds, strings).
R. STRAUSS
Till Eulenspiegel; etc.
Vermeland—Swedish folk song (strings).

Examples of music arousing *national feeling:*

ELGAR
March, Pomp and Circumstance.

TSCHAIKOWSKY
March Slav.

DE LISLE
The Marseillaise.

D. T. SHAW
The Gem of the Ocean.

Examples of music with *poetic thought:*

COUCH
Kathleen Mavourneen.

ELGAR
Salut D'Amour.

GRIEG
To Spring.

MASSENET
Meditation from Thais.

RUBINSTEIN
Romance.

Examples of *program (descriptive) music:*

DELIBES
Dance of the Automatons.

GRIEG
March of the Dwarfs.

JUON
Naiads at the Spring.

MACDOWELL
From an Indian Lodge.

MENDELSSOHN
Spring Song; Overture to Midsummer Night's Dream.

ORTH
In a Clock Store.

POLDINI
Waltzing Doll.

ROSSINI
Overture to William Tell.

PONCHIELLI
Dance of the Hours.

SAINT-SAENS
The Swan.

SCHUBERT
The Bee.

3. QUESTIONS ON INTELLIGENT LISTENING

1. As to *rhythm:* Is it clear, well marked (march, gavotte, minuet, mazurka, etc.); tiresome; confused; intricate or complex (rhapsody); syncopated (Negro music); monotonous (Indian, etc.); regular or irregular? What time? What tempo?

2. As to *melody:* Is it sad; pleasing; monotonous; joyful

(Dixie); fragmentary (rhapsody, short Indian music, etc.); dignified; original or ingenius; striking? Is it songlike (within range of about one and a half octaves, flowing rhythm, and not too rapid); or instrumental in character (big jumps, jerky rhythm, and very rapid)? Is it scalewise, arpeggio-like, varied, or jumpy? Is it above, below, or within the range of accompaniment?

3. As to *harmony:* Is it rich (sextette); varied; obscure; peculiar and unusual; elaborate; abundant (Schubert's Unfinished Symphony)? Is it major or minor; simple or complex? Is the accompaniment of chords or arpeggios? Is it thin and delicate, or full and rich? What is its range—close or wide?

4. As to *form:* Is it symmetrical (as in a march or folk dance; minuet from Mozart's Don Giovanni, etc.); classic, romantic (tone poem: Les Preludes, by Liszt); diversified (as in a rhapsody or art song; Wagner's The Ride of the Valkyries, etc.)? Is it a theme and variations? Is it 1-part, 2-part, or 3-part form? What sections are repeated? What is its classification as to form? Is it in sonata form, or a fugue? Is the texture homophonic or polyphonic?

5. As to *tone-color:* For what instrument or instruments is it written? For what voice or voices? Are there contrasts of color? Staccato, legato, crescendo, diminuendo, pizzicato, scale passages, chords, broken chords, etc., and pedal effects? Which instrument gives the first theme, the second theme, etc.?

6. As to *style:* Is the piece pleasing on the whole? What is the general mood? What is its climax, and how is it attained? What feeling or emotion does the piece express? What kind of piece is it? To what school does it belong? How does it compare with another of the same type?

7. As to *composer:* By whom? When and where did he live? Who was his teacher? Who were his friends? What important positions did he occupy? What were his traits of character? Had his personal character anything to do with the qualities peculiar to his own works? Or had his education, personal environment, or fortunes? If so, which of his works show this? What traits of nationality lie in his music?

For what kind of music is he noted (songs, church music, chamber music, symphony, lyric pieces, opera, etc.)? What are his chief works? What is his chief musical activity (virtuoso, conductor, composer, teacher)? Does he follow his predecessors, or does he strike out for himself? Are there any special circumstances that attended the writing of this music? What were the prevailing philosophical ideas as to art, religion, and life during his period as a composer? What did he do, if anything, to make music different from what it was before his time? If he made any advances, were they along the line of melodic or harmonic structure, form, orchestra, or what? Did he use more than one form of artistic expression, as, for instance, Schumann did in writing his critical essays or Wagner in writing his own librettos? Are his compositions historically identified with any particular movement—poetic, philosophic, or religious? Who were his contemporaries, literary and musical? What composer, if any, represented an opposite current of musical thought during the period of the composer under consideration?

8. As to title: What is the title? Does it reflect the character of the piece, or is it suggestive? How does the story, or other explanation, help us to understand the music?

4. FORM

No rule can be laid down for recognizing the excellence of a musical idea. The ability to appreciate the depth and beauty of a fine musical thought must come from continued musical thinking, by living with the music of the masters, and by absorbing the spirit of their nobility.

However, it is possible to assist the reader and student in gaining acquaintance with those qualities of excellence in musical composition and musical performance which are susceptible of definition.

Those who desire to cultivate an intelligent understanding and enjoyment of music ought, above all, to be acquainted with the *form, or structure, of music,* and the *history of music.*

Let us now point out some of the elementary principles

of form so that we may take the first step in developing the power of listening intelligently to music.

From the study of musical history we acquire knowledge of the period to which a composition belongs; of the state of development of the art; of the purpose and possibilities of composition at that time. In addition, we obtain much information regarding the composer, his training, his individuality, and of his life in general.

Let us consider in more detail the form in music. Fine buildings, pictures, and statues must be seen; *music must be heard*. The printed page of a composition is not music; it is merely the record of music. It is true that there are a few professional musicians who are capable of imagining the sound of a composition from reading the printed page. But still, this is not art. It is like imagining a picture from reading a description of it. Music is to be conceived primarily as presented to the sense of hearing. Now, if music consists of a series of consecutive melodic bits, each different from the other, the mind grasps nothing. In order, then, for the mind to become acquainted with these melodic bits, it is necessary to have them repeated. Thus, due to the fleeting nature of a musical thought, we have the first requisite of musical form—repetition. In architecture, sculpture, and painting (the arts which exist in the element of space), we come from the whole to the parts; but in *listening to music*, it is necessary to *remember the parts* as they come before the mind, and *then*, by dint of a feat of memory, to *combine these parts mentally into a whole*. Studying the methods of distributing repetitions, the composers were led to adopt a plan of construction, the organization of forms; and hence we find that *form* in music is synonymous with *design or pattern*. It is mainly because of the difficulty of combining parts mentally into a whole that so many feel that they "do not understand music." And again, it is because they do not understand it that many foolishly assume music to have no form or pattern and, therefore, is not a great art.

Every work of art must have design; and the greater the diversity in unity displayed by the design, the higher the art. Form in music refers to the structure that is observed by the composer. As in the case of architecture, sculpture, painting, and literature, the larger the composition, the more details there may be present in the form. All the fine arts exemplify, each in its own way, the same principles of form —namely a central idea which through repetition, contrast, or variety, and unity or symmetry, is emphasized in proportion to its relative importance to the secondary or subsidiary ideas. In architecture, "the simplest form is a plain, square building. But the highest art is to be found in a great Gothic cathedral, with its thousands of details, each beautiful in itself, but all similar in general character, and all forming part of a whole, which is the perfect embodiment of unity."

Form is necessary in music as it is in tangible things. *Form, or pattern, in music is the definite order or central idea in which musical ideas are presented.* Form is not a set of mechanical rules to be strictly observed on all occasions; but, rather, the result of an effort to say clearly and most beautifully whatever has to be said. Form is an arrangement of the parts and contents of that which is signified or represented. Form reveals itself chiefly through *repetition* (imitation, transposition, restatement), *contrast* (variation), and *symmetry* (unity). There is a symmetrical grouping of elements defining dimensions in space or time. Symmetry is founded on likeness—similarity; contrast is founded on difference. All music, from the shortest song, dance, or hymn tune to the most elaborate symphonic work, is based upon a definite form, i.e., *music is the orderly arrangement of the five elements or materials of music, namely: rhythm, melody, harmony, tone-color, and form.* It implies unity of tonality and of general rhythmic effect, as well as the unity in the grouping of the various parts (phrases, periods, movements), so as to weld them into an organic whole. Form takes in the rules or techniques for the construction of a composition; it is the framework which the composer uses for his musical structure. Everything is dependent upon form. We could not see a thing clearly unless it had some outline. Wherever many thoughts are to be brought together and united into a whole, like the tiny parts of a mosaic, there must be *order, symmetry, proportion*—there must be *form*.

What is true of music is also true of architecture, painting, or the other arts. Note the façade of any great church building or other fine example of architecture. Here we find a great variety of decoration in the shapes of doors and windows and other details, yet all these are made to fit into a design as simple as the form of a folk tune—a design in which there is balance and repetition, contrast and climax. The same qualities may be noted in Leonardo da Vinci's "Last Supper," or Rafael's "School at Athens." Here a great amount of apparently diverse detail is unified by a balanced and symmetrical form in the painting as a whole. However, the form and the idiom are incidental; it is the spirit that creates and the letter that killeth. Every great piece of music, in its welding of feeling and form, reflects some aspect of the human soul and of the life around us.

REPETITION

The first principle of form in all art is *repetition* (imitation, transposition, restatement). It is the simplest and most elementary of structural devices in art. Repetition was applied by instinct early in human civilization, for it is very easy for the mind to repeat any idea just uttered. Repetition in music, like repetition in architecture, is a means of obtaining the effects of continuity, coherence, order, and symmetry. Thus, it is a factor of importance for artistic work. The nature of our mental activities conditions the mode of presentation of the musical thought. Through repetition the composer emphasizes the musical thought and aids the memory of the listener. A composition in which phrase follows phrase without repetition would hardly be more than a vague wandering among tones, lacking sense or purpose. The repetition of phrases, or portions of a composition, helps to achieve clarity and constitutes the basis of its form. It is impossible for the mind to assimilate ideas unrelated to each other and not developed. Hence the necessity for reiteration of the same idea. Music goes as quickly as it comes. In music no series of sounds formed into a melody can long survive the substitution of other series unless there is some restatement or, at least, some reminder of the first. With volatile sound patterns, repetition is necessary to impress our minds. There must be sufficient repetition to establish the feeling of unity; all parts must be welded together into a whole. Furthermore, any musical effect when repeated is a different effect; the repetition changes it somewhat, for the second time a melody is heard it either sounds thinner or richer. This principle applies more or less to all art. Even the theme which gains by repetition will lose its force if repeated too often. But, inasmuch as music is an art existing in time, repetition is always used. Coherence in any time-art requires continuity.

In architecture, an art existing in space, the main design is brought out through the groupings of large units, such as towers and arches, together with repetition of smaller units, such as windows, doors, columns, and details of ornamentation.

In poetry, an art existing in time, the principle of repetition is very active. Ideas or thoughts must be repeated to become definitely fixed in our minds. The feeling of definite structure is obtained by a repetition of meter, verse length, construction of stanza, and rhyme, which is nothing but a repetition of sounds.

In painting, an art existing in space, the artist needs to present a theme only once and our eye will easily be attracted to the part of the canvas on which it appears, and we can look at it as often as we please.

In music a feeling of definite structure—form, design, or pattern—is obtained through the grouping of large sections with characteristic repetition of parts, the balancing of phrases of similar construction, the identical accentuation of certain motives, the repetition of rhythmic figures, and characteristic harmonic progressions. We cannot get a definite idea about a piece of music unless we know something about the structural plan. To be able to follow the subject, or theme, and to understand this structural plan, adds to our pleasure in listening to music. We do not think of the process after the habit is acquired.

There are various kinds of repetition (imitation). The repetition of phrases, or of portions of a composition, is not always literal. They may be repeated tone for tone; or the pattern of the theme may be repeated approximately so that it is recognizable as the gist of the theme and yet differ from it somewhat; or they may be merely suggested. Phrases often undergo slight changes which, without destroying their identity, give them various shades of meaning and also avoid monotony. It took centuries to develop the devices that seem to us so simple. Savages, like children, repeat monotonously. The logical development of material into new phrases, or portions of a composition, in such a manner that, though altered, the relation and the connection of the new matter with the old is still recognizable, is known as "thematic development." It is achieved by:

1. *Imitation:* One of the modifications most often employed is that of changing a few tones at the end of the phrase. The end of a phrase is called "cadence." By means of different cadences the phrase may be made to suggest that the thought is either complete or incomplete. The rhythmic-melodic theme may be literally repeated, but the accompanying harmony (variation in the accompaniment) may give it a different meaning each time; or it may be literally repeated in a different voice or part, transposing the melody into the lower or middle register.

There are other kinds of imitation: parallel motion may be employed; the theme may be inverted (by contrary motion); the theme may be augmented (by altering instrumentation); the theme may be diminished; or the accompaniment may be altered.

2. *Transposition:* The theme may be repeated on other degrees of the scale, i.e., higher or lower in pitch than at first. A radical and fascinating change of coloring is also obtained through contrast of major and minor keys; altering of harmony; and different succession of chords. As an example of transposing the second and concluding themes on their final appearance from major

to minor, see Mozart's Symphony in G minor, first movement, measures 227, 260.

Next to rhythm, *modulation* (changes in harmony) is the most stimulating and enchanting element in music. It is done by transforming the subject rhythmically while the harmony and melody remain the same; or by altering the melody with unchanged harmony and rhythm; or by elaboration and ornamentation of parts of the principal melody; or by altering the melody and harmony, leaving rhythm intact. *No composition of any scope can be considered great unless it abounds in beautiful modulations.* Just as organic unity depends upon a basic key or tonality, so variety is gained by modulation. Without it there is monotony; but with too much modulation there is irritating restlessness. By change of key, a new kind of variety is imparted to a melody. This does not interfere with, but secures, coherence and unity.

3. *Restatement:* The theme may be exactly repeated, but with a change of accent lifted (shifted in rhythm), especially when it does not follow the bar measure; or it may be exactly repeated after an interesting digression or contrast. Restatement may also be effected by altering the force and coloring of sound (legato, staccato, portamento, etc.); and by variety of contrapuntal treatment (transposition of motive into other parts, inversion by means of double counterpoint, etc.). Restatement after contrast is at the foundation of any large composition. It supplies that connecting link between the structure of the folk song and that of the most elaborate tone poem. Restatement is used for securing coherence and organic unity.

CONTRAST (VARIETY)

The second principle of form in all art is *contrast* (variety). Strictly speaking, contrast is nothing but the result of variety; for this reason we speak of contrast when referring to the principles of form in art. If interest is to be maintained in any work of art, the artist must use a comparatively small amount of material. However, there must be sufficient variation in the construction of the parts and contrasting sections among the parts to avoid the least monotony.

Every work of art in whatever medium—stone, color, word, tone or motion—must show a successful combination of coherence or unity of general impression with variety of detail. Coherence is established through the systematic repetition of phrases or portions of a composition. However, few compositions are constructed on phrase repetition alone. Phrases of a *contrasting* nature are needed to develop the structural balance in the musical work. The monotonous repetition (as pointed out before) of the same idea without variety is fatal to attention. True, to the uncivilized, the repetition of the same idea in the same way is not unpleasing; but to the cultured person, repetition without variety is very irksome. A certain amount of contrast is necessary in order to bring out a central idea. Thus, variety, which makes for contrast, provides for more changes of mood. This is a big step toward freer expression, which, in turn, makes possible a more definite and greater range of emotions.

Colonial architecture brings out interesting contrast by its two large wings, with a tower or a dome in the center, ornamented by a large porch with columns. If the dome were not there, the design would not be pleasing. To give a subject prominence in a picture, it is necessary to paint in a dark background or one that will enable the principal figure to stand out.

Systematic repetition, in some form or other, is the most important constructive principle in music. It is necessitated by the very intangible and elusive nature of the material used. *Sweet things taste sweeter in contrast with something acid.* In music no theme is of sufficient import to bear constant repetition. Then, too, monotony is less tolerable in music than in the other fine arts. The ear is too sensitive an organ, and we have no way of shutting off sound. We may shut our eyes at any displeasing sight, but the only way to escape annoying sounds is to be so far off as not to hear them.

In music, contrast sometimes is made by the repetition of

a theme that has been varied; sometimes by key—i.e., the piece begins and ends in the same key, but wanders in between into other keys; or by material—i.e., the piece opens and closes with the same rhythmic, melodic, and harmonic material, but in between there is introduced some new material, giving contrast either through variety in the treatment of details or through variety of actual subject matter. To bring into prominence a solemn idea, it is necessary to precede it by brilliant interludes. To make a theme joyous, slow and heavy music is introduced before, and so on.

We all crave contrast, a change of sensation; but a return to whatever is impressive at the outset gives us the feeling of organic unity. To repeat, because of the intangible and elusive nature of the material used in music, the composer cannot continually present new material without becoming diffuse. Instead, he must make his impression by varied emphasis upon the main thought. Otherwise the composition would become so discursive that one could not possibly follow it. This cyclic form of musical expression was discovered early after much experimentation. It has remained the leading principle in all great compositions. It is a permanent principle, derived directly from life and nature. *We return whence we came—everything goes in cycles.*

UNITY (SYMMETRY AND BALANCE)

The third principle of form in all art is *unity* (symmetry and balance). Goethe formulated the law of diversity in unity in these words: "The more perfect the being, the more dissimilar are its parts. Subordination of parts indicates high-grade organization." Unity signifies the combination of parts resulting in an effort that is esthetically pleasing— fitness, adaptability to other parts, consistency with general purpose. *Unity of design does form a perfect "whole,"* one in which *every part dovetails into another part so that we know and feel they belong together.* In short, every part of a composition should seem a natural, reasonable, logical sequence of what has gone before and should be related to what comes after it; yet there must be no monotony. The principle of symmetry obviously was taken over into music from the verses and rhymes of poetry. The metrical schemes of Greek and Latin poetry have dominated music for centuries, mainly in the form of song. The requirement for balance and proportion is the same in the shortest folk tune and in the most elaborate composition. The composer repeats his main theme or melody often enough to give the impression of unity; and, by means of contrasting themes, he avoids a feeling of monotony. The form of a musical composition is good when the balance and proportion between the elements of unity and variety are effectively maintained. All works of art show unity through contrast. *Object* and *design, system* and *organization—these are the fundamentals of form.* Music, like a painting, a story, a play, a piece of sculpture, or architecture, generally presents materials of a conflicting nature, but achieves unity through the very conflict, or contrast, which necessarily sustains our interest. *Some unity of musical design, of key, of tone-color, of mood, of style, or content inevitably binds together the different movements of a larger work.* We demand unity, yet we like contrast. We demand coherent music. We do not like incoherent pictures, futuristic paintings, and the like; we abhor shapeless buildings or statues; nor do we enjoy a play or novel not well organized. Yet we do not want mere evenness in any work of art. We really admire the structure made of varied materials, whether in stones, clay, bronze, colors, words, and thoughts. We are pleased if the artist has succeeded in bringing the contrasting materials to a final and inevitable unity; and if he has arranged his materials in such a way as to bring out the significance of unity through contrast.

In the sonata or symphony it is the "recapitulation" which gives us the solution of the problem. It is like the ending of the play or story, the final effect of the picture, the statue, or building after the observer has gained the right perspective and his eyes have become used to the necessary relationships of color and outline.

In music the simplest form is that of a folk song; but the most complete form is that which is most highly organized—the sonata, the symphony, and the symphonic poem. The various parts of these large compositions, like those of a great architectural structure, must be welded "together into a unified whole that will be effective as a whole, and not merely in its parts."

Unity is secured by repetition, either exact or suggestive, of musical ideas; by the regular occurrence of an accent or group of accents; and by the persistence of a given measure.

We are rhythmical by nature, and motion that is unrhythmical is displeasing to us. Rhythm, in the larger sense, signifies a measured flow, a regularly repeated movement or beat, leading the ear or eye insistently from one part to certain other parts of a musical, pictorial, or architectural work. A phrase standing by itself leaves our rhythmic feeling unsatisfied. There must be an answer to satisfy us. So, in music, there is balance of phrases, of sections—yes, even of whole movements. Rhythm, in another sense, also means any feeling of movement caused by the association of ideas. An association may not be strictly rhythmic, yet cause the feeling of movement; it implies a certain clearness of arrangement of the subject matter, expressing a feeling for order.

Asymmetry is the opposite of symmetry. Asymmetry is derived from prose recitation in a language, with its irregular accents and subdivisions. In its oldest form this musical "recitative" comes from both the Greek drama and the Hebrew psalmody. It became the main pattern (*accentus*) of the declamatory Gregorian chant of the medieval Christian Church; while the Ambrosian hymns used another style (*concentus*), thus preserving the metrical symmetry of ancient poetry. Later on, as music developed in the polyphonic contrapuntal styles and then in the sonata and symphonic styles, both symmetry and asymmetry were mixed in a great variety of combinations. This gave to music both the stability of symmetry and the vitalizing interest of asymmetry. Continual symmetry becomes tiresome; too much asymmetry is sometimes incoherent and tends toward a vague formlessness.

In painting, the aim of the artist striving for originality and variety is to oppose objects of dissimilar appearance but of equal force of attraction. Line, form, color, light, and dark may all be set against each other in order to distribute the interest equally within the frame. In addition, sentimental appeal must here also be recognized as of importance in the matter of balance or symmetry.

Within the restricted space defined by the frame, the eye seeks the central point around which all the many factors are balanced. This point is, in most cases, near the center. In general, if two diagonal lines are drawn across a picture, the main interest will often be found near this focal point. In order to effect an artistic balance, different things of the same value should be placed at about the same distance on either side of the central point of the picture. The larger the picture, the more urgent is the need for considerations of balance.

Almost every picture follows in its compositional arrangements some definite scheme—the triangle, circle, cross, or the letter S are recognizable in the original or modified form in many pictures.

Any work of art which expresses unity, or oneness, harmony with each and every desirable element, is bound to be rated a classic in due time. True, the world has many works of art, but only some of them have been so inspired in every particular phase as to give that complete satisfaction, one which is more easily felt than explained. Such masterpieces command the greatest respect and reverence. They almost defy analysis. Indeed, they cast a certain spell over us. They are practically beyond artistic criticism. Usually, they are simple in the extreme. Yet they always tell a great and easily understandable message by their beauty. While they are positive, they still leave room for suggestive interpretation. They possess perfect harmony of form and spirit.

Every masterpiece leaves us with the feeling that a maximum of expression has been obtained with a minimum of means and effort.

Unity is essentially a constructive necessity in a work of art. Unity gives pleasure that comes with contemplation of good order and the symmetrical or balanced opposition of the materials of art. The demands of symmetry are met by effecting a nice balance of one detail with another. The beauty of symmetry is that every part is of exactly the right proportion, neither too long nor too short, too wide or too narrow, when compared to any other part; but all "fit" in every way. Also, there is due proportion between the larger divisions of the work. The lines of the great Greek buildings are perfect, but the good lines of great Roman architecture are often hidden by all sorts of rich and splendid decorations. Like other principles of art, unity manifests itself in a subtle, rather than obtrusive, way; however, close examination will train us to observe readily its application. All types of musical forms or designs are simply the outcome in different ways of the fundamental principles of *repetition, variety, and unity.*

CLIMAX

The fourth principle of form in all art is *climax.* The tendency to rise when exaltation is depicted, and to fall when depression is depicted, has its origin in human nature. Excitement tends to quicken the pulse; depression to make the pulse beat slower. The emotional effects of a gradual rise to a climax and a gradual fall to the softest sound possible are well known to musicians. No doubt, we experience much satisfaction in reaching a culmination point—the *point of perfect attainment*—after a period of wandering. The reaching of a climax after a time of expectancy gives us great pleasure—*a feeling of elation.* In the same way, the composer whose music leads up to a climax is sure to move the feelings of his listeners. Music which contains no culminating point, no part that seems to summarize and vitalize what has gone before, causes in us a feeling of disappointment, of unsatisfied desire. We seem to have arrived at nothing in the end. The climax must be natural; it must seem inevitable.

In some cases, the rise to a climax, followed by a corresponding fall, is made on such a large scale that the movement seems to take its characteristic features from such a rise and fall. Again, there are cases where, instead of a gradual rise or a gradual fall, an abrupt transition takes place. The expected does not occur; but, on the contrary, something of a startling nature appears which for a moment threatens to disturb the continuity of the music. This also is a climax, in a way. Here music, being in its essence an appeal to our emotions, follows the feeling-flow that is found in many and diverse circumstances. Our lives are not always even and placid. At times we are confronted with startling happenings, which break the regular flow of our existence. Sometimes the more passionate expression is not found in a gradual development but in an unexpected one. There is charm in variety, and the interposition of the unexpected has a delight of its own, provided always that a certain continuity is felt.

5. STYLE

The influence of any epoch, race, or nation upon the fine arts gives to their over-all design what is known as style. We all are well aware of certain distinct characteristics that make style. Negroes, Eskimos, Hindus, Japanese, or Chinese are unmistakable. Equally distinct are the characteristics which the various races have given to the applied design with which they ornament their products.

We all recognize the stately lines of a Gothic cathedral; the laquered black, gold, and red riot of Chinese architecture; and so on. Most people appreciate the fact that, in working out a scheme that embodies design, it is not customary to mix styles. "Everybody would recognize the incongruous appearance of a Venetian gondolier on a Wisconsin lake, or of a cedar canoe on a canal in Venice. There are countless extremes which would be equally apparent as violations of an ever-present need for that fitness which we call harmony."

Classifications in painting, architecture, poetry, drama, and music cannot, and should not, be applied as rigidly as in the sciences of chemistry, botany, or zoology. The concepts of "classic" and "romantic" must remain flexible and dynamic in order to give us insight into the nature of art, and so encourage a better appreciation of the style of the artist and his relation to his era.

In the last analysis, *a good style* in the fine arts, as well as in the useful arts, *is simply an appropriate style*. The ultimate test is fitness. Whatever is unfit is thereby bad, no matter how popular it may be temporarily. Furs in summer are always in bad taste, although current fashion may proclaim them to be "in style" among the thoughtless.

A composition has style if it has proportion, i.e., if it does not contain anything that is not absolutely essential to make the work complete, if it contains no more nor less than what is needed to make a well-rounded whole. The musical ideas, the motifs, phrases, and sentences (or themes), etc., are well developed.

The classical artist subordinates *content* to form, but he is by no means all form and no emotion. The romantic artist subordinates *form* to content, but he is not all emotion and no form. In fact, no art work can exist if it possesses only one of the elements. An art work which has good form, but no feeling and inspiration, has neither life nor meaning. We have countless sonatas, symphonies, and fugues composed by musicians who followed all the rules but had nothing vital to say. No wonder such works have been relegated to oblivion.

The artist wants his message to have a strong, unified effect and yet, at the same time, to have *novelty, suspense, as well as repetition, contrast, unity, and climax*. He must have beauty of outline for his message.

As to *repetition:* If the artist repeats the same motif, or idea, over and over again, he becomes boring.

As to *contrast:* The work must be adroitly alternated with variety and contrast, novelty and surprise, within the pattern.

As to *unity (symmetry, or balance):* The artist seeks to organize all components of the art work into one cohesive design so that each part of the painting, edifice, or symphony will function organically within the total framework.

As to *climax:* It must contain an element of suspense, of movement and growth toward a climax—the high point of intensity.

It took composers several centuries of trial and error to find and develop the technique of form as we now know it.

In some of our great art songs (*Lieder*) the union of text and music is so complete that it is practically impossible for us now to conceive of the one without the other. The rhythm not only conforms to, but also accentuates, the meter of the poetry.

There is usually a definite character noticeable in works of art. As we have in literature the classic, romantic, didactic, and modern styles of writing, so we have in music various styles. Every work of art is subject to certain rules of formal construction and expression; and these rules are influenced more or less by the subject. The chief divisions in music, as in poetry, are the *epic, lyric,* and *dramatic*.

In the *epic style* description is most prominent. Feeling and representation are founded on an event which has to be narrated in a poetic manner. Strictly speaking, musical works do not possess the same sort of epics as poetry, but symphonies, oratorios, operas, ballads, and cantatas display elements of epic style.

In the *lyric style* feeling is not objective, but subjective (personal). Here expression and warmth of feeling are the chief ingredients of the music. The chief forms of instrumental music belong to the lyric style.

In the *dramatic style* the artist's conception of events and actions is realized through visible action on the stage. This visible action is performed by persons representing well-defined and positive characters.

Other divisions of style are: *brilliant, fantastic, devotional, sentimental,* etc. The form in which a composition is written serves to classify it. A group of composers who employ similar style in any given period is known as a "school." So we have the *classic; romantic; impressionistic; national; expressionistic; modern; and the ultramodern schools.*

The *classic school* is based on voice-writing, perfection of form, and beauty of tonal combinations. Rousseau defined music as "the art of combining sounds in a manner agreeable to the ear." The term "classic" implies logic of structure, proportion, interrelation and balance of parts, and the perfection of the form determining the manner of the expression. The element of pure beauty of sound, its confinement within formal limits, was the chief object of the classic composers. Instrumental music was written as though it were intended to be sung by two or more voices. Hence, the accompaniment was treated as a distinct melody by itself. Classic music employs intellectual, rather than emotional, expression, and is concerned with the logical development of ideas. But it is by no means unemotional. It has beauty of melody and harmony, but these elements are not used primarily to excite the emotions but, rather to hold intellectual interest. It has regularity and balance, exemplified by a structure based on the 4- or 8-measure phrase and period. It has a definitely established key, careful modulation to the next key, and a feeling for cadence (dominant, tonic chords). The orchestration is rather simple and obvious compared to that of modern music. The strings are most important, and the wood winds and brasses are used to reinforce them during climaxes. Contrasts are not too violent, and there is no ostentatious display for its own sake. The music is suave, tender, and dreamy, rather than full of pathos; its prevailing mood is one of grace and merriment, instead of grandeur. The melodies are simple, songlike, spontaneous, and flow naturally. The harmony is light and plain. There are no violent changes in tempo and dynamics. As the classic composer is a master of form, of purely musical design and organic development of musical ideas, the form is suitable to the content, has no stiffness, and is flexible. Finally, the music tells its message without the aid of a program; it conveys a sense of objectivity. Classic music seeks to be beautiful music alone; whereas romantic music usually is full of subjectivity. The beauty and harmony of classic music are not used primarily to excite the emotions, but, rather, to hold the intellectual interest. By leaving our imaginations free to interpret as they will, it may enhance even the power of emotion. Classic music is the most elevated type of music, and its appreciation demands theoretical knowledge and technical skill in performance. The classic school is represented by J. S. Bach, Haydn, Mozart, and Brahms.

The *romantic school* deals with a single poetic subject,

usually indicated by title, and it is conveyed through subjective emotion. We may describe the "romantic" as the release of the subjective and imaginative elements which shape the form, subordinating it to the expression of a passionate concept. Romantic music *aims at the particular, rather than the general.* Its most constant mark is the *tendency to specialize expression.* It employs the expression of personal emotion, achieved by striking contrasts, violent tempos, dynamic changes, vivid climaxes, and considerable ostentatious display for its own sake. It usually has a prevailing mood of grandeur and pathos. Romantic music does not have a strictly defined form. There may or may not be a suggestion in the title, and the listener can give reign to his fancy in interpreting the music in his own way. He may find a picture, a story, a mood, or poetic ideas. The romantic school is represented by Schubert, Schumann, Spohr, Mendelssohn, Liszt, Chopin, and partly by Beethoven.

The *impressionistic school* of music has Debussy as its head. Like the impressionistic school of French painting (Pissaro, Manet, Monet, etc.), this music is not concerned so much with the expression of emotion or sentiment. It stresses tone-color and the artistic effects of different sound combinations. It creates an "atmosphere," either subjective or objective. Debussy composed vivid impressions of night, lakes, and landscapes with new harmonies and delicate orchestral colors, suggesting the subtle play of light and shade. Besides his short, picturesque piano pieces, note especially the orchestral works, L'Apres Midi d'un Faune, La Mer, and The Sunken Cathedral.

The *national school* emphasizes the traits of individual peoples, such as the Teutonic fondness for sweet harmonies and symmetrical form. The excitable nature of the Hungarians is suggested in erratic rhythms and fitful tempos. The sturdy, vigorous English peoples show a preference for straightforward melody and regular rhythms. The music of the Italians is mostly all impulse, full of grandiose phrases that appeal to the ear, and a great deal of bad style; and so on. The national dance tunes have their characteristic rhythms, or tempos, their peculiar scales, or harmonies, etc.

These peculiarities are often determined by the traits of the people among whom the dance tune either originated or became popular. Often national music is based upon the folk music of the country, or music may be imbued with a national spirit through its text. It is not always easy to recognize the national traits of a composition, because some countries have characteristics in common; and, also, composers frequently study in foreign lands and adopt the manner of writing in vogue in that country.

Expressionism in music is highly subjective and stresses freedom of personal style. Expressionism looks for material and inspiration in voicing the inner experiences, the inner spiritual conflicts, the inner moods and feelings and experiences, rather than seek inspiration in the forms and images of the world about us. Schönberg's Pierrot Lunaire, Sextet, and his piano pieces are expressionistic.

The *modern school* values realistic description and, at times, uses direct imitation. It tells the story—and often a very definite one—through suggestive atmosphere, though it depends upon program notes to establish the desired connection between the story and the music. Modern composers employ such methods to great advantage, especially those who want freedom from the restraint of precedent in the use of rhythm, melody, harmony, form, and tone-color. The modern style upholds music that is either accompanied by action and finds expression in opera or strongly suggests action and is found in song, chorus, oratorio, etc.

The *ultramodern school* uses the same technique as the modern school, only in a more daring, experimental way. In seeking for new ways of tonal expression, the ultramoderns broke down the system of keys. In *polytonal music,* two or more keys are used at the same time, creating new effects. In *atonality,* music is written in no key at all, and each tone is quite independent of the others; the tone is its own center, for there is no well-defined system of key relationship. In rhythm, likewise, the ultramodernists stress *polyrhythm.* The rhythmic beat, which regulates the flow of music in a rigid grouping of a 2, 4, 3, or 6 pulse, is hardly used by them; in its place has come a flexible style which changes continually from one rhythm to the other, almost from measure to measure. Sometimes two or more rhythms are used at the same time. Leading composers are T. Harris, A. Copeland, D. Milhaud, B. Bartok, A. Schönberg, P. Hindemith, etc. They are the pathfinders who, in due time, will find their followers.

Realism portrays the "thing itself." Obviously, realism can be more easily practiced in literature and painting than in music; but it appears in music which is primarily dramatic. A realist composer is one who seeks a form of expression which shall be a counterpart of the subject, or rather, of the original emotion. From the point of view of esthetics, the realism of the subject is irrelevant; the term "realist" in art can only be applied to the means employed by the writer, the painter, or the composer to express no matter what subject.

Program music evidently follows a definite literary development. Often such music is inspired by the text of a poem and seeks to express the thought instrumentally. In giving a composition a title, such as The Swan, The Sorcerer's Apprentice, The Flight of the Bumble Bee, Autumn, etc., composers do not imply that they are actually attempting to depict the thing named, but, rather, that *the music expresses characteristics and emotions suggested by the title.*

When music makes a picture or tells a story, it is the keen ear, the alert mind, and the free imagination which bring joy and awaken within the listener that something nearer and further than the instruments, which is music.

Under the heading of the vague term "neoclassicism" come many recent compositions. Neoclassicism reflects a tendency on the part of modernists to revert to the principles of form as set by the classic masters. Neoclassicism is not achieved by imitating, editing, or transcribing classics or their formulas, but *by adopting new ways of expression to create new art founded upon traditional classic principles.* Brahms and Sibelius were the two great neoclassicists of many of the modern composers; rhythm is of much greater importance to them. Some modern composers, in their reaction against impressionism and all idealism in music, and in their desire to represent correctly the harsh mechanistic life of today, have tried to eliminate the human element from music and to make it merely the reflection of the age. The piano is thus treated primarily as a percussion instrument, and its percussive possibilities are exploited to the utmost.

Formerly the art of the pianist, or piano-playing, constituted the ability to produce a warm, good singing tone in melodic passages, a fluency sufficient to surmount any technical problems, a dependable command of beauty of tone, a strong sense of rhythm, close attention to expressive molding and polishing of a phrase, a firm grasp of structural design, and, behind it all, understanding of the composer's intention and the ideals and spirit of the times he represented—in short, a feeling for style.

Style includes the *general mood* of a composition as well as *climax*. Characteristic moods in a composition are: calm, dignified, stately, dreamy, martial, solemn, melancholy, gay, changeable, etc. A composition may have one or more climaxes. Naturally, each large division has its own point of greatest intensity; and the work, as a whole, should grow to a climax, generally near the end. It is up to the listener to perceive the exact nature of this climax.

Finally, a discussion of style must include the question: Is the piece pleasing as a whole? Are any parts commonplace or tedious?

There is individuality of style in a noted composer. Any composer who is not simply an imitator of others has certain tricks of expression—peculiar turns of melody; peculiar chord progressions; peculiar accompaniment figures; erratic rhythms; etc. These distinguish his music from that of his predecessors or contemporaries, and such original features give to his works an individuality of style.

6. CONSTRUCTION OF MUSICAL FORM

A. FIGURE, MOTIVE, PHRASE, PERIOD, DOUBLE PERIOD, MOVEMENT, CADENCE

In poetry we find syllables combined into different *feet* (the dactyl, anapest, iambus, trochee, etc.), poetic feet combined into *lines,* lines into *stanzas,* and stanzas into a complete *poem.*

In music, likewise, we find notes combined into *figures,* figures into *motives,* motives into *phrases,* phrases into *periods,* and periods into a complete *composition* (or *movement*). Thus, tones are combined into groups of various lengths and structure. As we have learned before, *form* in music is concerned with these groups. A quick survey gives us this summary:

| figure |

Figure: The smallest musical idea or unit of melody (or rhythmic fragment) is called a "figure"; it varies greatly in length and may consist of as few as two notes. A figure corresponds closely to a word in language, and it may begin or end on any beat of the measure. As the figure is the smallest unit in the musical composition, it is seldom complete in itself. The composer, like the painter, may construct his design by duplicating his figure or motive, using it as the basis of a larger idea. But the writer has no permission to repeat words *ad libitum;* only very rarely may he repeat a word for emphasis. Even at that, expression in music is much more concise and to the point than in literature.

| | Motive | |
| Figure | | Figure |

Motive: Two or more figures combined in a characteristic group of tones which make a complete germ of melody (or rhythmic pattern), achieve musical sense, and cover two measures, form a "motive." It is the idea from which a composition develops. The motive marks a slight break in the music, and the sense of incompleteness which it leaves demands an immediate continuance of the thought.

| | Phrase | |
| Motive | | Motive |

Phrase: Two or more motives combined to form a musical thought is called a "phrase." It is the smallest complete musical thought (like a simple sentence in grammar), and gen-

erally consists of the motive used in repetition or in sequence and developed. The phrase generally suggests a
more decided break in the music than the motive; and for
this reason is defined in its ending by a certain chord, or
chords, known as "cadence." This cadence indicates the
character of the phrase as *final, interrogative, or indefinite*.

(Note: In tonal architecture the contention that each
musical masterpiece originates in one single motive theme
or melodic passage, which implies every element and division of the piece of music, is of great significance. This motive principle exists, with varying technical manifestations,
in all the music known to us. Careful perusal will show the
thematic development of the musical art.

For example, the thematic principle of the music of the
polyphonic period was predominantly that of "imitation"
and "variations." Consider the purely imitative canon and
the imitations and variations of the fugue.)

The classicists Haydn, Mozart, Beethoven, and their
noted successors used extensively the principle of thematic
"transformation" through various melodic, harmonic, and
rhythmical means.

The art of tones is created from sound. By a magic interplay between the identical, yet different, cells, the higher
forms of life came into existence. Likewise, one musical
motive, one theme, releases another as an expression of its
own innermost idea. The theme lives through the motives
from which it is formed, the work through its themes; yet
the theme and the highest unit, the work (composition),
are each entities in their own right, announcing their own
message.

Every art has its unit of expression—the straight line, the
curve, the arch, the poetic stanza, and the prose sentence. In
the same way, a musical composition is a succession of
definitely organized units of thought and emotion in terms
of sound and rhythm. A phrase is the structural basis of all
musical form; it extends, when regular, through four ordinary measures in moderate tempo. Moreover, in the more
elaborate forms of composition, the phrase is freely expanded or contracted. To determine the length and character

of phrases, the student should first become thoroughly familiar with the sound and effect of the various cadences. He
should be able to tell when the periodic breaks occur at the
end of the phrases and, also, the character of each phrase as
tested by its cadence.

The word "phrase" here corresponds to the same usage
as in literature. However, the musical phrase is always
rhythmic in character. A succession of words without any
accent and no division into phrases would not be significant
in prose writing. Often our failure to punctuate properly in
writing, or to separate phrases intelligently in reading and
speaking, will give a wrong impression. In setting poems to
music, the musical phrase and the line of poetry usually
correspond. For example, the hymn Old Hundred consists
of two stanzas of four lines each, and the melody is composed of four phrases. The hymn How Gentle God's Commands as well as the hymn Softly Now the Light of Day
likewise consist of four phrases. Of course, sometimes the
phrases do not follow the poetic lines. Consider, for example,
the hymn Come My Soul, Thou Must be Waking; here the
stanza consists of six lines and the melody of four phrases.

The phrase divisions in music are of utmost importance.
They are necessary because we must listen to sounds in
their relationships to one another, and, as pointed out
earlier, *the human mind is able only to take in a limited
number of sounds grouped in such relationships to each
other*. Thus, it gives us a grouping by the aid of which we
are able to take in the meaning, or effect, of what we hear.
Throughout the development of form, there is a mechanical
balance of measures. To notice the phrase, then to recognize
it whenever we listen to the piece again, is the foundation
of all musical understanding and enjoyment.

| Sentence or Period |
| phrase | phrase |

Sentence, or Period: Two (or sometimes three) phrases
combined to form a complete musical thought is called a
"sentence," or "period." A sentence is the union of two
phrases extending consequently, when regular, through

eight ordinary measures in moderate tempo. Now, the first of the two phrases is called the *antecedent, or thesis;* it begins with a tonic chord, as a rule, and ends with a *semi-cadence.* The second of the phrases is called the *consequent, or antithesis,* and ends with a *perfect authentic cadence.* In other words, the first phrase is the *question,* and the second the *answer* (like a compound sentence in grammar).

The same structure is found in prose. Examine the sentence: "The woman is trimming her daughter's hat." The subject (first motive) is: "The woman"; the predicate (second motive) is: "is trimming." The statement, "The woman is trimming," is incomplete (corresponding to the antecedent phrase ending in a half-cadence) and demands a phrase to complete its meaning. The phrase "her daughter's hat" (two additional motives) is here used as the explanation, making a complete sentence (period). Music would be very rigid, like the sections of a fence connected by a post at a distance of so many feet, if all periods were equally of eight measures in length. The tiresome effect of much so-called "popular music" is due to the stereotyped metrical pattern. In order to get an elastic metrical design, three four-measure phrases are combined into a twelve-measure sentence.

The period, or sentence, may be developed or extended by means of repetition of the first, sometimes of the second, or of both phrases. To write a paragraph (division of the composition), more sentences must be added.

Division, or	Double period
sentence	sentence

Division, or Section: Two sentences, or periods, combined form the *double period or division (section).* It is a developed musical thought; and it consists, when regular, of sixteen measures in moderate tempo. A division may be expanded through the addition of extra measures; or it may be contracted by the logical omission of certain measures and by the overlapping of phrases.

The double period, or division, is one of the simplest musical forms, but it does not give the impression of a complete thought. The first period ends with *a cadence suggestive of incompleteness* and demands a second period *expressing completeness to balance the first.* Many hymns and short songs consist of but one double period.

| | Movement, or Part | |
| | Division | Division |

The composer, like the painter, may build his design by duplicating his figures or making them the basis of a larger idea. Expression in music is much more concise and intense than in literature. The musical figure, when used to build up a phrase, a period, or a theme, or even a section of development, may be varied and used in different ways to make a fine musical design and still be recognizable as a figure. These ways may be enumerated as follows: by *repetition; simplification; transposition; expansion; contraction; alteration;* etc. As an example of *simplification,* a figure may be made simpler by taking away some notes; of *elaboration,* a figure may be made more elaborate by the addition of a few notes; and so on. It is by such means that a composer creates the musical structure known as "development." Development refers to the various ways in which figures of one or more themes are used to produce impressive musical works. Sometimes figures also may be used for the creation of themes themselves; and figures may also be interwoven into the accompaniment of themes.

Intelligent musical understanding depends upon the realization of these structural aspects of music. Modern music, the forms of which were derived from folk songs and dance tunes, consists of a series of balancing phrases which stand to each other in the relation of question and answer.

Sections of a composition in which a subject is definitely stated are called "principal passages."

Sections of a composition which bridge over the interval from one principal passage to another are called "transitional passages."

A composition may also have an *introduction,* varying in length and scope, and an *ending,* called the "coda," bringing it to a close (and sometimes a *climax*) after the demands of the form have already been satisfied. The coda is free in form but establishes the key of the piece to which it belongs and brings it to a clear ending.

We see, then, that the form of a composition may range from a single sentence, or period, to an elaborate architectural structure made up of figures, motives, phrases, periods, double periods, movements, etc., all arranged in symmetrical and unified order.

Music is composed in such a way as to have a more or less regular arrangement of notes (*melody*) or chords (*harmony*) in matters of length, of relative quickness and slowness (*rhythm*), of groups or extended passages. Just as in the formal construction of material things there must be a design or form (pattern) having *repetition, unity, contrast (variety), and climax.* Form in music relates not only to the outline or shape of the contents, as in the graphic and plastic arts, but also to its periodicity and its punctuation, as in literature. Such punctuation is effected by means of accents and cadences.

Coda: This is an extension at the end of a composition, a summing up of the material. Its length is proportionate to the composition and may be a series of phrases or sections.

Codetta: This is an extension at the end of a phrase or section usually made up of material which has been used near the cadence of the last phrase. It may be two to four measures in length.

Next let us consider cadences. A *complete cadence* corresponds in musical punctuation to a period at the end of a sentence. The *perfect, final, or authentic cadence* consists of the chord on the fifth degree of the scale, followed by that on the first degree, or tonic, of the scale; thus V–I. The *plagal cadence,* associated with the church Amen in hymns, etc., consists of the chord on the fourth degree of the scale, followed by that on the tonic of the scale; thus IV–I. Both the authentic and the plagal cadences have different degrees of finality, according to the arrangement of their compound ones.

An *incomplete cadence* corresponds in musical punctuation to a comma, semicolon, or question mark. The *interrogative, or half-cadence,* ending on the accented beat, consists of the chord on the tonic of the scale, followed by that on the fifth degree of the scale; thus I–V. The *indefinite, imperfect, or deceptive cadence* may have various forms. Most often it consists of the chord on the fifth degree of the scale, followed by that on the sixth degree of the scale; thus V–VI.

(Note: Very often the content of the second phrase [consequent or antithesis] is a repetition of most of the first phrase [antecedent or thesis]. This is called "imitation." The imitation of a group of tones or other scale stops is an interesting method of melodic invention. The passage of chords, i.e., the use of a figure, motive or phrase above or below the original tones, is called a "sequence.")

(Note: *Sequential patterns, repeated phrases, and imitated figures* are the bases of nearly all music; therefore, these elements of composition need to be pointed out, discussed, and explained. When these cohesive factors are thoroughly understood, music loses its aura of mystery and may then be seen as a well-organized set of tonal patterns from which stem the expressive qualities of the art. Observe problems of key structure, simple cadence, form, and phrase construction. Also, observe the use of the *Leitmotif* —a musical figure to which some definite meaning is attached. It represents some person, thing, or dramatic event. See Mozart's Don Giovanni and Wagner's operas.)

A musical figure may be changed as follows:

1. *Transposition:* The figure appears intact on a different degree of the scale. Continued and regular transposition leads to "sequence."

2. *Expanding:* One or more intervals of the figure widened; generally, the outside notes are given in a wider interval.

3. *Contraction:* A narrowing of one or more intervals of the figure—the reverse of the preceding method.

4. *Augmentation:* The figure has notes of a larger denomination; generally, notes of double the original value are used.

5. *Diminution:* The figure appears in notes of a smaller denomination; generally, one-half of the original value.

6. *Repetition:* Certain members of the figure are repeated.

7. *Omission:* Fragmentary presentation of the figure.

8. *Irregular change* of order of notes; this is seldom employed.

9. *Reversion:* The figure played through backwards.

10. *Inversion:* The figure is presented upside down.

11. *Elaboration:* A variation of the original figure.

12. *Simplification:* The reverse of preceding.

13. *Ornamentation:* The addition of turns, trills, mordents, etc., to the figure.

14. *Rhythmic imitation:* The rhythm of a preceding model may be imitated on a single note. (See Liszt's Piano Concerto in E flat.)

15. *Combination:* Any of the foregoing methods of *transformation* may be used together. Note transformation by transposition, augmentation, and expansion.

B. ONE-PART (UNITARY), OR PRIMARY SONG FORM

The *unitary, or one-part song form,* is a simple composition complete in one period or sentence—eight measures in ordinary moderate tempo or sixteen measures in quick tempo—containing a development of a motive. It is the smallest musical form—one-sentence or one-period song.

However, often the double period of sixteen measures (even in moderate tempo) is used. In this form, the first period ends with a cadence suggestive of incompleteness and demanding a second period expressing completeness to balance the first. The second period usually resembles the first one, especially in the opening phrase. Many hymns and short songs are written in the form of the double period.

Examples:

J. S. BACH
Well-Tempered Clavichord, Prelude I.

BEETHOVEN   CHOPIN
Theme and 32 Variations.   Prelude I, Opus 28, #1.

SCHUMANN
Some of his Kinderlieder, Opus 79.

WEBER   W. H. MONK
Softly Now the Light of Day.   Abide With Me.

L. M. GOTTSCHALK   SCOTCH
Holy Spirit, Light Divine.   Blue Bells of Scotland.

GERMAN FOLK SONG
Fuchs, Du Hast Die Gans Gestohlen.

F. GLÜCK, 1814
The Broken Ring (German folk song). This song has only two phrases; its second phrase is lengthened by repetition in a somewhat altered form.

(Note: In some crude form or another music was in existence for centuries before the Christian era. The Egyptians, Assyrians, Chinese, and the Greeks all invented and developed various systems of tonal progressions, which eventually became our modern scales. Especially with the Greeks, song-writing and, to some extent, even part-writing in songs was common. But whatever music these ancient people enjoyed, with the exception of a very few numbers, has all vanished. Now the earliest music of any definite design of which we have record came into being in the primitive Christian Church in the form of chants and hymns. Of course, the early hymns were all of one voice, or part, and were sung or chanted entirely without the accompaniment of harmony.)

Examples of extended one-part 12-measure song form (3 periods; 3 x 4 measures):

GRUBER   J. W. LYRA, 1843
Silent Night, Holy Night   Der Mai Ist Gekommen
Zu Bethlehem Geboren

BEETHOVEN
Sonata in F♯ (12-measure main theme in second part).

C.   TWO-PART, OF BINARY SONG FORM

This is really the simplest complete elementary form consisting of two distinct sentences, or periods. One theme or melody is contrasted with another, known as the "counter-theme." In the *two-period independent form,* the phrases of the second period are made up wholly of new material. In the *two-period form with partial return,* the second phrase of the second period is made up from a phrase of the first period, with no change or only slight alterations. The *2-part, or binary form,* is often represented by the symbol: I II; or A B (8 + 8 measures or 8 + 4 + 4 measures).

The simplest folk songs and folk dances, as well as themes with variations, were written in binary form. Any composition in two parts is in the binary form. Each part may contain an indefinite number of sentences, or periods.

In the 18th century the old binary form was in use everywhere for instrumental music and was written as follows: the composition was divided into two parts by a double barline in the middle; both parts were repeated and, at the end of the first part, a modulation into the dominant key was generally made (see Suites by J. S. Bach and G. Handel).

By utilizing balanced phrases of contrasted keys, as well as themes in periods, instrumental music gradually worked out a structure of its own. (See examples in national dances and in works of early instrumental style by Corelli, Vivaldi, Couperin, Rameau, Purcell, and others.)

In the folk song we find both repetition and contrast—two principles of great importance in music. The folk song has been of great influence in the development of all music, especially that of the classic epoch of Haydn, Mozart, and Beethoven. Music, to be interesting, must have repetition as well as variety; and for this reason, the second part of a composition is different from the first. Then, too, a composition must also have unity—that is, the different parts must have some resemblance to each other, or else the piece will sound like musical nonsense. Therefore, most compositions end in the same key in which they begin, and we often find that the last phrase is more or less like one of the phrases in the first part.

The *2-part instrumental form* (8–8, or 16–16 measures) by reason of its simplicity and directness is often found in the short pieces of Schumann, Brahms, Debussy, Grieg, and Tschaikowsky. Fully developed, each part is at least a period and, to some degree, extended: 1) by repetition of either part; of each part; or of the entire piece; 2) by the introductory phrases; 3) by the codetta, coda; 4) and by the Postlude.

The binary, or 2-part form may be represented by this diagram: I II, or A B (I or A indicating the main melody [theme], and II or B indicating the contrasting melody). Either the first or the second part may be repeated; and in some instances both parts are repeated.

Examples:

Annie Laurie.   Santa Lucia.   America.
Yankee Doodle.   Annie of Tharau.
Soldier's Farewell.   There's Music in the Air.
My Old Kentucky Home. (This familiar melody is in the 2-part song form: A B. It has a first part, consisting of eight measures (sometimes repeated), and a second part, or *chorus,* also consisting of eight measures, the first four measures of which contain new material (introducing variety), while the last four measures are exactly the same as the last four measures of the first part, which establishes the unity of the song as a whole.)

Another type of the binary form may be represented by this diagram: I II I.

Examples:

Martha, Martha, Du Entschwandest (from Martha).
Scenes That Are Brightest (from Maritana).

Two-part form with partial return. This is a similar type, very much used, and may be represented by this diagram: I I II I (A A B A). The main theme is presented; then follows the contrasting part; after which the song closes again with the main theme. The repetition directly following the first statement of the main theme serves to fix the melody clearly in the mind of the listener; the succeeding contrast-

ing theme provides the necessary variety; and the final return of the main theme emphasizes its importance and gives
a most satisfying sense of completeness to the whole.

Examples:

The Minstrel Boy.   Last Rose of Summer.   Drink to Me Only.
To a Wild Rose.   All Through the Night.   Robin Adair.
Believe Me, If All These.

J. S. BACH
   Air for the G String (D major Suite).

BRAHMS   COUPERIN
   Waltzes, Opus 39.   Clavecin pieces.

SCHUBERT   KREISLER
   Twelve Ländler, Opus 171.   Rigaudon.

FOSTER
   Swanee River (Old Folks at Home).

The first four measures of Swanee River constitute a
phrase, as do the next four measures. These two phrases
combined are called a *period;* the *thesis, or antecedent,* establishes the key or tonality, the general scheme of *pulsation,
or time* (4/4, together with the basic melodic or rhythmic
idea of the song). The first phrase, however, arouses in us a
feeling of incompleteness; the second phrase, the *antithesis,
or consequent,* has the same key or tonality, the same pulsation or time, the same general melodic and rhythmic idea,
but a slight change of the melody at the end arouses in us a
feeling of satisfaction, of *cadence,* of completeness. Now,
the third phrase follows the same pulsation or time, thus
giving *unity;* but the tone lengths of the phrase are different
and the melodic idea is new. The fourth phrase is a repetition of the second phrase and serves to bring the song to a
strong unified close. Thus, phrase 1 and 2 balance one another and form a period; so do phrase 3 and 4, which form
another period; while, in a larger way, the entire period 1
balances the entire period 2.

In some instances the composer adds a final statement to
the forms outlined above, in order to give a more graceful or
more emphatic ending to the song. This added *ending or
Coda* (or *Codetta*) is illustrated in the following songs and

choruses—Form: I I II I Coda (or Codetta).

Examples:

Then You'll Remember Me.

A Life on the Ocean Wave.   Free as a Bird.

All the songs mentioned show a two-period form. However, more than two periods may be used in some cases, or the two may be differently arranged. Again, a composer may balance a period occasionally by a passage of a contrasting style. But music may be written according to an entirely different plan; and a period may sometimes be followed by a free episode.

We next take up the three-part form.

(Note: Ordinarily, we speak of the *small 2-part song form* having either eight or sixteen measures; and the *big 2-part song form* having 16–16 measures.)

D. THREE-PART, OR TERNARY FORM

The *three-part, or ternary,* form is a composition complete in three distinct sentences or periods (3 x 8, or 3 x 16 measures). The 3-part form is probably the most common type of musical construction, especially in the smaller forms. It is frequent in all piano literature, as well as in many violin and cello solos.

Three-part form with countertheme. The essentials of this structure are the existence of three distinct parts: a first or principal idea, or thematic section (period); a second idea, or section, giving a genuine contrast to the first in regard to key, melodic outline, and general treatment; and a third section of reassertion which repeats the material of the first idea, or section, so as to give unity and finality. The second section, or *episode,* may sometimes be in the same key as the first part. Between any two periods there may be a little passage linking them together. This is known as a "transition passage" when introducing new material, or a "returning passage" when it is followed by material used before. The repetition of the third section may be complete or only partial, or it may be varied or exact. This repetition gives the hearer a strong impression of unity and, at the same time, enables the composer to introduce still greater variety in the second part. An *introduction* and a *coda* at the beginning or end may add distinction to the design. Examples are Dvorak's Humoresque; Ach Du Lieber Augustin; etc.

Three-part form with episode. This is the same as the above, but instead of a countertheme (having two phrases and a cadence), there is an episode lacking some or all these points and composed in a more or less free style. An example is Mendelssohn's The Return (Songs Without Words, #41).

Three-part abbreviated form. This is similar to either of the above mentioned types, but the return of the first period is altered into a single phrase instead of a complete period. Examples are Mendelssohn's On the Seashore (Songs Without Words, #19); Schuett's Reverie; etc.

In the *extended ternary form* (*a lengthened song form*) used in the classic *minuet* and *scherzo* (or slow movements of sonatas and symphonies), as well as in many folk songs, marches, and dances, each of the three parts, taken by itself, is in complete binary form; and as the third section is generally a literal repetition of the first one, it is not written out; but at the end of the middle section (called the "trio," because it was originally written in three-voiced harmony) we find the direction, "*Minuet (or scherzo) de capo,*" meaning a return to the first section. Sometimes the first section is prefaced by a short *introduction,* while the third section may be followed by a short *coda,* or an additional phrase which brings it to a more finished ending. Thus, we have the following very pleasing arrangement: Introduction A B A; Coda.

I	II	III	
1 2	Episode	1	2
Binary form	New Subject	Repetition of I	
Statement	Contrast	Coda?	
		Restatement	
		The material of the coda may be taken from the first part or from the episode, or both or new material may be used	

The simplest way in which three themes may be represented is illustrated in the beautiful song Juanita, where the melody is composed of three periods, each supplementing and contrasting with the other.

Other examples:

BEETHOVEN
   Minuet in G; Allegretto (Sonata #6).

S. ADAMS
   Nancy Lee.

BRAHMS
   Ballade G minor, Opus 118, #3.

F. N. LOHR
   Out on the Deep.

GOSSEC
   Tambourin.

GHIS ?
   Amaryllis.

PADEREWSKI
   Minuet.

SCHUBERT
   Impromptu, Opus 90, #4; Moment Musicale, F minor.

SCHUMANN
   Träumerei; The Important Event (Scenes from Childhood).

F. ABT
   When the Swallows Homeward Fly. (The three parts of this fine song differ in length—the first part consisting of a period; the second of a phrase-group; and the third of an extended period.)

As composers realized more and more the importance of the opening sentence making up the composition, they also came to the conclusion that the music should appear again in the original key after having been presented in a contrasting one. In short, with a return to the main key there must also be a simultaneous recurrence of the main sentence, or theme, a restatement of it after the contrast.

The *ternary, or three-part form,* or *classic song-form with trio,* is used very often. Practically all the popular dances and marches are written in this form; other pieces are issued under the name of: Intermezzo; Minuet I, II; Passepied I, II; Musette; Magiore; Minore; Fris or Friska; etc. Naturally such pieces show rather long phrases; the waltz is apt to have phrases of 16 measures each, instead of the usual 8 measures. With little training anyone ought to be able to recognize the popular examples of this form, and pick out the periods, or name the Trio, with considerable accuracy.

Many larger pieces of music are composed on the plan

of a complete Classic Song-form with Trio, just as the single periods of a three-part song-form are grouped. In other words, one three-part song-form is followed by another three-part song-form, which in turn is followed by a repeat of the first three-part song-form (modified).

Examples:

GRIEG
   Sonata C minor for Violin & Piano, Opus 45, 2nd movement.

J. S. BACH   HAYDN   SCHUBERT
   Suites.   Piano Sonatas.   March Militaire.

There is also a song form with two trios.

Examples:

MENDELSSOHN
   Priest's March from Athalia; Wedding March.

SCHUMANN
   Scherzo from First Symphony.

(Note: Ordinarily, we speak of the small 3-part song-form as having 8-8-8 measures, and the big 3-part song-form as having 16-16-16 measures.)

Irregular-part forms are songs whose association or compounding of parts violates one or another of the essential conditions of the regular structural plan. To avoid monotony, a phrase may be two or three measures or even eight measures in length. The two phrases in a sentence, or period, may differ as to the number of measures. As a result of extension or contraction, a phrase of four measures may be replaced by a phrase of three measures (contraction); or a phrase of five measures may be put in place of a phrase of four measures (extension). The text in vocal music often requires phrases of unusual length.

Examples:

BRAHMS
   Theme and Variations (St. Anthony), Opus 56 (shows extension).

HAYDN
   Minuet from Emperor Quartet, Opus 76, #3 (shows extension).

Five-part Form—A B A C A. Parts 1, 2, 3 are the same as in the 3-part form; part 4 generally is a transposed or modified version of Part 2; part 5 is an exact or modified repetition of Parts 1 and 3.

(Note: Knowledge and appreciation of the phrase is absolutely essential to intelligent singing. The habit of singing according to phrases is of the utmost importance.)

5

VOCAL MUSIC

A. SECULAR MUSIC

1. FOLK SONGS

VOCAL music is divided into:

1. *Secular*—folk song; song; part-song; ballad; chanson; aria; recitative; *Lied* (art-song); madrigal; cantata; opera.

2. *Sacred*—chant; canticle; hymn; chorale; anthem; motet; mass; oratorio.

Monophonic (one-voiced) music is the simplest we know—the Gregorian or plain chant of the early Church.

Homophonic (one-voiced) music consists of a principal melody supported by an accompaniment of chords.

Polyphonic (many-voiced) music is made up of a number of seperate melodies, each with its own rhythmic values, which, taken together, form harmonies (contrapuntal); mass in 4, 6, etc. voices (fugue).

Simple song forms date back to the very birth of music. The earliest folk songs were composed at a time when few people could read or write, when books were printed in Latin, and when there were no newspaper, telegraph, telephone, steam and electric power, airships, radio, and TV. The earliest development of the folk song began with the traveling singers—the *troubadours* and the *Minnesingers*. Luther, the great reformer who established the Protestant

Church and promoted the German language, was also quite active in the development of music. It was during his time that congregational singing was introduced; and from this period our chorus was later evolved.

There may have been musically gifted persons who knew nothing of laws or rules of music yet had a creative ability which expressed itself in spontaneous melody. Other singers, hearing these melodies, passed them on down the years until finally they attained fairly permanent forms. We believe that some of the folk music of various countries came into existence this way, because the poets and composers of them are unknown. Some of the folk music was so perfect in its simplicity and naturalness that it had been little altered through the years. But, on the other hand, much folk music passing from one generation to the other by singing only has gone through many changes. In any case, real folk music is natural and spontaneous, rather naïve and artless, and carries with it an indisputable charm, partly due to the uncertainty of its origin and partly to this artlessness. A folk song is a song that has its origin in the joys, the sorrows, the work, the legends, the history of a people and has been sung extensively by them for many years, sometimes centuries. It is often based on a legendary or historic event, or on some incident of common life. Well-known composers often write in the style of such simple and artless folk music, thereby creating the same atmosphere. Such songs are also called "folk songs." There are wonderful songs of either sort, and they will endure through the ages. The song, whether long or short, has a most direct appeal and is the one musical form we all grasp and understand best. Folk songs of all countries reveal many different national characteristics. Folk songs and folk tunes have always had an influence upon the great composers of any given country; they are often used as leading themes in the more pretentious art forms.

The design of the folk song gradually grew larger and contained more variety; and through this process the foundations were laid for the masterpieces of modern instrumental music. Vocal music is more limited in range and power than instrumental music, but, at the same time, it is capable of a greater depth of emotional expression. It enhances the meaning of poetry and of thought. By the use of words, it presents definite ideas, and this may give vent to the highest aspirations of man. Instrumental music is capable of much more varied color contrasts, greater dynamic power, greater possibilities of power and utterance, and generally has fewer limitations than vocal music. As men's lives have become more ordered, as higher standards of living and thinking have appeared, the sense of beauty has grown, until, finally, this steady progress has resulted in the creation of permanent types. No doubt, the natural musical genius which every generation produces was responsible in the past for all the folk music of which every modern nation is now so proud. When the first folk songs were written, the art and science of music did not exist as we know it now. The folk song in itself is a lifetime study; and there is much literature on the subject.

A *folk song must appeal* to the heart and be the common property of the people. *It must express as much as possible* in the easiest and most natural way—a complete vehicle of feeling. *It must be very simple in form,* so that anyone may easily learn it; *tuneful* so that everyone will like it; and *sincere* so that it truly reflects the nature of the country and the characteristics of its people.

It will be seen, upon examination of folk songs, that the musical form is dictated by the poetic form. A stanza of four lines calls for a song of one period, or sentence.

A clear understanding of simple song forms will make it far easier to follow the more complicated structure of the sonata form and other types to be found in an overture, tone poem, sinfonietta, etc.

In songs of the folk-song type we find that melody is much less used by them in picturing moods than in the art-song (*Lied*) type. In folk songs the words have the same scheme of rhythmic accentuation as the music; the lengths of their phrases correspond, and the general character of the music reflects the general mood of the words. No provision is made in the music for a change of mood in the various verses. Occasionally, however, the composer does affect a change of melody and accompanying harmony in important parts of the text in order to convey their character. (See: R. Franz, Opus 4, #9; Die Heide Ist Braun; also, several songs by Brahms.) Ordinarily, however, the music can only follow the meaning of the words through variation in tempo and dynamics.

To repeat, when the composer sets the verses of a poem to music, he must plan his musical structure to express most fittingly the underlying emotions of the text. Where one prevailing sentiment is carried through all the stanzas of a poem, the natural plan would be to repeat the same melody for each stanza. All folk, national, and patriotic songs, and nearly all popular songs, are composed in this manner; and the style of composition in which the same melody is re-peated for each stanza is called the *strophe form*. Many of the world's great songs are in strophe form, as, for example, Schubert's Der Lindenbaum; the Cradle Song; By the Sea; Hark, Hark, the Lark; My Peace Art Thou; Who is Sylvia?; and Silcher's Lorelei.

To some extent, intercommunication does away with all peculiar differences, either tonal or rhythmic, or it fuses them into a musical language that is cosmopolitan rather than racial, national, or provincial. More and more, our railroads, autos, airships, telegraphs, telephones, radios, magazines, and newspapers are preventing the creation of genuine folk songs in all modern countries.

Some American folk-songs are Dixie Land; Jingle Bells; My Old Kentucky Home; Old Black Joe; Old Folks at Home (Swanee River); etc.

Play or sing and analyze:

> Annie Laurie—two phrases—design: A A B A
> Home Sweet Home—two phrases—design: A A B B
> The Minstrel Boy—two phrases—design: ?

Swing Low, Sweet Chariot is a 2-part song. The parts are nearly alike and are eight measures long. Each part is made up of two balancing 4-measure phrases, almost alike, except that the second phrase has a more definite ending than the first. It is in the key of F major, but the melody is based upon the *pentatonic scale*—c d f g a. Many Negro songs are built upon this primitive scale.

Another type of folk song is the *Christmas carol,* the oldest of which have lost almost all trace of their origin. During the early years of the Middle Ages, they were refashioned for service in the Church. There are five different kinds of carols, each one being designed for a particular service with the ceremony of the Christmas feast. Each separate part of the great festival had its own songs of praise and gladness. The number of carols is legion. Some are associated with a folk-song melody of their own, while others have undergone manifold variations by individual composers inspired by the passing mood or emotion.

1. *Krippenlieder:* H. von Laufenberg—In Einer Krippe Lag Ein Kind; Maria Durch Einen Dornenwald Ging; old French carols—Entre le Boeuf et l'Ane; March of the Kings; etc.

2. *Kirchenlieder:* The services of the Church formed the background of Truler's lovely carol, Nun kommt Ein Schiff Gefahren; Luther's famous arrangement of Gelobet Seiest Du, Jesus Christ; M. Praetorius' old hymn, In Dolci Jubile, known in England as Good Christian Men, Rejoice; Er Ist Gewaltig and Stark, Der zu Weihnacht Geboren Ward; Thou Didst Condescend to Be Poor and Weak—the spirit of humility runs through all like a silver thread.

3. *Sternsingerlieder:* These songs were sung in patrician homes by children dressed as the three kings of the Orient and carrying a star in token of the mystic sign that led them to the manger in Bethlehem. This custom is still preserved in South Germany and parts of Silesia. The little "star-singers" on Christmas Eve sing such tunes as, Mit Gott so Wollen wir Loben Gern; Nun Reisen wir Froh Nach Unserer Sonnen; etc.

4. *Hirtenlieder,* or *shepherd songs:* These were very popular, simple, tiny ballads unfolding the immortal story in all its pristine beauty. Later on they were woven into Christmas plays.

5. *Kirchenlieder,* or *children's songs:* Notice the ever popular, Es Ist ein Ros' Entsprungen; Luther's Kirchenlied auf die Weihnachten; O Tannenbaum; Gruber's incomparable Silent Night, Holy Night, conceived in the Bavarian Alps. They are all rooted deep in the hearts of a simple people.

6. *English Christmas songs:* God Rest You, Merry Gentlemen; The First Nowell; Hark, the Herald Angels Sing.

7. *American Christmas songs:* O Little Town of Bethlehem; It Came Upon a Midnight Clear; Carry It On; Adeste Fidelis (O Come, All Ye Faithful); Christ Was Born in Bethlehem.

These carols are all lovely little tunes of praise and adoration, filled with the sweetness of peace and good will. The simple note of familiarity that pervades them does not affect the deep reverence with which the divine mystery is approached. The beauty of an old song lies in its appeal to the heart; and inasmuch as memory is something beyond the bounds of time, the loveliness of these old carols depends upon the measure of the soul's response to the message they convey.

2. SONGS (STROPHE SONGS)

A *lyric song* is the expression of some dominant emotion, such as love, ecstasy, contemplation, patriotism, etc. It is also known as *strophe song,* i.e., a song in which successive stanzas of verse are sung to the same music. In the broad sense of the word, there are many good old songs which are neither folk songs, art songs, ballads, nor arias, etc., but which are written according to musical rules. Such songs are found in the best music textbooks.

Of course, the so-called "popular songs" have no place in these pages. As a rule, they are trashy songs of lilting rhythm and more often than not have foolish words.

Form of the lyric song:

1. The unit, or stanza form: I (A); the music is composed of a single sentence, or period.

2. The binary, or 2-part form: I II (A B); there are two more or less contrasting divisions.

3. The ternery, or 3-part form: I II I (A B A); a contrasting division is followed by a return to the first division. Often a short refrain is added to which nonsense words are sometimes sung.

Many beautiful strophe songs exist. However, this style of composition contains two possible defects: the character of the melody and accompaniment may fit only a few stanzas and be unsuited to others, or the music may become monotonous on repetition.

Mendelssohn wrote some charming lyric songs, but he scarcely influenced the development of the *Lied*. His songs have fluency and grace, rather than poetic depth. They are extremely regular and conventional, and they break no new paths.

Examples:

LOHR
   Out on the Deep.

MOLLOY
   Love's Old Sweet Song.

TROTERE
   In Old Madrid.

SCHUBERT
   The Linden Tree; Impatience; The Miller's Flowers; To Wander.

MENDELSSOHN
   On Wings of Song.

PINSUTI
   Bedouin Love Song.

National or patriotic song: A song identified with the history of a nation either by sentiment or by long use. Such songs have been written in almost every great crisis and have sprung into favor because they voice in an intense manner the popular feeling.

Examples:

CAREY
   America.

P. J. HAYDN
   Austrian Hymn.

R. DE LISLE
   The Marseillaise.

A. VON LWOFF
   Russian Hymn.

P. PHILE
   Hail, Columbia.

J. S. SMITH
   Star Spangled Banner.

War song: Wars have always produced songs, and people keep on singing them long after fighting has stopped. Usually, only the inspirational songs survive rather than those associated with actual episodes of the war.

Examples are Emmet's Dixie; Old Dan Tucker; etc.

Popular song: This is a song that is in use among all classes of people and is of very recent origin. Generally speaking, the popular song is a little more elaborate than the folk song.

Examples:

BARNBY	HARRISON
Sweet and Low.	In the Gloaming.
KNEASS	J. B. SPILMAN
Ben Bolt.	Flow Gently, Sweet Afton.

Ode (*Ode,* Greek—a song): The setting to music of a lyrical poem.

PART-SONG

The *part-song* is a composition for at least three voices in harmony, without accompaniment. It is essentially a melody with choral accompaniment, the upper part usually being the most important.

Examples:

PEARSALL	MENDELSSOHN
O Who Will O'er the Downs.	O Fly with Me.
A. SULLIVAN	J. BARNBY
O Hush Thee, My Babie.	Sweet and Low.

The *two-part* song is a composition for two voices, in which the second voice is merely a supporting accompaniment.

Examples are Donizetti's Long Live Valor (Daughter of the Regiment); Dancing Song (Hungarian folk song); etc.

The *three-part* song, or trio, is a composition for three voices.

Examples:

F. ABT	A. SULLIVAN
Rest.	Out on the Ocean.

The *four-part* song, or vocal quartet, is a song for four voices.

Examples:

H. Hadley	Gounod
Bugle Song.	Send Out Thy Light.

(Note: In the 15th and 16th centuries such great masters as H. Finck, H. Isaak, H. L. Hassler, L. Senfl, H. Schein, etc., wrote excellent German part-songs. The main difference between these songs written by the old masters and the more modern songs is that the old masters simply arranged some of the beautiful folk melodies, whereas the later composers tried to write original songs. The older part-song is based upon a folk melody—a *cantus firmus*—usually given to the tenor. The other voices are written in counterpoint to the *cantus firmus*. Some songs were homophonic, i.e., written with underlying chords.)

THE BALLAD, OR NARRATIVE SONG (COUPLET)

The *English ballad* is a simple song which describes an event or narrates a story through a number of verses. All kinds of stories may be told in the ballad, as well as moral reflections upon the stories. The verses are sung to the same melody; and they have a simple accompaniment. Though each verse depicts some new development in the story, there is no change in the melody to express the difference in mood or picture. All that is required is for the rhythm of the music to fit the meter of the poetry. A ballad should be easily understood. Zumsteg, and others, have written excellent narrative songs; Carl Loewe is the master *par excellence* of the ballad.

Examples:

Brahms	Schubert
Verrat.	Erlking.

Schumann
Belshazzar.

H. Wolf
Der Feuerreiter; Die Geister am Mummelsee.

See also:

> Barbara Allen; Kathleen Mavourneen; I've Been Roaming;
> My Pretty Jane; On Venice Waters; The Lass With the
> Delicate Air; When Love is Kind.

CHANSON

The *chanson* is a native song of France. It is a song of
dainty and graceful character usually based on a love theme.
It is similar to the Italian *canzone*, a part-song in popular
style which places more emphasis upon daintiness and grace
in the melody.

Examples:

B. GODARD
Florian's Song.

Chanson Provençale.
Lorraine.

ARIA

An *aria* (*air*) is a sustained melody following a recitative
in either an opera or oratorio. The aria is a monologue consisting of a theme and its development. As a means for expression, the aria tends to fall into somewhat distinct classes,
according to its melodic and harmonic treatment and its
consequent fitness for certain types of feeling. The melody
of the aria may be sustained and lyric, or florid and dramatic; some lyric subject or passion may be expressed. In short,
it is a lyric or dramatic melody of a single voice, accompanied by instruments. There is no settled form; it may be in
the large 2-part or 3-part song form, or in the form resembling the rondo, or sonata-allegro form.

Lyric arias are: I hear You Calling Me; Little Gray Home
in the West.

Dramatic arias are: Invictus; The Road to Mandalay;
The Two Grenadiers; Vesti la giuba (Pagliacci).

The *coloratura aria* is intended for vocal display, and
words are of small importance. This style of singing dazzles
the unthinking public. The coloratura singer is a vocal ath-
lete who values superior technic over the real art of song.
The *aria di bravura* (*bravura aria*) is usually given to a fe-

male voice; it is nothing but a series of trills, scales, turns, or various similar embellishments for the display of vocal agility.

Bravura or coloratura arias are: Delibes' Bell Song (Lakme); Donizetti's Mad Scene (Lucia di Lammermoor); Handel's Why Do the Nations? (Messiah); Rejoice Greatly (Messiah); Every valley; etc.

Aria de capo: The first part of the aria was always repeated. It was developed by A. Scarlatti and used in his operas. It is a vocal song-form with trio, consisting of a section, a contrasting section, and the repetition of the first section (or partial repeat). The first section was in the principal key and some related manner; a second section contrasted with the first in key and manner; and a third section was either a repetition of the first or an intensified variant of it. This kind of solo has great value as a purely musical form and resembles the longer song forms generally. The *aria da capo* was homophonic, i.e., it had a dominating melody and an accompaniment mainly harmonic.

Examples are Mendelssohn's Oh, God have Mercy; It is Enough; etc.

(Note: It is customary after the conclusion of the second part to allow a short portion of the first part to reappear as *Coda,* thus attaining the desired contrast. In the arias by Mendelssohn and other later composers, the coda enters (instead of a full return of the main theme) in the same manner.

Arias really were solos, but duets in similar form gradually were employed for musical and dramatic climaxes. In such duets the voice parts were often handled in rather exact contrapuntal fashion.

An example is Handel's He Has Despised (Messiah).

Aria parlante: This is a song somewhat in a spoken style, the forcible enunciation of the text being the special feature. It is less abrupt than the recitative; and the music is designed for declamatory effect. The *aria parlante* was the precurser of the recitative.

An example is Rubinstein's Der Asra.

Aria cantabile: This is a song of marked sing-style; a

quiet, slow, and smooth melody, usually in a slow tempo, with few slips, and supported by compact harmony expressive of peaceful or meditative emotion.

An example is Handel's He Shall Feed His Flock (Messiah).

Aria buffa: This is a comic-opera aria, a song with humorous words.

An example is Rossini's The Barber of Seville.

Aria di portamento: This is a song which used the *portamento* (a sweep of the voice toward the tone coming next, before the time of the tone given is entirely finished). The melody is made by skips and more prominent accents, expressive of heightened but not agitated feeling.

An example is Mendelssohn's Jerusalem (St. Paul).

Aria di mezzo carattere: This is a song of ordinary character and style, rather declamatory or descriptive in the voice-part, and usually provided with an accompaniment of importance.

An example is F. J. Haydn's With Verdure Clad.

Aria d'imitazione, or imitative aria: This is a song which stresses the imitation (usually more in the accompaniment than in the voice) of such sounds as singing birds, moving water, festivity, warfare, etc.

Arioso: This is a form of recitative in which there are passages of melody without the formation of a complete air. This kind of song is common in modern opera. It is a type of music similar to the aria but less marked as to its divisions and without the separable character of a set number.

Examples are J. S. Bach's Cantata #61, Nun Komm, Der Heiden Heiland (arioso for bass); Puccini's operas; etc.

Arietta: This is a small aria—a song less elaborate than the aria.

Recitative: This is a declamatory, intoned song, used in opera and oratorio, often connecting the different parts of a scene. It delivers the words in the same irregular rhythms in which they would naturally be spoken. There are two kinds of recitative—*recitativo secco* and *recitativo stromentato.*

The *recitativo secco* has absolutely no form except that

of the text, the music being almost without rhythm or definite melody. Known as the "unaccompanied recitative," it has practically no orchestral support, except wholly detached chords which are struck only when the harmony changes. It is obvious that the interest centers on the words and not on the music, which simply brings out the meaning of the words. The declamation ranges from simple narration or conversation up to passionate recitation, whichever the story or the character speaking happens to suggest.

Examples are Handel's Comfort Ye (beginning with the words, "The voice of Him . . ."); Mozart's Magic Flute, Act I, Finale (The Wisdom, etc.); Don Giovanni; Marriage of Figaro.

The *recitativo stromentato* is accompanied throughout by the orchestra. Between the passages of the recitative, the instruments usually play illustrative melodic passages which bring out clearly the feeling of the text. It is known as the "accompanied recitative," a recitative that resembles a dramatic song. Many of the old opera scores contain examples of these recitatives, or musical declamations, much resembling speech, though always with a definite pitch verging more or less upon the *arioso,* or informal song.

Examples are Handel's Comfort Ye (Messiah); Mozart's Don Giovanni; etc.

Scena: This is a solo for voice which expresses various dramatic emotions and uses a variety of styles. It is either a wholly independent work or a part of an opera. It generally contains some recitative music; a smooth aria section, (known here as a *cavatina*); and an aria or other part devoted to more brilliant display. A *cavatina* is a brilliant melody, without much ornamentation, but generally very expressive.

An example is Mendelssohn's Infelice (an independent *scena*).

The vocal *rondo* is generally like the orchestral rondo form. The theme can remain unaltered at each appearance; or it may change key and, in some degree, its harmony.

For an example of a strict vocal rondo form, see Gluck's I Have Lost My Euridice.

The *cabaletta* derives its name from *caballo* (Spanish, a horse), because of the galloping style of its accompaniment.

Melos (Greek—melody): This is a sort of melodic recitative which R. Wagner named and introduced in his later works.

Melodrama: Strictly speaking, the melodrama is not a vocal form. It demands a reader to speak the words to a musical accompaniment of piano or orchestra; however, it surely deserves more attention than has been given it.

Examples:

R. COLE
King Robert of Sicily; Hiawatha's Wooing; Pierrot Wounded.

FIBICH
Hippodamia (a trilogy).

M. VON SCHILLING
Das Hexenlied.

R. STRAUSS
Enoch Arden.

THE ART SONG, OR LIED

The *art song, or Lied,* is the highest development of vocal music. It is a poem set to music which is in perfect accord with the text, the result of the musical inspiration of a single mind.

The great German song-writers, Schubert, Schumann, Franz, Wolf, Brahms and R. Strauss, are the founders of this type of song. It is a song in which the music reflects and interprets the meaning of the poem throughout and does not repeat with each stanza. Where the mood of each stanza changes, or where the music portrays or accompanies dramatic action, the melody follows the varying emotional or dramatic character of the verse. Every phrase of the music must exactly correspond in meaning to its poetic line. The rhythm of the music must correspond with the meter of the verse; but, in addition to this, the general mood of the music must fit at every point with the changing imagery and shifting mood of the words. Each thought, each delicate shade of meaning become more evident through the music. It is a perfect blending of the two distinct elements in a song—the poetic and the lyric, or words and melody. Indeed, the moments are rare when skill, insight, and luc are all equal to the opportunity and produce an all-around satisfying whole—a masterpiece.

The voice part contains no tone that will make the same kind of appeal as a ballad or popular song. Hence, it must not be compared with any other kind of song.

The new idea of the expressive use of melody brought about the development of the art song and led to a different type of construction, known as the *"durch-komponiertes Lied"—through-composed song*. Both melody and accompaniment change continually with the varying moods of the words, instead of letting the music stop and start again after each strophe. Often we find that the music for successive verses is different. In the Lied the form of each melody belongs to the particular poem to which it is set and to no other. All the effects are blended into one expression to show us clearly that they belong to the same work of art. Thus, we justly estimate the composer not according to the vividness of his details but according to the beauty of his whole composition. This includes the *introduction, interlude,* and *postlude,* which are often used freely in songwriting. Some organic connection must exist between these and the song proper. Such a song obviously permits a much greater variety of expression than folk music or folk poetry.

As much of the melody may be in the accompaniment as is in the voice part. The success of this art form depends upon the fusion of words, voice part, and accompaniment into a perfect whole—a living whole in which, in addition to the poem, rhythm, melody, and harmony are inseparable.

The words should always be understood before the music is heard. In subject matter, the poem used may be classified as reflective, fanciful, descriptive, realistic, convivial, serious, sacred, secular, patriotic, or as a lyric of love, of battle, and so forth.

Form and style of an art song are almost inseparable, and both are dictated by the subject matter. The simpler the emotion to be portrayed, the simpler, as a rule, are the form and style. The mood and style may be tender, dreamy, intense, fanciful, exalted, pathetic, etc. Hence, we find that songs range from those of a purely lyric nature, in which emotion is the product of pure contemplation—as in songs celebrating the charms of a maiden, the calmness of the night, sweet flowers, or the loveliness of spring—to those in which the dramatic element is almost as much in evidence as it is in opera. There are some art songs in which emotion is the product of personal passion, as in Franz's Im Herbst; Schubert's Erl King, Doppelgänger, and Der Tod und das Mädchen; and Schumann's Ich Grolle Nicht.

In several of these songs we find the application of the "Leitmotif" (see Der Doppelgänger, Morning, and others). Schubert introduced it; Schumann, Brahms, and Wolf brought it to its highest development; and Wagner used it with such wonderful skill and on an unprecedented scale in his music dramas.

The accompaniment may be of considerable importance in the creation of form, especially vocal forms. Often the accompaniment presents only a background which is set so as to bring out distinctly the melody of the solo voice. In other cases, the accompaniment re-enforces the plain rhythm, as, for example, in marches and dances. But the accompaniment may also, by means of characteristic rhythms, deepen and strengthen the expression of musical pieces. We may note this in many modern songs. The accompaniment also may serve as a sort of framework by connecting the strands of rather loosely woven and freely recited melodies that express various different ideas and so become a unified whole. The accompaniment may also be a dialogue with the solo voice, may stop the solo at a suitable place and go with it in unison, or be a more or less contrasting voice. In short, the accompaniment may be subordinated to the solo voice, go with it, or become the leading voice for the time being. Often the *Ritornello* is used—a short theme or melody in the form of a prelude, an interlude to connect the different sections, and a postlude, especially if the theme consists of the same melodic material. Thus, the accompaniment has a chance to appear as the leading melody while the solo voice pauses, holds a long tone, or exe-

cutes a trill, etc. Other means of varying accompaniments
are: chords, arpeggios, tremolo, scale passages, etc. As
examples, see the *Lieder* by Schubert, Schumann, Brahms,
etc.

(Note: A most striking example of the difference between the strophic form and the through-composed song
form is shown in the two settings of Heine's famous poem,
Die Lorelei. In writing the music to these verses, Silcher
has caught, in the most wonderful way, the dreamy, mystic
spirit of the German people and has put it into a strophic
setting which will always be dear to the German heart.
Liszt has set the poem to music in the through-composed
form. His melody and accompaniment follow the constantly
shifting sense of each line in the most subtle and realistic
manner. He has presented a very striking and effective
miniature music-drama.)

The *Lied* began with Haydn and Mozart. Incidentally,
the singer's voice—his instrument—has undergone no change
in all the centuries that man has been an artistic being.

F. J. Haydn (1732–1809). Like his other music, his songs
have rugged simplicity and straightforward spontaneity, as
well as depth of feeling in his slow movements. Songs: She
Never Told Me Her Love; etc.

W. A. Mozart (1756–1791). His music possesses intuitive
grace and melodic charm; it shows careful work and refined
perfection; most of it is in a happy vein, but in some pieces
there is a peculiar sadness and depth of feeling as if he
sensed the tragic futility of all human endeavor. Songs:
Abendempfindung; An Chloe; Das Veilchen; Unglückliche
Liebe; Trennung und Wiedervereinigung; Zu meiner Zeit;
Komm lieber Mai; Wiegenlied.

Beethoven (1770–1825). He was sometimes scornful of
the traditional limitation regarding orchestral instruments
and the voice, but he wrote nothing that could not be sung.
He merely forced singers to be better musicians and better
performers. In his vocal music he anticipates the romanticism of Weber and Schumann while yet preserving something of the classicism of Gluck and the majestic Bach. His
An Die Ferne Geliebte was the first through-composed cycle

of songs, each having a character of its own, but part of a larger entity that combined all. Here the songs are so bound together by the accompaniment that the piano part plays about as an important a role as the voice in the creation of the poetic mood. Other songs: Adeleide; Die Ehre Gottes; Vom Tode.

F. Schubert (1797–1828). His more than 600 songs instituted a new balance between the melodic form and emotional meaning. Every phrase is singable; every song is lyrical. The poems are of good quality, and his piano parts continually rival the voice as a means of reflecting and communicating the text. Schubert was a master of modulation. He gives his vocal line a new feeling by the restless changes of keys into which the accompaniment leads the voice. Thus, his songs have a new freedom, a new elasticity; yet all his songs abound in melody, varied in character as they are. Not too much praise can be given to the spontaneity, variety, and originality of his melodies. Indeed, he is the very foundation and embodiment of the German *Lied*. Note especially: The Erl King; The Wanderer; The Post; Die Allmacht; Der Wegweiser; Frühlingstraum; Die Forelle; Rastlose Liebe; Der Atlas; Du bist die Ruh' (part strophic and part through-composed); Der Doppelgänger (this song is romantic music, for the music is joined indissolubly to a romantic poem and would have little meaning apart from it); Meerestille; Der Leiermann; Ungedult; Wohin; and his song cycles: Die Schöne Müllerin; Die Winterreise.

C. M. von Weber (1786–1826). While he does not figure as an important composer of songs, he was quite a positive influence because of the *Lied* character of the airs in his fine operas.

K. Loewe (1796–1869). His songs are striking examples of his poetic feeling and power of musical expression. Usually they consist of short, varied melodic sections so arranged as to tell a story directly and vividly. His story-telling ballads must be well sung—they are recitations in music. Ballads: Edward, Archibald Douglas, etc.; songs: Die Uhr; Erlking.

R. Schumann (1810–1856). He was a master of the *Lied*.

There is an intimate charm, an elegiac tenderness about his best songs that have hardly been surpassed. He made the piano part still more important to the song and depended increasingly upon the accompaniment to set the mood of the text. He exercised a finely cultivated taste in the choice of his texts and has written many touching and rather youthful songs that combine a fluent lyricism with a distinct treatment of the piano, achieving a perfect unity of expression. The cycles, Dichterliebe and Frauenliebe und Leben, are among the most remarkable of all song literature. Songs: Im Walde; Die Lotus Blume; Die Drei Grenadiere; Stille Tränen; Widmung; Liebesbotschaft; Der Nussbaum; Hidalge; etc.

F. Liszt (1811–1886). He wrote songs of varied character. However, like Chopin (who also wrote charming songs), he treated vocal music as secondary to his other forms of composition. Songs: Die Lorelei; Mignon; Der König von Thule.

R. Franz (1815–1892). He was a song composer of rare spirituality. He preferred serene and idyllic poetry as well as poems of ethical content. He did not care for the passionate and the dramatic, and realism was repugnant to him. Tenderness and gentle pathos were his most characteristic expressions. He used the strophic form freely, but his melodies suggest less the folk song than the songs of Brahms. The sincerity and the lyrical charm of his simple songs deserve not to be neglected. Note especially: Im Herbst; In Meinem Auge; Schlummerlied; The Rose Complained; For Music; Dedication; My Mother's Eyes.

J. Brahms (1833–1897). Brahms brought the *Lied* to its most melodious expression and gave it its greatest perfection of musical structure. His accompaniments are rich and varied and surpass those of Schubert and Schumann. In excellence of workmanship and depth of thought and poetry it is doubtful whether songs by any other composers surpass his. Surely, the world should know more of his 200 songs—too few are sung. In some songs he used the same melody for successive stanzas of quite different meanings, leaving to the accompaniment and to the singer the necessary changes of

mood. Note his: Feldeinsamkeit; O Kühler Wald; Der
Schmied; Wie Melodien; Die Mainacht; The Saphic Ode;
An die Nachtigall; Botschaft (the perfect love song); Von
Ewiger Liebe; Vergebliches Ständchen; Wiegenlied (a stro-
phic song); Liebeslieder; Zigeunerlieder; Four Serious
Songs; etc.

H. Wolf (1860–1903). Esthetically, his songs are the
culmination of the German *Lied*. He wrote his melodies so as
to give the texts a maximum of expression. It was the poetic
content that determined the shape of the musical form, the
styles and contours of his songs. His melodies, though rarely
lyrical, are delightful to sing for anyone able to grasp the
principles of their wonderfully plastic line; the melodies
often border on declamation, whereas some of those of
Brahms' contrast with their folklike singing. Wolf went beyond all other *Lieder*-writers in completely fusing words and
music. He set his texts so as to give the feeling that words
and music must have been created together by the same
artist. In any of his songs we can hardly find a stress that is
unjustified or an accent that is misplaced. The piano parts
of his songs are as important as the vocal parts, and often
they seem to be almost complete in themselves. His *Lieder*
abound in increased freedom of his song form; he used the
method of the through-composed song. Obviously, he was
the most dramatic of composers of the *Lied*. Note especially: Morning; Zur Ruh'; Biterolf; Verborgenheit; Auch
Kleine Dinge; Gesang Weylis; etc.

R. Strauss (1864–1949). The most celebrated of recent
composers for orchestra, the stage, and the *Lied*, he has written songs that reflect keen insight into the texts selected
from modern German poets. Some of his songs are humorous or sentimental; they show the tenderer side of his nature
and often have an individual charm of melody brilliantly
marked by picturesque accompaniments. Songs: Traum
Durch Die Dämmerung; Morgen; Freundliche Vision; Serenade; Ruhe Meine Seele; Ich Schwebe; etc.

Moussorgsky (1839–1881). A writer of songs of distinction, his works are Russian but rarely oriental like those of
Borodin or Rimski-Korsakov. Some of his unique songs are

purely lyrical; others are characterized by a declamatory setting, the music serving to put the various points of the poem in strong relief. Note the sardonic humor of such songs as The Goat, The Flea, The Seminarist. He is spokesman of peasants and children, as he contrives to speak their language as well as characterize them with unique fidelity. Cycles: The Nursery, Death, No Sunlight; songs: Gopak; Hebrew Song; etc.

Tschaikowsky (1840–1893). This fine composer wrote a hundred or more songs, most of which are elegiac. See Nur Wer Die Sehnsucht Kennt; Don Juan's Serenade; etc.

Other outstanding Russian composers are: *Rubinstein* (Der Asra; etc.); *Tanieff* (The Minuet; The Birth of the Harp; etc.); *Rimski-Korsakov* (left about eighty songs, mainly lyrical); *Gretchaninoff* (Oh, Do Not Sing Again; etc.) *Stravinsky* (The Cloister; etc.).

Grieg (1843–1907). His songs have an individual touch because of his personality and the melodic idioms he derived from the folk ideas of his people. The songs display a poignant coloring of harmony and a freshness of his melodic inspiration; they are original, yet he achieves his effects by means of simplicity. Songs: Ein Schwan; Erstes Begegnen; Die Alte Mutter; Im Kahne; Ich Liebe Dich; The Dream; From Monte Pincio; Solveijg's Song.

Jensen, another Scandinavian composer, wrote very fresh and attractive songs.

Mendelssohn (1809–1847). Note his fine songs: Der Blumenkranz; On Wings of Song (part strophic, part through-composed); Suleika; also, duets for female voices Gruss; Ich Wollt' Meine Liebe; Abschiedslied der Zugvögel Maiglöckchen; etc.

Debussy (1862–1918). Many of his songs convey the same fugitive, illusive quality, the same passing impressions and the same sort of atmosphere, rather than definite emotions, as his impressionistic piano music. Songs: Green Mandoline; La Chevelure; Beau Soir; Nuit d'Etoiles; Le Balcon; La Flute de Pan; Recueillement; Les Cloches; Fantoches; etc.

Other good French *Lieder*-writers are: *Berlioz* (La Cap

ive); *Gounod* (Le Soir; Venice); *Massenet* (Elégie; Les
)iselets; Crépuscule; Si tu Veux, Mignonne); *Reynaldo
Iahn* (D'une Prison); *C. Franck* (La Procession; Pruis
\ngelicus; Marriage of the Rose); *Duparc* (Chanson Triste;
[estament; Soupir; Phidylé; Invitation au Voyage); as well
ıs *V. d'Indy* and *A. Bruneau.*

G. *Fauré,* greatest of French *Lieder*-writers, produced
ome sixty songs. His songs are full of sentiment, but they
ıre rarely sentimental, much less naïve. They have clarity,
;race, and delicious sensibility, and there is amazing supple-
ıess in his modulations. Many of his songs show exquisite
vorkmanship, vitality, and a luminous quality. They also
ıave beauty of melody and subtle suggestion in the piano
ıccompaniment. See Après un Rêve; Nell; Claire de Lune;
]'est l'Extase; En Sourdine; etc.

Among American *Lieder*-writers we note: *Chadwick*
The Ballad of Trees); *MacDowell* (The Sea; Thy Beaming
]yes); *S. Homer* (The Pauper's Drive); *G. Spross* (Will-o'-
he-Wisp); etc.

MADRIGAL

The *madrigal* is a shepherd song (*mandra*—a flock; *gal*
-a song). It is a short, charming secular composition usu-
lly for three to eight voices, each of which has a melodic
ole. The words—usually from a lyric, pastoral, amorous, or
lescriptive poem—are rather unimportant; for when the
ame words are used over and over again in different voices
vhich answer each other, their meaning becomes confused
nd more or less lost. The interest resides in the beautiful
levices by which the musical idea is developed.

It is *a capella* (unaccompanied) and is written in imi-
ative counterpoint, i.e., a melody announced by one voice
; imitated by the others in turn, each line of words with a
lifferent fragment of melody (not a continuous fugue).

The madrigal, as a musical form, came into being at
bout the same time as the fugue, and its vitality is no less
ısting and permanent. It originated in the Low Countries
oward the middle of the 15th century. Spreading to other
[uropean countries, it reached its greatest perfection in

Italy and in England. It is strictly polyphonic, all parts being equally melodic, and it requires a nimble counterpoint and mastery of imitation on the part of the composer. It has not been improved since its inception. All in all, we may consider the Italian madrigal the finest of all secular vocal music. Its greatest masters are Luca Marenzio; Gesualdo, Prince di Venesa; and Monteverde. In many Elizabethan madrigals the music and poetry possess equal charm, and it was imperative that the composer always devise a rhythmic and melodic setting that would preserve and enhance the attractiveness of the words.

Madrigal-singing is a delightful form of vocal exercise. The melodic structure demands self-reliance and independence, two things which are of great value to singers. Europe has many famous madrigal societies, especially those in England.

Examples:

DI LASSO
 I Knew a Young Maiden.

WILBYE
 Oft Have I Vowed; Stay, Corydon, Thou Swain.

   See also, *The Triumph of Oriana*, a collection of madrigals in praise of Queen Elizabeth by O. Gibbons, J. Benet, T. Morley, J. Wilbye, T. Weelkes, M. Cavendish, T. Bateson, etc.

CANTATA

The *cantata* is somewhat similar to the oratorio, but usually it treats a secular subject. It is generally shorter than the oratorio, though not necessarily so, and it is often less contrapuntal. It is a short lyric drama, or story, adapted to music but not intended to be acted. The form is extremely flexible, using chorus, solos, recitatives, and interludes; and it varies with the particular resources at the disposal of the composer. There are some sacred cantatas generally intended to be part of a church service, and treating religious subjects in a brief or informal manner. All of the 120 cantatas by J. S. Bach were composed for church services.

During the 16th century a cantata simply was any vocal work, as distinguished from one for instruments.

In Italy, beginning about 1650, and for about a hundred years thereafter the cantata specifically meant a "solo scene, secular or sacred, in which recitatives and arias alternated, often with elaborate accompaniments for a solo instrument." This was really an outgrowth of the prevalent opera. However, this type of cantata was of small importance artistically, as it had little independent development. It became popular in the services of the Catholic Church and was composed by all the leading composers from Carissimi onward.

In Germany, during the 17th century, a cantata was a work in which Bible passages sung by a solo voice in recitative or arioso were interspersed with congregational chorales, or with choruses in similar style. The idea was to unite some thread of story or some logical series of thoughts with expressions of devotion or meditation; and it was often quite subjective and even somewhat sentimental in character, reflecting the warm Protestant piety of the people. It differed from the operatic Italian cantata by calling for participation on the part of the congregation.

Around 1700, there arose in Germany a demand for poetical texts especially prepared for semidramatic treatment which dealt with the special character of the Sundays and holidays of the Lutheran calendar. It was evidently a result of the interest in the opera, to which the Germans reacted promptly. The first of such texts were written by the poets E. Neumeister (d. 1756, a clergyman of Weissenfels and Sorau); S. Franck (d. 1725, of Jena and Weimar); and, Chr. Fr. Henrici (Picander, d. 1764, of Leipzig). The musical setting of such texts at once was taken up by musicians and became very popular.

The *modern cantata* may be considered a less pretentious oratorio. Usually, it has an aria, arioso, and a recitative. It is written for various voices accompanied by instrumental music. There are solo cantatas, ensemble cantatas, and chorus cantatas. Many choral works, both sacred and secular, may be regarded as cantatas. G. Bantock, the English composer, has tried to create a new form of cantata consisting of separate movements for voices alone. (See his Atalanta in Calydon.) Here the voices are divided into several groups, and the various groups are treated like the individual parts in an orchestra work. The composition is in four parts, and the contrasts of style are similar to those of the symphony's movements.

Examples:

J. S. Bach
  Church Cantatas.
	Telemann
	  Church Cantatas.

M. Bruch Fair Ellen; Epic Cantatas—Fritjof; Odysseus; Arminius.	

Chadwick
  Judith.
	Gaul
	  The Holy City.

Handel
  Apollo and Daphne.
	Hadley
	  In Music's Praise.

Parker
  Redemption Hymn.
	Rheinberger
	  Toggenburg.

A. Sullivan The Golden Legend; The Prodigal Son.	

Stainer
  The Daughter of Jairus.
	D. Taylor
	  The Highwayman.

OPERA

The *opera* is a composite of poetry, singing, instrumental music, acting, dancing, lighting, and scenic painting—in short, it is a drama set to music. It is dynamic, has swift dramatic action, ardent romanticism, sensuous melodies, brilliant effects, tense emotional climaxes, and relies for its emotional effect on the inner conflicts of individuals. The component parts of an opera are: recitatives, solos, duets, trios, quartets, choruses, etc.; and they are usually preceded by an instrumental overture. Music is a means of intensified self-expression, so an opera singer must convince the audience that his emotions alone impel the orchestra to play the music of the composer. Music is used in opera for "background" purposes, for providing "atmosphere," and the like.

The first and the last essential is for the listener to understand not only what the characters are doing but what they are thinking and feeling as the situation develops. In other words, the opera-goer must understand what the opera is about and the thoughts and emotions of the music.

Popular taste in opera is curiously unstable. No group shows so little intelligent interest as opera-goers; and of all those who consider themselves musical, none have shown such low standards of taste. Since the beginning of opera, the indifference and complaisance of the general public has constantly defeated the finest efforts of expression. The composers have always realized that all the elements of their art serve expression and must be kept subordinate to it. The public, on the other hand, has always considered these subordinate means as ends.

The assimilation and understanding of the music demand intelligent listening and a consciousness of the dramatic tensions involved in opera. A description of the themes (a survey of the tonal landscape) or a learned explanation of the manner in which melodies and motives are interwoven and express the situation on the stage are merely secondary.

The music of opera is an outgrowth of the language in which it was conceived and created and from which it is tonally and psychologically inseparable. Opera is a union of words and music, which is indivisible. No substitution of elements other than those which constitute its original identity is possible. All that the best and most sensitive translation can achieve is an approximation of the original. The genius of a language is the genius of the music which it inspires; the music emanates from the words.

In music, teamwork is as necessary as it is in running a fine business or a good school. The beauty, proportion, and expressiveness of the whole require that each individual be in his proper place. But the general opera public shows too little artistic taste to realize this and has disastrously pampered the vanity of singers and encouraged them to turn dramatic action into a rather gaudy display of personalities. Thus we have the *star system*. Gluck, in his preface to the opera Alceste (1767), wrote: "I have been very careful never to stop a singer in the middle of a piece either for the purpose of displaying the flexibility of his voice in some favorable vowel, or that the orchestra may give him time to take breath before a long-sustained note. . . . In fact, my objective has been to put an end to abuses against which good taste and good sense have long protested in vain."

A. Scarlatti (1659–1725) was the innocent cause of the deterioration of opera in Italy, a circumstance due to his perfection of the aria form. This caused the prima donna to vie with the male soprano and contralto for prestige both on and off the stage; and it constituted a power at once fictitious and inimical to artistic progress. Thus, the opera in Italy straightway became hedged in with conventionalities which interfered with its steady progress, degenerating into a quasi-spectacle, with some noted popular singer as the central figure. Writers on music complained that the art had not yet become established there upon true principles. They also lamented "its degeneracy and corruption" and "its having ceased to copy nature and to appeal to the heart." Gretry declared that, during the years he spent in study at Rome, he never witnessed the success of a serious opera. "If the theater was crowded," says he, "it was to hear a certain singer; when he left the stage, the people in the boxes played cards or ate ices, and those in the pit yawned." In some operas the dramatic element is almost negligible. Even nowadays, as formerly, people will go to any opera (no matter which one) as long as they may hear their favorite singer. Audiences really do not take the drama very seriously when they stop the action at the end of every aria in order to applaud the singer.

In 1646, the opera was transplanted from Italy (A. Scarlatti, etc.) to France (Lully, etc.) by Cardinal Mazarin; and, about the same time, to Germany (Kaiser, and others); and somewhat later to England (Purcell, etc.).

Considering the popularity of opera as an art form and as a fashionable entertainment for over two centuries, it is surprising that the standards of judgment touching it have such feeble and fleeting authority. Hardly any form of popular entertainment is acclaimed so enthusiastically as a new opera, yet none forgotten so quickly. Opera is a mixed art form; it is always in a state of flux; and it is subject to changes of taste in music, the drama, vocal art, histrionic art, politics, and morals. Indeed, opera has so many elements outside of the province of music itself that its interpretation actually has little to do with purely musical standards. In general, the sustaining of an illusion created by the story, words, actions, costumes, scenery, and lighting effects must be considered of primary importance.

Opera has no definite form, but the different schools of opera show various distinctive characteristics and styles. Peri and his followers wanted opera to be declamatory, with the music heightening the effect of the action. But this ideal was not strictly adhered to; and in the time of Handel, opera had become a sort of singing concert. Thus came the *Singspiel*. The *Singspiel* was a German form of dramatic entertainment in which music was interspersed with dialogue. "Grand opera" on French and Italian stages was employed continuously throughout, recitative being used instead of spoken text. Gluck and his school conceived the idea that the music should illustrate the dramatic actions and situations as demanded by the text, although Gluck still kept up the structure of separate operatic numbers. Gluck was the first to write operas in which dramatic action and poetry had an equal part in the musical whole. He turned the undramatic Italian *"opera seria"* into a real "dramatic opera." According to Gluck, "the true mission of the music is to second the poetry, by strengthening the expression of the sentiments and increasing the interest of the situations, without weakening or interrupting the action by superfluous means for tickling the ear or displaying the agility of fine voices." This declaration influenced all German operatic composers.

Later on it needed a Mozart to make opera fluent and vivid once more. Mozart improved the lighter form of Italian *"opera buffa,"* the comic opera. Rossini and his school then entered the field, catering to public taste and inducing it to welcome a revival of the singing-concert idea, though with generally less musical content than even in Handel's time. Rossini developed a somewhat newer and finer style of Italian *opera buffa;* while Bellini, Donizetti, and others composed in the sentimental opera style of Rossini. In France, the *opera buffa* became the "opera comique," especially through the work of Boieldieu, Auber, and others. Von Weber and his school developed a German kind of opera, the "romantic opera." Meyerbeer, with Spontini, Rossini, Halevy, etc., fostered the French "grand drama," in which the orchestra is the main exemplifier of the musical action and the individual characters are "identified" and associated with certain melodies (*Leitmotifs, or leading motives*).

Wagner was the first to make consistent use of the leitmotif, and his ideas of opera have been used by composers of all nations since his time. He and his followers brought about a change in public taste, as Wagner was the first to do away with separate numbers. His works were formed into a plastic whole, instead of being a set of more or less meaningless tunes loosely joined together. He put into his music real expressive power and dramatic force; he studied his texts and characters; and opera again was changed from an entertaining vocal display to a true art work. His great music dramas proved that music of a most advanced type could be made to support and intensify the text in marvelous fashion. Opera since Wagner's time aims to be highly dramatic and usually is cast into a continuous, complete whole. Verdi, in his last works, passed from the style of Rossini to one approaching the Wagnerian music drama.

Modern opera shows any number of the individual ideas of various schools, groups of composers who follow certain fixed ideals. The Italians love melodic flow, vocal display, and sonority in their works, often at the sacrifice of dramatic sincerity and musical worth; no profundity or greatness of inspiration—they prefer simplicity. The Germans, an introspective people, demand above everything else sincerity and musical truth.

The main trends followed since Wagner are given below. Besides these main trends, there are others which have not yet become firmly established, but which show that composers are always trying out new ways and means to express their thoughts and emotions.

Verism (*Italian, verismo—naturalism*): In the "veristic"

opera, dramatic action takes first place and is always very "theatrical." Usually, it deals with terrible passions, brutal loves, murders, and crimes, etc. It aims to show life in the raw and usually succeeds, making it a tingling, exciting thing in its music and action. Verdi was the first great verist; he was followed by P. Mascagni and Puccini.

Italian:

GIORDANO
Siberia; Fedora; Mala Vita.

LEONCAVALLO
I Pagliacci.

P. MASCAGNI
Cavalleria Rusticana.

PUCCINI
La Tosca; Girl of the Golden West; Manon Lescaut.

G. VERDI
Rigoletto; Il Trovatore.

R. SANDONAI
Conchita.

French:

BIZET
Carmen.

A. BRUNEAU
Kerim; La Rêve.

German:

D'ALBERT
Tiefland.

WOLF-FERRARI
Jewels of the Madonna.

Tragic opera (opera seria): The kind of opera that is confined to music and singing, and of which the recitative is a principal feature.

Italian:

ALFANO
Resurrection.

BELLINI
Norma.

DONIZETTI
La Favorita; Lucia di Lammermoor; Lucrecia Borgia.

LEONCAVALLO
La Bohème.

FR. LEONI
The Oracle.

GIORDANO
Andreas Chenier.

V. GNECCHI
Cassandra.

PUCCINI
La Bohème; Madame Butterfly.

A. PONCHIELLI
La Gioconda.

ROSSINI
Semiramide.

SPONTINI
La Vestala.

R. ZANDONAI
Francesca da Rimini.

German:

GLUCK
  Orpheus and Euridice.

E. KORNGOLD
  The Dead City.

R. STRAUSS
  Symphonic one-act opera, Electra; Salome.

R. WAGNER
  Rienzi; Rheingold; Siegfried; Walküre; Götterdämmerung; Tristan and Isolde.

French:

AUBER
  La Muette de Portici.

BOITO
  Mephistopheles.

H. FEVRIER
  Monna Vanna.

C. GOUNOD
  Romeo et Juliet.

J. HALEVY
  The Jewess.

C. ERLANGER
  Aphrodite.

MASSENET
  Manon; Herodiade; La Navarraise.

E. LALO
  Le Roi d'Ys.

J. NONGUES
  Quo Vadis.

REYER
  Sigurd.

A. THOMAS
  Hamlet.

MEYERBEER
  L'Africaine; Le Pròphete.

E. MORET
  Lorenzaccio.

Russian:

H. GLINKA
  A Life for the Tzar.

MOUSSORGSKY
  Boris Godounov.

Spanish:

R. LAPARRA
  La Jota.

American:

H. HADLEY
  Cleopatra's Night.

Romantic Naturalism: In such operas an attempt is made
to give "real-life" characters and stories a romantic, sentimental treatment instead of a brutal, natural one, unlike the
verists. They feature an admixture of the grave and lively.

German:

VON FLOTOW
  Martha; Alessandro Stradella.

I. BRÜLL
  The Golden Cross.

HUMPERDINCK
Hänsel and Gretel; Königskinder.

A. LORTZING
Czar und Zimmermann; Undine; Waffenschmied.

H. MARSCHNER
Hans Heiling.

MOZART
Magic Flute.

V. NESSLER
Trumpeter von Säkingen.

L. SPOHR
Jessonda.

R. STRAUSS
Frau ohne Schatten.

L. THUILLE
Lobetanz.

K. KREUTZER
Nachtlager in Granada.

R. WAGNER
Flying Dutchman; Lohengrin; Tannhäuser.

VON WEBER
Euryanthe; Freischütz; Oberon.

Italian:

BELLINI
La Sonnambula; I Puritani.

G. PUCCINI
Girl of the Golden West.

G. ROSSINI
William Tell.

G. VERDI
Aida.

French:

G. MEYERBEER
Robert le Diable.

CHARPENTIER
Louise.

J. OFFENBACH
Tales of Hoffman.

A. THOMAS
Mignon.

Russian:

RIMSKY-KORSAKOV
Fairy ballet opera, Le Coq d'Or.

Spanish:

E. GRANADOS
Goyescas.

English:

PURCELL
Dido Aeneas.

GILBERT & SULLIVAN
Yeoman of the Guard.

American:

D. TAYLOR
Peter Ibbetson.

Nationalism: In "national," or "folk," operas the composer uses "folk-tune" themes in the style of some particular country or people. There are many beautiful operas of this kind, written by composers of many lands.

Bohemian:

JANACEK
Jenufa; Kata Kabanova; Memoirs of a Dead-House.
J. WEINBERGER
Schwanda, the Bagpiper.

Internationalism: This style uses a "world language" in opera, with short, abrupt motives, complex rhythms, and endless repetition.

Hungarian:

B. BARTOK
Duke Bluebeard's Castle.

Russian:

STRAVINSKY
Emperor's Nightingale.

Lyric drama: The French lyric drama has two convincing dramatic situations—a type of musical declamation that grows out of the inflections of the French language, a certain literary quality in the libretto; and a sweet lyricism that is quite different from the dramatic melody of the Italians.

French:

BRUNEAU
La Rêve.
C. GOUNOD
Faust; Mireille.
MASSENET
Griselide; Jongleur de Notre Dame; Thais; Werther.
X. LEROUX
The Wayfarer; Le Chemineau.

L. DELIBES
Lakme.
R. LAPARRA
La Habanera.

MEHUL
Joseph in Egypt.

Italian:

V. BELLINI
I Puritani.
MONTEMEZZI
L'Amore de Tre Re.

LEONCAVALLO
Zaza.
G. VERDI
The Masked Ball.

German:

GLUCK
   Iphigenia in Aulis; Iphigenia in Tauris; Alceste.

BEETHOVEN
   Fidelio.

R. WAGNER
   Parsifal.

American:

H. PARKER
   Mona.

V. HERBERT
   Natoma.

Lyric comedy:

Italian:

PERGOLESE
   Il Maestro di Musica; Le Serva Padrona.

CIMAROSA
   Il Matrimonia Segreto.

A. PARELLI
   A Lovers' Quarrel.

G. VERDI
   Falstaff.

French:

H. RABAUD
   The Cobbler of Cairo.

German:

R. STRAUSS
   Rosenkavalier; Intermezzo.

English:

GILBERT & SULLIVAN
   Mikado; Pinafore; Patience; Princess Ida.

Comic opera or *Opera buffa:*

Italian:

DONIZETTI
   Don Pasquale; Elixir of Love; Daughter of the Regiment.

G. ROSSINI
   Barber of Seville; L'Italians in Algeri; La Cenerentola.

PUCCINI
   Gianni Schichi.

French:

M. RABAUD
   Marouf.

ROUSSEAU
   Le Devin du Village.

German:

LEO BLECH
That Was I; Versiegelt.

D'ALBERT
Tiefland; Abreise.

CORNELIUS
Barber of Bagdad.

H. GOETZ
Taming of the Shrew.

MOZART
Don Giovanni; Cosi Fan Tutte; Marriage of Figaro.

O. NICOLAI
Comic fantastic opera—Merry Wives of Windsor.

JOH. STRAUSS
The Bat.

R. WAGNER
The Meistersinger.

H. WOLF
The Correquidor.

Bohemian:

F. SMETANA
The Bartered Bride.

American:

DE KOVEN
Robin Hood.

R. PLANQUETTE
Chimes of Normandy.

Sentimental opera: This type presents a simple, happy tale.

Italian:

V. BELLINI
La Sonambula.

DONIZETTI
Linda de Chamouni.

P. MASCAGNI
L'Amico Fritz.

French:

AUBER
Fra Diavolo.

German:

K. GOLDMARK
Cricket on the Hearth.

The *Singspiel:*

German:

H. KOCH
The Devil Is Loose (1727).

Ballad Opera:

English:
J. GAY & PEPUSCH
The Beggar's Opera.

Impressionism: The "impressionistic" opera is not brutal; it reproduces "impressions" in music and has no large sentimental themes, no clear outlines in its music. Its main feature is vague "color" and beautiful tone handled in a delicate and refined way. Its subjects are usually unreal and symbolic; it does not show life as it is, but carries us in music and story to lands of revery. See works by Respighi, Malipiero, Pizetti, etc.

French:
DEBUSSY
Pellèas et Mélisande.

RAVEL
L'Heure Espanole.

Spanish:
DE FALLA
La Vida Breve.

Hungarian:
B. BARTOK
The Castle of the Knight.

Expressionism: The "expressionistic" opera is a symbolic form of play, i.e., other meanings underlie the stage action. It is rich in color and "sense music," combining the strongest kind of sex interest (morbid and unhealthy) with fantastic fairytale imaginings in story and music, the modern and the ancient, and developing the motive of sacrifice and renunciation.

German:
A. BERG
Wozzeck.

F. SCHRECKER
Treasure Hunter; Branded; Bell-Chime and the Princess; The Distant Tone.

American:
SCHÖNBERG
Expectation; The Lucky Hand (both expressionistic in dramatic technique and *atonal* in music).

Other (*recent*) operas:

BLACHER
   The Flood; The Night Swallow.

BUSSER
   La Carosse du St. Sacrament.

DELIUS
   Koanga; Hassan; Fenimore and Garda.

W. EGK
   Peer Gynt; Columbus; Circe.

VON EINEM Danton's Death.	FARINA Tempo di Carnevale.

HAAS
   Tobias Wunderlich; The Marriage of Job.

HOLST The Perfect Fool.	JANACEK From a Death House.
HINDEMITH Cardillac; News of the Day.	KRENEK Life of Orestes.

ORFF
   Carmina Curana; The Moon; Catulli.

POULENC Les Mamelles de Tiresies.	SCHOECK Don Renado; Penthesilea.

R. STRAUSS
   Danae's Love; Friedenstag; The Silent Woman.

STRAVINSKY
   The Soldier's Story; Emperor's Nightingale; Mavra;
   The Rake's Progress.

SUTERMEISTER Raskolnikov.	WEIL Mahagony.

Historical opera:

German:

K. GOLDMARK Queen of Sheba.	R. WAGNER Rienzi.

French:

   G. MEYERBEER
      Les Huguenots; Robert le Diable.

AUBER La Muette de Portici.	HALEVY La Juive.

Italian:

   ROSSINI
      William Tell.

American:

> F. CONVERSE
> The Sacrifice.

Mexican:

> A. GOMEZ
> The Guarany Indian.

Eclecticism: In eclectic operas the composer, in order to express his own original thoughts, borrows ways and means of expression, rhythms, tone combinations, etc., already existing for use in his own work. They are really original works, but using already established modes of expression.

German:

> K. GOLDMARK
> The Cricket on the Hearth; The Queen of Sheba.

> KIENZL
> Kuhreigen.

Russian:

> BORODIN
> Prince Igor.

> RIMSKY-KORSAKOV
> Snowmaiden.

> TSCHAIKOWSKY
> Eugene Onegin; Pique Dame.

Bohemian:

> FIBICH
> The Fall of Ancone.

Hungarian:

> F. ERKEL
> Hunyadi Laslo.

French:

> F. DUKES
> Allegorical grand opera—Ariane et Barbe-Bleue.

> JAN BLOCK
> The Tavern Princess.

Danish:

> H. BOERRESEN
> Kaddera.

American:

> C. W. CADMAN
> Shanewis; Dooma; Witch of Salem.

In order to appreciate opera, we should not only have a knowledge of form, but we should know and be able to recognize the more important themes. We must be able to listen to the orchestra, as well as to the singers, and have some knowledge of the plot; in short, we should be acquainted with the nature and purpose of operatic music. This may be obtained from music history and an examination into the internal evidence of opera music itself. True, few persons have the time to make such an examination; but the historical facts ought to be ascertained, especially when they are easily available in books.

The purpose of operatic music is to illustrate and vitalize the text. Unless it does this—or tries to do this—such music is not an art. Its value as a separate musical form is to enable the composer to express ideas, as distinct from sensations. Opera is not a work of art unless it is a play in which an attempt is made to express dramatic emotions in music. Consequently, the first and fundamental basis of judgment of an opera should be: Is there fidelity of its music to the text? The second question to be answered—and to serve as a basis of judgment—is: How eloquently does the music express the emotions contained in the text? The third question to be answered—also to serve as a basis of judgment—is: Is the music beautiful in itself?

The framework of an opera is the libretto. "Obviously, if the libretto is weak, or incongruous, the music is likely to be poor. The appropriateness of the music is the first requirement. If it is inappropriate, it does not make any difference how melodious or symmetrical it is—it is not good. It is by this test that so much of the old Italian opera music fails, pretty as it is." People usually read the libretto to learn the story of the opera, but they do not judge critically how the music voices the emotions contained in the text, and for this reason they fail in their appreciation. To quote Mr. Henderson: "Rossini's Semiramide affords the finest example of offense in this matter; and the reader who desires to know what an artistic opera should *not* be, will do well to study the charming music of this score in the light of the text." In the later works of Wagner, there are no set arias, duets, or ensembles; but the musical form follows that of the text, which is written freely, as it should be in the spoken drama. The result is that the music embodies in a faithful manner the emotions of the text. Indeed, Wagner's music dramas are the finest exponents of the true method of writing opera. In these works we find music, poetry, painting, and acting united as far as possible in any organic unity. Not only that, Wagner, through his work in opera practically revolutionized modern music, both with regard to content, form, and orchestral color.

To be sure, opera is the most popular form of musical entertainment, because in it music is made easy to understand by means of text and action. Opera is a most wonderful artistic creation, and it includes the vocal, scenic, poetic, lyric, dramatic, instrumental, choreographic, pictorial, and sculptural arts, besides history and pageantry. However, as program music, it is obviously not the highest form of music, because in it music is only a component part of a whole and is governed absolutely by the text. The only sort of unity possible or desirable in opera is unity of the underlying idea and of the musical style. Does it not follow from this that absolute music, i.e., music unaccompanied by a text, is the highest form of the art, simply because of its own inherent beauty?

Operas are classified according to the content and the nature of their words and their scope and treatment, such as: grand-opera seria (romantic, tragic, heroic, historic, realistic, impressionistic); comic opera; light opera—opera buffa (operetta, singspiel, etc., containing absurd situations, satirical comedy, and light music). Wagner's music dramas are usually classed as grand opera.

To write a genuine opera demands extraordinary intellectual endowment which finds expression naturally in music. This is quite different from the purely musical endowment of men like Bach, Beethoven, or Brahms.

The marks of a beautiful and reasonable opera are: a highly imaginative and significant drama in which action and reflection hold a proper balance, one which expresses truly and dramatically some great and moving passion or some elemental human motive; a complete union of the body and spirit of the drama with the body and spirit of music. A real opera has the same unity which exists in any of the other artistic forms. It is *one,* not several things.

Reasons for the continued popularity of opera are:

1.   The actual preference on the part of the public for the human voice over any instrument. Coupled with this is the delight the public takes in extraordinary vocal feats.

2.   When singing is combined with fascinating orchestral music, good acting, lovely costuming, fine scenery, and splendid lighting effects, the appeal is irresistible.

A few interesting questions:

1.   What kind of an opera is it?
2.   What is the nature of the plot, and where is the story laid?
3.   Is the music consistent with the words and the dramatic action?
4.   How many acts has it?
5.   Has it a formal overture or a prelude?
6.   Has it a fine ensemble—duets, trios, quartets, quintets, or sextets?
7.   Has it a ballet?
8.   Has it good chorus music? As opera, chorus music must be memorized and acted; generally, it is simple in construction. The chorus of the oratorio has no such restrictions, and thus often may mark the height of contrapuntal art.
9.   Are there vivid contrasts?
10.   What do you know about the composer?

There are three immortal comedies which are classed as grand opera: Mozart's The Marriage of Figaro; Rossini's The Barber of Seville; and Wagner's The Meistersinger.

Operas suitable for children:

BALFE
The Bohemian Girl.

FLOTOW
Martha.

HUMPERDINCK
Hänsel and Gretel; Königskinder.

MASSENET   MOZART
Cendrillon (fairy opera).   Marriage of Figaro.

OFFENBACH
Tales of Hoffmann.

ROSSINI
William Tell; Barber of Seville.

SMETANA   THOMAS
The Bartered Bride.   Mignon.

PLANQUETTE   VERDI
The Chimes of Normandy.   Aida.

WAGNER
Flying Dutchman; Tannhäuser; Lohengrin.

VON WEBER
Der Freischütz.

B. SACRED MUSIC

To repeat, vocal forms may be divided into *church mu-sic* and *secular music*, and each category again into *unison* and *part-songs*. The *Gregorian song* is entirely unison; it is a collection (made at the time of *Pope Gregory II*, d. A.D. 694) of liturgical melodies for the whole year. With few exceptions, the *Gregorian song* is the oldest music we have which is still practiced. It is very important for the study of Catholic church music not only because of its high musical value, its expressive melodic content, but also because its melodies have served as *themes or cantus firmus* for count-less part-songs, such as motets, magnificats, masses, etc.

The traditional psalm song was taken over by the early Christian Church service from the Jewish Temple service. The Greek-Christian liturgy practiced psalmody in the form of the *antiphone*, i.e., an exchange between two choruses singing in unison, a men's and a boys' choir. *Bishop Am-brosius of Milan* is credited with having introduced the antiphonic psalmody into the occidental churches. Nowa-days, psalmody means a hurried recitation upon one tone or only a few tones, with rising and falling of the voice at important interpunctations. This singing accompaniment to the accentuation of the words is also known as *accentus*. The notes are not divided into measures, and the first and last tones are held a little longer.

Chants and *canticles* (songs of praise), or other music in *plain song, or plain chant,* make use of the Gregorian modes. They form a part of various church services (Protestant Episcopal Church).

Chant: A short song consisting generally of a long reciting tone, on which an indefinite number of words and a melodic phrase or cadence may be intoned.

Single chant: This consists of two strains, the first of three measures and the second of four measures in length.

Double chant: It has the length of two single ones.

Antiphone: In the Christian Church, the antiphone is a verse first sung by a single voice and then repeated by the whole choir; or any piece to be sung by alternate voices.

1. HYMN

The *hymn* is a short religious song or part-song in stanzas, characterized by a devout spirit of worship or of exalted praise. It is designed to be sung by the congregation in the style that is effective for mass singing; and, therefore, it combines simplicity of form with fervor of sentiment. Hymns are divided into phrases corresponding to the lines of the sacred poem. Four-line stanzas of hymns are in the single-period form, antecedent and consequent, each extending for two lines; eight-line stanzas of hymns are usually in the two-period form, sometimes independent, sometimes with partial return.

Examples:

J. BARNBY
    O Paradise; Now the Day is Over; etc.

J. B. DYKES
    Lead Kindly Light; Holy, Holy, Holy; Alford; etc.

A. EWING   DE GIARDINI
    Jerusalem the Golden.   Come, Thou Almighty King.

HANDEL   W. MONK
    Awake, My Soul.   Abide With Me.

A. Sullivan
Onward, Christian Soldiers.

Old Hundred (Doxology). This melody derived its name from its association with Psalm 100, and may be traced as far back as 1551.

2. CHORALE

The *Chorale* is a hymn tune sung during church service by the congregation. The chorale is homophonic; it is based upon a melody sung by one voice, for which the other voices provide the harmony. It is strong and rugged in character, of stately dignity and transcendent beauty. This style of music came into the Church through the German Reformation. With the Lutheran Church came congregational singing and the need for a new style of composition, which should not only make the participation of the people in the singing possible, but should also stimulate them to sing by freeing the familiar melodies from the elaborate and ingenious but soulless counterpoint which fettered them. The chorale had a great influence on the rapid spread of the new ideas throughout Germany. The chorale is sung slowly and with dignity, in keeping with the sentiment of the text, with the last word of each line sustained. All chorales are strophic in form, consisting of from four to ten lines, and each strophe ends with a strong cadence and a pause (⌒).

Our idea of measured rhythm in music, and its notation in symbols, came from the application of prosody to music. (Rhythm is to music what meter is to poetry.) The chorale took the place of the Gregorian chant or plain-chant. The phrasing is regular in chorales, and each phrase is followed by a definite pause. Chorales become the foundation on which rests the basis of the art of music of later centuries. Chorales not only affected the structure of vocal music, but also of instrumental works. So the themes of measured music consist of phrases of 2 or 4 measures in length, separated by pauses which correspond to the punctuation of written language.

Examples:

J. S. BACH
: From Ill Do Thou Defend Me (Passion of St. Matthew).

J. CRÜGER (1647)
: Now Thank We All Our God.

M. LUTHER
: A Mighty Fortress Is Our God.

LUTHER-BACH
: From Heaven Above to Earth I Come.

ISAAC-BACH
: Now All the Woods Are Sleeping.

LUTHER-BACH
: Out of the Depths I Cry to Thee

DECIUS-BACH
: To God On High All Glory Be

NEUMARK-BACH
: If Thou But Suffer God to Guide Thee.

Offertory; Offertorio (Ital.); *Offertoire* (Fr.); *Offertorium* (Ger. and Latin) is the *anthem* or *motet* sung by the choir at the time of the collection of the alms from the congregation during the communion service. The Offertory may also be a piece of organ music performed during this time.

Example: Fr. Couperin—Offertory from Solemn Mass for use in Parishes.

3. ANTHEM

The *anthem* is a part-song or piece of music set to sacred words with accompaniment, usually to verses of the Psalms or other portions of the Bible or the liturgy, and is sung or chanted. It may be for one, two, three, or four voices, though seldom more than five parts. Originally, the term conveyed the idea of a hymn (antiphone), a choir answering choir in alternate parts, the one sung by one side of the choir, the other by the second side, or of responsive singing between choir and priest; but, at present, the anthem is a separate sacred composition sung as a part of church service. Anthems are written with or without solo voices, with or without organ or orchestral accompaniment. Anthems are generally much more ambitious and varied in style than hymns. A hymn, if sung by a congregation, is usually given in the soprano part as a unison melody.

There are three kinds of anthems: 1) *verse anthem,* which generally has only one voice to a part; 2) *full anthem with verse,* the latter performed by a single voice, the former by all the choir; 3) *full anthem,* performed by all the choir.

Examples:

GOUNOD   H. SMART
   Send Out Thy Light.   The Lord Is My Shepherd.

4. MOTETTE (MOTET)

The *motette* is a contrapuntal song similar to the madrigal—a part-song—but with sacred words (French, *le mot,* the word), having an introductory song followed by several fugal subjects, the whole ending with the exposition of the last subject, a repetition of its introduction, or a special final subject. Usually, each of the voices had its own text independent of the others. It was the most popular form of composition during the 13th and 14th centuries in France, from whence it was taken up in the Netherlands and in Italy. It had no instrumental accompaniment in its earliest form, and later the accompanied motet became very popular. At first, it appears to have been a secular song, but was adopted, with necessary modifications, by writers of sacred music. For the Latin text some excerpt from the Bible was taken, but often texts for motets were written expressly for an occasion. Almost anything could find its expression therein, as long as it kept to a rather dignified and solemn tone. The motet attained marked importance during the 16th century as a popular form in liturgical polyphony. It was used in Roman Catholic worship and usually was divided into two sections running continuously. It was freer in form than the fixed parts of the mass, and it never formed a permanent section of the ritual. The motet written for a particular holy day is sung between the Credo and the Sanctus of the mass. Often the motet is founded on the Gregorian tones of the text, and the mass founded on the same theme, so giving the whole service a musical unity.

There were *wedding motets* expressing good wishes; *funeral motets* expressing the praise of the dead; and the like. J. Deprès, Orlando di Lasso, Palestrina, Byrd, O. Gibbons, Tallis, J. S. Bach, and Handel have composed fine motets. Bach's motets, strictly speaking, are really cantatas; they have an entirely different structure.

The motet has also been used freely as a secular composition. The history of this form rather closely parallels the growth of that unaccompanied madrigal (its nonliturgical counterpart), which it rivaled in beauty and wealth of output.

Examples:

J. S. BACH
Seven Motets (Peters Ed.).

ARCADELT
Ave Maria.

DUFAY
Salve Virge.

J. DEPRES
Ave Vera Virginitas.

T. LUIS DE VITTORIA
Domine Non Sum Dignus (4-part); Jesu Dulcia Memoria.

5.   MASS

The *mass* is music for church service of the Roman Catholic Church. It is written for chorus, solo, organ, or orchestral accompaniment. The mass uses a *cantus firmus* which sometimes is taken either from a Gregorian chant, a motet, or from a secular song. Considerable thematic development is the rule. The mass is always composed to the same prescribed text. It is the most elaborate form of sacred music next to the oratorio, to which it is closely related. It reaches its highest point in the genius of J. S. Bach. There are six principal parts in the traditional mass, following the *Introduction;* a *Kyrie eleison* (Lord have mercy upon us); *Gloria in Exelsis* (Glory to God in the Highest—including also the *Qui tollis, Quoniam,* and *Cum Sancto Spirito*); *Credo* (Creed—containing also *Et Incarnatus, Et resurrexit,* and *Amen*); *Sanctus* (Holy is God)—with the *Honsanna; Benedictus qui venit* (Blessed is He); and the *Agnes Dei* (Lamb of God—Give us mercy and peace), the latter part of which, the *Dona nobis pacem*, is often treated by itself.

Great composers of the mass are: Palestrina; J. Deprès; di Lassus; Hassler; Vittorio; Haydn; Mozart (12th Mass, etc.); Schubert; Cherubini; Rossini; Weber; Gounod (Messe Solemnelle, etc); Bruckner; and others. Other composers of the mass are: J. S. Bach (Mass in B minor, the greatest of all masses; etc.); Beethoven (Mass in D). They all wrote elaborate masses, but they are rarely heard in church service, as these works are considered too long and too operatic in style. In fact, these masses are intended for concert performance.

The *requiem* (*Missa pas Defunctis*) is a mass in honor of the dead. It is generally shorter than the regular mass; it omits the Gloria and contains instead a *Requiem Aeternam dona eis* (Eternal rest given to them), *Lux aeterna* (Eternal Light), and *Dies Irae* (a 13th century Latin poem describing the Day of Judgment). The Dies Irae poem, composed by Thomas de Celano, is subdivided into Dies Irae, Tuba Mirum, Recordare, and Lachrymosa, as separate numbers. *Te Deum laudamus* (We praise Thee O God), an ancient Christian hymn, is used by the Roman Catholic Church.

Requiems have been composed by Palestrina; Vittorio; Anerio; Vecchi; Mozart; Cherubini; Brahms; Verdi; etc.

(Note: The Gregorian chant is based upon a melodic and rhythmic system different from the church tunes of our time.)

Examples:

Kyrie and Gloria, from the Ordinary of the Mass.
Tenebrae factas sunt (describing death of Christ on the Cross).

6. ORATORIO

The *oratorio* is a composition on a large scale for chorus, solo airs, recitatives, duets, trios, quartets, full orchestra, and sometimes organ accompaniment, given in concert form but without scenery, costuming, or setting. The text is sacred and usually based upon biblical themes or events. Besides sacred oratorios, there are also secular ones. The oratorio appeals to one's highest nature; contemplation is pre-eminent. It has lyricism of an introspective nature, rich harmonies, sublime choruses, spiritual exaltation; it is majestic and depends for its strong emotional effect on the choruses. The chorus assumes greater importance than the soloists. Dignity and grandeur are distinctive qualities.

Passion is the name for the musical dramatic representation of the suffering of Christ on Golgotha, according to the words of the scriptures. It is a special form of oratorio developed in the German Lutheran Church. In short, the Passion is a German transformation of the oratorio imported from Italy, treating the narrative of Christ's suffering and death in recitative, with intertwining airs and choruses, introducing the German chorale, and thereby evolving a new composition of great dignity, devotional expression, and exalted pathos. As early as the 12th century it was customary to give a Passion to commemorate Good Friday. The active persons were the priests, taking the part of Jesus and the apostles, and the people were represented by the chorus. In the 17th century, the Passion was changed into a different form. Schütz was the originator of the new form, while J. S. Bach brought it to the highest development.

The older oratorio consisted for the most part of set movements bound together by recitatives, which enabled a continuous story to be told.

The modern oratorio differs from the older style in that the set pieces are not used and the work is made continuous. The solo voice no longer has airs written according to some type of musical form; neither are the choruses' elaborations of a musical pattern, nor are the same words repeated again and again. The voice and orchestral parts are skillfully interwoven. The oratorio and the opera now have their musical elements of expression in common.

In the long and varied career of the oratorio and the opera, the attempt to unite the two arts of music and literature has resulted in many different styles and forms which are difficult to group under a single head. Generally speaking, two styles of oratorios are used—the epic and the dramatic. In the *epic oratorio,* the singers merely narrate the text in the vocal guise (Handel's The Messiah); in the *dramatic oratorio,* each singer represents a certain character (Handel's Samson). A combination of the two styles is found in Mendelssohn's Elijah, and St. Paul.

The *Stabat Mater* is a medieval Latin poem depicting the sufferings of the Virgin Mary at the Cross. The poem was written by Jacobus de Benedictis in the 13th century. It has received numerous musical settings. Other shorter Latin poems that are often set to music include *Ave Maria, Veni Creator, O Salutaris.*

Examples:

J. S. BACH
    The Passion, According to St. Matthew.

BEETHOVEN
    Mount of Olives.

BRAHMS
    German Requiem.

ELGAR
    The Dream of Gerontius.

C. FRANCK
    The Beatitudes.

HANDEL
    Judas Maccabeus; Messiah; Israel in Egypt; Joseph; Samson; Solomon; Japhtha; Saul; Belshazzar.

GOUNOD
    The Redemption.

HAYDN
    The Creation; The Seasons.

R. KAISER
    Passion.

LISZT
    St. Elizabeth.

MENDELSSOHN
    Elijah; St. Paul; Hymn of Praise.

PARKER
    Hora Novissima.

PARRY
    Job.

PIERNE
    The Children's Crusade.

ROSSINI
    Stabat Mater.

SAINT-SAENS
    Christmas Oratorio.

SCHUMANN
    Paradies and Peri.

SCHÜTZ
    The Passion, According to St. Matthew.

SPOHR
    The Last Judgment.

STRAVINSKY
    Oedipus Rex.

6

INSTRUMENTAL MUSIC

INTRODUCTION
DEVELOPMENT OF INSTRUMENTAL MUSIC

WE pointed out before that the folk-song and the folk-dance tunes are the first and simplest patterns in music. From them many different forms were evolved during the classical period of musical history. Instrumental music is one of the greatest achievements of the 17th century. It began as a mere adaptation to choral music; and, little by little, composers found out the changes that were necessary or inevitable when the music was to be played rather than sung. Thus was evolved a style of its own. Gradually, men became more proficient on the various instruments and combined these into groups; so the early simple forms developed into the more intricate and complicated "old" suite, sonata, quartet, theme and variations, symphony, and tone poem.

Much music is written in the song form but is not intended for singing. Similarly, many compositions bear the names of dances that have nothing to do with dancing as such. Many of these gavottes, minuets, tarantellas, mazurkas, waltzes, etc., of Chopin and others, are simply idealized dance forms.

We need to remember that the most elaborate piece of music may show a form that is really related to the simple *A B A, or I II I, form*—namely, *statement, contrast, and restatement*—and that most of the melodies, whether slow or fast, show rhythmic patterns that go back to actual dance measures. If the ear has become accustomed to recognizing the various patterns in the simple forms, it will gradually acquire the habit of following the formal outlines of more elaborate works, so that eventually a fugue, a sonata, a symphony, or a tone poem may become as clear to the listener as the plot of a story or play.

A *composition*—musical or literary—*is a development of ideas*. Music contains ideas which must be recognized if we are to listen intelligently. A musical idea is the smallest number of tones having individuality and independence—notice the motive, phrase, or theme. An idea may be expressed through various keys, rhythms, tempos, and orchestral colors for the purpose of giving variety, but its individuality must not be destroyed. The criterion of artistic genius is: the creation of something containing variety while also preserving the sense of unity.

Instrumental works are divided into two classes: *absolute* (*abstract, or pure*) music; and *program* (*representative*) music.

Absolute, or classic music, i.e., music without any words or descriptive material, which does not appeal through associations with literary and illustrative ideas to make its meaning clear, depends largely upon form for its effect. Form, i.e., definite laws of structure and development, is the chief factor in making music coherent, and, in a sense, articulate or expressive.

Proportion, balance, repetition, contrast, unity, recognizable musical ideas and infinite resources in handling the fluid medium of sound—all combine to convey emotions, imaginative conceptions, and even suggestions of all sorts of things in nature and in life without the aid of words, specific titles, or any implied program.

Absolute music must have well-balanced proportions, clear and understandable harmonies, and clearly defined melodies. It emphasizes form, or design; and as perfection of form is an intellectual process; this kind of music makes an intellectual appeal. Absolute music is pure; it depends upon nothing but its own inherent beauty. It can release the spirit from all other conceptions of a definite nature and express what is inexpressible through any other medium. It can stir the emotions, the imagination, and the spirit of man. It can suggest things that only man's spirit can understand, things that lie deep in our subconsciousness. In form and content it is governed by the same law of order that saves the universe from chaos and underlies all beauty in nature. The beauty is there for those who have ears to hear; and what it may mean or suggest depends upon the inner feeling of the listener. Absolute music is concerned with musical imagination only and contains no indication that the experience or thought is derived from the external world. It represents nothing but itself, as it is related to nothing outside itself. Works of this type have no precise titles. Any designation will do—such as fugue, prelude, sonata, variation, rondo, andante, adagio, etc., and will be applicable to a large number of pieces of quite the same character.

For examples see works by Bach, Buxtehude, Scarlatti, Palestrina, Handel, Haydn, Brahms, as well as some compositions by Beethoven.

(Note: Unless they are writing program music, good composers, as a rule, do not attempt to evoke a definite image in the mind, as the painter does in a picture, but rather to create a definite atmosphere. If the listener will examine, for example, the titles of R. Schumann's Opus 68, he will realize at once what this means. Some titles exceed others in their definiteness in expressing the musical contents of the piece; while in others atmosphere, and not picture, predominates.)

Program (*romantic*) *music* is a type of music that tells a story, suggests things in nature and life, or portrays racial or national characteristics without the aid of words but with a specific title, description, text, or any implied program. Generally speaking, the more definite and detailed a program is, the easier it will be for the music to make us aware of what we hear. This definite title creates in our minds a picture of what the music is trying to express through sounds, such as character, an actual picture, a definite, plain, or dramatic story (narrative) from history, myth, or poetry, some observation of nature—bird calls, wind, rain, storm, etc. —or human life. It suggests to us poetic ideas. Program music places content above form and may be merely suggestive and poetic or realistic. It is free from formalism; it supplies more for our emotions than our intellects.

For many centuries music was invariably associated with other things, with ritual and the dance, with poems and dramas, with religion, war, and ceremonial events. No wonder most people think only in terms of expressing this or that "through music," even though our civilization has produced absolute music.

Every connection of music with other ideas diminishes the hearer's responsibility as an active listener. Whenever words give a clue, or associated ideas lend a meaning, the activity of the listener is lessened. His imagination is guided; his emotional reactions are motivated. Clearly, the addition of music to other ideas presents no great difficulty. It surely enhances most ideas to which it is added. But to combine music with other ideas on terms of equality requires genius of the highest order, because the essence of music is so different from anything else.

Music written with some literary background in mind need not be less valuable than that which was created out of "purely musical emotion." It communicates to us a conception of inherent beauty and organic unity. In listening to program music, we have to consider the program plus the music and must decide continually how the music carries out the literary idea. It requires a well-balanced, creative mind to write fine program music, to adjust the pictorial and emotional elements in a piece of music to the point where esthetic criticism approves of all. Naturally, opinions differ as to the value of program music, of both the objective and subjective order. Tastes differ and *few people hear or think alike.*

It is unfair to expect program music to be as effective when we do not know the story as when we do; also, a good story cannot make up for poor music. Considering these points of view, we may thoroughly enjoy both program music and absolute music. Each has its special beauties, and the true music-lover enjoys them all.

No doubt, absolute instrumental music (fugues, toccatas, sonatas, symphonies) requires the highest degree of purely musical inspiration. It is an art form in pure sound capable of stirring the emotions, the imagination, and the spirit of man. Of course, this does not mean that program music cannot be great. But great program music is music that can stand alone. Note, for instance, Haydn's Surprise Symphony; Beethoven's 6th "Pastorale" Symphony; Berlioz' Symphony Fantastique; R. Strauss' tone poems; and the mystical works of Scriabine. Such music, devoid of its program, still retains its greatness. It can stand alone.

Often the progress of a program conditions musical form. Such a possibility frees the composition from rigid adherence to any of the existing plans of musical composition.

The division of instrumental music into "representative" and "presentative" has value only as a means of classification. In a deeper sense, all arts are presentative as well as representative, impressive as well as expressive, for they exist primarily to give pleasure and secondarily only to give instruction or to reproduce nature.

Examples of Program Music:

A. BAX
November Woods; Tintagel; The Garden of Fand.

BEETHOVEN
Overture to Fidelio (Leonore); Overture to Egmont; Overture to Coriolanus; Symphony Eroica, #3; Symphony Pastoral, #6.

J. S. BACH
Phoebus and Pan (illustrating the braying of the ass).

H. BERLIOZ
Overture to Roman Carnival; Overture to Romeo and Juliet; Symphony Fantastique.

BORODIN
In the Steppes of Central Asia.

DUKAS
Sorcerer's Apprentice.

DEBUSSY
Children's Corner; The Afternoon of a Faun.

C. Franck
Le Chasseur Maudit.

C. Gounod
Funeral March of a Marionette.

Gluck
Orpheus (depicting vividly the flames of hell).

d'Indy   Holbrooke
Trilogy, Wallenstein.   The Raven.

Ippolitov-Ivanov
Caucasian Sketches.

Liszt
Liebestraum; Waldesrauschen; Mephisto Waltz; tone
poems; Les Preludes; Orpheus; Tasso; Francesca da
Rimini; Mazeppa; etc.

Mendelssohn
Overture to Fingal's Cave; Italian Overture; Scotch
Overture; Calm Sea; Spring Song; Spinning Song; Mid-
summernight's Dream; etc.

H. Purcell
Masque, Venus and Adonis (illustrates braying of
hounds when Adonis goes a-hunting).

Rachmaninoff
The Island of the Dead (after a painting by Böcklin).

Rimski-Korsakov
Scheherazade; Flight of the Bumble Bee; The Russian
Easter; Sadko.

Schubert
The Bee.

Schumann
Davidsbündler Dances; Papillons; Kreisleriana; Kinderscenen.

Smetana
Six tone poems, My Fatherland; string quartet, Aus
meinem Leben.

Saint-Saens
Dance Macabre; Carnival of the Animals; Le Rouet
d'Omphale; La Jeunesse d'Hercule.

Tschaikowsky
Symphony #4, #5, #6; Overture to Romeo and Juliet;
Overture to Francesca da Rimini; Ballet of the Seasons;
Nutcracker Suite; etc.

R. Strauss
Tone poems, Till Eulenspiegel; Don Juan; Don Qui-
chote; Tod und Verklärung; Heldenleben; also Sprach
Zarathustra; etc.

I. Stravinsky
Ballets; The Fire Bird; Petrouchka; Sacre de Printemps.

R. Wagner
All his operas.

1.   POLYPHONIC FORMS

There are two great classes of forms—*polyphonic* (*contrapuntal*), or *many-voiced,* in which two or more mutually
independent melodies are heard simultaneously; and *homophonic* (*monophonic*), or *one-voiced,* in which a melody appears either singly or is accompanied by chords.

The *homophonic* forms make their repetition within the
limits of a single-voiced melody having a subsidiary accompaniment. The single-voiced melody has a succession of
tones conceived as an organic part of a succession of chords,
but of which the accompaniments are formed. Thus, harmony is the support of melody by chords; while counterpoint is the support of melody by melody. *Homophonic
music runs vertically.* Its simplest form is the song, and its
highest, the symphony. The entire range of musical works
within the homophonic domain may be approximately divided into three general classes, or styles, of compositions:

1.   The lyric—element of melody predominates
2.   The étude—element of harmony predominates
     (exercise, study, etc.)
3.   The dance—element of rhythm predominates.

The *polyphonic* (many-voiced) forms make their repetition (at a distance of one or more measures) in a second
voice, which is always sung or played by a first voice. It is a
melody repeated at different intervals by different voices,
and forming its own harmonies—*counterpoint* (*puntus contra punctum,* "point against point," or note against note).
Counterpoint is the science of making two or more voices,
or parts, move together with such freedom that seemingly
they are independent, each part with a design of its own.
In other words, it *is the science of combining melodies,* in-

stead of supporting a melody by chords. *Polyphonic music runs horizontally,* each part creating a harmony with other parts by overlapping rather than by a definite concentration on several tones at a time, as in a chord. This means that when polyphonic music produces definite harmonies, they occur by accident, not by design. Through all such music there runs a clear pattern of interlocking melodies. Counterpoint is an important branch of music; and to a good composer its mastery is indispensable. Contrapuntal music had its origin about the year 1250 and was developed into a science by the early Flemish composers. Note the excellent use of polphony in: *Palestrina* (1525–1594), Motet; Sicut Servus; *O. Gibbons* (1583–1625), Madrigal; *a capella,* The Silver Swan; *J. S. Bach* (1685–1750), Concerto for two Violins; *Mozart* (1756–1791), Overture to Magic Flute.

The subject, or melody, against which the counterpoint is to be written is called the *"cantus firmus,"* and the counterpoint itself, *"discantus."*

Counterpoint can be single, double, triple, quadruple, quintuple, etc.

Single counterpoint: The position of the *discantus* and the *cantus firmus* are fixed and cannot be inverted (above or below each other).

Double counterpoint: The position of the two voices can be inverted so that the lower part may become the subject, and the subject the lower part, etc., thus producing new melodics and new harmonies.

Triple counterpoint: The writing of three voices or parts in such a manner that they may be placed in any order, above or below each other, yet form correct progressions in any of the six resulting positions.

Quadruple counterpoint: This is rather a mathematical problem than music, for each note is so rigidly dictated by rule that all freedom is lost.

There are five different varieties of counterpoint:

1. The different parts show note against note; that is, the *cantus* and the *discantus* have notes which are struck simultaneously, and are of equal length.

2. Two (or sometimes three) notes of *discantus* (accompanied part) show for each one in the *cantus firmus* (fixed theme).

3. Four notes against one of the subject.

4. *Syncopated counterpoint*—each note of the *discantus* begins when a note of the *cantus firmus* is half-done.

5. *Florid counterpoint* (free counterpoint) makes use of all the preceding kinds in a single composition. It is most usually found in classical works, and is said to have been introduced by Jean de Muris (University of Paris, about 1330).

The polyphonic instrumental works of J. S. Bach and his school were called by such names as: prelude; canon; invention; fugue; toccata; fantasy. But as a complete account of these forms here would lead too far afield, we will confine ourselves to a description of a few.

Imitation is a less demanding and often more attractive form than the canon. A melody may be imitated in an inverted form—turning the notes upside down; or letting them move in the opposite direction (contrary motion) to the original design; or it may even have some of its individual intervals augmented or diminished by moving them half a tone upward or downward. The imitation may take place at any interval or at any part of the measure.

The principles of polyphonic music are most simply illustrated in the round and canon.

The *round* is a composition for two, three, or more voices, so arranged that, although each singer or player has the same part, by starting at different times a harmonic effect is produced. As each voice comes to the end of the song, it starts over again from the beginning.

Examples:

Three Blind Mice.   Merrily, Merrily.
Lovely Evening (Old German).
Sumer Is Icumen In (Old English; oldest round known)
Come Mirth (St. Paxton, 1735–1787).
Early to Bed.   The Huntsman.

When the imitation is strict and continuous, a *canon*

results. The canon (from the Greek, *strict rule,* or law) is a composition in which the several voices begin one after another, each successive voice intoning precisely the same melody and the rhythmic pattern. Because the repetition is exact, the canon is said to be in *strict imitation.* Imitation is usually in the octave, above or below; but it may also be in the 2nd, 3rd, 4th, 5th, 6th, 7th, 9th, or 10th. If the imitation uses the same tones as the subject, the canon is *in the unison;* if it uses those a tone higher, the canon is *in the second;* etc.

Canons can be in the song form, rondo, or similar forms.

Canons are classified as: *simple canon* (one subject is exactly imitated, at any interval or distance, by one or more voices); *double canon* (two subjects are similarly imitated by two or more voices); *free canon* (the subject is imitated, but not exactly, mutation or changes taking place in the imitating voice); *canon in contrary motion* (the imitating voice inverts the subject, instead of repeating it exactly); *endless canon* (*infinite canon*) (so contrived that the theme is begun before the parts which follow are concluded; and while the imitating voice giving the last part, the subject accompanies this with its first phrase, so giving further material for imitation, leading into the canon again, making it endless); *canon in augmentation* (the imitating voice reproduces the subject, but in notes of a larger denomination); *canon in diminution* (the subject is imitated in notes of a smaller denomination). Then there are: the *Circle Canon,* the *reversible canon,* and the *enigma canon.* The *finite canons* end with a cadence. (See Rätsel by Weitmann; other varieties of canons may be found in Richter, Cherubini, Stainer, Jadassohn, Gurlitt, etc.)

Examples:

J. S. BACH
Goldberg Variations.

BEETHOVEN
Quartet C minor, Opus 131, second movement. (Note the imitation which begins when the second instrument takes up the melody after it has been introduced.)

DVORAK
Slavonic Dance #7. (The same tune is given out by
the oboe and bassoon, the bassoon beginning a measure later than the oboe.)

C. FRANCK
Violin Sonata, 3rd movement (first theme in canon).

HAYDN
Quartet D minor, Opus 76, #2 (minuet is in strict
canon).

FR. KIEL   A. KLENGEL
Canon for Piano, Opus 1.   Canons et Fugues.

REINECKE
Dialogue, Opus 107, #22.

SCHUMANN
Album for the Young, Opus 68, #27; Opus 124, #20;
Etudes Symphonic; Variations.

Invention: This is a short piece in contrapuntal style
aimed to show ingenuity, somewhat in the informal style of
an improvisation. It usually has two motives, one contrasting
with the other.

Examples are J. S. Bach's 15 Two-Part Inventions; also,
Three-Part Inventions.

Inversions: They are a special type of form in double or
triple counterpoint. At the beginning comes the theme and
one or more counterthemes, and the whole piece is developed out of these motives by means of inversions of voices,
as well as various combinations of these inversions.

(Note: *Symmetrical Inversion,* according to B. Ziehn, is
the strict inversion of a complete 2- or 3-voice part so that
each tone going upward is answered in the same interval
by a tone going downward, and vice versa; at the same time,
they also change their voices—i.e., the soprano voice becomes
the bass, the alto becomes the tenor, and vice versa. The intervals [major, minor, diminished, augmented, etc.] are
retained as originally written in the complete melody, or
theme, but the tonality changes completely and so often
causes entirely new chordal combinations.)

Fugue (from Latin *fuga*—flight): A fugue is a composition written in strict polyphonic style according to laws laid
down by the older masters, of which J. S. Bach is the ac-

cepted head of the school of fugue-writers. It represents the highest form of polyphonic music—*it runs horizontally*. In this form of composition one part seems to fly before the other, the voices joining in a continuous chase. The constant motion is the characteristic of the fugue. Among all musical forms the fugue follows strict logic. A fugue really is the art of creating an artistic whole from a single motive of a few tones. It becomes more interesting as it proceeds; it moves uninterruptedly to a climax; it moves toward a goal and reaches it. Some of the most powerful, dynamic, and intense works of art are found in fugal forms. A fugue sounds rather complicated, yet its structure is really a simple one. The fugue really demands an active attention to details, and it should be listened to with care. A number of great fugues should be heard several times, and a count should be made of the entries of the subject; also, the ways in which fragments of the main material are used either as a whole or in part should be noted, as well as the presence of any new material. The fugue consists of one movement, but with it is very commonly associated a *prelude* of some kind, the two together making a work in two movements. The fugue includes somewhat distinct sections or parts.

The required parts of a fugue are:

A. *Exposition:* This consists of the *subject*, the *answer*, and the *countersubject*, *episodes*, and *strettos*, which alternate with one another. The subject is the theme, the fundamental melody. It usually is four measures long, and is introduced without any accompaniment. The subject may be only a few notes in length; it need not be beautiful in itself, as the merit of the composition depends rather on the manner in which it is treated; finally, the subject should be a complete musical phrase and, generally, end on an accent. The answer is the correlative of the subject; it is simply the subject repeated by a second voice, immediately, at a different pitch, either in the fifth above or in the fourth below. The answer may be rather exact (real) or it may contain mutations (tonal); it generally enters at the end of the subject, but this rule is not invariable. Meanwhile, the first voice goes on, very often using a second theme, known as the "countersubject." The countersubject is that part of the melody which is so constructed as to form the accompaniment to the answer. The countersubject serves as an accompaniment to the subject or the answer, as they appear after the first entrance of the subject, in the exposition, but it is more than a mere accompaniment, for it is intertwined in all possible combinations with the subject and answer. It should be in double counterpoint with the subject, appearing either above or below. After this a third voice takes the theme, now on some octave from its original pitch, and known again as the subject. In the meantime the second voice, which has finished the answer, takes up the countersubject in a transposed position; while the first voice, which has finished the countersubject, becomes a free part for the time being. This process continues until the subject or answer has appeared in all the voices and the countersubject in all but one. Up to this point, it is called the "exposition."

A fugue begins with one of the voices giving out the subject; then soon another voice comes in with the subject, so now there are two voices going on together; then comes a third voice with the subject, and so on, until all the voices have had their turn, very similar to a round. However, there is this difference: the first voice brings in the subject in the proper key of the fugue; the second brings in the subject in the key of five tones higher or four tones lower; the third brings it in the old key again; and so on.

B. The *Development:* A development portion now follows in which all the voices are used, giving subject, answer, or new material and episodes (or digressions) often of considerable extent, the whole section culminating in an extended passage on a sustained or repeated bass-note, known as *pedal-point or organ-point.* The development concludes with a closing section in which there is a return to the original key. Sometimes this portion of the fugue is brought to an ending by a short duet between the voices, which is called a "codetta."

A fugue, like a story, has *episodes.* The author leaves the main plot of the story for a moment and goes on to tell a little incident that is not really part of the main plot but still has something to do with it. A fugue has episodes like that; they usually are made up of some little bit of the subject or countersubject. The first episode takes us into some other key, and then the subject comes in again; then follows a second episode and a further entry of the subject in still another key; and so on, to the end of the fugue, where the subject comes back at last in the old key—the main key of the piece.

The development of fugal material is largely a matter of variety of keys. It consists of a series of episodes, passages in free style. Very often their material is derived from the subject, or countersubject, or both, but they also may be wholly independent. Each episode leads to a new key in which all the subjects appear.

J. S. Bach, in his major fugues, often leads from the exposition to the dominant key; then to the relative minor; then the super-tonic-minor; the mediant-minor; and, finally, to the dominant or subdominant. In the minor fugues this succession is often used: dominant minor, relative major, subdominant major, and dominant or subdominant minor.

C. The *Recapitulation:* Finally, by way of restatement, the original key is brought back. The theme, as subject and answer, is again presented by all the voices in turn, sometimes in reverse order and often with a crowding or overlapping of the entries, one voice entering with the subject before the other has finished it. This is called the "stretto," the whole leading to a climax of great intensity. The subject of the fugue ends in its own key.

The *Coda* appears after the last Stretto, and it often features the subdominant prominently. It ends with a *ritenuto*.

The wonder of the fugue lies in the fact that so much is made out of so little material, that it achieves unity in variety in such a compact and logical manner. Really, there is only one melody, the countersubject being derived from it. The fugue supplies only a contrast of keys and possibly an inversion and augmentation or diminution within the limits of its own subject, while the sonata displays a strong thematic contrast.

If we know how a fugue is made, it is not very hard to understand it; until at last, listening to a fugue (or playing it) becomes a great pleasure in our lives. It is worth a little study and effort. A fugue is entirely, or almost entirely, contrapuntal. It may be in three, four, or five voices. When listening to a fugue, ask yourself these questions:

> How many voices has this fugue?
> How many episodes after the exposition?
> Has it any stretto?
> Can you remember the subject and identify it not only as it first enters in each voice, but later on as it reappears again and again?

(Note: The fugue was not fit to express the lyrical and dramatic qualities of the opera. Something new demanded to be expressed, and new ways were found for expressing it. The richer harmonic resources of the new music expresses the new ideas about life.)

Music, like the other fine arts, has evolved from the simple to the more complex (quantitatively); but it does not follow that the contents involved have risen higher in any valuational sense (qualitatively). The simple folk song or chant may be just as profound in "content" as a big symphony. Complexity of means of expression has nothing to do with complexity or profundity of content.

In the fugue the musical content is not the theme itself but what is done with the theme; in a sonata the musical content comes into existence only with the changes the theme undergoes.

The problem of form in music, as we all know, is peculiar, *because the art of music exists in the dimension of time.* Any auditory conception of *a musical whole requires the aid of repetition*—one of memory's most useful helps. By a liberal use and artful manipulation of the device of repetition the fugue satisfies our formal requirements with rather little labor. One other point: it is peculiar to music that it has the ability to propound two or three contrasting ideas simultaneously. Thus, the fugue deliberately narrows its expressive potentialities.

Devices used in fugues:

1. *Inversion:* The theme, or subject, is turned upside down, while retaining its identity by means of its rhythm.
2. *Augmentation:* The length of notes is doubled, while their relative length, or rhythm, is carefully maintained.
3. *Diminution:* The length of notes is halved, while their relative length, or rhythm, is carefully maintained.
4. *Shifted rhythm:* The position of the theme is shifted in the measure, so that all the accents fall differently.

Fugues may be classified as follows:

Single fugue: A fugue with a single subject.

Double fugue: A fugue having two subjects in succession. (See J. S. Bach's The Art of the Fugue; Mozart's Requiem, 1st movement—Kyrie eleison.)

Triple fugue: A fugue having three subjects in different combinations. (See J. S. Bach's Fugue E major, Triple Fugue for Organ; and C♯ minor Fugue.)

Four-voiced fugue: A fugue so identified by the number of voices (subjects) used.

Real Fugue: A fugue in which the answer uses exactly the same intervals as the subject.

Tonal Fugue: A fugue in which the intervals of the subject are changed in the answer to keep the fugue in the same key.

Diatonic fugue: A fugue constructed according to diatonic scale without accidentals.

Chromatic Fugue: A fugue in which a wholly chromatic subject is used.

Chorale Fugue: A fugue with a chorale inserted at the end of a section, or at the real end. (See Mendelssohn's E minor Fugue for Piano, Opus 35; M. Reger's Psalm 100.)

Gegenfuge (Contrast Fugue): A fugue in which the subject is answered by inverting it. (See J. S. Bach's Art of the Fugue #5, 6, 7, 14.)

Gregorian Fugue: A fugue classified according to Gregorian scale used (doric fugue, etc.).

Augmented Fugue: A fugue in which the answer is augmented.

Inverted Fugue: A fugue in which the answer is inverted, etc. (according to treatment given the answer).

Strict Fugue: A fugue composed according to the rules.

Free Fugue: A fugue not written according to the rules.

Fughetta: A very short fugue consisting of an exposition and a few episodes.

A *fugal passage* is a passage that suggests fugal treatment, often with omissions, reductions, and other freedom of treatment. Therefore, it is not a definite form but a sort of improvisation, a free fantasy in the style of imitation.

Intelligent and fair criticism of a fugue is only possible to one who is fully acquainted with its laws. However, any person can make a pretty good estimate of a fugue who knows the general principle of polyphony. The listener to a fugue should identify the subject and watch for the answer. He should notice whether it is direct, inverted, augmented, or diminished. At the same time, he should hear the counter-subject and try to remember it. After that, he should follow the interweaving of the melodic parts and discover whatever ingenious and striking effects are produced by them. After all, the main question is: Does it sound well? Is it beautiful within the field of polyphonic writing, or is it ugly? If it has balance, symmetry, clarity, and logical development, it has beauty. "The fugue is an intellectual piece of music, and it must be studied with the intellect." He who listens for rhythm and melody only will be disappointed in all fugues, even those of J. S. Bach.

The polyphonic in music was developed in the interval between 1100 and the time of J. S. Bach, 1750. With the growth of the new interest in chords and harmonies, and the settling of the system of keys and scales, which was completed in the time of Bach, harmony became the major interest of composers, and polyphony was used less and less often. That is why music from Bach's time on sounds so much more familiar to us; the composers were thinking in terms of harmony, as we do. Before that time, for thousands of years, music probably consisted of only one part—that is, all in unison. No records exist to prove that the primitive and ancient peoples had part-music. The only authentic knowledge we have is that *organum, or double melody,* was invented in the 10th century A.D. Nothing has been added to the laws of the fugue since Bach's day. One who desires to comprehend fully the scope and power of polyphonic church music should study the *a capella* music of *di Lasso* and *Palestrina;* while for perfection in the instrumental form, he should devote his attention to Bach's fugues. To quote Mr. Henderson: "In studying the polyphonic works, one should recognize their intellectual and emotional characteristics. First, note the profundity of the musical learning. Contrapuntal writing is the most learned kind of composition, because every measure must be made in obedience to fixed laws. Second, note the mastery of musical material. Third, note the serenity of the emotional atmosphere—one seeks in vain for the note of dramatic passion which found its way into artistic music after the birth of opera, and the adoption of the melodic style of the folk song."

Let us not be ignorant nor take the wrong attitude with reference to polyphonic music; let us try to understand its character and its style of construction. At its best (as in J. S. Bach), it is very expressive—but it must be performed and listened to intelligently.

The most important set of compositions for the piano, no doubt, is Bach's Well-Tempered Clavichord. It contains 48 beautiful preludes and fugues in all the keys, both major and minor. Another important work in this line is Bach's Inventions in 2- and 3-parts. They are written in a simpler polyphonic style, and some of these little pieces serve as the best possible introduction to J. S. Bach. Bach's fugues are very elaborate works; some of the greatest were written for organ. *Bach's music can be heard for a lifetime, never losing its appeal, but continually unfolding new beauties.* It has the power of any great work of art—first, it makes us long to know it better; and second, it has power to arouse and hold our steady affection.

Examples of fugues:

J. S. BACH
Well-Tempered Clavichord (Ditson Edition #352, 353) Volume II, #7, is a clear example of a 4-voiced fugue, a tonal fugue, and a free fugue.

BEETHOVEN
Fugue, Quartet in C, Opus 59, #3.

C. FRANCK
Prelude, Choral and Fugue.

HANDEL
Hallelujah Chorus (Messiah); Fugue in D major; Fugue in A major.

MENDELSSOHN
Lord Our Creator (Elijah); Prelude and Fugue, E minor, Opus 35, #5.

MOZART
Jupiter Symphony (last movement in fugal form); also Overture to Magic Flute (in fugal form).

RHEINBERGER   A. SCARLATTI
Fugue in G minor.   Fugue in A minor.

SCRIABINE   SMETANA
Le Poem de l'Extase.   Overture to Bartered Bride.

WAGNER
Overture to Meistersinger.

J. S. Bach's Fugue in C minor, #1, from The Well-Tempered Clavichord, is made up of seven strettos, and has no episodes.

Structure:
A—Statement, measures 1–10, C minor.
B—Contrast, measures 11–19, in various keys, begin with E.
A—Restatement measures 20–21, C minor.

Thematic treatment measures:
1–2. Subject in alto.
3–4. Subject answered in soprano (imitation) countersubject in alto.
5–6. Episode 1, motive A in soprano.
7–8. Subject in bass, countersubject in soprano; fragments of motive C in alto.

9–10. Episode 2, motive A tossed between soprano and alto; motive B in bass.

13–14. Episode 3, motive B in soprano; motive C in other two voices.

15–16. Subject in alto; countersubject in soprano; motive C in bass.

17–19. Episode 4, motives A and B variously distributed between all three voices.

20–21. Subject in soprano, in tonic key again; countersubject in alto; motive C in bass.

22–25. Episode 5, motives A and B in all voices.

26–28. Climax; subject in bass; motives B and C in the other voices.

29–31. Coda; subject in soprano.

2. HOMOPHONIC FORMS

In time contrapuntal music became controlled and dominated by rule and intellectual distinctions, and little chance was left for flexibility and originality. This, of course, hampered the development and function of the art of music as such. Music must have beauty, great freedom of expression, and give esthetic enjoyment. An overemphasis of intellect at the expense of feeling will not do. Consequently, harmony began to be developed, and *homophonic forms* came into existence. It is harmony rather than counterpoint that has dominated composition from the time of Haydn to this very day. Another reason for the development of homophonic forms was that, around 1600, composers turned their attention away from nonrhythmic vocal church music (Gregorian chant or plain song), which was in the nonmeasured or recitation style, to purely instrumental music. Naturally, composers turned to the rhythmic folk tunes of the people, and developed a melodic type in which there was a clearly defined scheme of pulsation, definitely measured tone lengths, and regularity of construction. As a result, dances were the first successful instrumental pieces. In time, these various dance forms were not used only for dancing but also for performance as pieces of concert music. Once free from the restriction of the dance, the music was gradually refined—idealized—by the better composers and became more complicated in construction. These tunes were then strung together into suites, partitas, rondos, etc. (See examples by J. S. Bach, Handel, Haydn, Mozart.)

In homophonic forms the song idea prevails. The one-voiced melody has a subordinated accompaniment, and the system of repetition is designed so that melodic thoughts are presented symmetrically by the one voice. Homophonic music is clear and definite in its plan of construction; its rhythm is very obvious; and its phrases and cadences are easily followed. Folk songs, hymn tunes, dances, as well as overtures, sonatas, concertos, symphonies and tone poems, are all music in the homophonic style.

3. THE DANCE

Since the dawn of time, long before there was music, men have marched bravely and proudly to battle, expressing courage in their defiant figures, or slowly and dejectedly walking behind the bier of a king or hero, expressing sorrow in every dragging footstep or drooping pose. Older than the march and the song (*canzona*), the *dance* is really as old as mankind. Even many of the early religions adopted dancing as part of their ceremonies. Obviously, dancing stems from man's need of expressing *what* and *how* he feels—a need for expressing emotion in movement. The sun-worshipers used circular dances; and in the Bible we read about the dances around the Golden Calf or the bull Apis.

The dance has not only a great value in itself but it is of unusual importance because many other musical forms are derived from it. The march, gavotte, minuet, waltz, song, hymn—all bow to the rhythm created by dancing. The periodical repetition of a rhythm in a more or less symmetrical way forms the musical accompaniment to that wonderful manifestation of life which is the dance. The music for the dance has far more importance than most people imagine. All people have danced the war dance, the love dance, the hunting, the harvest, the snake dance, and even the dance of religious frenzy, long before the first progressive savage devised the rhythm-marking tom-tom to animate the dancers and heighten the effect.

The dance was *first*. It was the primitive but accurate

expression of life-experience through motion. Psychologically, it brings about and sustains that mood of joy and physical well-being that finds its simple expression in rhythmic bodily movement. Thus, bodily movements on the esthetic level form the art of dance. Dance music at first consisted of merely a marked rhythm beaten out on some instrument of percussion. This rhythm grew out of, and was demanded by, the dance itself; and it, in turn, was intended to guide, control, and stimulate the dancers. It served the immediate purpose of keeping the dancers in step.

The dance clearly defines the measure of space and of time in the field of the art of sound—music and poetry; it also is concerned with form or shape in the field of the arts of sight—painting, sculpture, and architecture. By releasing creative movements, the dance frees the personality for all types of expression. By arousing the sense of space and cultivating it in a visual-motor activity, the dance becomes a functional basis for the creation of visual forms. The dance is a combination of steps, as music is a combination of tones. The rhythmical element is predominant in both, expressed by the numerical symbols 2 and 3 (double and triple time).

Steps and tones divide time into periodical figures. For instance, the ancient Romanesca had five steps and the same number of notes, as in the modern waltz we have three circular steps repeated two times, corresponding to the rhythm of two measures.

In the dance, perhaps more so than in poetry, we have the origin of the accent (long or down beat), which is the very essence of rhythm. The accent of the dance was transmitted to vocal music when the ancient Greek prosody was slowly discerned.

Gradually, vocal cries were added in time with the dance, expressing its mood—the cry of pain, pleasure, or desire; the shout of triumph or defiance; the wail of the death agony; the yell of delirious frenzy; etc. These were then developed, refined, and put together into expressive and pleasing melodic phrases till the song evolved from the dance. The fine arts received scant encouragement during the Dark Ages;

but the troubadours and minnesingers brought about revival of dancing as well as of song. There were also various religious dances—the Flagellants had a penitential dance which they used in time of plague and other calamity. In the 15th, 16th, and 17th centuries—during the time of polyphonic music—dance music was not neglected. Wagner called Beethoven's Symphony in A major the "apotheosis of the dance."

At first, composers wrote music for dances with choreographical intent; while, later on, writers of oratorio, opera, symphony, etc., used those same rhythms for their own musical ideas, aside from the dance. It was the stimulating rhythm of the dance which inspired many modern opera-composers to introduce not only the dance in the form of incidental ballet but to use many of their rhythms for their songs.

If we examine carefully a modern opera, we will be able to notice traces of rhythm derived from popular medieval songs, dances, marches, pastorales, and barcarolles. Lully, Rameau, Handel, Gluck, Cavalli, and others had in their operas many gavottes, chaconnes, sarabandes, etc., as in more modern operas we have marches, polkas, galops, tangos, waltzes, mazurkas, etc. Even the sublime Wagner recognized that dance rhythms were important factors in some of the most highbrow works.

Clearly, dance music reflects the tastes and needs of the social environment and differs with each time and place. Yet everywhere the emotional responses are more or less the same.

Each nation has developed its own musical idiom, like its spoken language, because dancing and singing are such deep-rooted impulses and so very close to the life of the people. The art of dance, of all the arts, perhaps shows in its structure and form the greatest resemblance to that of music. The individual "art dancer" is like a solo singer or violinist performing a piece. A "group of dancers" is a body of performers which unites to tell a tale of some kind by means of the dance with music (rhythm and sound). Like music, the dance has no direct reference to reality, or nature, as has painting or sculpture, but is fleeting and temporal; and again like music, the dance pleases through a succession of regular and symmetrical groupings.

The art dance is rhythm personified. In the ballet and in the pantomime, the bodily positions and the facial expressions clarify and emphasize the aims of the composer. Made supple through practice, the human body presents the loveliest, most complete plastic reproduction of ethereal, fleeting tones. The finest art dances give reality to dream pictures. In ballet music many see the triumph of the art of tones.

There are three factors which contribute to our pleasure in witnessing the art dance.

First, we enjoy the attractive personality of the dancer, especially if she or he be unusually graceful. We may look upon this as the material of our enjoyment—the expressing medium. There is the power of intricate beauty in itself, which excludes any emotion aroused by the association of ideas.

Second, the figures performed by the dancer correspond to the formal aspect of music, the form or pattern. This may be regarded as the idea in which we take pleasure—the thing expressed. The form contemplated as a whole gives us enjoyment and also serves as a framework which combines and unifies the more or less expressive material of music into a totality which only exists by and for itself. It is the plot or story which unifies all the elements of the dance. Without form, we would be lost in a bewildering chaos. It is evident, of course, that dance figures resemble the melodious themes in music. But these dance figures worked into an exquisite whole are still vastly inferior in variety, interest, and value to those melodious themes woven together into a unified, harmonious pattern or form.

Third, we enjoy the spirit and animation which the dancer infuses into the movements. This may be regarded as the emotional response—the perceiving mind. This factor corresponds to the symbolic element in music. It expresses that which we have so often vaguely felt but have never ourselves been able to express. We do not only wish to see pretty movements, but movements reflecting inner conditions—"graceful, coquettish, agile, languid, tender, lively, passionate, furious movements, movements imbued with life and suggestive of the personality behind them."

Sometimes this, sometimes the other, factor will be the cause of our enjoyment. At times we are carried away by the attractiveness of the face, well-proportioned limbs, and appropriate attire of the dancer. At times the form or pattern of the figures of the dance will stand out, and our pleasure will depend upon the contemplation of the beauties of the design. Then again, the symbolic or expressive element will assert itself, and the dance becomes rich in the utterance of the meaning and secrets of life. As in music, we experience a sympathetic arousal and furtherance of our feelings, a reciprocity of sentiment and emotion, a delightful interplay of stimulation and response. Again, as in music, when all factors are potently active, we experience some of the most blissful moments of which human consciousness is capable. Everything now expands into a living cosmos animated by love, hate, energy, tranquility, strife, peace, passion, despair, and triumph; everything now is within reach, and we enter into the very life of the dance (or the tones). We seem *to be* the dancer. We feel all the pangs and discords of the dance, but they are all united in a harmonious, magnificent totality.

OLD CLASSIC DANCE FORMS

There are two types of dances—those whose music is intended for dancing, and those whose music is idealized. Dance music, above all, must mark clearly the rhythm of the dance, in addition to a striking and pleasing melody. Idealized dance forms contain the general plan of the dance and, in addition, have perfection of construction, of harmony, and of form, which really put the emphasis upon themselves and not directly upon the dancing. The old classic dance forms are derived from dance music but are not intended for dancing purposes—they are idealized dance forms.

THE OLD SUITE (16TH CENTURY)

In the chapter on homophonic forms it was pointed out that dances were developed from the rhythmic folk tunes of the people; and that, in time, the various dance forms were used not only for dancing but also for performance as concert music; and furthermore, as these dance tunes were naturally too short for a pretentious musical work, such pieces were gradually freed from the restrictions of the dance and became more refined and complicated structures. The methods had developed by which this could be accomplished; one, by writing variations to the original dance tune; and the other, by writing a series of dances in contrasting styles, but all in the same key. Such a series was called a *suite, or partita,* in Germany; it was also known as *lessons* in England; *odres* in France; and *Sonata da camera* in Italy.

The German orchestral suite, as a form comprising a succession of dance movements, came into existence at the beginning of the 17th century. In 1601, N. L. Hassler published at Nuremberg his *Lustgarten Neuer Deutscher Gesänge, Balletti, Galliarden and Intraden,* in which, while there were vocal movements, there was also a succession of pieces for instruments alone. Then came similar works by other composers—Heinrich Steucius, Valentin Haussmann, Christoph Demantius, Johann Groh, etc. But these musicians did not give the title "suite" to such works, which also included parts for wind instruments, although it would seem that stringed instruments were considered of greater importance.

A suite is a succession, a cycle, a series (from the French *suivre*—to follow). It is a composition consisting of a number of unrelated movements in dance form joined together to make an artistic whole, and having contrast and symmetry. It was formerly very popular because it contained something for the mood of everybody—calm or lively, sad or merry.

All movements are in the same key, or closely related keys and mode, but a change in rhythm and character is made by means of contrast of slower or quicker tempo or duple or triple time. All are in the 2-part, or binary, form —usually with some division repeated.

The Old Suite often begins with a *prelude* (*intrada, fantasia, preambula,* or *overture*). The middle movements of the Old Suite could be varied. If this were done by means of slight embellishments, the variation was known as "Les Agrements"; while a more decided alteration (variations) was called a "*double.*" The *Intrada,* in the Old Suite, frequently took the form of a *march.* When the regular order of the Old Suite was disregarded, careful composers often gave it some other name. Bach called it an "overture."

(Note: The four works for orchestra by J. S. Bach that are known to us as "suites" were entitled "overtures" by their composer. This title was given to them by other composers of similar works, because the overture, or opening movement of the composition, was the chief feature of the whole and contained the most elaborate workmanship. The form and character of that movement were derived by Bach and other composers from the *Lully, or French Overture*—a form that began with *a slow section, followed by an Allegro* that was either a strict fugue, or fugato, and closed *with a return to the slow section.* There should be mentioned, too, Johann Kusser, who, having lived for a time in Paris and having been on friendly terms with Lully, brought out in 1682 his *Composition de Musique Suivant la Méthod Français Contenant Six Overtures.* But there are others—Mayr, Fischer, Aufschneiter, von Moffat, etc.—who, like J. S. Bach, put dance tunes together. However, the 18th-century composers came more intimately into contact with the style of Bach's suites. The D minor Suite for Orchestra by Joseph Fuchs plainly points the way; nor should there be forgotten the overture-suites by Telemann. Then, too, there is an overture-suite by Johann Ludwig Bach of Meinigen, written in 1715, as well as four similar works by Johann Bernard Bach, a distant relative of the immortal Sebastian.)

Since about 1620, every suite has the following essential movements:

1. *Allemande*—flowing in quadruple rhythm.
2. *Courante*—lively and emphatic.
3. *Sarabande*—melodious and often serious; in slow triple rhythm.
4. *Gigue*—lively and brilliant; either in triple rhythm or with triplet divisions of the beat.

The composer was at liberty to introduce other dance forms between the sarabande and the gigue, such as gavotte, bourrée, branle, musette, loure, pavane, passepied, minuet, tambourin—all known as "intermezzi." Occasionally, even a small fugue or an air with variations was introduced.

The *air* is simply a melody. It is not fixed in rhythm, yet most of the airs of the older composers are in even rhythm and of moderate tempo.

Air with Variations: This movement consists of a melody given out first in its simplest fashion and then repeated several times, each repetition introducing some variation of rhythm, harmony, or melody. Sometimes it comes after a *Toccata,* a technical display piece; or a *Toccatina,* a somewhat less brilliant piece. The air was a plain melody; while the *Burlesca* was a playful number, as was the old *Scherzo.*

(Note: The so-called "overture-suite" was a product of the late 17th century, when composers, including J. S. Bach [English Suites], were considerably influenced by French works of similar character, notably the works of J. H. Lully. Most of them have long been forgotten, but it is of interest to recall the "Lustmusik" of George Bleyer, court musician at Rudolstadt, who published his collection of dance movements at Leipzig in 1670. They were written "in the contemporary French manner.") See: *Denkmäler Deutscher Tonkunst* (Johann Fischer—Suites); *Denkmäler der Tonkunst in Oestereich;* also, V. d'Indy, Suites.

It was customary to speak of Bach's "Six Sonatas for Solo Violin," composed while he was active at Cöthen. In reality, the 1st, 3rd, and 5th are sonatas; the 2nd, 4th, and 6th are suites, or partitas. The difference between a sonata and a suite, or partita, was generally the difference between the old *Sonata da chiesa* (church sonata) and the *Sonata da Camera* (chamber sonata). The *church sonata was made up of serious music, often containing a fugue;* while the *chamber sonata consisted mostly of dance movements.*

In the Old Suite the first part goes from tonic to dominant; the second part goes from dominant to tonic. Each movement has its distinctive characteristics. Variety is imparted by the use of different rhythms and tempos. In fact, variety was the main purpose in the choice and order of the movements. The Allemande was usually considered to be introductory (in addition to a possible Prelude); the Courante contained material requiring more close and technical attention; the Sarabande was of decided lyrical and emotional value; and the Gigue originally was full of life and humor, but later was treated with much contrapuntal intricacy.

The special rhythmic or metric pattern that belonged to the given dance was prominent throughout. Whether or not melodic themes were used was of secondary importance. The treatment might be homophonic, contrapuntal, harmonic, or any mixture of the three. It required much skill to keep within the strict bounds of the melodies and the characteristic metric pattern yet achieve unity, variety, and, at the same time, interest.

The general mood of each movement of the Old Suite varies from the serious and dignified to the bright and gay.

The *Old Suite, or classic suite,* is the invention of *Johann Jacob Froberger* (1605–1667), and the order in which he played the movements in his clavier suites became the classic and established succession of dance movements in the suites of composers who followed him.

Famous composers of the Old Suite were Corelli (1653–1713); D. Scarlatti (1683–1757); H. Purcell (1658–1695); Handel (1685–1759); J. S. Bach (1685–1750); Couperin (1683–1753); Rameau (1683–1764); Gluck (1714–1787); Mozart (1756–1791); and Johann J. Froberger.

Bach's English Suites, French Suites, and German Suites, or Partitas, written for the harpsichord represent the finest music of that type in the entire literature. Handel's Twelve

Harpsichord Suites also rank among the great masterpieces of musical art. Handel abandoned the precise order of movements, and his suites are very free, even the dance names being discarded in some of them. It is not uncommon to find six *doubles* in succession. Sometimes, in the Old Suites, a movement could be duplicated, and two courantes, two minuets, or two bourrées appear.

The Old Suite formed the bridge, on the one hand, between the crude folk song, primitive dance tunes, inventions, and fugues, and, on the other, between the sonatas, symphonies, concertos, trios, quartets, quintets, etc., of Haydn, Mozart, Beethoven.

Examples:

J. S. BACH
Suite #2, B minor, for strings & flute.

CORELLI
Suite for strings.

COUPERIN
Suite in G minor.

GRIEG
Suite from Holberg's Time, Opus 40.

GLUCK
Suite from Iphigenia in Aulis.

HANDEL
Suite #5; Suite from the Water Music.

H. PURCELL
Suites I to VIII.

A. SCARLATTI
Sonata for Flute & Strings.

ALLEMANDE

The *allemande* is a graceful dance in moderately quick 4/4 or 2/4 time; it is of cheerful, quiet character, a fairly serious piece, but energetic; its meter is iambic. Well known in France at the time of Louis XIV, it was probably of German origin; it is still popular with the peasants in certain portions of southern Germany and in Switzerland. (The allemande is known also as "German dance.")

This form always commences on the upbeat; and its principal characteristic is a continuous movement in 16th notes in smooth and regular rhythm. It uses a theme or motive of a quiet and sober character; has no strong accents; and has a simple accompaniment. It is in 2-part form (binary);

each movement is repeated; and usually it is written in contrapuntal style.

Examples are J. S. Bach's French, English, and German Suites; and J. J. Froberger's Allemande.

JIG

The *jig* (French, *gigue;* Italian, *giga*) takes its name from a Norman musical instrument resembling the cornamuse (bagpipe), which originally played it, and was known since the 13th century. Probably of Celtic origin, it is a sailor's dance in England and Ireland. It was referred to as "jigge" by John Garland in 1230. There are four kinds of gigues: English, Spanish (also called "loure"), Canaries, and Italian. At present the name "jig" is given to any dance tune of a lively, droll, and grotesque expression.

The *Spanish gigue, or loure,* is slower and has a more pompous, magniloquent expression. It is an old dance, usually in 4/4 time.

The *canaries* is full of life and bustle, but of a simple, even childlike, expression.

The Italian *giga* is used by Handel and sometimes by J. S. Bach (French Suite #4) and has had a certain influence on modern music. (See Beethoven's Kreutzer Sonata for Violin & Piano, last movement.)

The English *jig* usually is in 6/8 or 9/8 time; also in 12/8, 12/16, or 3/8 time; mostly, it will be found to have a basis of rapidly moving groups of three notes. Its tempo is very rapid and lively. Generally, but not always, it begins on the upbeat. Often this folk dance contains fugal treatment; and it was the final movement of the Old Suite, being of lively and brilliant character. The form is binary.

Examples:

HANDEL
    Gigue in G minor (9th Suite).

LULLY
    Ballet Suite, Noce Villageoise, arranged by Rosenthal, #2.

SAINT-SAENS
    Jig from the opera ballet Henry VIII.

VERACINI
Giga (Sonata in D minor for Violin & Piano).

COURANTE

This is a dance in triple time; and there are two distinct variations.

Courante in 3/2 time, alternating with 6/4 time, is of French origin. It was a ceremonial dance at the court in the 17th century. The name is derived from the French word *courir*—to run. Of lively tempo, it begins with a short note, an upbeat. The courante has a predominance of dotted notes, especially dotted quarter notes, in a rapid, running style. It has a curious mixture of 3/2 time and 6/4 time, which, although equal in duration, represent different grouping of notes in the matter of natural accents. It is of binary form.

The courante in 3/4 time is of Italian origin. It is quick and light, with regular rhythm and lively tempo; and it begins with a short upbeat. It is characterized by running passages in 8th notes, or 16th notes, and sometimes in triplets. A bright, running sort of piece, it is in 2-part or binary form.

Examples:

French:
> LULLY
> Air and Corrente.

Italian:
> VERACINI
> Corrente (Sonata in D minor for Violin & Piano).

LOURE

The *loure* is a dance probably named after the "loure," an instrument similar to the bagpipe used in Normandy. The loure is written in 3/4 or 6/4 time; it is of rather slow tempo, with accented rhythm. Of binary form, it is a lower species of the gigue, which does not replace, but precedes it, when used in the Old Suite. Rhythm: ♪ ♩ | ♩. ♪ ♩ |
An example is J. S. Bach's French Suites.

PRELUDE

A *prelude* (Latin, *praeludium;* German, *Vorspiel*) is a composition in free form intended as an introduction. Usually, it is shorter than an overture, and what it introduces is often merely another piece of music, instead of a play or an opera. Originally, it was used as an introduction to suites and fugues and often has two to three different themes. Sometimes it was put between the sarabande and the gigue as a contrasting movement. This type of *praeludium* is not a dance, like the other movements of the Old Suite, but a free and generally contrapuntal composition. Sometimes it was called a *sonata, sinfonia, concerto, intrada, preambule, fantasia, overture, or toccata.*

(Note: The word *"sinfonia"* [symphony] formerly had an altogether different significance from that which it bears at present. It meant a *prelude,* a *postlude,* or an *interlude.* See the pastoral symphonies of Bach's Christmas Oratorio, Handel's Messiah, or any instrumental passage appearing in a vocal work.)

The *chorale prelude* is a short composition (generally for organ) that treats the melody of a congregational hymn. It was a favorite medium for German masters of the 17th and 18th centuries. At least two organ composers exercised a marked influence upon J. S. Bach, namely, *Dietrich Buxtehude* (1637–1707) and *Johann Pachelbel* (1653–1706). Pachelbel's 78 Choräle zum Praambulieren (1693) are fine examples of the earlier chorale prelude.

Bach composed a large number of these pieces, in fact, five collections. The earliest of them was the *Orgelbüchlein* (Little Book for Organ). The remainder of the extant preludes on the melodies of hymns (chorale preludes) by Bach date from his residence in Leipzig.

The Wagner *prelude, or Vorspiel,* is an outgrowth of the dramatic overture. In the prelude to Lohengrin, Wagner limits himself to a single suggestion—the coming and going of the Holy Grail; while in the prelude to the Meistersinger, he foreshadows the plot of the opera itself. The prelude leads directly into the opera.

Examples:

J. S. BACH
    Preludes (English Suites).

CHOPIN
    Preludes.

HELLER
    24 Preludes for Piano.

C. FRANCK
    Preludes.

JARNEFELT
    Prelude.

RACHMANINOV
    Prelude in C♯ minor; Prelude in G minor.

M. REGER
    Preludes.

REINECKE
    Prelude to King Manfred.

R. WAGNER
    Preludes to Lohengrin, Meistersinger, Rheingold, Tristan and Isolde.

SARABANDE

This is a stately dance in 3/4 or 3/2 time, and of slow, solemn tempo. Of Spanish or Moorish origin, it is supposedly the invention of a dancer named Sarabande. Later it was adopted by Italy; but it is no longer used as a dance. At first this dance was very lascivious—anything but modest—and Philip II, indeed, suppressed the dance toward the end of his reign; yet Richelieu danced the sarabande in a ballet performed before Anne of Austria. Little by little, it became a dance stately, serious, and noble. In the 16th century it was danced only by the "dames" richly dressed in silk brocade, adorned with precious stones, and with a long train. It employs the following rhythmical outline, or some modification of it— ♩ ♩. ♪ ♩ ♩ |*or* ♩ ♩. ♪♩. ♪ ♩ *or* $\frac{3}{2}$ ♩ ♩. ♩ —the distinct accent is on the second beat. It always commences on the down-beat, and its form is binary. It is of more harmonic style than the courante, and was the slow (third) movement of the Old Suite. The sarabande is rather majestic, serious, and dignified in character, somewhat grave, melancholy, even though elaborate ornamentation of the melodic line is frequently used. The chords progress as entities and serve as accompaniment to a line of melody. They thus show a tendency toward the harmonic conception that developed so strongly in the last three centuries. Sometimes the sarabande is followed by variations called *"doubles."*

Examples:

J. S. BACH
    His sonatas contain excellent sarabandes.

CORELLI
    Prelude and Sarabande.

HANDEL
    See his sonatas. Aria from opera Rinaldo (Lascia ch'is pianga).

TELEMANN
    Sarabande and Gavotte.

DOUBLE

The *double, or variation,* was somewhat like the Old Suite in structural plan. It became well known in the early 18th century. It was a series of movements developed out of a single song or dance tune used as a theme. Each successive movement stated the theme either intact, but with various embellishments, or disguised it by means of various treatments. The unity of form of the double inhered in the identity of the theme. The double often formed a part of the Old Suite.

An example is J. S. Bach's Partita for Solo Violin, #2, B minor.

BOURREE

This dance resembles the gavotte; it is in duple or quadruple time—2/2, 2/4, 4/4. It is virile and of lively tempo, generally played with two beats to a measure: allegro, much like the gavotte, but brighter, quicker, heartier.

It begins on the fourth beat of the measure, and the phrases and sentences end on the third beat. Often the second and third beat are connected by syncopation. There are two sections, both repeated, and the bourrée is in binary form.

According to some authorities, the dance is thought to be of French origin, from Biscay. A popular dance of the people, a peasant dance, it found its way to the French court of Catherinë de Medici (the court of Henry II), as well as her daughter (Marguerite de Valois) in 1565 and quickly became fashionable. But although in time it became obsolete as a polite entertainment, it never has gone entirely out of existence. The *bourrée* is still danced in the villages of Auvergre, and at the *"bals musettes"* in Paris.

Examples are J. S. Bach's Bourrée, 5th French Suite; Suite #3 for Orchestra, D major.

TAMBOURIN

This is a very brilliant dance, usually in 2/4 or 4/4 time, and of rather lively tempo. Its form is binary. In the accompaniment, the bass repeats the same tone in imitation of the *tambourin*, or *galoube*, which used to accompany the flutist's melody. The tambourin originated in Provence, a province in the southeast of France, and was in vogue in the first half of the 18th century.

Examples:

GLUCK
Tambourin from Iphigenia in Aulis.

LECLAIR
Tambourin in D major, Sonata for Violin & Piano.

RAMEAU
Tambourin.

PASSEPIED, OR PASSAMEZZO

It is of French origin, from Bretagne at the time of Louis XIV. Originally a sailor's dance, it has been in use since the 16th century. As a round dance, it was most popular also in England. According to Sir Hawkins, the name *"passamezzo"* was derived from *passer*, to walk, and *mezzo*, middle or half; the dance is a diminutive of the galliard. But other writers have inclined to the belief that the passamezzo was a lively variant of the *pavan* and that its name is merely an abbreviation of *"passo e mezzo,"* i.e., a step and a half. In executing its steps, one foot was passed above the other—hence its name. It strongly resembles the minuet; in 3/4 or 3/8 time; and in animated tempo. Characteristics: It is light and dainty and begins on the third beat.

Examples:

J. S. BACH
English Suite #5.

DELIBES
Passepied (Le Roi s'Amuse).

LULLY
Ballet Suite, Noce Villageoise, arranged by Rosenthal, #5.

RESPIGHI
Old Dances and Airs for the Lute.

RIGAUDON

The *rigaudon, or rigadou* (*Rigaud*—French; *Rigadoon*—English) is of French origin (Provence). It was brought out in the court of Louis XIII; and it probably received its name from the author of a sailor song named Rigaud, a dancing master in Marseilles. Sometimes the rigaudon was also sung by the dancers. The old dance songs were sometimes called "ballets," from the Italian word *ballere,* to dance. The rigaudon is in 2/4 or 4/4 time, with a quarter upbeat. The tempo is rapid—allegro. The music is of lively and gay character; and its form is either binary or ternary.

Examples:

KREISLER
Rigaudon.

RAMEAU
Rigaudon in G (Dardanus); Pieces de Clavecin (1724).

RAVEL
Rigaudon Suite, Le Tombeau de Couperin, IV.

PAVANE (PADUANA)

The *pavane* came from Padua, but the name was probably derived from pavone, padovano (*pavo*—peacock in Latin), in imitation of the slow, pompous strut of this bird. Originally, it was sung as well as danced. In binary form, it is in 4/2 or 4/4 time. The tempo is slow and solemn, impressive, stately. One of the most aristocratic and pompous dances, it is sometimes called "grand ball," and was very popular at the time of Louis XIV. At times it was accompanied by the tambourine. In the last measure there was a hold, and here the "dame" used to give the "chevalier" the demanded kiss. (See: "Pavane," in J. Rosenmüller's *Studen-tenmusik* (1654).)

Examples:

FAURE
Pavane.

LULLY
Ballet Suite, Noce Villageoise, arranged by Rosenthal, #1.

RAVEL
Pavane (modern example).

BRANLE

The *branle* is a dance in duple time, in moderate tempo, and with a refrain after each strophe if it is used as a dancing song. It is part only of the Old Suite of the 16th and 17th century.

See Henry Expert for good examples.

GALLIARD, OR ROMANESCA

The *galliard, gagliarda, gallarda, gaillards, romanesca, romanesque* is an old Roman dance, now almost obsolete. It is usually in 3/4 time, but there are examples in 2/2 time. Of vivacious, spirited, though not rapid tempo, it flows along smoothly at first, but hurries before the close. It is a quick, nimble dance of merry character, pulsating with a flowing melody, and has five steps. It somewhat resembles the minuet; in fact, the galliard is considered the forerunner of the minuet. Often the galliard was combined with the more stately pavane. Its form is binary.

Examples:

ARRANGED BY ACHRON
La Romanesca (for violin—old 16th century air).

LISZT
Galliard (piano arrangement).

RESPIGHI
Old Dances and Airs for the Lute (Four Pieces for Orchestra).
The King of Denmark's Galliard.
The Earl of Essex's Galliard.

VILLANELLA

This is a lively movement, usually in 6/8 time. Besides a dance, it was in the 16th century an Italian unaccompanied part-song. Light and gay in character, its text was naïve and occasionally indecorous.

Examples:

RESPIGHI
 Old Dances and Airs for the Lute.
TELEMANN (1681–1767)
 Suite (Overture) #5 in D, Villanella.

FARANDOLE

A folk dance of Provence and Italy, it is said to be of Greek origin. The dancers join hands in a chain and follow the leader in a jolly procession through various evolutions. The man in the first row signals the couples with a handkerchief, a ribbon, or flag. It is a circle dance of exciting character. In 2/4, 4/4, or 6/8 time, the rhythm is marked throughout by the *galoubet* and the throb of a *tambourine*, native instruments of Provence and Languedoc. The tempo is rapid and gradually becomes quicker towards the end. It is in 2-part form.

Examples:

BIZET
 L'Arlesienne Suite #2.

PUGNO
 Farandole.

SALTARELLO

Of Italian origin—from *saltare*, to leap, to dance—it is so-called from the leaping, springing, or jumping movements. It is either in 3/4, 6/8, 12/8, or 2/4 time, with triplets to each beat. The saltarello is very quick and fiery in tempo, but a trifle slower than the tarantella. It has a jumping rhythm and may be played with or without castanets. It contains more skips than the tarantella; and its form is either binary or ternary.

An example is Mendelssohn's Symphony #4, finale.

FORLANE

The *forlane, furlana, or forlana* (Italian) is an old Venetian dance. It was very popular, and much used by the gondoliers, who danced it in pairs, using the same arm motions as in rowing. It was once thought to have originated in Friula, perhaps because the people of that region were known as "Furlani." The forelane, as well as other Italian dances, found its way into France at the end of the 16th century. J. S. Bach and Rameau used the forlane in their works. It is of gay and joyous character; in 6/8 or 6/4 time; and of quick tempo—somewhat like a slow jig. The form is binary.

Examples:

J. S. BACH
    Forlane in Suite in C.

PONCHIELLI
    Forlane in opera La Gioconda, at end of Act I.

RAVEL
    Forlane in suite Le Tombeau de Couperin, #2.

WOLF-FERRARI
    Forlane in opera The Jewels of the Madonna.

TARANTELLA

Of Neapolitan origin, the name is derived from the tarantula (a large, poisonous spider), or from Taranto, a city in Italy. The popular superstition used to attribute to this dance a supernatural power of curing the poison bite of the tarantula. It is always in 6/8 time, an exceedingly rapid, wild dance, with a strong rhythmic swing and a feverish dash. It is either in binary or ternary form. The tarantella is danced in Italy and in Spain by trained dancing girls.

Examples:

N. W. CALKINS
    Tarantella.

CHOPIN
    Tarantella, Opus 43.

HELLER
    Two Tarantellas for Piano, Opus 85.

MASSENET
    Tarantella, La Danse, from Scenes Neapolitan.

SAINT-SAENS
    Tarantella for Flute and Clarinet.

SICILIANA

A pastoral dance or dance song of the Italian shepherds, originating in Sicily. It is in 3/8, 6/8, or 12/8 time—

♪. ♫♩ ♩♪ ♩♩ ♪

Tempo is allegretto or andantino. Slow and graceful, it is of gentle and soothing character. The siciliana is in binary or ternary form, or a rondo.

Examples:

HAYDN
Symphony in D, second movement.

KREISLER
Siciliana.

SCHUMANN
Sicilienne, Opus 68.

BOLERO

The *bolero,* also known as *cachcha or giatana,* of Spanish origin (Andalusia), is a rather recent folk dance that has been taken over as an art dance, a dance of the ballet class for couples or for a single female dancer. It is similar to the polonaise, but has not its dignity and loftiness. The bolero is frequently written in a minor key and in 3/4 time, with a brisk, well-marked rhythm ♪ ♫ ♪ ♪ ♪ ♪. The tempo is moderate. It is now almost always accompanied by the clacking of castanets held in the hands of the dancer. These instruments of Moorish origin have a clicking sound which is very fascinating. The bolero is in ternary form. The Cuban bolero is in 2/4 time.

Examples:

CHOPIN
Bolero, Opus 19, piano solo.

RAVEL
Bolero (extremely popular).

WEBER
Bolero from opera Freischütz.

JOTA ARAGONESA

The *jota Aragonesa* is a Spanish national dance which takes its name from Aragon, the port of the country in which it originated. It is generally accompanied by singing, and, like much of Spanish music, it has a slightly mournful sound, as if the dancers were not quite happy. It is in 3/4 or 3/8 time, and of lively tempo. The form is binary.

Examples:

BIZET
    Carmen Suite #1.

DE FALLA
    Jota.

SARASATE
    Jota Navarra.

CHABRIER
    España Rhapsody, for orchestra.

E. GRANADOS
    Jota Aragonesa.

FOLIA

An old dance of Spanish origin (or possibly Portuguese), it is now obsolete. It is in 3/4 time, slow and stately in character. The *folia* was known in Italy as *follia di Spagna,* and in France as *folies d'Espane.* Samples of old dances were given by Francesco Salinas (1513–?) in his *Musica,* printed in Salamanca, 1577.

An example is Corelli-Lonard's La Folia.

FANDANGO

A dance song of Southern Spain, it was brought there by the Moors. The *fandango* has been popular since the 16th century. It is danced only by a male and a female, who do not touch each other, not even their hands. The music usually is in the minor key. It is in 3/4 or 3/8 time and has the characteristic Spanish rhythm. The tempo is lively, and it usually is accompanied by a song and a tambourine or castanet. The form is binary.

Similar dances are the: *rodeno* (*Rondina*); *branadina; murciana; gitano; polo; tirana;* and the *melanguena.*

The *melanguena* is a popular dance in triple time, closely related to the fandango, and accompanied with castanets or a tambourine and guitar.

An example is Chabrier's Espana Rhapsody, for orchestra.

SEGUIDILLA

The *seguidilla* is a Spanish dance. It is in 3/4 or 6/8 time, and of quite rapid tempo.

Other national Spanish dances of this sort are the *jaleo* and *guaracha*.

An example is Bizet's Seguidilla, from the opera Carmen.

TANGO

The *tango* generally is considered to be a Spanish dance, though it really is of African origin. It came to Spain by way of the Moors and was brought to Cuba by Negro slaves. It is very popular in Argentina, and was popularized in the United States about 1911. The time is varied—though usually in 4/4 or 2/4 time—and it consists mostly of eighth-notes. Its tempo is generally rather slow, but in some cases it becomes faster toward the end. It is danced with reckless abandon. The form is either binary or ternary.

Examples:

ALBENIZ
  Tango in D.

I. CERVANTES
  Cuban Dance #1.

E. DONATO
  A Media Luz (Argentine tango).

E. V. MALDEREN
  El Tango de Rêve.

HABANERA (HAVANAISE)

The *habañera, contradanza criolla* (Creole country dance) is Cuban. Evidently, the name is derived from the Spanish word *Havana;* but in reality it is a very old African dance introduced into the West Indies (Cuba) by the Negroes, and thence brought to Spain. It is in 3/4 or 6/8 time, with frequent triplets. The tempo is rather slow. Its character is graceful, and it usually is accompanied by the tambourine, which marks its peculiar and persistent rhythm. It is in 2-part form.

Examples:

BIZET
  Habañera, Carmen Suite #1.

CHABRIER
  Habañera.

RUMBA

The *rumba* is a well-known dance, somewhat like the tango; it became popular in the United States in 1929. It is in 2/4 or 4/4 time, of rather lively tempo. Its rhythm is more animated than that of the tango, as some of the percussion instruments keep up a steady succession of eighth-notes, with accents at unexpected points in the measure, while others emphasize the syncopated figure played throughout by the brasses.

An example is M. Menendez's Green Eyes. Also Max Reese—Rumba (La Gitana).

MAXIXE

The *maxixe* is a very prominent Brazilian dance of the older generation; it is usually in 6/8 time and in a rather rapid tempo.

ECOSSAISE

The *Ecossaise* (*Ecossais*—French) is of Scotch origin. It consists of two parts; usually it is in 2/4 time, of quick tempo, and of lively character. Its form is binary.

MORRIS DANCE

A rustic dance, the *morris* was probably derived from the Moors in Spain. It was later danced by the Christian militants. From Spain it was introduced into Italy, Germany, and England about the 15th century. In northern England it became very popular at the time of Henry VIII and was danced at village festivals and on processions on May Day. The participants wore fancy costumes and impersonated fictitious characters, such as Robin Hood, etc. It is still danced in Corsica, where it simulates the struggles of the Crusaders against the Saracens, the conquest of Jerusalem ending the dance. It is also still danced in Greece, Montenegro, and other nearby countries. It is the dance of the Christian heroes. Usually it is played in 3/4 time in moderate tempo. Its form is binary.

Examples:

E. GERMAN
Three Dances from Henry VIII.

P. GRAINGER
Country Garden Dances (Shepherd's Hey).

HORNPIPE

Originally, an old popular Scotch and English shepherd's dance, its name is supposed to be derived from the reed instrument (shepherd's pipe, or horn) said to have been played in England as late as the time of Charles II. Now the name generally is given to a sailor's dance. In Handel's day it was in triple time, simple or compound; but now (since about 1760, when it was performed in theaters by prominent dancers), it is more commonly in 4/4 time, in even rhythm, and of very rapid tempo—merry, cheery and energetic. It has a peculiar charm. The sailor's *hornpipe* is still very popular in the British Navy. It is in 2-part form.
Examples:

Arkansas Traveler.	Sailor's Hornpipe.
College Hornpipe.	Turkey in the Straw.
Devil's Dream.	Rory O'More.
Garry Owen.	Elizabethan Shepherd's Dance.
Green Sleeves.	Miss McLeod's Reel.
Old Irish Jigs.	The Irish Washwoman.

Handel's Concerto Grosso, Opus 6, #7.   Dixie.

REEL

The *reel* is an Irish and Scotch dance performed by two or more couples gliding or whirling in figure-eight movements. It is of Danish origin and is in great vogue in Norway, Denmark, and Sweden. It is a very animated dance of rapid, even rhythm; either in 4/4 or 6/8 time; a jolly tune played in a lively tempo. It is in binary form.

An example is P. Grainger's Molly on the Shore (based on two folk tunes from County Cork in the south of Ireland).

HAY, OR HEY

The *hey* is a rustic dance of England. It is a circular arrangement, much used at May-Day gatherings. Sometimes words were sung to it.
Examples:

P. GRAINGER   ?
    Shepherd's Hey.   The Hayloft (Barn dance).

STRATHSPEY

The *strathspey* is a dance somewhat slower than the reel and has the so-called "Scotch snap"—a 16th note followed by a dotted 8th note.

SPRINGDANS AND THE HALLING

The *springdans* (Skocna) is a Norwegian dance in 3/4 time and somewhat lively tempo and character.

The *halling* is another Norwegian dance in 2/4 time, a boisterous affair for men only at which the dancers try to kick the low rafters of the barn while they swing around.

An example is Dvorak's Slavonik Dances, Set 1, #5, #7. Grieg has illustrated both dances in his shorter works.

FURIANT

An example is A. Dvorak's Slavonic Dances, Set 1, #1, #8.

GALOP

The *galop* is supposed to be of German origin, although it is very popular also in France. It is a tumultuous dance movement in 2/4 time. The tempo is very quick. The spirit of the *galop* is a furious desire for dancing. It is a round dance; a spring dance; similar to the polka, but much quicker. Its form is ternary; and usually there is a short introduction, trio, and coda (3 x 8 or 3 x 16 measures for the actual dance). Liszt, in his *Galop Chromatic,* makes it an harmonic, thematic art work and a virtuoso piano piece. Johann Strauss has composed marvelous *galops.*

SCHOTTISCHE

The *schottische, or Scotch dance,* is a modern round dance in 2/4 or 4/4 time, with even rhythm; and in the character of a slow polka. It is of moderately slow tempo, having a number of short notes in each measure to which the performers take three moderate steps and two quick ones. Its form is binary.

An example is Rollison's Golden Trumpets.

TWO-STEP

The *two-step* is a popular modern American dance in fairly rapid 2/4 or 6/8 time and even rhythm. There are countless examples.

FOX TROT

The most popular American dance, the *fox trot* has an unusually catchy rhythm; it is in 4/4 time and of moderate tempo.

Examples:

E. DAWSON, F. FURBECK
Typical Tangle Tune.

GERSHWIN
I Got Rhythm (from musical comedy, Girl Crazy).

GRISELLE
Cubist.

G. KAHN, M. BLOOM
You're Breaking My Heart.

AL WILSON, I. BRENNAN
In My Old Plantation Home.

E. SMALLE
Sweet Love.

DUMKA

The *dumka* is a Bohemian dance of sad, melancholy, and doleful character. The word "dumka" has been used in Slavonic music for folk ballads, and, particularly in Little Russia, for folk songs of a lyrical and elegiac character, usually in the minor key.

Examples:

DVORAK
Slavonic Dances, Set 1, #2.

TANSMAN
Dumka (Four Polish Dances for Orchestra, #3).

TREPAK

This is a Russian dance which is rather impetuous, with much expenditure of energy on the part of the dancers and much stamping of heavy-heeled boots.

Examples:

A. RUBINSTEIN
Russkaya Trepak (Dance Russe).

TSCHAIKOWSKY
Trepak (Nutcracker Suite, #4); Violin Concerto, 3rd movement.

HOPAK

The *hopak* is a furious Russian dance. Its most conspicuous step is often seen on the stage, the feet being thrust forward in violent alternation from a crouching posture. It usually is in 2/4 time and of agitated tempo.

Examples:

MOUSSORGSKY-RACHMANINOV   ?
Hopak.   Ukrainian Hopak.

KAMARINSKAIA AND ZIGANKA

The *kamarinskaia* is a lively Russian dance for men. It has exerted much influence on music; and Tschaikowsky made it into a symphonic movement.

The *ziganka* is a Russian peasant dance in 2/4 time, and of lively tempo.

CHACONNE

The *chaconne* is an old dance which probably originated in Spain (Andalusia) at about the end of the 16th century; it is also known as the *giaconna* (from the Italian *ciesco—* blind). Some say that it received its name from the game of Blind Man's Buff; others claim that it was invented by a man named Chacon; still others hold that it was so named because it was made popular by a blind man. At any rate, in early days it was not approved by the moralists.

It is in 3/2 or 3/4 time, although examples in even rhythm (4/4 or 2/4) have been found. It is of moderately slow tempo; developed out of a recurring theme of eight measures; and *the theme must always be kept continuously in the bass*. Almost always it begins on the first beat of the measure and generally is in the major key. As to style: it is a graceful, slow and dignified dance, resembling the passecaglia. It originated as a device in which a passage was continuously repeated in a composition. Even as early as the 13th century, the tenor part in motets was subjected to the repetition of a short motive; and the same device was carried out by M. de Fuenilans in his Fantasias for Lute, which he dedicated to Philip II of Spain in 1554. As a form, the chaconne arrived at its apogee with J. S. Bach. His example in the D minor Partita for Violin Alone is the freest and noblest treatment in existence.

Toward the end of the 17th, and in the early part of the 18th century, the chaconne was the conventional ending for an opera. J. B. Lully (1632–1687) often used it in the finale of his operas; and it was employed by Gluck in the closing section of his Orfeo ed Euridice (1742); but there were numerous instances of its exploitation in operas and ballets of other 17th- and 18th-century composers.

The name "chaconne" is also given to a set of variations on a *ground basso* (*basso ostinato*—a continually repeating bass figure above which the upper voices are moving), usually eight measures long.

Examples:

J. S. Bach
    Chaconne for Violin Alone.

Vitali, Tomaso
    Chaconne.

D. Buxtehude
    Chaconne in E minor, for Organ, transcribed for orchestra by C. Chavez.

Dubois
    Chaconne in E minor.

Durand
    Chaconne, Opus 62,

Beethoven
    Chaconne, 32 Variations for Piano.

Lully
    Ballet Suite, Noce Villageoise, #4, arranged by Rosenthal.

Brahms' chaconne in the E minor Symphony, last movement, is an outstanding example of a later chaconne. There are 31 variations of an 8-measure theme; after which comes a rather broadly developed finale. These 8-measure variations follow one another without any connecting melodies, except a 4-measure melody interpolated before the coda variation.

PASSECAGLIA

The *passecaglia* (*passecaille*, French) is an old French dance, although the name, according to M. Littre, is derived from the Spanish *passer*, to walk, and *calle*, street; the combination suggesting that a passecaglia was originally a tune played on guitars and the like in the streets by wandering musicians. As a dance, it was negotiated by one or two performers, and it survived in France for more than two centuries. In the 17th and 18th centuries the passecaglia, as well as the chaconne, became popular with composers as variation forms. Both were originally dances, and as such were written by Gluck and others of his time. Yet at that period and before it, the passecaglia was treated also as a purely musical form, as may be seen in the works of Buxtehude, J. S. Bach, Frescobaldi, Mazella, and others.

The passecaglia is in 3/2 or 3/4 time, and it developed out of a recurring theme of eight measures; its tempo is slow, rather bombastic in character. Its form is binary. Usually, it is in the minor key; but otherwise it closely resembles the chaconne in form. Both consist of a long-spun, ever changing contrapuntal superstructure developed over a persistently repeated theme—an elaboration upon a *ground bass*. In the passecaglia the theme, repeated again and again, *under or over* a continuous stream of music, can be placed in any voice-part; *while in the chaconne the theme must always be kept continuously in the bass,* and this ground bass provides a simple foundation for a concentrated and emotionally charged musical thought. But, of course, there are exceptions to that rule.

Examples:

J. S. BACH
Passecaglia (for two-manual harpsichord with pedals). Transcriptions for orchestra by: Fr. Stock, L. Stokowski, R. Goedicke, O. Respighi, H. Esser.
Passecaglia in C minor for Organ; Crucifixus, Mass in B minor.

BUXTEHUDE
Passecaglia for Organ.

BRAHMS
Finale, 4th Symphony (founded on a majestic 8-measure theme in triple time).

KARG-ELERT
Passecaglia in E minor for Organ.

H. KAUN
    Passecaglia for Two Pianos.

PACHELBEL
    Passecaglia for Organ.

M. REGER
    Passecaglia for Two Pianos (for orchestra by: A. Jung;
    P. Grainger; N. F. Schaub. A. von Webern; J. Jongen;
    Ilse Fromm-Michaelis; G. Scott; J. Weinberger; etc.).

GAVOTTE

The *gavotte* is of French origin; its name is supposed to
have been derived from that of the people of the "Pays du
Gap" in the old province of Dauphine, southern France.
The peasants of this place are called "Gapmen" or "Gavots."
The gavotte was distinguished from other dances of the day
in that the participants lifted their feet, instead of shifting
them along the floor. Even in the 16th century it had become familiar at the court balls in France. Perhaps the
popularity of it was not unconnected with the evolutions
of the dance, for kissing of each other by the dancers was
a prominent and important feature.

In the 16th century the gavotte became popular with
the composers of music for the stage and with the artists who
danced in the theaters. It was first used for theatrical purposes, as it was considered too strenuous an exercise for the
dainty ladies of the court. Its great popularity as a spectacle
led to its adoption in a slightly modified form as a regular
dance of the court. The gavotte gradually became more dignified; the steps became slower, the figures more sedate. It
became the chaste dance of the 18th century, with its elegant and ceremonial reverence, but with mutual exchange
of kisses—a *bal très gallant*.

It is in duple time, 2/2, 2/4, or quadruple, 4/4. The entire dance is dominated by a persistent rhythm, with a pace
that remains unvaried except at the end, which should be
somewhat slower, in accordance with the custom of Bach's
time. The gavotte is a dance of lively and energetic character, genial and skipping. It always commences on the
last half of the measure, on the third beat, cadences falling
on the first half of the measure; and it ends with the first

half of a measure. The style of the gavotte has some similarity to that of the Bourrée; its phrases are generally short.

The gavotte is sometimes followed by a second gavotte, which is written in the same key if Gavotte I were in the major; but in tonic major if Gavotte I were in minor. Sometimes Gavotte II (or trio) was written on an *organ-point;* in which case it was often called a *"musette,"* named after a medieval instrument which continuously sounded a bass note, like a bagpipe. (See J. S. Bach's English Suite, #3, #6.) Its character should always be rustic.

The *organpoint, or pedalpoint,* is a prolonged bass note over which there are frequent changes of harmony. It occurs especially at the end of a composition where the organpoint, as a rule, appeared on the dominant of the key, and usually begins with a chord. To be of good effect, it must be clear at the beginning and at the end, whereas in the middle the most extraneous harmony may be introduced.

The general mood of the dance is joyous in Gavotte I and more quiet in Gavotte II.

An old French gavotte and rondo is Amaryllis, arranged by Ghis; we do not know who actually composed it. Evidently, it was written before King Louis XIII of France was born; and it is probably the oldest instrumental composition. It is in 4/4 time and in 3-part form. It was a favorite piece at the court of Henry III, and was first performed at the wedding of his daughter Margaret to the Duc de Joyeuse, October 15, 1581, at the Palais au Petit Bourbon. It was sung to the words: "Le son de la Clochette auquel Circe sortit de son jardin," etc. It was a custom in those days to give a lady some pastoral name, and under such a title to dedicate to her music or poetry as a mark of chivalry; hence the name Amaryllis.

Examples:

J. S. BACH
Gavotte in D, Sonata #6, for Cello; Gavotte in E, Partita #6 for Solo Violin; Gavotte, English Suite, #6.

GOSSEC   MARTINI
Gavotte.   Gavotte in F.

RAMEAU
    Gavotte in D major; Gavotte in E minor.
GRETRY   LULLY
    Gavotte Colinette à la Coeur.   Gavotte Roland.

The *modern gavotte* has the same general characteristics
as the old gavotte, but it is nearly always in the ternary
form.

Examples:

H. FLIEGE   GABRIEL-MARIE
    Gavotte Circus Renz.   La Cinquantaine.
GLUCK-BRAHMS   GODARD
    Gavotte in A.   Second Gavotte.
A THOMAS   VON WILM
    Gavotte from Mignon.   Gavotte, Opus 81, #10.

MUSETTE

The *musette* is a pastoral dance, now obsolete, of shep-
herd-like character. It is in 6/8 or 2/8 time and of moderate
tempo. Its chief characteristic is a drone bass which sustains
the genial, smooth-flowing melody. Its name was derived
from the musette—an old French instrument of the bagpipe
species which enjoyed great popularity in the time of Louis
XIV and XV of France. The ladies of the court played upon
costly musettes, and the instrument was introduced into
court ballets and, subsequently, into the opera.

Now the name "musette" is used for a lyric piece in 6/8
time and very slow tempo. Of course, the organpoint is still
important.

Examples:

BACH-POLLAIN
    Musette for Cello.
ANNA M. BACH
    Bach for Beginners, Book 1, Musette for Piano.
RAMEAU   GLUCK-PASTERNACK
    Musette for Violin and Piano.   Musette.

MINUET

The *minuet* (Italian, *minuetto*, from the Latin, *mintus*,
small) originated in Poitou, France, and took its name from

the small, mincing, dainty steps of the dance—*pas menus*.
Like the bourrée and the gavotte, it found its way to the
select ballrooms of the French aristocracy, and both Louis
XIV and Louis XV were devoted to it. In 1653, Louis XIV
danced it to Lully's music for the first time at Versailles.
It soon became the most popular of court and society dances
until the beginning of the 19th century. The minuet was not
restricted to the ballroom. It was frequently used as one of
the movements of the suite, where, quite often, one minuet
was followed by a second. The latter was often written in
three voices, for which reason it was called a "trio." Handel
employed the minuet for the closing movements of overtures
to operas and oratorios.

There are two varieties of this dance: the *old minuet*,
and the *modern minuet*. Both are in 3/4 time, and both are
very graceful, dainty court dances.

Old Minuet: A slow, stately dance, very ceremonious,
French in form, tranquil and dignified in character, aristocratic. It has a pause or long note at every fourth measure.
It commences and is accented on the last beat of the measure. This minuet was sometimes followed by a second minuet, which, in order to contrast with the first, was written
for three instruments; and for this reason was called a "*trio*."
The first minuet was for violin and bass. The word "trio"
is still used in modern music, but its original meaning is lost;
and it now signifies an "episode." Both of these two dances
(the *minuet* proper and the *trio*) might be in either binary
or in an all ternary form, and they were combined to effect
a large 3-part form, often with a coda. The key relationship
between minuet and trio usually consists of a change from
major to minor, or vice versa.

Examples:

HANDEL
    Overtures to operas and oratorios.
LULLY
    Minuet from La Bourgeois Gentilhomme.

Modern Minuet: It was Haydn who made the minuet
quick instead of slow. He gave the dance the jolly, rakish

character which distinguished it in the latter part of the century. But Haydn was not the first to introduce the minuet into the symphony. Johann Stamitz had done that before him, and there is a symphony by George Matthias Monn (1717–1750), written during the period of Haydn's youth, which contains a minuet. The modern minuet is lively, instead of being dignified; simple and jovial, instead of being aristocratic; and it commences on the upbeat. It is always in 3-part form.

Mozart's minuets are characterized by refined wit and artistic design. Some of his minuets are on such an elaborate scale that it may not be easy at first to recognize the different parts as they appear in succession. For example, in the minuet from the Jupiter Symphony, the first part itself consists of two subsections or lesser parts, each of which is repeated. Then comes the true second part—the *trio*—which also contains two subsections that are repeated. The third part, of course, is the same as the first part, lacking the "repeats."

Beethoven's minuets are charming. With him the scherzo did not entirely supercede the minuet, because he used the minuet in his Eighth Symphony.

The minuet is one of the most important dances which in a great way influenced instrumental music. In the time of Haydn and Mozart, the minuet was very popular in fashionable Vienna society. Quite naturally, they selected this dance to introduce into their large works—sonatas, symphonies, string quartets, trios, etc. The same, by the way, happened to the waltz.

Usually the minuet form is made up of two complete 3-part song forms, known as *"Minuet and Trio."* The whole first part, or minuet, is heard after the trio, thus making the movement a large 3-part song form.

Examples:

J. S. BACH
Minuet in B.

BIZET
Minuet from L'Arlesienne.

BEETHOVEN
Minuet in G.

BOCCHERINI
Minuet (has Trio).

CZIBULKA
Minuet of the Fly (for string instruments; from comic operetta Bajazzo).

GLUCK
Minuet.

HAYDN
Minuet Sonata in G; Minuet and Trio from Surprise Symphony.

MOZART
Minuet from Don Giovanni; Minuet in D major; Minuet, G minor Symphony.

PADEREWSKI	REINECKE	SCHARWENKA
Minuet.	Minuet.	Minuet.

POLONAISE

Strictly speaking, the *polonaise, or polacca,* is not a dance at all, but the music to a ceremonial procession. The piece was in existence at least 150 years before J. S. Bach's time, although the characteristic rhythm was not so marked then as now. It came into the limelight in 1753, in Cracow, then the Polish capital, on the occasion of the coronation of the young French Prince Henry d'Anjou as King of Poland. This coronation ceremony was one of the most magnificent affairs ever witnessed. Poland was then at the height of her power, wealth, and splendor. She was oriental in her love of lavish display and extravagant personal adornment. An important feature of this grand festival was a presentation ceremony to introduce the members of the court and aristocracy to the new king. All the lords and ladies of the realm, arrayed in their most sumptuous apparel, assembled in one of the lower halls in the royal castle, formed in a glittering procession, and marched in stately pomp up the grand staircase to the dais, where the king awaited them. There they were presented to his majesty by a master of ceremonies.

Suitable music for the march was written by a local composer. The music was intended not only to mark the rhythm of the march but to add to the pomp and beauty of the occasion; and it embodied the peculiar racial characteristics and national traits of the Poles.

So the polonaise, or polacca, came into being. Crude and

primitive though it may have been, it has gradually developed into a definite, complete, and quite elaborate musical form. This form has been used the world over by many composers; and it became the musical accompaniment to a festival cortege.

It is in 3/4 time, and is agreeably and strikingly rhythmical:

♪ ♫ ♫ ♫ ; *or* ♪ ♫♫ ♫ ♫ ; *or* ♪ ♩ ♫ ♫ ♫♫ ♩. ♫

The last measure of each movement of the polonaise usually consists of four 16ths coming on the first beat of the measure; followed by a quarter-note falling on the second beat; and then by an eighth note on the third beat. The characteristic of ending with a short note on the third beat is very marked. The main cadence has a feminine ending.

Its tempo is very moderate. It is always a promenade march, not a dance; and it is always Slavonic in its general tone and aristocratic in its manner and mood. The polonaise expresses court etiquette and the reserved official manner used at court functions; it takes the place of the Grand March as the opening number at refined balls—the March aux Flambeaux and the Dance Ceremonie are nothing more than polonaises.

However, as time went on, just as in the case of the waltz, the music of the polonaise was broadened and elaborated so as to include in its scope the expression not only of its original mood but additional ideas, feelings, and fancies, even incidents connected with or arising out of it. For example, we may recall the days of Poland's glory with widely different emotions, with pride and exultation over her past; with hope for her present state of existence; and so on. Any of these moods may be legitimately expressed in the polacca.

To sum up: The polonaise contains every contrast possible. The melody has runs, skips, and artificial groupings; and syncopation occurs freely both in the melody and the accompaniment. The accompaniment has various rhythmic changes in its construction, and the melody is often completed with the third beat of the measure. Bach, Handel, and others wrote it in the binary form; but the modern polonaise, as developed by Chopin, is written in the ternary form.

Examples:

J. S. BACH
Polonaise, French Suite for Clavier, #6; Brandenburg Concerto #1.

CHOPIN
Polonaise Militaire; Polonaise in A.

ANDERSON   LISZT
Polonaise Brilliante.   Polonaise in E major.

MACDOWELL   MEYERBEER
Polonaise, Opus 46, #12.   Fackeltanz.

MOUSSORGSKY
Polacca, from the opera Boris Godounov.

WIENIAWSKI
Polonaise de Concert, Opus 4, for violin & piano.

See also, polonaises by Oginski, Kurpinski, Moniuszki, M. Moszkowski, P. and X. Scharwenka, etc.

MAZURKA

The *mazurka, or masurek,* is of Polish origin. The power of dance music to express national characteristics was not fully shown until Chopin, in his polonaises and mazurkas, developed, enobled, and idealized these popular styles of Poland. The mazurka is the national dance of the Poles. Most often the mood is one of unrestricted gaiety. It is a vehicle for a wide scale of emotions, ranging from sad to gay, from fiery and violent to dreamy and melancholy. Sometimes, when sung in slower tempo instead of danced, it is called the *dumka (revery).*

Its characteristics are: leaping melodies, jerky rhythms, some degree of syncopation, and irregular accentuation of the weak beats of the measure—generally on the second beat; but in order to give variety, the third and first beats are occasionally accented. It is in 3/4 or 3/8 time, of pronounced rhythm; the tempo is moderate, somewhat slower than the waltz. It is usually in ternary form; but some of the smaller mazurkas of Chopin and others are written in binary form.

Examples:

CHOPIN
Mazurka in B.

ENGELMANN
Mazurka, Opus 730, #4.

J. B. LAMPE
Mazurka (three step).

SAINT-SAENS
First Mazurka, Opus 21.

MLYNARSKI
Mazurka for Violin & Piano.

J. STRAUSS
Dithyrambe.

GODARD
Second Mazurka.

J. HUBAY
Mazurka, Opus 15, #1.

MOSZKOWSKI
Mazurka, Opus 10, #3.

W. D. SMITH
Mazurka.

WIENIAWSKI
Obertass.

KUJAWIAK

The *kujawiak*, a Polish peasant dance, originated in Kujavia. It is closely related to the mazurka (Mazur), but it is quieter, somewhat melancholy, slower and simpler. It is in 3/4 time and of moderate tempo. The characteristic rhythm of this dance places the accent on the second beat of the measure; whereas the mazurka often has the accent on the third beat. The form is ternary.

Examples:

TANSMAN
Kujawiak (Four Polish Dances, #2).

WIENIAWSKI
Kujawiak for Violin & Piano.

KRAKOWIAK

The *krakowiak, or Cracovienne* (French), is a Polish peasant dance, very popular around the district of Cracow. It usually is in 2/4 time— ♩ ♫ ♫ *or* ♪ ♩ ♪ . It is of moderate tempo. The accent is on the second beat, usually brought about by the syncopation—a frequent accentuation of unaccented beats—but it is lively and graceful, rather than passionate.

OTHER POLISH DANCES

The *Oberek* is a Polish peasant dance, related to the

Mazurka, and very much like the Kujawiak, but much quicker. Often it is in 3/8 time. An example is Tansman's Oberek (Four Polish Dances, #4).

The *polka-mazurka* is about the same in style as the mazurka, although slower, and with the unexpected accents on the third beat. It is a variant of the polka, which joins to the polka the slower mazurka step.

The *polka-redowa* is faster than the mazurka and has no unusual accents.

The *varsovienna* is a Polish (Slavic) dance in 3/4 time. Its tempo is faster than that of the mazurka.

The *redowa, redowak, or redowaszka,* is a Polish dance in 3/4 time, sometimes alternating 3/4 and 2/4 measures.

CZARDAS

The *czardas,* of Hungarian origin, is a Hungarian Gypsy dance of a romantic kind. It is either in 2/4 or 3/4 time; of impassioned character; with sudden alterations of tempo and great varieties of effect. If begins with a slow movement, the *lassu,* in common time, gradually increasing its tempo to one of wildness and liveliness, until the second movement, or *fris,* is reached. Its form usually is 3-part.

Examples:

HAUSER
    Hungarian Rhapsody for Violin & Piano.
HUBAY, J.
    Hejre Kati.

POLKA

The *polka, or Pulka* (Bohemian, a half-step) is of Bohemian origin; it is the national dance of the Bohemians. Its success has had no parallel in the history of dancing, for it conquered the world within a decade. It was introduced into Vienna in 1839; in 1840, it became the rage of Paris. In 1840, also, it was introduced into the United States at the inauguration of President Polk. It is in 2/4 time. The rhythm is: ♪ ♫♫♩ ♫♫ . The tempo is moderately lively—

merry, hopping (*hüpfend*—skipping). The form is usually ternary—short introduction, trio, and coda.

Examples:

VON BLON
Dear Violet.

BENDEL
Invitation à la Polka.

L. DELIBES
Pizzicato Polka.

DVORAK
Slavonic Dances, Set 1, #6.

SMETANA
Polka from opera The Bartered Bride.

JOS. STRAUSS
The Dragon Fly (a charming polka-mazurka).

JOH. STRAUSS
Thunder and Lightning; Tik-Tak; Pizzicato.

TANSMAN
Polka (Four Polish Dances, #1).

WALLERSTEIN
Jenny Lind's Favorite Polka.

RUBINSTEIN
Le Bal.

RAFF

Heel and Toe Polka.   Polka de la Reine.

QUADRILLE

The *quadrille, anglaise, française, or kontretanz,* is a dance in cycles of usually six tours, or parts, consisting of a corresponding group of melodious dance tunes in various keys and various time—6/8 and 2/4 or 4/4 time. It is known in England, France, Germany, and the United States (*square dance*). An announcer tells the couples what they shall do. The dancers are placed in opposite rows and made to go through certain figures, accompanied by rapid 4-measure or 8-measure phrases in the music. It resembles our Virginia reel.

Examples:

J. S. BACH
French Suite, #3.

J. S. KNIGHT
The Lancer's Quadrille.

MARCH

The *march* is a composition of strongly marked rhythm, designed to accompany the steps of a group of men. Of German origin, it is about 250 years old. Germany has done the most to standardize and popularize the march in its present form. German love of symmetry and order made not only for regular march music but also made sure that it be simple enough for everybody. All definitely rhythmical compositions are program music by their very content. When actual marching or dancing is added, they take on an extra pictorial and dramatic quality.

Marching and dancing have always had a strong appeal to people of every country. People march together on various occasions—they march in parades; they march at graduations; they march in wedding processions and in funeral processions; and they march to war. For every kind of *march or procession* there is suitable music. A march sets the tempo for the marchers and helps them to keep in step, but it also serves to express their feelings, which may be gay, pompous, serious, or sad, according to the nature of the occasion. The rhythm of a march has a definite appeal, aside from the melody, harmony, form, and tone-color. The beat of a drum alone is sufficient for men on a march. Whatever is added to this rhythm tends to give a march its particular character.

The Welch march of the *Men of Harlech* (written probably in 1468) and the *Dessauer march* (of German origin) are the oldest marches in use today.

Marches are usually in ternary form; and they frequently have two trios.

There are four principal varieties of marches: the *quick march;* the *slow march;* the *triumphal march;* and the *funeral march*.

1. *Quick March, or Quickstep:* This is in 6/8, 2/2, or C time. The initial march is part I; the trio is part II. Both parts are of about equal length. The trio sometimes is in the subdominant; sometimes it is in the relative minor key.

Examples:

BIGELOW
    Our Director.

E. E. BAGLEY
    National Emblem.

VON BLON
    Emperor Frederic; Under the Flag of Victory; Return of the Colors; etc.

J. FUCIK
  Thunder and Blazes.

E. F. GOLDMAN
  On the Farm; On the Go; On the Road; On the Air;
  On the Campus; On the Mall; Stepping Along; etc.

R. B. HALL
  10th Regiment; 20th Regiment; Fort Pophan.

F. H. LOSEY
  Eastern Star; Firebrand; Lucky Strike; Spic and Span.

A. PRYOR
  Captain Cupid; On Jersey Shore; Heart of America;
  The Baby Parade; etc.

SAINT-SAENS
  French Military March, from the Algerian Suite.

J. P. SOUSA
  Stars and Stripes; El Capitan; King Cotton; Hands
  Across the Sea; Semper Fidelis; The Thunderer; Wash-
  ington Post; etc.

F. VON SUPPE   JOH. STRAUSS, JR.
  Boccaccio March.   Radetsky March.

C. TEIKE
  Old Comrades; The World in Arms; Staunch and True.

BARNA
  Rakoczy, or Hungarian March. (Barna was a Gypsy
  violinist, a court musician to Prince Rakoczy. Berlioz
  immortalized this very exciting Hungarian national
  march in his Damnation of Faust. Notice the brilliant
  recurrence of rhythmical aspects of original motive.)

2. *Slow, or Parade, March:* It is in 4/4 time, usually
short, and used mainly by the troups marching in parades,
saluting the colors.

Examples:

FREDERICK THE GREAT
  Fredericus Rex #1 (Cavalry Parade March).

FREDERICK THE GREAT
  Fredericus Rex #1 E (Mollwitzer March, 1741).

FREDERICK THE GREAT
  Fredericus Rex #1 F (March of 1756).

?
  Hohenfriedberger March (1745).

?   ?
  Dessauer March.   Torgauer March (1760).

?
  Pariser Einzugsmarsch.

3. *Triumphal, or Festival, March:* It is also called *grand march* or *march brilliante*. It is in 4/4, 12/8, or C time. The tempo is usually somewhat slower, and the rhythm more majestic than that of the quick march. The music suggests the pomp and ceremony of the occasion.

Examples:

BEETHOVEN
In Moto d'una Marcia; Turkish March, Ruins of Athens. (Notice evidence of unity in the recurrence of melodic and rhythmic original motive.)

ELGAR
Pomp and Circumstance.

V. HOLLANDER
March.

GOUNOD
March of the Queen of Sheba; Soldier Chorus, Faust.

MENDELSSOHN
Athalia, Priest March; Wedding March, Midsummer Night's Dream (has two trios).

GRIEG
March of the Dwarfs; Norwegian Bridal Procession.

MEYERBEER
Coronation March, Le Prophète.

LACHNER
March, Suite in D minor.

RAFF
March Leonore, Symphony #5.

SCHUBERT
March Militaire, D major.

PROUT
March Triumphal.

SCHUMANN
March Quintet, Opus 44; Carneval, March of the Davidsbündler. (Exception—in 3/4 time.)

SODERMANN
Swedish Wedding March.

SAINT-SAENS
March Heroique.

WAGNER
Tannhäuser March; Kaisermarch; Huldigungsmarsch.

VERDI
March from opera Aida.

TSCHAIKOWSKY
March Slav.

Majestic religious march:

GLUCK
March, opera Alceste.

MOZART
March, opera Magic Flute.

WAGNER
March, opera Parcifal, Knights of the Holy Grail.

4. *Funeral March, Marcia Lugubre* (Italian), *March Funèbre* (French), *Trauer Marsch* (German): It is usually in 4/4 time; and its rhythm suggests the solemn tolling of bells. Part I, of course, is in the minor key (except Handel's Death March in Saul, which is in major key). It expresses the sorrow we feel at the loss of someone dear to us. Part II (trio) is in the major key, representing the disembodied spirit; it suggests peace and rest.

Examples:

BEETHOVEN
March Funèbre, Eroica Symphony; March, Sonata in A, Opus 26.

BRAHMS   CHOPIN
March Funèbre.   Funeral March, Sonata in B minor.

GRIEG
Asa's Death, Peer Gynt Suite.

HANDEL
Death March, from Saul.

MENDELSSOHN
Trauermarsch (Songs Without Words).

WAGNER
Siegfried's Trauermarsch, from Götterdämmerung.

GOUNOD
Funeral March of a Marionette. (This is a dirge of another sort. It begins with excitement; suddenly, a musical crash proclaims a toyland tragedy, followed by an exclamation of horror. Now the jerky, stiff-legged procession of wooden dolls moves forward; the sound of marching is accompanied by wails of the chief mourners and an outburst by all the company. The march to the cemetery is interrupted by the animated musical discussion, ends too sadly, and with some degree of haste to get back to normal again.)

WALTZ

The *waltz* is a modern dance of German origin. The name is derived from the German word *waltzen*, to turn, or whirl. The waltz was formerly known as *"Deutscher Tanz," German dance*. Mozart, Hummel, Haydn, Schubert, and Beethoven often composed waltzes in sets and so earned a few ducats writing for the Vienna court. The German dance was exceedingly simple in melody, harmony, and accompaniment; it was a lilting dance, rather a Ländler, with sharply accented beats, divided into two parts, each generally eight measures long. Its spirit was decidely folkish, alike in its sentimental strains as in its physical aspects. Naturally, the minuet was more elegant. Usually, Mozart's German dances showed much inventiveness, even though the simple pattern offers rather little scope for marked individuality. The trios of his Deutsche Tänze often contained parts of folk music, generally in the minor key. (See Mozart, K. 568, K. 571, K. 586.)

The waltz is the love dance of modern civilization. It expresses the romance, the poetry, the subtle glamour and fascination of sex in its refined, idealistic, but irresistible potency.

In most of the older dances, the figures are executed by several couples. Partners are temporarily shifted; at times the evolutions are more complex and the social element more in evidence. In the waltz, however, there is a complete isolation of the couples. Each couple is enveloped in its peculiar, exclusive atmosphere of swift, graceful motion, almost intimate mutual absorption—alone for the moment in the midst of the whirling crowd and ingratiating music. This is its chief fascination and expresses the mood of the waltz.

No doubt, love with its subsidiary emotions is, and must remain, the oldest, most universal, and most potent factor in human existence. It is also the motive power in many important human actions and the determining element in most human experiences. No wonder that a motive of such vital and universal interest to the human race, which has served as the main theme in most of the great dramas and stories since literature began, should also be utilized by the composer. In the waltz love surely finds diversified expression.

Naturally, in connection with this concrete idea of the love dance, many other subsidiary emotions and suggestions arise which are associated and incident to it. Waltz music, at first intended to guide, control, and stimulate the dancers, gradually developed and expanded so as to include and utilize all these subsidiary emotions and incidental suggestions; till today some of the waltzes are no longer strictly dance music but complete art works. They are elaborate tone pictures of the ballroom scenes and moods, portraying vividly the complexities of human life and passions. Wagner said: "One of Strauss' waltzes as far surpasses in charm, finish, and real musical worth hundreds of the artificial compositions of his contemporaries as the tower of St. Stephen's surpasses the advertising columns of the Paris boulevards."

One of the first to develop the waltz was Schubert. He made the melody more brilliant and the harmony more elaborate. Weber also improved the waltz. Schubert and Weber together raised the waltz into the realm of art. They developed and expanded its form, introducing into it suggestive, descriptive, and more profoundly emotional elements.

Great development was given the waltz by the popularity of Weber's Invitation to the Dance. This wonderful composition stands as the most remarkable, world-famous, and epoch-making example. It was the forerunner of the fine waltzes of Chopin, which, in turn, have been the models from which our modern waltzes are constructed. Other composers have contributed liberally and ably to this most popular form of idealized dance music. The concert waltzes of Liszt, Schütt, etc., are played more today than ever. These waltzes add greatly to the delight of music. We need the lighter music to give contrast to the more serious kind. Moszkowski has composed four masterly waltzes for the piano. They all are concert numbers of some magnitude and fairly surpass all previous works in complexity of construction, technical brilliancy, wealth of musical content, and imagination.

The story of the waltz is a bit of Viennese history, for the waltz as such was born and nurtured in Vienna, the city that had known floods, plagues, invasion, and wars; the city that was, and remained, obsessed with the idea of the brevity of life; the city of carnivals and night life; the city of players, singers, and composers—Vienna the brilliant, and festive, and pleasure-loving.

The nameless minstrels of town and country gifted with rhythmic improvisations, as well as the great composers Mozart, Haydn, Schubert, Weber, Beethoven, all contributed the elements that formed the Vienna waltz. From the folk dances and Ländlers of Bavaria and Bohemia, from towns and countryside, from cafés and wineshops, came suggestions and inspiration for the waltz. In dance forms and rhythms they borrowed, perfected, and laid down new patterns. At first a theme of a few measures, it branched out until several themes were strung together. Introductions, trios, and codas were added; and so with Gungl, Lanner, and the Strausses the waltz reached full, pulsating maturity. All Vienna waltzed, and the dance spread like wildfire. The waltz was a compound of brilliance, vitality, esprit, abandon, glitter, and sentiment, the perfect expression of a romantic city eager for a gay life and seeking escape from a haunting emptiness. The waltz now invaded cafés, theaters, ballrooms, and homes. It was introduced into the social life of Vienna about 1730 and soon gained a sure and permanent foothold in popular favor, despite some opposition, and before long it spread throughout the whole world.

The *Vienna, or quick, waltz* is characterized by fire, energy, and tender expression. For actual dance purposes, these waltzes remain unequaled today. They are strictly rhythmic and full of *Lebenslust,* still embodying the sprightly grace, the exaggerated, flirtatious spirit of the primtive waltz. It gets a slight accent on the second beat, a typical Viennese device.

Of course, all waltzes are in 3/4 time. The phrases are rather marked, being generally of 8, 16, or 32 measures. Most waltzes are in ternary form. The modern concert and dance waltzes are in sets of four to five numbers of contrasting melodies and keys, with a *coda* made up of the principal themes, in addition to a brilliant *Introduction.*

The artistic value of the waltz lies in its easy, graceful, changing, delightful melodic invention. It is the most flowing of the modern dances and yields itself readily to dreamy, legato effects; but to obtain the full effects of these, it is well to contrast them with a brighter, skipping theme.

As in the Old Suite, in which the dances were changed to individual, idealized pieces, the waltz also has been made into individual concert pieces.

(Note especially: *Chopin*, Waltzes; *Brahms*, Liebeslieder Waltzes; *Berlioz*, Waltz in Symphony Fantastique; *Liszt*, Mephisto Waltz; *Tschaikowsky*, Waltzes in Symphonies #4 and #5; also his Waltz of the Flowers; etc.)

Examples:

CHOPIN
Minute Waltz; Waltz de Salon; Valse E♭, Opus 18; Valse C♯ minor, Opus 64, #2; Three Valses, Opus 70.

CZIBULKA
Love's Dream After the Ball.

DRIGO
Valse Bluette.

DELIBES
Ballet Music.

VON DITTERSDORF
German Dance.

GILLET
Loin de Bal.

E. GRIEG
Waltz, Opus 12, #2.

GUNGLE
Venus Reigen; Dream of the Ocean; Les Adieux; Immortellen; etc.

V. HERBERT
Kiss Me Again; Kiss in the Dark.

IVANOVICI
Danube Waves; Carmen Sylva; La Belle Roumaine; Oriental Roses.

E. KALMAN
See his various operettas.

KREISLER
Liebesfreud.

LANNER
Styrian Waltzes, Opus 6, 11, 165, 202.

LEHAR
Merry Widow Waltzes; Gold and Silver.

LISZT
Valse Impromptu in A♭.

MILLÖCKER
See his many operettas.

MOSZKOWSKI
Various waltzes.

RUBINSTEIN
Caprice; Valse Brilliante.

SCHUMANN
Papillon (has old German waltz in it).

E. SCHÜTT
A la Bien Aimee.

SIBELIUS
Valse Triste.

JOHANN STRAUSS
Village Swallows; Music of the Spheres.

JOHANN STRAUSS, JR.
Artist's Life; Blue Danube; Emperor Waltz; Roses from the South; Frühlingsstimmen; Morning Journals; Tales from the Vienna Woods; Thousand and One Nights; etc.

TSCHAIKOWSKY
Waltz of the Flowers; Waltz from Serenade for Strings Opus 48 (second movement).

E. WALDTEUFEL
The Skaters; Summer Evening; Ever or Never; La Berceuse; My Dream; Les Sirens; Return of Spring; To Thee; Très Jolie; Dolores; etc.

VON WEBER
Six Waltzes; Invitation to the Dance. (This brilliant number emphasizes the difference between the lively waltz and the slow Ländler.)

F. WINTERNITZ   VOLLSTEDT
Rêve de Jeunesse.   Artist's Dream; Jolly Fellows.

ZIEHRER
Vienna Beauties; Woodland Songsters.

LANDLER

A *Ländler* is written in 3/4 time; it is a little slower than the waltz. It originated among the German peasants in the 18th century, and is very popular in Austria, Bavaria, Styria, and Bohemia. The music of the Ländler differs from that of the minuet chiefly in the accompaniment, which is more rhythmic and monotonous, the first beat of each measure being accented by the bass, while the second and third beats are played more lightly.

Examples: See Mozart, Beethoven, Schubert—*Deutsche Tänze, or Ländler.*

THE BALLET

Civilization and art are intimately connected. People have always felt the need to satisfy their instincts *to sing, to act,* and *to dance.* Thus, they compose songs and plays about what interests them; and they also express their joys or sorrows by moving rhythmically to music. Dance music is entertainment; it emphasizes physical appeal more directly than any other type of music. When singing and acting are combined, we have opera of one kind or another. Many operas also present a combination of music and dancing designed to tell a story in simple pantomime. Such dancing we call *"ballet."* The ballet represents actions, characters, sentiments, passions, and feelings by mimic movements and dances in which several dancers perform together and show their skill. *The ballet is pantomime set to music*, and the dancing shades off into a sort of acting drama in which all that is spoken in drama is said by gesture; usually, it is a series of dances in varying styles and rhythms. A ballet may have several acts and be as long as an opera. In such a complete work each dance helps to illustrate or unfold the plot. The ballet was brought into prominence in our time by the fine work of the Russian dancers.

The highest beauty and poetic fancy has certainly been reached in the ballet. The music and the dance must blend absolutely to express feeling and passion, for neither art seems to exist for itself but only as a support for the other. It is full of rhythmic and plastic life, picturesque and poetic in its conception. The music, besides being romantic and passionate, should have rhythm and melody; the solo dances resembling arias and the ensemble more like a chorus. While resembling ordinary dance music, the ballet, in order to raise itself to a true art, must contain in addition poetical ideas, a characteristic outline, and a definite expression of feeling in dramatic form.

The following composers have written outstanding ballets: *Adam* (Giselle); *Berlioz* (Ballet des Sylphes); *Bohm; Delibes* (Coppelia; Sylvia; etc.); *Chaminade; Glazounoff; V. Herbert; Stravinsky* (Petrouschka; Apollon Musagète; etc.); *Tschaikowsky* (Sleeping Beauty; etc.); *Ponchielli* (Dance of the Hours).

OTHER INSTRUMENTAL FORMS

FANTASIA

The *fantasia, fantasy, or fanciful piece,* is one in which the composer, free from the restrictions of conventional form of design, may give reign to his imagination and go as far as his own sense of artistic proportion allows. A free development of one or more themes usually follows a prelude and precedes the fugue (Bach's largest organ form). It may consist of one or several movements. Quite often it derives its form and content, in part at least, from some literary or pictorial ideas of the composer, such as a story or a landscape. If the composer depicts a scene, he may imitate actual sounds, such as the purling of a brook, the singing of birds, etc. It may then be classed as program music. Ordinarily, the movements of a fantasia are more closely connected than those of a suite or a sonata. A theme used in one movement will sometimes appear in another. Fantasias for organ or for various combinations of instruments were common before Bach's time.

Examples:

J. S. BACH
  Chromatic Fantasy.

CHOPIN
  Fantasia in F minor.

LISZT
  Rhapsody #11 (also, paraphrases and fantasies).

MENDELSSOHN
  Fantasia, Opus 28.

RAFF
  Villanelle, Opus 89.

MOZART
  Fantasia #3 (involves no program idea).

SCHUBERT
  Fantasia, C major.

SCHUMANN
  Fantasia, Opus 17.

CAPRICCIOSO

The *capriccioso* is a work in free form, somewhat resembling the fantasia, yet not as earnest in style. It is lighter, more "capricious," and even bizarre. The form should not hamper the quality of style. The word *caper* (Latin) means *goat* and suggests the familiar phrase "to cut a caper." *Caprice, capriccio, capriccioso,* and *capricciette* are musical terms that indicate a free-and-easy leaping movement.

Examples:

KREISLER
  Caprice Viennois.

MENDELSSOHN
  Rondo Capriccioso.

ETUDE

An *Étude, or Study,* is a short composition by which the player may gain mastery of one or more technical difficulties, such as scales, runs, chords, arpeggios, trills, octaves, sixths, double stops, etc. It is a complete piece of music, whereas an exercise is not. *Études* have inspired pieces of great brilliancy, in which difficult passages are used as a setting for musical ideas. Paganini, Chopin, Dancla, Liszt, Rubinstein, and others have written *Études* of real musical merit that demand the acme of skill.

The *Étude* is usually written in a kind of unit form, without evident breaks or changes; or in 2-part, and sometimes in 3-part, form. It necessarily does not involve strong contrasts. *Étude*-writing requires an intimate acquaintance with the instrument and its needs; consequently, they are composed by experienced teachers or performers.

See *Études* by: Bertini, Czerny, Clementi, Cramer, Burgmüller, Duvernoy, Foote, Heller, MacDowell, Moscheles, Raff, Liszt, Schumann, Wollenhaupt, etc. Also, *Études* by: Dancla, Fiorillo, Gavinies, Dont, Kreutzer, Paganini, Rode, Kaiser, Rovelli, Wieniawski, etc.

TOCCATA

The word *"toccata"* (Italian, *toccara;* French, *toucher—to touch, to feel*) at first was used as a technical term for any keyboard composition requiring full, sonorous chords followed by quick runs, and originally meant the same as sonata, fantasia, or free prelude; but later the term was applied only to brilliant examples of the staccato style. Very likely, it was invented as a musical form by Merulo (1532–1604). A study in which some difficulties of execution were always present, it generally preceded a fugue. The characteristic mark of the modern toccata is the moving along throughout in notes of short value. It still is a study but is more generally founded on the treatment of a single figure—a rapid, flowing, continuous succession of figures or passages. The toccata is not a very long piece, but often demands a brilliant and showy execution.

Examples:

RHEINBERGER
Toccata

R. SCHUMANN
Toccata, Opus 7.

For old-style toccatas, see those for organ by Fresco-baldi, Buxtehude, Froberger, J. K. Kerll, Pachelbel, Scheidt, etc. in *Denkmäler der Tonkunst in Oesterreich;* also J. S. Bach's Organ Toccatas in D minor; Piano Toccatas in D minor; G minor; E minor.

RICERCARE

The *ricercare* is derived from the Italian word *"ricercare,"* *to seek, to find* (the theme). Frescobaldi was the first classic master of this form. It is a piece containing a number of de-velopments in fugue style of a given theme, as well as of rhythmical variations of that theme. Some ricercari have four or more developments; often the rhythm of the theme also is changed—4/4 time is changed to 3/2, or to 6/8, or 9/8 time, etc.

Examples:

BEETHOVEN
String Quartet, Opus 133 (fugue).

B. FROBERGER
Ricercare.

RITORNELLO

This is a short repetition of the concluding phrases of an air; a passage which is played while the principal voice pauses; the introduction to an air or any musical piece.

DIVERTIMENTO

The *divertimento* (Italian), or *divertissement* (French), is music for festive occasions, usually composed for several instruments. It consists of five to six individual numbers of march, minuet, and other similar forms. Like the serenade, the divertimento is a cyclic form of short movements, often beginning and ending with a march. However, the serenade generally is written for orchestra, and the divertimento for solo instruments. It also somewhat resembles the modern suite, but it is more light and informal in character. Tschai-kowsky made it a single suite movement.

An example is Mozart's Divertimento in D.

TRANSCRIPTION

A *transcription* is an arrangement of an original composition for another instrument—piano for orchestra, a song for a violin solo, etc.—either condensed or extended, in which the arranger has used his own idea. The term is often used in the sense of "paraphrase" or "fantasia" with operatic melodies.

Examples:

> MENDELSSOHN-ACHRON
> On Wings of Song (violin solo).
> WAGNER-WILHELMJ
> Walter's Preislied (violin solo).
> WAGNER-WILHELMJ
> Romanze (Albumblatt, violin solo).

BADINERIE

The *badinerie* is a short composition which does not imply any particular type of dance form, but merely suggests a mood of jollity and badinage. Foolery, toying, tumbling, juggling, and a kind of apish gamboling characterize the music. A badinerie usually is written in lively 2/4 or 4/4 time.

An example is J. S. Bach's Rejouissance, from Suite in D.

SALON MUSIC

Salon music really means "music for the drawing room." It means also that the music is not of the highest type or requiring serious attention, but is written merely to please, in a more or less superficial manner. It has none of the development of the sonata or of the carefully worked out intricacy of the fugue, the suite, etc. Instead, it has light but pleasing melodies and rich harmonies in the form of broken chords (arpeggios). Of course, salon music is not necessarily trashy music, nor is it necessarily easy to compose. While it may include works of interest and value, of dexterity and expression, it does, however, lack the depth and earnestness of master works; it is brief and to the point, brilliant and showy at times, and occasionally songlike and devotional.

Examples:

C. Bohm   Leybach
   The Fountain.   Fifth Nocturne.
Thome
   Simple Aveu (Confession).

IMPROMPTU

The word *"impromptu"* is derived from *"in promptu"* (Latin, *in readiness*); and it denotes a fantasy, a composition that is not developed according to the regular laws of form, a piece of music having an improvisational and informal character. It is a little tone picture which expresses a definite mood. It usually portrays one thought, and its form is simple, consisting of one theme and a second theme which balance each other. The impromptu usually is in 3-part song form. Impromptus, and other lyric pieces, represent excellent opportunities for various color treatment; and for this reason they appeal strongly to composers of the romantic school.

Examples:

M. Bruch   Chopin
   Impromptu for Piano, Opus 12.   Impromptu.

MacDowell   Schubert
   Impromptu for Piano, Opus 46.   Impromptus.

SCHERZO

The *scherzo* (Italian) means "jest" and is the name for a capricious, humorous composition, usually in quick tempo, rhythmically and harmonically piquant, having strong accents, shifts of accents (syncopation), clever staccato, and large melodic skips of fine articulation; hence, it requires delicate rendering. Generally, it occurs between the slow movement and the finale, or between the first and slow movement of a sonata or symphony, taking the place of the minuet formerly used at the time of Haydn and Mozart; but it may also be an independent piece of music, usually in 3-part form.

For examples, see Scherzos by Beethoven, Brahms, Bruckner, Chopin, Mahler, Mendelssohn, Schumann, etc.

RHAPSODY

The *rhapsody* is an irregular, formless composition of impassioned and intense character. It is often used to represent the wilder strains of folk music. It wanders from one theme, key, or tempo to another at the will of the composer. While some works of this type, such as Dvorak's Slavonic Rhapsody, are thematically original or nearly so, the majority are founded on folk music, as, for instance, Delius' Brigg Fair, G. Holst's Summerset Rhapsody, or V. Williams' Norfolk Rhapsody. Liszt has given the rhapsody a charming and effective character; his Hungarian Rhapsodies are among the truly characteristic pieces for the piano. The rhapsody may be in any rhythm. The Hungarian rhapsody, as represented in the gypsy music of that country, contains the *"lassan,"* tender and slow in character and serving the purpose of an introduction, and the *"friska,"* a bright and dashing movement ending with a frenzy. Besides Liszt, Brahms and Dohnanyi, etc., composed fine rhapsodies.

POTPOURRI

The *potpourri* (French) is a medley of tunes or bits of melodies taken from a popular musical work and strung together to make a continuous whole and provide contrasts. A good potpourri, however, should begin and end in the same key. Potpourries from famous operas, operettas, musical shows, etc., are the most common examples.

MEDLEY OVERTURE

The *medley overture* is introductory music made up of passages from popular airs. Richard Clark, a violinist in the orchestra of the Drury Lane Theater, is said to be the originator of this type of music. It has no definite form; merely a collection of melodies from singspiel, musical shows, songs, etc., well contrasted and arranged to lead to a climax.

See examples by Auber (Overture to Fra Diavolo); Herold (Zampa Overture); Bellini; Bizet; Boieldieu; Donizetti; Rossini; S. Romberg; Strauss; F. von Suppe; etc.

Examples of overtures of *incidental music* to a play:

BEETHOVEN   MENDELSSOHN
 Egmont Overture.   Midsummer Night's Dream.
V. WILLIAMS
 The Wasps.

LYRIC PIECES

After intrumental forms of music had been worked out to a high degree of perfection, composers began to use music mainly as a medium for expressing their own personal feelings rather than for mere tonal beauty, as had their predecessors. Inasmuch as this subjective expression required greater elasticity of treatment, they invented new forms to suit their needs or sometimes made use of the conventional forms, with occasional modifications. The songs by Schubert are beautiful examples of lyric pieces. Such lyric songs, by the way, embody some vivid emotional experience; they are the most personal kind of music we have. Others who also possessed this great gift for personal expression now transferred their melodies to other instruments besides the voice.

When the piano was perfected, it made possible the rendering of lyric melodies. Before long, many composers wrote such pieces, not only for the piano but also for other instruments. Mendelssohn called his lyric pieces "Songs Without Words"; while Chopin, Liszt, Schumann, and others gave them various names, such as "Nocturne"; "Romance"; "Revery"; "Träumerei"; "Albumblatt"; "Aubade"; etc.

A true lyric piece, like a brief lyric poem, is clear and simple in structure; it voices but a single mood and, as a rule, is short and unified in style. It is either in binary or ternary form.

The performer must understand the mood of the lyric piece and be able to reproduce it in order to convey a definite meaning. Yet the performer must be individual whenever he recreates tone pictures that are entirely subjective. In fact, he who expects to recreate moods cannot be outside of them; he cannot be objective, but must be within the mood. In short, he must be subjective. Modern art is subjective and can therefore not be handled objectively. Just as a lyric poem creates quite different pictures for different readers, so lyric music must do the same. To fulfill its purpose, it must stir the soul.

Berceuse, cradle song, lullaby, Wiegenlied: A lyric composition in either 2-part or 3-part form, and generally with a lulling 2/8 or 4/4 regular and tranquil rhythm representing the rocking of the cradle. It is known the world over.

Examples:

D. ALARD
  Berceuse.

FR. BRIDGE
  Cradle Song.

GODARD
  Berceuse, from Jocelyn.

GRIEG
  Slumber Song (Romantic School; free treatment as to form).

GOUNOD
  Dodelinette (*dodeliner*, French, to rock gently).

HAUSER
  Wiegenlied.

ILYINSKY, A.
  Berceuse.

MOSZKOWSKI
  Berceuse, Opus 38.

BRAHMS
  Lullaby.

CHOPIN
  Berceuse.

JAERNEFELT
  Berceuse.

SIMON
  Berceuse in G.

Barcarolle, Boat Song: A lyric piece in wavelike 6/8 time; in slow tempo; giocoso and quietly; suggesting the motion of a boat gently rocked by the waves. It is a vocal or instrumental composition in the style of the Venitian gondolier's song. It is usually written in the ternary form, often with a Coda, and generally with modifications of Part I on its reappearance.

The *gondoliera* is similar to the barcarolle but carries a definite suggestion of Venitian effects.

Examples:

CESEK
  Barcarolle.

CHOPIN
  Barcarolle.

EHRLICH
Barcarolle in G.

GODARD
Venetian Barcarolle.

MENDELSSOHN
Venetianisches Gondellied, #6, #12, #29 (Songs Without Words).

NEVIN
Gondolieri, Opus 25, #2.

HELLER
Boat Song.

OFFENBACH
Barcarolle (Tales of Hoffmann).

RHEINHOLDT
Boat Song.

A. RUBINSTEIN
Third Barcarolle; Fourth Barcarolle.

SAINT-SAENS
A Night in Lisbon.

L. V. SAAR
Gondoliera.

P. SCHARWENKA
Gondellied, Opus 63.

H. SITT
Barcarolle.

TSCHAIKOWSKY
"June" Barcarolle (in 3-part form, with coda).

Spinning Song: A lyric instrumental piece or song. Long ago, the yarn for making cloth was spun by hand. This task usually was performed by the women of the household, who would assemble in a room set apart for the purpose and chatter or sing gaily as they ran their spinning wheels.

Examples:

MENDELSSOHN
Spinning Song, #34 (Songs Without Words).

DVORAK
In the Spinning Room.

KULLACK
Spinning Song.

SAINT-SAENS
The Spinning Wheel of Omphale.

SPINDLER
Spinning Wheel.

WAGNER
Spinning Song from Flying Dutchman.

Hunting Song, Chanson de chasse (French), *Jagdlied* (German): A lyric instrumental piece or song of gay and spirited character.

Examples:

GURLITT
Hunting Song.

KUHLAU
Hunting Song.

KÜCKEN   KREUTZER
    The Huntsman.   Night in Granada.
MENDELSSOHN
    Hunting Song, #3 (Songs Without Words).
ROSSINI
    Overture to William Tell.
TSCHAIKOWSKY
    La Chasse, from The Seasons.
WEBER
    Lützow's Wild Hunt (song); A Hunting We Will Go
    (song).

Nocturne (French), *notturno* (Italian), *Nachtstück*
(German): Literally, a night-piece; a quiet, dreamy or sentimental composition, usually of lyric character, reflecting
the calm of eve. Field was the founder of this favorite form
of drawing-room music. Generally, it is in the large 3-part
form, often with a coda, and usually with modifications of
Part I on its reappearance.
    Examples:

CHOPIN
    Nocturne in B major, Opus 33 (2-part form with short
    coda).
DEBUSSY   J. FIELD
    Clair de Lune.   Nocturnes.
G. GOLTERMANN   LISZT
    Notturno for Violin and Piano.   Liebestraum, #3.
MENDELSSOHN
    Nocturne from Midsummer Night's Dream.

Songs Without Words, Lieder Ohne Worte (German):
Since Mendelssohn's time this has become a common term
for somewhat showy instrumental pieces. Songs without
words must be singable in character and must have a certain dramatic import; but it is not necessary for the composer
to attach any definite meaning to the work.
    In his forty-two Songs Without Words, Mendelssohn has
proven his mastery of the style by using the simple song
form of A B A (without Trio) 42 times in constantly new
variations. The use of the Reprise, i.e., taking up again section A at the close, is handled very skillfully; the same is true

of the fine thematic development of the Coda. For example, take song #6: Introduction 6 measures, A 4+6 measures, B 8+1 measure, A 6 measures; finale, 6 measures. The reprise in section B comes nine measures later than expected. Thus Reprise A and Coda are one, the reprise being only hinted at but not carried out. A Postlude concludes the piece.

The simple song form also has been used very skilfully and effectively by Chopin in his waltzes, mazurkas, impromptus, scherzos, preludes, and études. Also by Brahms: four ballads, Opus 10; eight capricci and intermezzi, Opus 76, Opus 116, 117, 118, 119. Some of these show interesting changes and are partly mixed forms.

Arioso (Italian), *arietta* (small aria): A short melodious movement in the middle or at the conclusion of a recitative. It differs from the aria in that it has no thematic articulation, being a short lyrical movement. Often the term is used for short melodious pieces.

Arabesque: A composition in which the theme is surrounded by delicate tonal embroideries. It is an excellent equivalent of the intricate and exquisite tracery that decorates Moorish or oriental buildings, in which the figures of animals, plants, and even human beings are interwoven.

An example is Schumann's Arabeske.

Albumblatt, album leaf: A short informal lyric piece suggesting improvisation. It usually is in the song form.

An example is R. Wagner's Albumblatt (violin solo).

Aubade: A morning song or serenade.

An example is Schubert-Liszt's Hark, Hark, the Lark.

Bagatelle: A short, unpretentious piece, usually in song form, having an improvisational and informal character.

Ballade: A lyric piece, poetic, rhapsodical, emotional, and dramatic in style, with some degree of narrative suggestion.

An example is Chopin's Ballades; also, see ballades by Liszt, Brahms, Schumann, etc.

Ballata (Italian): Sometimes means "Ballade"; but most often it refers to a song-dance, from the Latin word *"ballare,"* to dance.

Cabaletta: A pleasing melodious piece in simple style. The accompaniment is in triplets, or similar notes, to suggest a galloping horse.

An example is Lack's Cabaletta.

Canzonetta (Italian): A little songlike melody.

Cavatina (Italian): A smooth, pleasing melody, singable in character, with a certain dramatic import. It is in 2-part or 3-part song-form. It is a lyrical vocal solo or instrumental piece of simple character; but it is not necessary for the composer to attach a definite meaning to the work.

Examples are Raff—Cavatina; or Aulin—Cavatina.

The *elegy, or dirge,* (*eligia,* Italian), is a melodious, expressive piece of sad and mournful style.

Examples are S. Youferoff's Elegie; P. Juon's Elegie; Massenet's Elegie; C. V. Rychlik's Elegy; etc.

The *entr'acte* is a composition to be played between the acts of an opera similar to the intermezzo.

The *intermezzo* (*intermedio,* Italian) is a short lyric piece in free style; an *interlude;* a short movement usually connecting other numbers—between the acts of an opera or a play, the verses of a hymn, etc. The word means "between the halves"; and the composer is allowed complete freedom. It may sometimes be a prayerful piece.

Examples are Bizet's Intermezzo from L'Arlesienne; Mascagni's Intermezzo from Cavalleria Rusticana; etc.

(Note: The oldest intermezzi were composed of madrigals; at times they were relieved by instrumental numbers, likewise madrigals. Later on the ballet divertissement took the place of the intermezzo. It exists in the drama as the interpolated ballet and as entr'acte music. The name also signifies the same as "episode," probably used for the first time by Schumann for a connected series of piano pieces. Schumann evidently regarded them as intermediate numbers for a concert program. Besides Brahms and Heller, many other composers also have made use of the title "intermezzo.")

Légende, or legend, suggests legendary romance or supernatural mystery of epic-lyric character (dramatic), as if the music were telling a tale. It is usually in 3-part form. An example is Wieniawski's Legende.

The *novelette* is a striking composition that seems to tell an adventure or a story; it is freely constructed and romantic in character. It does not express anything definite, and is often used for pieces of any length in which occur rapid changes of themes and rhythmical combinations of the boldest sort. The term probably was first used by Schumann (Opus 21, Noveletten).

The *novellozzi* is a composition with strong literary suggestion. An example is Godard's Novellozza.

The *pistacchio* is a melody made up of various single pieces taken from different sources, i.e., works of different composers. In an operatic pistacchio, words are set to melodies already existing.

The *pastorale* is a composition suggesting scenes and emotions of rustic life. It is naïve and simple in character, and often a drone bass is introduced, imitating a bagpipe and giving a rustic effect. It is related to the siciliano and expresses the music-making of shepherds on their pipes. It is of simple rhythm, melody, and modulation, and usually is written in triple time (6/8 or 12/8).

Examples are J. S. Bach's Pastorale, from his Christmas Oratorio, Pastorale for Organ, Sonata for Flute in E major; Sonata for Violin in G major; Tschaikowsky's Manfred, Opus 58, III.

The *poem* suggests poetic-romantic feeling; it is similar to the romanza. An example is Chausson's Poeme for Violin & Piano.

The *romanza* expresses romantic feeling, or it may tell an actual story. It is of lyric character, like a song. Melodic invention and lyric feeling predominate. Originally a song or ballad, it may be written in 2-part or 3-part song form, or in rondo form; but usually it is free in style. It may be in any rhythm, but must be passionate.

Examples:

BEETHOVEN
Romance in G; Romance in F.

FAURE
Romance Sans Paroles.

PROTHERO	A. RUBINSTEIN
A Welch Romance.	Romance.
SPOHR	SWENDSEN
Romance.	Romance.
TSCHAIKOWSKY	WILHELMJ
Romance.	Romance.

The *reverie* is a composition of dreamy and tender style, usually in 2-part or 3-part song form. It may be in any rhythm, but 3/4 time is best adapted to its quiet effects. Examples are R. Strauss' Reverie and A. Wormser's Reverie.

The *vinata, or ninetta* (Italian) is a vintage song, a wine song, a drinking song.

Examples of other lyric pieces:

Adagio Pathetic—B. Godard. Allegro Scherzoso—C. Cui.
Ave Maria—Bach-Gounod; L. Cherubini; Schubert.
Au Matin—B. Godard. Adoration—F. Borowski.
Andante Religioso—C. V. Rychlik; Thomé.
Air—Lully. Aria in E—Porpora.
Canzona—C. Bohm. L'Etincelle—G. Papini.
Humoreske—Dvorak; A. Heft; T. Aulin; Tschaikowsky.
Hymn A St. Cecile—Gounod. Habanera—E. Chabrier.
Hymn to the Sun—Rimski-Korsakov.
Meditation—Massenet (Thais); Glazounow.
Melody (Melodie)—Dawes; A. Rubinstein (Melody in F);
  Tschaikowsky, Opus 42.
Près de la Mer (Esquisse)—A. Arensky.
Sérénité—Vieuxtemps. Simple Histoire—C. Dancla.
Souvenir—Drdla. Spring Song—Mendelssohn.
The Swan—Saint-Saens. Träumerei—Schumann.

RONDO

Originally the word *"rondo"* referred to a tune adopted to a round dance.

The necessity of repetition of the principal musical idea led to the establishment of the *rondo* form. The rondo is an instrumental piece with a main theme A or I, then one, two, or more subsidiary themes, B C or II III, etc., in contrast, which are presented in rotation, always alternating with the main theme. A rondo may end with the A theme (or theme I), or with a *Coda,* the latter made up of old or new material. The main theme should occur at least three times or more. A rondo may also have an *introduction.*

The tempo of the rondo is usually fast, and it is most generally written in a light, fluent, jocose, free style and with dainty expression. This makes the rondo a popular form for a movement of a sonata, a symphony, or string quartet.

Generally speaking, there are three types of rondos, but almost anything that cannot be classed elsewhere is apparently put among the rondos, if possible; thus there are also *irregular rondos.* Sinding's Rustle of Spring, therefore, is a rondo on two themes. There are too many repeats in this piece to allow it to be classed as a 2-part song form, admitting that the periods may sometimes be repeated together instead of separately.

Rondo Type I: In its earlier state the rondo began with a subject (melody) of one or two periods. After wandering through several keys, and introducing much more passage work, it returned to the main theme. This rondo form with one or two subjects was used by composers from Couperin (1688–1733) to Haydn (1732–1809). Thus, we have a main theme(or section); a second theme (or section); and a return to the main theme. The main theme and the second theme may be repeated together, in which case it is called Rondo Type I by repeats—A B A (I II I).

Examples:

BRAHMS
 Allegretto, from Second Symphony. (An extended rondo Type 1 by recurrence of second and main

theme. This is a fine example of the variety that may be given to the main theme. Note altered rhythm, new keys, and unexpected modulations, all done with great skill and without obscuring the main lines of the form.)

CLEMENTI
Rondo in F.

COUPERIN
The Little Windmill.

MOZART
Sonata in D #15 (Adagio Movement).

Rondo type II: Later composers introduced a second subject, and still later composers a third subject; but the first was always repeated after each one. This rondo form, with two or three themes, was used much by Mozart and Beethoven. Thus we have a main theme, a second theme, main theme, third theme, and main theme again. The effect of monotony may be avoided if the themes are fairly long and the second and third themes are in strong contrast to the main theme—A B A C A; I II I III I.

Examples:

BEETHOVEN
Sonata Pathetique (slow movement).

MOZART
Piano Sonata #1 and 2 (final movements; Litolff edition).

MOSZKOWSKI
Spanish Dance, Opus 12, #1.

Rondo type III: It consists of a main theme, a second theme, main theme, a third theme, main theme, second theme, and main theme again. It is not often used: A B A C A B A; I II I III I II I.

An example is Beethoven's C major Sonata, Opus 53, last movement. (Main theme, measures 1–62; second theme, 62–114; main theme, 114–174; third theme, 149–212; main theme, 212–243; second theme, 243–302; main theme, 302–441.)

(Note: Many compositions are very similar in form to the rondo, but they really are mixed forms—partly song form or sonata. Note especially Schumann's piano works—Novelleten, Opus 21; Faschingsschwank, Opus 26. Here a main theme alternates with several side themes. Inasmuch as each of these side themes is complete in itself, like the main theme, the interest which the classical rondo arouses because of its colorful repetitions is missing.)

Other notable composers of the fine rondos are: Field, Hummel, von Weber, and Mendelssohn (Rondo Capriccioso).

SERENADE

The *serenade, or Ständchen* (German), is literally an evening song; but it may be used both for morning and evening as a mark of esteem and good will toward distinguished persons. The Italian *serenata,* implying a serene night (*la sera,* the evening) came to be accepted as a general name for the rhapsodies sung by lovers beneath the windows of lady loves. A *serenade* is a lyric song, or set of songs, or an instrumental symphonic work.

It expresses the wooing of a lover and tender and dreamy sentiment in keeping with the stillness of night.

The old instrumental serenade was a cyclic form containing a number of short movements, often beginning and ending with a march. Quite characteristic, however, was the introduction of a minuet between every andante and allegro; but the form was not a fixed one. Mozart's "Haffner" Serenade contains eight movements, three of them minuets. Generally, the serenade is written for orchestra, while the *divertimento* is written for solo instruments. There are many exceptions, however. Beethoven called his Trio Opus 8, a serenade. Serenades formerly were compositions in which wind instruments predominated, being best suited for out-of-door performances.

With its introduction into the concert room, the scope of the serenade became more extended in form and orchestration; and as time passed, the title was applied to works consisting of several movements of free structure and romantic temper—something after the style of the suite and the divertimento. Thus, the serenade denotes a nocturnal love song of soothing and tranquil character. While the serenade was more frequently composed in the 18th century, there are more modern examples of this form; as, for instance, the serenades for string orchestra by: Brahms, Brüll, R. Strauss, Novak, Weiner, Fuchs, Milhaud, etc.

Examples:

ALBENIZ
Serenade Español.

AMBROSIUS
Serenade.

BEETHOVEN
Serenades for String Trio.

C. BOHM
Spanish Serenade.

VON BLON
Serenade d'Amour.

BRAHMS
Serenades, Opus 11, Opus 25.

DRIGO
Serenade from Les Millions D'Arlequin.

DRDLA
Serenade in A.

R. FUCHS
Serenade.

GABRIEL-MARIE
Serenade Badine.

CHAMINADE
Serenade.

HAYDN
Serenade.

V. HERBERT
Serenade.

MOSZKOWSKI
Serenata.

PIERNE
Serenade.

POSZNANSKI
Serenade Italienne.

RACHMANINOFF
Serenade.

SCAMBATI
Serenade Napoletana.

SCHUBERT
Ständchen.

SCHUMANN
Serenade.

TITLE
Serenade.

TSCHAIKOWSKY
Serenade Melancholique; Serenade for String Orch.

DE VORE
Serenade d'Octobre.

WIDOR
Serenade.

R. VOLKMAN
Serenade.

THEME, OR AIR, AND VARIATIONS

This is a popular form for harpsichord or organ. Monotony is more unendurable in music than in any of the other arts. Composers were always busy inventing new devices to vary their thoughts so that the interest of the listener might be continually sustained and refreshed. Thus, there was developed the variation form. It is one of the oldest musical forms; and, from the 16th century on, gives the composer a chance, within its narrow limits, to prove his agility and ingenuity. By "variation" is meant the representation of some musical thought or idea under different aspects. A similar theme is taken and repeated with modifications of melody, rhythm, meter, harmony, key, tonality, or any combination of these. Few composers have denied themselves the pleasure of taking a simple theme, either original or borrowed, and transforming it in such ways as their fancy might suggest; and few music-lovers have failed to experience the pleasure that comes of following the theme through its successive transformation and recognizing it under all its various disguises.

There are two main kinds of variations: 1. The *ornamental variation,* showing brilliance and virtuosity, retaining the harmonic base of the theme and surrounding it with passages and figures, runs, trills, arabesques, etc. 2. The *character variation,* showing a varied remodeling of the theme, transforming the theme into something new, giving it a different character, going away from the original theme, but without losing its connections. Both kinds of variations are desirable, and each has been developed by great composers. At any rate, the theme of either type of variation must be short—a sort of small song form, which, because of its symmetry, its cadences, its simple, clear harmony, is especially suitable and easy to grasp so that the ear may recognize it readily in whatever form it may reappear.

The *theme and variation* came into existence when modern music was not fully developed. At first, it consisted of the simple representation of some folk tune, with a subsequent variation of this tune in different ways by the addition of all kinds of interesting features, displaying the cleverness of composers in manipulating their materials. No form has been discovered which could extend for more than a few phrases or periods, so composers began to develop a form by repeating a theme under different guises. It was used as a vocal and an instrumental form. William Byrde (1543–1623), a favorite composer to Queen Elizabeth, is said to have first used the variation form. In time it became a great favorite with all the great masters. The art of writing a good theme and variation is one of the most important demands on the technic of composing.

The oldest and simplest variation form is the *ground bass*, or *basso ostinato*. It is a composition in which a theme of four to eight measures is continually repeated in the same bass, each time with a different upper part. It was very popular at one time. The chaconne and the passecaglia, originally dance forms constructed on a ground bass, were turned into variation form by J. S. Bach. (See his suites, as well as those by Handel. The *ground bass* was also much used by H. Purcell.)

Variation forms are divided into "strict" and "free."

Strict Variation (*ornamental*): The original form of the theme is closely preserved. The theme generally is in ordinary form of two periods, or sentences, nearly always repeating each part. Most of the variations are in the same key. Though each variation repeats enough of the material of the original theme to make the composition as a whole seem unified, yet it introduces some element of variety so that no two variations are identical.

Examples:

J. S. BACH
  Goldberg Variations.

BYRDE
  The Carman's Whistle.

HANDEL
  Air and Variation (The Harmonious Blacksmith).

HAYDN
  Variations on the Austrian National Anthem; Andante from Surprise Symphony.

MOZART
  See many of his piano or violin sonatas.

Free Variation (*character*): The original form of the theme is not preserved. Beethoven, in his later works, was the founder of this form. It is also much used by modern composers. Since Beethoven, the finest variations have been written by Liszt, Schumann, Brahms, Wagner, Grieg, and Tschaikowsky. Variations on a theme may constitute an entire composition (like those by Brahms), or the movement of a sonata or symphony (like those by Mozart, Beethoven, etc.). Variations usually are in slow tempo, and they may be of different kinds—adding a few notes to the original, changing rhythm, additional complex rhythm, putting the melody in the bass, adding ornamentation, changing tonality from major to minor, or vice versa, etc. The form requires imagination, skill, ingenuity, resourcefulness; it hardly lends itself to a highly emotional content. But the inventiveness of the musical mind can easily be studied in a theme and variations.

Examples:

BEETHOVEN

> 5th Symphony, 2nd movement, andante; Sonatas for Violin & Piano, Opus 12, #1, 2nd movement; Six Variations on an Original Theme, F major, Opus 34; 32 Variations in C minor; 33 Variations of a Waltz Theme by Diabelli, Opus 120 (a great masterpiece).

BRAHMS

> Variations on Themes by Paganini, Opus 35; Variations on a Theme by Haydn; Handel Variation, Opus 24.

ELGAR

> Enigma Variations (here the theme never appears).

C. FRANCK

> Symphonic Variations for Piano & Orchestra.

P. DUKAS

> Variations on a Theme by Rameau, for piano.

CHOPIN

> Variations B major, Opus 12; Variation on a Theme by Mozart, Don Giovanni, Opus 2.

GRAINGER   GRIEG

> Shepherd's Hey.   Ballade, Opus 24.

GLAZUNOV

> Theme and Variation, Opus 72.

J. HAYDN

> Surprise Symphony, G major, 2nd movement.

D'INDY

> Istar (here the theme does not appear until after the last variation).

MENDELSSOHN

> Variation Serieuses, Opus 64; Andante con Variazone in E, Opus 32.

M. REGER

> Variation on a Theme by Bach, Opus 80; Variation on a Theme by Beethoven, Opus 20, for Two Pianos.

SAINT-SAENS
   Variation for Two Pianos on a Theme by Beethoven.

SCHUBERT
   Impromptu, Opus 142, #3; Variation on the song
   Death and the Maiden (string quartet in D minor).

SCHUMANN
   Symphonic Études, Opus 13; Quartet in A (assai agi-
   tato). Carneval, Opus 9.

R. STRAUSS
   Don Quixote.

TSCHAIKOWSKY
   Theme and Variations, from Suite #3.

THE MODERN SUITE

The *modern suite,* or "set" of pieces, is an orchestral
composition in several movements. It has greater freedom
in the treatment of the instruments as well as in type of
movements than the old suite. What the composer will include in his suite is surely a matter of individual temperament and choice. However, a sufficient clue to the kind of
movement intended is usually conveyed by the title. *Some
composers,* like Lachner, etc., *made the suite into a definite
form;* while *others,* like Bizet, Grieg, Tschaikowsky, etc.,
*arranged suites from their ballet music or their incidental
music for some play.* The harmony and orchestration of the
modern suite are usually more complex, and there is practically no restriction upon the keys that may be used for its
several movements. The modern suite is sometimes constructed without pauses between the several movements.

In the modern suite we often find descriptive or program-
matic elements. The orchestra employs these elements for a
great variety of tonal effects.

The modern suite resembles the old suite, or classic suite,
in the contrasts of rhythm and tempo in the several movements.

Examples:

BIZET
   L'Arlésienne Suite, #1 and #2.

BRAHMS
   Serenade (in form of a suite).

D'ALBERT
First Modern Suite.

F. BUSONI
Turandot Suite.

CARPENTER
Adventure in a Perambulator.

A. COPELAND
Music for the Theater.

H. COWELL
Tales of our Countryside.

DEBUSSY
The Children's Corner.

DVORAK
Suite for Small Orchestra.

A. GRIEG
Peer Gynt Suite, #1 and #2.

O. GRIMM
Suites in Canon Form.

IPPOLITOV-IVANOV
Caucasian Sketches.

JADASSON
Serenade in Form of a Suite.

GRUENBERG
Jazz Suite.

CH. IVES
Three Places in New England.

L. LACHNER
Suites.

MACDOWELL
Modern Suite, #1, #2, Opus 10, Opus 14; Indian Suite.

MOSZKOWSKI
Suites.

J. RAFF
Suites for Piano.

RAVEL
Mother Goose.

RIMSKI-KORSAKOV
Scheherazade.

SCHUMANN
Papillons, Opus 2; Carnival, Opus 9; Kinderscenen, Opus 15.

SAINT-SAENS
Henry VIII Suite, #1 and #2.

SIBELIUS
Suite King Christian II.

A. SHEPHERD
Horizons.

STOESSEL
Hispanis.

STRAVINSKY
Suite from The Fire Bird.

D. TAYLOR
Looking Through the Looking Glass.

TSCHAIKOWSKY
Nutcracker Suite; Third Suite (consisting of four movements: a) Elegy; b) Valse Mélancholique; c) Scherzo; d) Air with Variations). He is considered the most successful of the composers who wrote modern suites.

CONCERTO

A *concerto* is a brilliant composition for a solo instrument, a dialogue between solo voice and orchestra (or piano), with orchestra accompaniment, generally based upon the form of the sonata-allegro. A concerto is usually a 3-movement composition; but sometimes concerto movements merge into one another with no pause. This is occasionally true of the symphony as well. The form of the concerto is somewhat modified so as to provide for technical display and to give abundant opportunity to the solo instrument. In the classic concerto the *exposition* is regularly given twice, once by the orchestra alone (*tutti*), and once by the soloist, with more or less of orchestral accompaniment. *Some ultramodern concertos are written in one movement and otherwise disregard the classic form and style.*

Most concertos are written for piano, violin, cello, oboe, clarinet, or flute solo. Of course, concertos may also be written for more than one instrument of the same kind, or even for instruments of different kinds (double concerto). Naturally, the best concertos are not merely instrumental solos with accompaniment but are really orchestral works, with one or more threads of solo music interwoven into their texture. If no orchestra is available, a piano may take its place as accompaniment.

The term *"concerto"* was probably first applied to music for a solo instrument and accompaniment by S. Bargaglia in a manual published in Venice in 1587. Michelletti published his *Sinfonie et concerti a Quadro* in 1691, and *Concerti Musicali* in 1698. But it was G. Torelli who determined the form of the grand solo for violin and adopted the term "concerto grosso" to mean a concerto with a greater number of instruments. Then came Corelli, the first of the modern violinists and violin composers.

The concerto for piano was brought to perfection by Mozart. In the history of the concerto (as well as in the history of other forms of music), Mozart was very important. He began early in his career to occupy himself with the creation and development of concertos—especially the piano concerto.

A feature of the concerto is the *Cadenza* near the end of the first movement and sometimes in the last movement; here the soloist usually plays alone, displaying his virtuosity. The cadenza generally is based on motives and themes of the first movement. Cadenzas are intended to be brilliant technically and also interesting musically. Often they are written by the composer of the concerto or by other masters, who saw no harm in an exhibition of skill when combined with genuine musical themes.

Examples of violin concertos: J. S. Bach (A minor; E major; G minor; Concerto for Two Violins); Beethoven (D major); M. Bruch (G minor; D minor; Scotch Fantasy); C. Burleigh (E minor); Conus (E minor); Dvorak (Concerto); Mendelssohn (E minor); DeBeriot (Nine Concertos); C. Goldmark (Concerto); F. J. Haydn (C major); Ernst (F♯ minor); Glazounoff (Concerto); Kreutzer (Concertos); E. Lalo (Symphony Español); Mozart (Six Concertos; Concertanto Symphony for Violin & Viola); Paganini (D major); Rode (Concertos); Saint-Saens (B minor); Sibelius (Concerto); Schumann (Concerto—newly discovered); Spohr (Nine Concertos); Tschaikowsky (D major); Vieuxtemps (Five Concertos); Viotti (Twenty-Four Concertos); Wieniawski (Concertos); etc.

Examples of piano concertos: Beethoven (Five Concertos); Brahms (Concertos—his second, in B flat, has the four movements in full sonata form); Chopin (Concertos); Field (Concerto); Grieg (Concerto); Haydn (Concerto); Hummel (Concerto); Godard (Concerto); Liszt (Three Concertos); MacDowell (A minor; D minor); Mozart (Twenty-One Concertos); Rachmaninov (Three Concertos); Schumann (A minor); Gerschwin (Concerto); Tschaikowsky (Concerto); etc.

Cello concertos were composed by Haydn; Goltermann; Dvorak; Boccherini; V. Herbert; F. Stock; and others.

Mozart also wrote a double Concerto for Two Pianos; Concerto for Three Pianos; Concerto for Bassoon; Concerto for Flute and Harp; two Concertos for Flute; four Concertos for Horn; Concerto for Clarinet.

The old *concerto grosso* is more like a suite. It employs two or more solo instruments, with the supporting accompaniment (filling up—*ripieno*) of a small orchestra. It is a composition for a small group of solo instruments (*con-*

certino, small concert) and the contrasting *tutti* of the orchestra (*concerto grosso*—big concert). The dialogue of these two groups and the manifold application of the themes and counterthemes make a pleasing composition.

Examples:

J. S. BACH
Six Brandenburg Concerti.

CORELLI
Christmas Concerto, G minor.

HANDEL
Concerto Grosso, #1, #2, #3, #4, #5, #6.

LOCATELLI   TORELLI
Concerto Grosso, Opus 1, #2.   Concerto Grosso.

VIVALDI
Concerto Grosso, Opus 3, D minor.

E. BLOCH
Concerto Grosso for Strings & Piano.

OVERTURE

The word *"overture"* comes directly from the French verb *ouvrir,* to open, and means an *opening piece.* Usually it is more extended, more self-sufficient, and more positive in its form than the prelude. Originally an overture was an orchestral number serving strictly as a *prelude or introduction* to an opera or oratorio, and it came into existence when the opera began, about 1600. For a long time the overture was very indefinite in form. At first, it consisted merely of a brief flourish or a series of airs strung loosely together, a medley of melodies or themes taken from the opera, oratorio, musical comedy, and operetta. Thus, it acts as a guide to the spirit and atmosphere of the work it precedes; but in its highest form the overture represents an independent musical idea of beauty. Usually, the overture has little development, as the main interest is in the well-contrasted themes.

There are several types of overtures:

The French overture. It was invented by Lully (1632-1687), and was copied quickly all over Europe. The type is: Adagio, Allegro, Adagio. Its form consisted of a slow movement in common time (repeated), generally called the *"grave,"* followed without pause by a fugue, which may be set in another key and in different time. After the fugue, a part of the whole of the *grave* was repeated, or some other flowing melody in moderate tempo was given. Occasionally, it was extended to four movements through the addition of some kind of stately dance form, like the gavotte or minuet. The French overture became very popular; Bach, Handel, Kaiser, Hasse, Telemann, and other composers of the 18th century adopted it.

Examples:

J. S. BACH
  Suite #3, D major, first movement.

HANDEL
  Overture to Messiah (a good example of the fully developed French overture).

The Italian overture, or sinfonia. It was introduced by A. Scarlatti (1659–1725), and was quite different. The type is: Allegro, Adagio, Allegro. Its form consisted of three distinct movements, the first and last of which were fast. The middle movement was scored for fewer instruments and had a different character from the preceeding and the following movement. It was a sort of short symphony, with glowing melody in moderate tempo. The third movement often was contrapuntal.

An example is J. S. Bach's Symphony in B (two lively movements and one grave between them, to be played without pause).

The *Dramatic overture*. This is a work which aims to give a suggestion or a resumé of an opera that follows. Such an overture is not restricted in form. Gluck wrote the first real dramatic overtures. The so-called "overtures" written before his time had little or nothing to do with the operas they preceded. Usually, they provided an instrumental flourish in order to obtain the attention of the audience. Gluck led the reform; he made the dramatic overture a real statement for what was to follow, at the same time preserving an independent musical structure. He wrote: "My idea is that the overture should indicate the subject and prepare the spectators for the character of the piece they are about to see." Gluck sometimes kept his overtures separate; but more often he allowed them to lead directly into the opera.

Gluck carried out his ideas magnificently in his Overture to Iphigenia in Aulis. Beethoven's Overture to the opera Fidelio, Leonore #3, not only gives a literal quotation from the later scenes of the opera, but also provides a fine dramatic treatment of the instrumental music itself. The whole overture follows a definite sonata-allegro form, with exposition, development, and restatement, in spite of the wealth of thematic material and the idealistic nature of the musical narrative. Beethoven always kept the overture as a separate piece. His Egmont Overture approaches the classical overture in form. The Overture to Anacreon by Cherubini draws its material largely from the opera itself. Later on, Gluck's idea was brought to perfection by Wagner, in his overtures to Tannhäuser, Tristan and Isolde, and Parsifal. Wagner knew how to reach marvelous effects by skilfully working his musical elements into a most pleasing structure. He is a great master of form, and his forms vary in the different overtures and preludes. Note also Schumann's Overture to Manfred and his Overture to Genoveva.

Analysis of Cherubini's Overture to Anacreon: The main movement is preceded by an introduction (*largo assai,* D major, 2/2 time) which consists of ten measures of prefatory chords in the full orchestra, followed by a section in which the two horns and various wood-wind instruments alternate in conversational passages. This leads through a *fortissimo chord* into the *allegro.*

The main section of the overture (*allegro,* D major, 4/4 time) is not written in sonata form, but is a freely constructed movement based almost entirely upon the subject presented by the violins four measures after the allegro begins. Some use is made in later portions of the piece of the little figure with which the cellos open the movement. There is a long continued *piano,* which is maintained for nearly fifty measures after the subject has been announced. Then follows a lengthy *crescendo*. Rossini afterwards often used these celebrated effects in his overtures.

Concert overture: In time overtures began to be written for separate performance and were quite complete in themselves. This incited composers to give more attention to their form and structure. The *concert overture,* usually written on the plan of a first movement of the sonata-allegro, with no repeat of the exposition but designed as a complete work in itself, is not attached to any opera or play. It is a separate, independent composition intended for concert performance. Often it is based upon some external suggestion of scenery (pictorial) or literary (poetic) idea. Usually, this overture bears a distinctive title, which may or may not have some descriptive significance. The concert overture offers an excellent opportunity for tone-painting. Though its length is generally greater than that of the dramatic overture, its popular style makes it a great favorite with the public. All the audience needs is some information as to the content of such a work, i.e., some explanation of the intention of the music.

Examples:

BEETHOVEN
Consecration of the House (in style of a free fugue); Fair Mesulina; Coriolanus.

BERLIOZ
Roman Carnival.

BRAHMS
Academic Festival Overture.

ELGAR
Froissart Overture; Cockaigne Overture; Falstaff Overture; In the South Overture.

GOLDMARK
Sakuntala; In Springtime; Prometheus.

GRIEG
In Autumn.

HINDEMITH
News of the Day.

KELER-BELA
Hungarian Lustspiel Overture.

MACKENZIE
Over Britannia.

MASSENET
Phèdre.

MENDELSSOHN
Fingal's Cave (Hebrides); Overture Calm Sea; Midsummer Night's Dream.

DVORAK	LEUTNER
Carnival Overture.	Fest Overture.
TSCHAIKOWSKY	R. WAGNER
Overture 1812.	A Faust Overture.
WALTON	VON WEBER
Portsmouth Point Overture.	Jubel Overture.

Classical overture: It is written on the plan of the first movement of the sonata-allegro form, with no repeat of the exposition—no repeat of the first three divisions (first, second, and closing themes) before the development. Mozart adapted this form and produced some of his fine opera overtures. They are full of life and marvelously reflect the spirit of the dramatic action. Von Weber used this form, slightly modified; and, at the same time, he chose his themes directly from the operas that followed, unlike the other composers in the sonata-movement form.

Examples:

MOZART
Overture to The Marriage of Figaro; Overture to Don Giovanni; Overture to Magic Flute; etc.

WEBER
Overture to Freischütz; Overture to Euryanthe; Overture to Oberon.

Examples of overtures to operas:

AUBER	BEETHOVEN
Fra Diavolo.	Leonore #1, #2, #3.
DVORAK	HUMPERDINCK
Bartered Bride.	Hänsel and Gretel.

MENDELSSOHN
Overture to Oratorio St. Paul (written in style of a free fugue).

MOZART
Magic Flute (written in style of a free fugue).

NICOLAI
Merry Wives of Windsor.

ROSSINI
William Tell; Barber of Seville; Italians in Algeria; Tancred; Semiramide.

J. STRAUSS, JR.	SCHUBERT
Die Fledermaus (The Bat).	Rosamunde.

Thomas
   Mignon; Raymond (The Queen's Secret).
Wagner
   Flying Dutchman; Rienzi; Meistersinger; Tannhäuser.
Weber
   Preciosa; Peter Schmoll.

Wagner's Overture to Tannhäuser has two distinct and contrasted ideas:

   1) Pilgrim's Chorus: religious; sustained tones; hymn of faith and courage is heard from distance, comes near, then dies away.
   2) Venusberg: motive; worldly—a persistent, delicate movement; attractive, enticing—subtle influence of evil.
   Pilgrim's Chorus—signifies triumph of good over evil.

SONATA

The word *"sonata"* comes from the Italian *suonare*, to sound (*suonate*, a sounding piece) and was, in the 17th and 18th centuries, first given to works for an instrument, as contrasted with a cantata, or singing piece. *Frescobaldi* was the first composer to use the word, and his sonatas were in one movement. Other composers enlarged this form. *Corelli* (1653–1713) gave it two movements, of which the first was in binary form having two themes of contrasted character and keys, a transition, and a return of these themes. Gradually, the sonata form began to approach its present shape. *Scarlatti* (1683–1737) gave a more melodic and homophonic character to his sonatas; *Kuhnau* (1667–1722) first gave three movements to the sonata; but *Phil. E. Bach* was actually the first to give a modern style of treatment to the binary form, to use the movements with proper contrast, and to evolve a rondo form that could be used in contrast with the sonata movement of Corelli; it is to *Haydn*, however, that the world owes this great gift to the art of music—he produced the true sonata-form. *Mozart* improved the sonata, and *Beethoven* perfected it. The sonata is, perhaps, the most important of all instrumental forms.

In early music there were two varieties—the *sonata da camera*, or *chamber sonata*, a work of light character which was little more than a suite, a succession of varied and independent dance movements essentially secular in style; and the *sonata da chiesa*, or *church sonata*, a group of abstract movements in more serious style, generally comprising a fugue or some other contrapuntal movement derived ultimately from the old choral music.

It took a long time to realize that instruments could play an independent role in music, instead of performing merely a voice part or a simple dance tune. The less music used the support of words and rhythmic dance steps, the more elaborate became the attempts of composers to develop a form that would allow music to speak for itself, without benefit of even a descriptive title. They wanted music to be logical, sufficiently varied as to be continually interesting, and with some appeal to the emotions as well as to the intellect.

The early forms of instrumental music were a mere transfer of polyphonic vocal music to instruments. As madrigals became too complicated for the human voice, it was natural, first, to accompany certain parts with viols, lutes, etc.; and, in time, to turn over the whole composition to various instruments. The early *canzones* were of fugal type, with a complicated interplay of instrumental voices but no real development of contrasting ideas.

At first, composers used the popular rhythms of the day and developed the *Old Suite*, a group of fairly short movements based on popular dances in various rhythms and tempos, but all in the same key.

They transformed *interludes* into madrigals and operas, and wrote overtures that preceded the performance of vocal works. All this gradually gave rise to a distinctive instrumental style which was independent of the older vocal style. As they became more efficient and more confident of their ability to think along purely musical lines, they began to create the more extensive form of the *sonata*, usually a group of movements showing dramatic contrast of theme and key with thematic development and organization. All the movements aim at an impression of organic unity, of structural organization, and of the diversity of mood and material which marks the sonata.

The early sonatas were written by Corelli, Vitali, Locatelli, Vivaldi, Bach, Handel, Scarlatti, Nardini, Galuppi, Paradisi, Kuhnau, etc.

Historically speaking, the earliest conception of the sonata form, and the origin of the symphony, are traceable to *Phil. E. Bach* (1714–1788)—the one known to history as the "Berlin," or "Hamburg," Bach. He was the third accomplished son of the immortal J. S. Bach. Phil. E. Bach's sonatas, although not fully developed, bear the form which Haydn first used for the quartet and the symphony, and whose inner contents he worked out. The sonata now has become definitely a work for a solo instrument, and also the first movement of a concerto, a symphony, as well as a trio, string quartet, quintet, sextet, etc.

The history of the sonata ends with *Beethoven*. Not much of significance has been added to his proclamation.

Since Beethoven, the sonata has been the form in which the music-lover has found deep satisfaction of his demands for the expression of various emotional experiences. Obviously, the sonata is also the culmination of all former experiments on the part of composers to find a medium for a unified, complex, and sustained work.

There are two definitely conflicting formal tendencies to be observed in the *sonata* and the *fugue*.

The essential characteristic of the sonata lies in the clash of opposing forces and of strongly contrasted ideas or moods —*it progresses from diversity to unity*. Two themes are presented, and the subsequent course of movement is spent in bringing them into an equilibrium. The two themes go through different keys and various, unexpected happenings. Everything is more or less arbitrary; *the sonata is the statement of a problem and its solution*.

The sonata form expands and develops into considerable

complexity from a single theme and its answering theme. Interest is maintained by exposing definite possibilities, unfolding what is already latent in the theme itself. The composer can only develop what is there already .

The modern sonata is an outcome of the old concerto, the two old sonatas, and of the general development of instrumental expression and technic. In modern music the *sonata* is an instrumental composition of three or four movements. Each of these movements is a piece in itself—a complete whole—and may be in any one of several different forms. The distinctive quality of the sonata consists in the form of the *first movement;* and as this first movement is generally an allegro, most writers refer to the sonata form as the *"sonata-allegro"* form. This first movement is somewhat intellectual in character, rather earnest and serious. The themes are of varying character; by way of development, the thematic material is woven into an exquisite pattern and worked up to a brilliant climax. The *second movement* is often slow and expressive, rather lyrical and emotional. Here feeling is most important, and simplicity is often the main characteristic. The *third movement* is usually animated in style; its character is light and playful or else bizarre or brusque. Usually, it is a scherzo, or its equivalent. The *fourth movement,* or Finale, is usually dashing and brilliant.

All these movements are strung together into a whole, with an underlying unity of larger scope. They are all in closely related keys, but of decidedly contrasted rhythm and style. The different movements quite often express distinct moods, such as admiration, meditation, humor, triumph, and the like.

A sonata is the extreme application of certain essential principles of structure. These same principles are also found in the construction of a good lecture:

1. The assertion of a subject of discourse.
2. The illustration of its truth by examples and elucidations of what is implied.

3. A final restatement, but with a greater force made possible by the previous discussion.

Similarly, a novel consists of:

1. A description of the general situation and a presentation of certain characters more or less antagonistic to each other.

2. Development of the plot and of the characters themselves, who are now put to the test.

3. Solution of the plot and final perspective of the characters.

Unlike the other movements of the sonata and symphony, the slow movement has no settled form. Style, rather than form, is here of greatest importance.

In as much as the sonata form is so vital a part of the concerto, symphony, string quartet, trio, quintet, octet, etc., it is well worth the careful attention and study of all listeners who really want to understand and enjoy music. The variety of style and artistic possibilities of the sonata provide sufficient freedom for the composer to give the fullest expression to his musical ideas. It often has resulted in music of the greatest value, music that comes as a revelation to the trained listener, and appeals to his highest emotions.

The sonata-allegro form (first movement) is divided into three minor parts, or sections. These are: 1. The *Exposition;* 2. The *Development;* and 3. The *Recapitulation.*

So we have this outline:

Possible *Introduction.*

I. First Section: *A* or *Exposition.*
  a) Theme, or Subject I (main theme): bright, gay—in tonic key.
  b) Connected by *link, or bridge* (transitional passage).
  c) Theme, or Subject II: theme goes into one of the related keys, usually the dominant.
II. Second Section: *B* or *Development* (free fantasy). The essential details of the two main themes are

used separately and in combination, in various keys and many rhythms, and lead to a climax. The composer here gives free reign to his imagination and does whatever he pleases, so long as he holds the interest of his hearers and neither becomes verbose nor indulges in mere mechanical manipulation. The material of the themes may be worked up into the most striking and beautiful tonal designs.

III. Third Section: *A* or *Recapitulation.*
    a) Theme I in tonic key.
    b) Connected by *link, or transitional passage,* which is now slightly modified, and must end in the tonic key.
    c) Theme II now in the same key as Theme I.

Possible *ending, or Coda:* It is of considerable length and importance, and uses any of the above themes.

The sonata-allegro form in the minor key:

Possible *Introduction.*

I. First Section: *A* or *Exposition.*
    a) Main theme, or subject (in the minor key).
    b) Bridge passage, leading to a half-cadence in relative major.
    c) Second theme, or subject, in the relative major.
II. Second section, or *Development,* free in style and key.
III. Third Section: *A* or *Recapitulation.*
    a) Return of main theme, in tonic minor.
    b) Bridge passage.
    c) Return of second theme, in tonic minor or major.

Possible *Coda:* If there is a coda, closing theme may be in the tonic major, allowing the coda to establish the tonic minor key.

The sonata may or may not have an *introduction;* after which comes the *exposition,* i.e., the *first theme, or subject,* is given in a clear fashion and in the tonic key. This may be slightly developed before the second theme or subject is given; or there may be an interlude of some additional material. Now comes the *second theme, or subject*. It is announced in a definite manner. It should be of contrasting character and in a different key, usually the dominant, or in the relative minor, or some other related key of the first theme, or subject. The second theme may also receive some slight development. In general, the first theme is striking and resolute in character; while the second should be more lyrical and tender. Between the two themes is a short, modulating *bridge passage*.

Then comes the *development section*. This part is hardest for the listener to follow. So far he has heard rather well-defined melodies, but now he is to follow imitations, changes of rhythm and key, changes of tone-color, and the like. It is the development section which makes the sonata form differ from the enlarged song form. The more interesting a composer makes this development section—that is, the more logically and ingeniously he handles his materials—the finer and more important becomes his entire movement. To be sure, there are movements in some sonatas, concertos, quartets, and symphonies that do not deserve the term "sonata form," because they are not well worked out.

The *recapitulation* usually consists of a restatement of both of the subjects, but with the opening melody now in a related key and the second subject in the tonic. However, both themes may appear in the same (tonic) key, etc. The recapitulation gives the movement the balance that comes from any return of theme after other material has been used. Then there may be a *coda* at the close, sometimes of considerable length. It is absolutely essential that the movement end in the key in which it started.

It is advisable to study the first movement of various sonatas, concertos, quartets, quintets, symphonies, etc. They provide good material for analysis. Each of them should be heard often, until at least the main themes and the chief details of form and instrumentation are quite familiar.

Henderson very aptly calls the three parts of the sonata

form "*preposition, discussion,* and *conclusion.*" The sonata was the representative musical form of the classic era. A knowledge of the sonata form is absolutely necessary in order to understand and enjoy compositions written in the *classic style.* The characteristics of the classic era are: I. *Symmetry of form;* and 2. *Subordination of profound musical learning to a pleasing style.*

We repeat: the movements of the sonata are broadly related, but quite capable of independent performance.

When the sonata is in four movements, they are usually as follows:

I.   Quick (allegro or vivace); often preceded by a slower introduction.

II. Slow (andante, largo, adagio, or maestoso).

III. Minuet, or Scherzo—often with Trio added.

IV. Quick—the Finale; sometimes a rondo, or another sonata form, or a theme with variations.

The sonata da chiesa, or church sonata, as perfected by Corelli and his contemporaries, is grave and dignified in character. It is usually written for from one to three solo stringed instruments, with an accompaniment on a figured bass. It consists of four (sometimes three) movements— slow, quick, slow, quick; or quick, slow, quick. Shortly before 1700, this type was used for the harpsichord as well; and in the early 18th century, sonatas were written for solo clavier, solo violin, or for a very small group of such instruments. Of course, the details of treatment differed according to the instruments used. The first quick movement was of chief interest, and within the movements the material was generally presented in two sections, progressing from tonic to dominant and back again (as in dance forms), or in the manner of exposition, development, and recapitulation. There was a constant tendency to get away from the comparative formality of polyphony and to use methods that were homophonic or harmonic (suggesting the method of the later and modern sonata), although the importance of a second subject was not yet generally recognized. Nor was there seen a need for a harmonic plan which controlled the process of development. In many sonatas, dance forms, fugues, or variations were used as movements, without any connection with the rest. Only occasionally was the tonal unity increased by some connection between the subjects used in the different movements.

The sonatas of *Haydn* and *Mozart* show clearness of form; they are lyrical and of pleasing cheerfulness. Mozart's overtures, as well as his Don Giovanni, Magic Flute, and Marriage of Figaro, should be listened to and studied with care not only for the great beauty of their contents but because they are our earliest examples of the overture in complete sonata form.

The piano sonatas of Beethoven show much dramatic power, and the last five are free in form. Both *Bach* and *Beethoven* represent the ideal creative artist, combining greatness of conception and overwhelming inspiration with a masterly command of form. The sonatas of *Liszt, Mac-Dowell,* and some modern composers also are free in form; they are broad piano rhapsodies in style and spirit.

Although the sonata-allegro form is chiefly used in the first movement of the sonata or symphony, it may also be employed in other movements and in separate compositions. There are many classical overtures, as well as sonatas, in which each movement, from beginning to the end, is in this form. But sometimes, though very rarely indeed, the first movement of a symphony or sonata is *not* in the sonata-allegro form. (See *Beethoven's* Sonata in A flat, Opus 26; *Goldmark's* Rustic Wedding Symphony—rather a suite than a symphony—etc.)

The great value of this form is that it gives scope to the composer to display a beautiful set of themes and to work out their development. In modern times, some composers, notably *Schumann* and *Liszt,* have endeavored to give the sonata a much freer and more extended form, especially in building up a continuous development.

Sonatas for Violin and Piano:

BEETHOVEN	BRAHMS	J. A. CARPENTER
Sonatas.	Three Sonatas.	Sonata.

R. COLE
Sonata, D major.

C. FRANCK
Sonata, A major.

GADE
Two Sonatas.

J. M. LECLAIR
Sonatas.

DE LAMARTER
Sonata in E flat.

PUGNANI
Sonatas.

A. RUBINSTEIN
Sonata, Opus 13.

TARTINI
Sonatas.

CORELLI
Sonata, E minor.

FOOTE
Sonata, Opus 20.

HANDEL
Six Sonatas.

GRIEG
Sonatas.

MOZART
Sonatas.

PURCELL
Sonata, G minor.

SJOGREN
Sonata, Opus 19.

VERACINI
Sonatas.

FAURE
Sonata, Opus 13.

GODARD
Sonata, Opus 12.

HAYDN
Sonata, G major.

LOCATELLI
Sonatas.

PROKOFIEF
Sonata, D major.

RAFF
Sonatas.

SCHUMANN
Sonatas.

VIVALDI
Sonatas.

SCHUBERT
Sonatas, Opus 137, #1, #2, #3.

Note these Piano Sonatas:

BEETHOVEN
Sonata, Opus 27; Opus 10, #1, #2; Opus 14, #1, #2.

HAYDN
Sonata #1; F major; Opus 3; Opus 5; Opus 7.

MOZART
Sonata, #14; #15; #18.

MACDOWELL
Sonata, Opus 57; Opus 59.

SCHUBERT
Sonata, Opus 120.

Here is the first movement of Beethoven's Piano Sonata in F minor, Opus 2, #1, analyzed:

A—Measures 1–48.
  8 measures, first subject in F minor.
  12 measures, episode.
  21 measures, second subject in A.
  7 measures, closing group.
B—Measures 49–100.
  52 measures made up largely of thematic material used in measures 1–48.
C—Measures 101–152.
  8 measures, first subject in F minor.

11 measures, Episode.
21 measures, second subject in F minor.
12 measures, closing group and coda.

An analysis such as this teaches us many interesting facts about the composer's method:

1) Is he systematic in the presentation of ideas?
2) Does he employ repetition—use over and over again the same thematic material?
3) Do parts correspond to parts? Hence, is there much of both: similarity and identity?
4) Is his structural plan progressive? What is the law of growth?

Note first movements of these string quartets:

BEETHOVEN	BRAHMS
Opus 59.	Opus 47.
DVORAK	HAYDN
Opus 96.	Opus 54, #1.
MOZART	SCHUBERT
#1.	Opus 29.

Form of Symphony #1 by Beethoven:

A. Exposition—
    a) Slow Introduction.
    b) Theme I; allegro.
    c) Transition to subordinate theme 2 (in key of G minor).
    d) Repetition of a part of subordinate theme; closing section, developed from theme 2.
B. Development (several sections made up of material from parts of principal and subordinate themes).
A. Recapitulation—
    g) Return to principal theme (b).
    h) Return to theme 2 in key of C (instead of G, as before); this theme is repeated in minor.
    i) Coda, in key of C.

SONATINA

The *sonatina* is a little sonata-allegro. It is short and similar in structure; but it has neither pathos nor grandeur. It differs from the sonata proper mainly in having little or no development of the theme, or else a development of only a few measures. It begins with a first and a second theme, contrasted and joined like those of the sonata, but lighter in style. The second section especially is not as important as the second section of the sonata. The recapitulation consists of two themes, this time both in the tonic key. The coda is short. Hardly ever has the sonatina contained more than three short movements. The second theme usually is not introduced by means of modulation to the dominant, as in the sonata, but by way of half-cadence. (See Beethoven's Sonatina, Opus 49, #4.) The rondo form is often used in the sonatina, and the slow movement frequently is merely a song form of the simplest character. The sonatina form may be used for a sonata movement. Lyric pieces and opera overtures sometimes use this form also.

Examples:

BEETHOVEN
Two Sonatinas, Opus 49; Opus 72.

BUSONI
Four Sonatinas.

CLEMENTI
Sonatinas.

DUSSEK
Sonatinas.

A. FOERSTER
Six Sonatinas.

KUHLAU
Sonatinas.

M. REGER
Piano Sonatinas.

SCHUMANN
Sonatinas, Opus 18, c.

CHAMBER MUSIC

Chamber music is most often written in the sonata-allegro form. It was played at first only in the chambers of wealthy amateurs, and its name is derived from the Italian *musica di camera*. All music for combinations of instruments smaller than the orchestra is called "chamber music." The *string quartet* (first and second violin, viola, and cello) is the most common form of chamber music. Other combinations are the *piano quartet* (piano, violin, viola, cello); *piano trio* (piano, violin, cello); *piano quintet* (piano, first and second violin, viola, cello); and various combinations for strings, wood winds, or brass instruments. In addition, many sonatas have been composed for single instruments and piano.

In chamber music the grandeur and brilliance of the orchestra are absent; but this is made up for by the great skill exercised in writing clear and interesting parts. There are marvelous trios, quartets, quintets, sextets, septets, octets, etc., by Haydn, Mozart, Beethoven, Schubert, Schumann, Mendelssohn, Brahms, and others.

SYMPHONY

The word "symphony" was first used by the Greeks— being a compound of *syn,* together, and *phone,* sound—as a name for the intervals, i.e., tones sounding together. It later began to mean the simultaneous sounding of tones of different quality. Hence, the word came to be used to designate compositions not only for different instruments but for combinations of instruments whose tone qualities are radically different. In other words *"symphony"* is the name for a great polyphonic composition for full orchestra of eighty to one hundred players, with combinations of string, wood wind, brass, and percussion instruments. Each part is played by a single performer, or group of performers, and hence becomes subject to a very personal attention. These parts are blended together by the baton of an expert conductor, resulting in a composite of tone produced by the players, each one contributing his fund of expression to the general effect.

The form of construction of the symphony is the same as the sonata-allegro, but it is usually of larger proportions and has in it a greater variety of rhythmic and tonal material. Then, too, heightened tone-color is an added element. All this increases the possibilities of dramatic effect. The symphony is an elaborate composition, generally in four movements, one of which—always the first—must be in the *sonata-allegro* form. Now and then these other movements are different from those of the sonata, and national dances may be used. Dvorak used the melancholy dumka and the wild furiant; while Tschaikowsky introduced the brilliant Russian dance kamarinskaia. Rubinstein's Ocean Symphony, by the way, contains seven movements. Unity in the four movements may be achieved either through the use of closely related keys, as in the works of Haydn and Mozart, or through continuity of ideas based on some poetic or dramatic "program," as in the works of later composers. Variety is attained, as in the suite, through contrast of rhythm, tempo, mood, etc., in the several movements. The symphony is considered the highest type of instrumental music thus far evolved. No other type offers similar opportunities for sublimity of invention, perfection of workmanship, and direct transference of abstract moods and emotions.

The symphony still is the form in which the composer gives utterance to big emotions. If any fundamental changes ever occur in its form, they are likely to be changes of the inner structural make-up of an individual movement. Thus, the form may become freer—thematic materials introduced in a less hurried way, and the divisions into first, second, and closing groups less clear, if there be any at all. It is difficult to tell much about the nature of the development section of the symphony or the extent of the recapitulation. For this reason, it is more difficult to listen to the modern symphony than it is to the older ones, whose examples of form are better understood and quite familiar to us.

What nation making a claim of culture does not have the symphony? From Moscow to San Francisco, from Budapest to Edinburgh, it may be heard. Schopenhauer, the keen philosopher, calls music "the melody to which the world is the text," and calls the symphony her "best playground, upon which she celebrates her grandest feasts."

The chief difference between a symphony or any other form of artistic expression—such as a work of sculpture, a painting, a novel or a play—is that a symphony is not a record or a picture of something else, but it is *itself* only.

Pure music manifests man's will. It comprises all his actions, all his thoughts, and all his feelings. It expresses in a fluent, free, and beautiful form those deeper impulses which cannot be made known by words. Life itself is inexplicable. A great symphony reveals, in the short time of somewhat less than an hour, all of life's hidden elements. It is perfection. Here our ceaseless longing for happiness and heaven, which we have sought in vain, becomes not only a reality but perhaps the only possible reality; for who knows but that everlasting happiness or a definitely located heaven might not be endurable?

The symphony, as a form of pure music, is our highest attainment. It speaks in its own terms. Opera, on the other hand, speaks in terms of character in action, of costume, of scenery, as well as of music.

By the middle of the 18th century, violin-making had reached its highest development through the skill and industry of the great Italian masters, Stradivarius, Guarnerius, and Amati. In its train now followed the gradual development of the orchestra and its literature, for which the public taste was becoming more and more keen. The symphony is the product of a long course of development, beginning when instruments were first played alone, without vocal or choral music. In fact, those brief instrumental interludes between sections of a vocal work were at one time known as "symphonies." *Johann Christian Bach, Abel, Wagenseil, Stamitz*, and other Mannheim composers, wrote the first symphonies. And Haydn profited much by his intensive study of the works of these men, as they had already achieved an improved standard of form and orchestration. Haydn took up their work and carried it forward to a higher point of perfection. Properly defined, the present-day symphony is "a sonata for orchestra."

The history of the sonata is also the history of the symphony. According to R. Wagner, the symphony had its source in the early folk songs and folk dances; in which connection, he says in his *The Music of the Future*, "That peculiar work of art, the symphony, was founded and developed on the simple basis of stringing together several song and dance melodies, letting the changes take place in accordance with their expressive character, and connecting them by transitions, in which the art of counterpoint proved particularly useful. Haydn was the gifted master who first extended this form and made it wonderfully expressive by the inexhaustible changes in the motives, as well as in their connections and transformations. While the Italian operatic melody retained its poor construction, it had, nevertheless, when delivered by talented singers gifted with beautiful voices and warm feeling, received a sensuously beautiful coloring. This sweet euphony had been hitherto unknown to German masters, and was entirely wanting in their instrumental music. Mozart first realized the charm; and while giving to Italian opera the richer development of instrumental composition, he imparted, on the other hand, the sweetness of Italian singing to orchestral melody. Beethoven then took possession of the rich and promising inheritance left by Haydn and Mozart. He developed the symphonic work of art to such astonishing breadth of form, and filled this form with such marvelously various and entrancing wealth of melody, that we now stand before his symphony as before a landmark of an entirely new period in the history of art; for in this symphony a phenomenon has arisen, the like of which has never existed in the art of any period or any nation."

(Note: "*Scherzo*" literally means "a joke"; actually, it is an instrumental playful movement, usually in 3/4 time. In form the scherzo resembles the minuet, from which it is derived; but it is usually in a much quicker tempo and of a more vivacious, lively, gay, and playful character. The dancelike character of the minuet themes is absent, the treatment is freer, and development is possible. Some composers use a 2/4 rhythm. Beethoven was the first composer to employ the scherzo as the title to one of the movements of his Second Symphony. He often emphasizes the rougher side of musical humor in his scherzos. Chopin made an independent movement of the scherzo; and his scherzos for piano are a new departure in this field. Brahms replaced the scherzo with an *intermezzo*, not always playful, but still retaining a trace of the minuet influence in its double movement.)

Examples of great symphonies:

BEETHOVEN
Nine Symphonies.

BERLIOZ
Romeo et Juliet; Fantastique.

BRAHMS
Four Symphonies.

BORODIN
Symphony.

BRUCKNER
Nine Symphonies (all very dramatic).

V. D'INDY
Symphony #2.

DVORAK
Symphony #6, New World.

ELGAR
Symphony.

C. FRANCK
Symphony in D minor.

HAYDN
Military; Surprise (including all those in the Solomon set); etc.

GOLDMARK
Rustic Wedding. (Strictly speaking, this is a suite; its movements do not conform to the symphony model in formal structure; it has five movements; its first movement, instead of being in the sonata form, is a set of variations entitled Wedding March.)

G. MAHLER
Nine Symphonies (Program music with the program omitted, they should be classed as tone poems.)

MENDELSSOHN
Symphony #1, Scotch; #2, Italian; Reformation Symphony.

MOZART
Symphony in E minor; Symphony in E flat; Jupiter; etc.

GLAZOUNOW
Symphony.

PROKOFIEF
Classical Symphony.

RAFF
Leonore; Im Walde (both are program symphonies).

RACHMANINOFF
Symphony.

SCHUBERT
All his symphonies.

SCHUMANN
Symphony #1, B flat; #2, C major.

SIBELIUS
Symphonies.

SHOSTAKOVICH
Nine Symphonies.

R. STRAUSS
Domestic Symphony.

TSCHAIKOWSKY
Symphony #4; #5; #6, Pathetique (the most dramatic in modern symphonic literature).

Outline of Mozart's Jupiter Symphony

First movement (Allegro Vivace).
> Part I—Exposition:
> > a.   Principal theme in C major.
> > b.   Secondary or counter theme in G major.
>
> Part II— Development: The two themes introduced
> in the first part undergo various transformations
> and appear in new keys.
>
> Part III—Recapitulation: The principal theme reap-
> pears in its original form and key, and the sec-
> ondary theme returns in its original form, but
> transposed to the key of the principal theme, C
> major.

Outline of Beethoven's Fifth Symphony in C minor

First Movement (Allegro con Brio)
> I.   Exposition (measures 1–124 repeated):
> > a.   First theme in C minor.
> > b.   Second theme in E flat major.
>
> II.   Development (measures 125–252): The two
> themes of the first part undergo various transfor-
> mations and appear in new keys.
>
> III.   Recapitulation (measures 253–372): First theme
> reappears in its original form and key, and the sec-
> ond theme returns in its original form, but in the
> key of C major.
> > Coda (measures 373–502): A sort of summing up
> > and rounding off of the movement, like the epi-
> > logue of a play.
>
> Second, or Slow Movement (Andante con Moto).
> > Theme A (measures 1–22); theme B measures
> > 23–49).
> > Variation 1 (measures 50–98).
> > Variation 2 (measures 99–184).
> > Variation 3 (measures 185–205).
> > Coda (measures 206–247).
>
> Third Movement (Allegro).
> > Part I (measures 1–140).

Part II trio (measures 141–236).

Part III (measures 237–323).

Coda (measures 324–373). It leads directly into the next movement.

Fourth Movement (Finale—Allegro).

I. Exposition (measures 1–85).

II. Development (measures 86–206).

III. Recapitulation (measures 207–294).

Coda (measures 295–444).

SINFONIETTA

The *sinfonietta,* or *symphonietta,* is a short little symphony, usually in one movement, having little or no development of the themes. It is the adaptation of the sonatina form of composition to the orchestra and is less grandiose in character and lighter in style. There are many examples on hand, especially by modern composers.

TONE POEM

The *tone poem, or symphonic poem,* is the most important of modern forms. A tone poem is a work of the dimension of a symphony, but written on quite a different plan. It is free in form, with varying tempo, and contains a description of a special subject. It was devised by Liszt at about 1840. Liszt wrote a series of thirteen works for the orchestra in which he used, in the main, the same themes throughout the whole of each work but presented them under a variety of guises. Much also depends upon a program which the music seeks to convey by means of different emotions aroused by the varied presentations of the themes. The tone poem is the antithesis of "absolute music," which merely seeks to express its own inherent beauty.

The form of the tone poem is determined by the nature and requirements of its subject, rather than by the purely esthetic considerations of *repetition, contrast, symmetry,* and *climax,* which govern the form of absolute music. It is an orchestral work with themes and episodes and development; but the development is generally continuous and not confined to a single section of the composition. It consists usually of several well-connected sections, or episodes, constituting a musically and dramatically consistent unit which has sufficient contrast, balance, and development, leading toward a climax.

The symphonic poem has three characteristics:

1. It is programatic. The tone poem is intended to express some poetic idea, to describe some definite event or scene, or even to relate a story.

2. It is put in form of a single movement. The tone poem has no set form; the form is governed by the story or idea it has to express.

3. It usually has a principal subject of such plasticity that the composer can create a varied content by presenting it in a number of transformations.

A tone poem generally has a program or descriptive title which may or may not have much to do with the music.

Outline of Liszt's tone poem, Les Préludes

(The idea is derived from Lamartine's *Meditationes Poétique:* Life on earth is but a series of preludes to a life hereafter.)

Part 1. What is the meaning of life?

Part 2. The enchanted dawn of every life is love.

Part 3. The storm whose deadly blast disperses youth's illusions.

Part 4. The peace and solace one finds amid the calm beauties of nature.

Part 5. Man's readiness to forsake the tranquillity of pastoral life and throw himself headlong into strife and turmoil whenever and wherever duty calls.

Part 6. Man's exultation when, through strife, he has gained "full knowledge of himself and of his strength."

Examples:

DEBUSSY   DUKAS
Afternoon of a Faun.   The Sorcerer's Apprentice.

C. FRANCK
  Les Djinns.

GERSHWIN
  An American in Paris.

HANSEN
  Pan and the Priest.

HONEGGER
  Pacific 231.

LISZT
  Les Preludes; Mountain; Tasso; Mazeppa; The Battle of the Huns (after a painting by Kaulbach); etc.

SAINT-SAENS
  Le Rouet d'Omphale; Danse Macabre.

E. SCHELLING
  A Victory Ball.

SIBELIUS
  Finlandia.

SMETANA
  The Moldau.

SOWERBY
  Praire.

R. STRAUSS
  Till Eulenspiegel; Death and Transfiguration; etc.

TSCHAIKOWSKY
  Francesca da Rimini.

7

NATIONAL MUSIC

FOLK MUSIC AND MODERN MUSIC

IN analyzing the distinctions between music and the other fine arts, we learned certain basic principles which underlie all art—namely, *form or design, content or expression,* and *nationality or group spirit.*

We next take up this group spirit or nationality.

Physical geography has a very great deal to do with the comfort or discomfort of peoples, and this is reflected in their occupations and their lives as well as in their culture, whether it be through the medium of music, architecture, sculpture, painting, literature, or dancing. Thus, all art becomes immediately identifiable with the country from which it emanates. Not alone is the rhythm of music affected by the nature of the landscape, the temperature, and the different local forces of nature, but the rhythms in architecture, sculpture, and the other arts also find themselves under the spell of nature's elements. Without this consistency of natural laws, there would be very little variety in the impulses of life. All music would be monotonous and uninteresting. In addition, this expression of each country has not come without a vast amount of historical experience. No doubt the predominating and characteristic emotions and attitudes of a people arise from their lands or their cities, and they exist as surely as the vision concretely is there for the eye to see. You sort of "feel it." Every nation has expressed its feeling for beauty, romance, joy, vitality, and stress through its national music. In music, as in all art, the true artist is rooted in his national origin. Hundreds of gifted musicians have given the best within them of emotion, imagination, and musical inspiration to their compositions, thereby greatly promoting culture.

France, Italy, and Germany were the only three great nations which counted in the history of music during the 18th century. If some artist were born in another country, he usually left his native land, went to France, Italy, or Germany, studied there, and adopted the traditions of the people among whom he wished to live. In time, toward the close of the 18th century, even the differences in the French, Italian and German styles tended to disappear.

Then, during the 19th century, we see nationalistic tendencies accented throughout Europe. Romanticism had taken over the idea of a "return to nature"; it had encouraged an interest in the everyday joys and sorrows of the common people. Nationalism turned this idea into a stronger love for the beauties of one's own fatherland; it placed an interest on, and enthusiasm for, the traditions and folkways of one's fellow citizens. Musicians now were striving to express in their works the genius peculiar to their own people or race.

Not only in literature and painting but also in music came the rise of a decided nationalistic movement which fostered some important art works of the period. Writers, painters, and composers became inspired by the national folklore. Music turned more and more to the folk tunes and folk dances of various countries, and this folk culture became a treasurehouse. Idiomatic melodies as well as characteristic rhythms, under the impetus of strong emotional associations reinforced by patriotic feeling, offered a new, rich field to music.

For an appreciation of national music we must always take into consideration the traits and environments of the people from which it sprang. Folk music has specific characteristics and style, native to the country from which it comes. It is a national product, with peculiar melodic, rhythmic, harmonic, and instrumental characteristics. Thus, the folk music of a nation becomes valuable data for historic, ethnological, and anthropological studies, just as much as architecture, painting, literature, or dancing. Then, too, the folk music of a country influences in one way or another, but always substantially, the individual creations of great composers. That is why, among other reasons, such great works have always a national character.

True, music is a sort of universal language; but each nation has used this language in its own way. Each country has its characteristic songs and folk dances. Folk songs are a basic and organic part of the life of a people. To the peoples of most nations, folk music is inseparable from many arts of daily living. In each of them it has played a vital role. The traditional music of the people is the basic fund from which gifted composers have always drawn. A creative genius can be neither a hermit nor a mere theorist. Of course, he has to live his inner life, but always in contact with the outside world. The work of a genius is a social phenomenon, yet it is a purely individual one; that is to say, the message of a genius is an expression both of his own being and of the world that surrounds him. As long as the creative artist is a man of the people, his work is always national. The participation of the man of genius in the world means his awareness of all social, political, religious, artistic, and other cultural problems. They are the avenues by way of which he receives a message.

Differences in National Music. When we bear in mind the fact that music springs directly from the daily life of the people, it is easy to understand that there is naturally as great a difference between the music and the other arts of the peoples of various lands as in their languages, styles of dress, occupations, and daily habits and customs. Nationality or group spirit in music is revealed in the peculiar character of life in certain localities or among certain peoples. Latin races love poetry, romance, and gaiety. This is in direct contrast to the steady, plodding nature of the Teutons, or the fearless freedom of the Slav. As mentioned before, the customs, and later the arts, of the various nations often were, and still are, influenced by climatic conditions as well as by racial and political forces.

Broadly stated, the following features are apparent in all national music: 1. *The use in their folk songs of different scales and modes,* especially a decided preference for one or all of the various minor scales, such as normal, melodic, harmonic, and Hungarian (normal minor with an augmented 4th, which produces a weird effect). 2. *The importance of variety in rhythm.* 3. *The use of characteristic instruments* by the different nations. The mandolin is popular in Latin countries; balalaika, in Russia; ukulele, in Hawaii; guitar, popular in Spain, Portugal, and Southern Italy; bagpipe, originally used in the British Isles, now considered the national instrument of Scotland; lute, originally used in Latin countries of medieval days, now used in Europe generally; harp, originally Irish, now used everywhere; castanets and tambourine, used mainly in Spain and in certain parts of France and Italy; tom-tom, used by the Indians; etc.

Examples of music showing nationality or group spirit:

BEETHOVEN
Sonata #7, Opus 30, #2, for violin & piano (uses German folk song).

BIZET
Suite L'Arlesienne (makes use of old French folk songs).

BRAHMS
Hungarian Dances.

CHOPIN
Polonaise Militaire.

DE FALLA
The Three Cornered Hat; etc.

DVORAK
Slavic Dances; Songs My Mother Taught Me; The Moldau.

GRAINGER
Shepherd's Hey (uses old Morris Airs).

GRIEG
Norwegian Bridal Procession; Peer Gynt Suite.

SARASATE
Spanish Dances.

SIBELIUS
Finlandia.

SMETANA
Bohemian Cradle Song.

SODERMANN
Swedish Wedding March.

TSCHAIKOWSKY
March Slav; 1812 Overture.

WOLF-FERRARI
Intermezzo #2, from Jewels of the Madonna—Italian.

Similarities of National Music. There are certain musical characteristics which are recognizable in the music of all nations and of all times. These are expressed in songs or instrumental pieces which portray such emotions as love, death, war spirit, pride of native land, courage, loyalty, hero worship, religion, etc. In turn, music reflects the various customs and occupations of the people, such as weddings and other festivals, usually expressed in folk songs and folk dances by the use of individual rhythm and scale formations. Very often an entirely different effect is obtained by a slight change in the music.

The song of a mother to her child is universal in character. Of course, there may be some rhythmic and melodic differences in different national cradle songs, but the dominant idea is the same.

Examples of music of tender devotion:

ALARD
Berceuse.

BRAHMS
Lullaby.

FR. BRIDGE
Cradle Song.

GODARD
Berceuse (Jocelyn).

HAUSER
Wiegenlied.

REGER
Wiegenlied.

Love, also, is universal in character. As a matter of fact, the universality of a love song is not easily disguised even by the employment of characteristic national instruments.

Examples of music expressive of love:

GERMAN FOLK SONG
Du, Du, Liegst Mir im Herzen.

IRISH FOLK SONG
Kathleen Mavourneen.

ITALIAN FOLK SONG
O Solo Mio.

SCOTCH FOLK SONG
Annie Laurie.

CHARPENTIER
Depuis le Jour (from opera Louise).

SAINT-SAENS
My Heart at Thy Sweet Voice (from opera Samson and Delilah).

R. WAGNER
Isolde's Liebestod; Siegmund's Love Song (from opera Walküre).

Death, likewise, is universal. A funeral march is recognized even before the listener can tell the country from which it originated.

Examples of music expressive of grief:

BEETHOVEN
Marche Funèbre (from Eroica Symphony, #3).

CHOPIN
Funeral March.

GRIEG
Asa's Death (from Peer Gynt Suite).

WAGNER
Siegfried's Trauermarsch (from opera Götterdämmerung).

War, too, is universal. The stirring battle song arouses a feeling in the heart of the listener which is not entirely the result of nationality. The group spirit is active everywhere.

Examples of war songs:

AMERICAN
The Star Spangled Banner; Yankee Doodle; Rally 'Round the Flag.

IRELAND   FRANCE
Tipperary.   The Marseillaise.

GERMANY
Ich Hatt' einen Kameraden.

HUNGARIAN
Rakoczy March (Magyars).

Religion, tranquillity, joy, and humor are feelings *expressed in all countries,* with but slight change in the musical methods employed.

Examples of the musical expression of religion and tranquillity:

M. BRUCH   GREGORIAN
Kol Nidrei (Hebrew).   Kyrie Eleison.

HANDEL
Total Eclipse (Sampson); I Know That My Redeemer (Messiah).

CRÜGER
Nun Danket alle Gott.

LUTHER
Ein' Feste Burg.

MENDELSSOHN
But the Lord is Mindful (St. Paul); O Rest in the Lord (Elijah).

PALESTRINA
Gloria Patri; Popule Meus.

C. V. RYCHLIK
Andante Religioso; Elegy.

THOME
Andante Religioso.

WAGNER
Amfortas Prayer (Parsifal); Good Friday Spell (Parsifal); March of the Grail Knights (Parsifal); Prayer of the King (Lohengrin); Elizabeth's Prayer, and Pilgrim's Chorus, Tannhäuser).

Folk songs are divided into two classes—the *true folk song*, of which the author and composer is *not known;* and the *composed folk song*, of which the author and composer is known, and whose melodies and harmonies are so simple and true that the people have adopted them as their own.

The oldest folk songs were created by anonymous musicians whose names are not recorded in history. Their main characteristic is simplicity, which necessarily is inherent in all folk music, and is the product of instinct and taste spontaneously aroused, not of formal analysis or patient working out on paper. All folk music depends for its success upon the ease with which it can be perceived, remembered, and repeated by anyone without special training. Both folk songs and folk dances have a fundamental rhythm that is emphatic and regular, either duple or triple; and the phrase structure is so constructed that the form is plain and easily kept in memory. If a great amount of folk music lacks variety, tending after a while to sound alike, that is because of a lack of formal design which gives coherence to the music. Folk melodies are beautiful and simple tunes which have outlived generations and bring comfort, heal sorrow, and make for better understanding among men. We accept these tunes as we accept the air and sunshine, for their great and fine thoughts have become a part of our lives. These songs have been passed on from mouth to mouth and often have traveled far. They were not printed, and so were subject to the alterations and the influence of many minds. At last these songs emerged from time, a symbol of the spirit of all the people instead of an individual.

Folk songs and folk dances *reflect the environment and heredity of different people. Generally speaking, the songs* of the North are rather rugged and heroic, while those of the South are more graceful, tender, and dreamy.

True folk songs, as well as composed folk songs, have given inspiration to all great composers, and they are frequently used by them as themes to be developed in their masterpieces.

While listening to folk songs and folk-dance tunes, ask:

1. What are the customs, ideals, or events that made the song or dance tune?

2. Is the tune reminiscent of the sea, mountain, fields, vineyards, cities?

3. Does the tune reflect play and custom?

4. Does the tune reflect ideals—devotion, love, honor, patriotism, death?

5. Does the tune inspire happy or sad feelings?

GERMAN FOLK SONGS

From the earliest times in Germany there was strong interest in music. It is the consensus of opinion that Germany, during the modern epoch, has given more great music to the world than any other nation. No wonder, when we remember the fact that from his babyhood the German child is surrounded by music in the house, church, and school. The German people display their intellectual and serious side in the regard they show for the art of music. They are naturally inclined to meditation, and their sentimental revery disposes them to take special pleasure in music from which all extramusical interest is excluded, and which finds the essential principle of its development within itself. Generally speaking, the *German shows fondness for sweet harmonies and symmetrical form.* German songs have *regular formations, straight melody, simple lyricism, homely sentiment, and not much ornamentation.* In these songs we are impressed with that intense loyalty to fatherland and that love of home which are notable features of the Teuton character. Germany was the cradle of the symphony; and the country stands pre-eminent for its many fine music schools. (The Leipzig Conservatory was founded by Mendelssohn in 1843.)

Almost a thousand years ago, the Minnesingers and the Meistersingers were noted for their wonderful recitations of poems and songs. Their achievements have been chronicled and immortalized by R. Wagner in his operas Tannhäuser and the Meistersinger.

Many folk tunes, some of them student and drinking songs, were brought into the Church at the time of Luther. They were provided with sacred words and are still sung in most of the Protestant churches throughout the world. In fact, the true history of German music begins after the Reformation, because musicians before that time were only imitators of the Dutch masters of counterpoint.

German folk songs are of an intimate kind; they are sentimental but vigorous, and, in spite of their simplicity, highly organized and compact. They reflect deep emotion as well as simplicity. The songs come directly from the hearts and souls of men and women close to Nature and sensitive to the realities of life. German songs describe some phase of folk tradition and custom, such as dancing under the Linden trees to celebrate rest from labor, a special festivity, etc. German musicians have helped to glorify the national heritage by writing music about the life of a hero or king; praising the beauties of their forests, rivers, mountains; using an historical event that had great emotional significance; and so on. The folk songs have been used to sing children to sleep; to celebrate births of infants; to give dignity to wedding ceremonies; and to bury the dead.

Thus, composers used music in order to communicate to their listeners the spirit of their country. The language of folk music is simple, direct, and unmistakable. Folk songs tell us much about the heart of a nation; and they have been sung in struggles, catastrophes, and war, voicing the lamentations of the people, their excitement, and their strength

Festival Overture; Beethoven's Sonata for Violin & Piano, #7, Opus 30.) The German folk song has been the basis of the early church and school music in the United States. Thus, it is but natural that German folk music seems to us less exotic than some of the lesser known music of other countries.

Much of Austria is practically German in language, custom, education, and art, but especially in music. The development of the two countries has been similar and connected. Several great composers and players have studied and worked in both territories. Perhaps special mention should be made of the most beautiful Viennese dance music of Strauss (father and sons), Lanner, Gungl, Ziehrer, etc.

The modern opera has been revolutionized through the influence of R. Wagner's marvelous music dramas. Every town of any size in Germany has its opera house, usually subsidized by the government. For many years Germany led in chamber and symphonic music, as well as in great orchestra-conductors.

(See: *Volkslieder aller Nationen der Erde,* by L. Koehler.)

Examples of folk songs by unknown composers:

Alles Ist Hin.	Als der Grossvater.
Du Du Liegst Mir im Herzen.	Ein Jäger aus Kurpfals.
Es Zogen Drei Burschen.	Gaudeamus Igitur.
Kommt a Vogerl Geflogen.	O Tannenbaum.
Preiset mit Viel Schönen Reden.	Muss i Denn.
Fuchs, du Hast die Gans.	Guter Mond.
Heimliche Liebe.	Zu Lauterbach.

So Viel Stern am Himmel Stehen.
Wenn Ich ein Vöglein Wär'.

Examples of composed folk songs:

ABT	BRAHMS
When the Swallows Homeward Fly.	Lullaby.
GLÜCK	GRUBER
Das Zerbrochene Ringlein.	Stille Nacht.
HAYDN	KINKEL
Deutschland über Alles.	Soldier's Farewell.

KÜCKEN, F. W.
 Ach, wie Ist's Möglich Dann (Thuringian).

LUTHER
 Ein' Feste Burg.

LYRA
 Der Mai Ist Gekommen.

SCHUBERT
 Der Lindenbaum.

SILCHER, F., (1789–1860)
 Aennchen von Tharau; Lorelei; Lebewohl; Ich Hat'
 Einen Kameraden; etc.

WERNER
 Heidenröslein.

WILHELM
 Die Wacht am Rhein.

FRENCH FOLK SONGS

The influence of the music and the instruments of the Far East, brought into France by the Crusaders, left a definite impression on French folk music.

The ballet was introduced into French opera in the 17th century and has ever since remained very popular. We are also indebted to France for the development of the system of notation and for the *opéra comique*.

French folk songs differ much in character, according to the part of the country from which they come—Provence, Bretagne, Gascony, etc. There are simple, unaffected songs from Normandy and delightful children's songs and lullabies from the South. Some very beautiful folk songs and dances are the French 9th century: Complaints on the Death of Charlemagne; the 11th century, O Marie, due Maire; the old melody, Chant des Livres, often sung at country weddings; and the folk song of Brittany, Le Clerc du Trémolo. Probably the oldest and the quaintest folk songs are those which owe their origin to the music of the Catholic Church. Traces of this church music are even to be found in popular dance tunes. The graceful and charming *chansons* have wit and polish. Most of the folk songs of France are marked by exquisite poetry and naiveté and have a cool, limpid quality. Many of them have that lightness, that exquisite daintiness, that volatile, mercurial temperament which is so marked an attribute of her people.

(See *Sixty Folk Songs of France*, edited by J. Tiersot.)

Old French folk songs:

The March of the Three Kings (A most original tune, it is very old, a noel in the form of a sturdy march. It opens the orchestral prelude to Bizet's L'Arlésienne.)

Gailon, La, La, Gai le Rosier (Another type of folk song of a later period which is more characteristic of the French people of today.)

Duke of Marlborough (Malbrouck) (It was sung when Godfrey of Bouillon captured Jerusalem on July 15, 1099, during the first of the Crusades. It is the original of the well-known, We won't go Home 'till Morning, or, He's a Jolly Good Fellow.)

At Pierrot's Door.	Au Clair de la Lune.
Carmagnole.	Mignonnette (La Roux).
Luck a-Traveling.	Slumber, Baby.
The Woodpecker.	Sur le Pont d'Avignon.

De Saboly-Ai; La bonne fortune (Ah! Great is our Fortune) Noël Provençal (1670).

Listen, Lordlings.	Pretty Pussy.
Pull a Cherry.	Ça Ira.
Pussy Willow.	First Nowell.

Ah! Vous dirai—je, Maman. Il était une Bergère.

Composed folk songs:

COUPERIN
Aubade Provençale.

R. DE LISLE
The Marseillaise (Probably the most inspiring song of liberty the world has ever known, written by a French officer in April, 1792. Volunteers were about to leave Strasbourg when the mayor of the city, who gave a banquet on that occasion, asked the artillery officer de Lisle to write a song in their honor. Both words and music were written in a single night, and its name was originally Chant de Guerre de l'Armée du Rhin. Parisians, ignorant of its real authorship, named the song Hymn de Mars. The song was written for the soldiers of Luckner's army, who sang it as they marched on the Tuileries, on August 10, 1792. The French Revolution had begun with the storming of the Bastille on July 14, 1789.)

Other French songs:

Chant du Départ.	Chant des Partisans.
Voici la Noël.	Le Mirage de St. Nicholas.
Ma Normandie.	Les Filles de la Rochelle.
A la Violette.	La Vieux Châlet.
Alouette.	La Mère Michel.
Sur la Route de Louvières.	Le Petit Homme.
Monsieur de la Palisse.	Compère Guilleri.
Le Bon Roi Dagobert.	La Belle Attendait.
Auprès de ma Blonde.	Il Pleut, il Pleut, Bergère.
Ron, Ron, Petit Patapon.	Le Tour Prends Garde.

César Franck, the distinctly French composer, may be called the father of modern French music. In him already we find that mysticism which is so characteristic of it. C. Debussy is the most important modern French musical personality. In his music the influence of poetry and painting is clearly noticeable. His main ideas are derived from the country and the landscape, just as in poetry and in painting. To him the country suggests a certain harmonic system, a technique of the orchestra that frees the instruments from all collective restraint. He was strongly influenced by the poet Verlaine and others. Debussy's music charms, caresses, seduces. He is a master who detests the colossal. Ravel and Fauré wrote enchanting songs and instrumental music of flexible and striking rhythms. Honegger's music is characterized by a diatonic rigor and extreme chromatics.

ITALIAN FOLK MUSIC

The national strain in art in Italy is exceptionally clear. The Italian composer, for instance, runs to melody and emotionality; and harmonic attributes are subject to the sensationalism of his melody. Mascagni's Intermezzo, from the opera Cavalleria Rusticana, could not possibly have been written by any other composer than an Italian.

Italy is the land of sunshine, beauty, and artistic tradition. Song is the natural expression of the Italian heart—songs of lovers, songs of boatmen and fishermen, songs of workers in the field, songs of children. Italian folk songs show much variety, ranging from the barcarolles of the Venetian gondoliers and the street songs of Naples to the music of Sicily, where there are still to be found traces of the old Hellenic civilization. Their many *songs reflect and express this graceful and beauty-loving spirit,* and they are characterized by the most seductive charm. They are filled with a carefree spirit, and are a perfect expression of the sensuous joy of living. *The Italian sings of his joy in life, of that which appeals to the senses.* In Italy, "popular music is familiar music." The opera is very popular, and many fine operas are produced. Excellent singers come from Italy; Italy marks the birthplace of the opera and oratorio; and it is a chief source of all forms of art, especially painting and sculpture.

The various kingdoms of Italy were united by the great Garibaldi, general under King Victor Emmanuel, in 1860. Thus, at present, the Italian commonwealth is no longer divided into various principalities.

Examples of folk songs by unknown Italian composers:

The Dove (Tuscan). Mamma Mia (Neapolitan).
O Solo Mio (O Sun I Love—Neapolitan).
Vieni Sul Mar (Neapolitan). Evening Prayer (Sicilian).
Bella Napoli. To Rosella.
Slumber, Slumber, Oh, My Dearest.

Composed Italian folk songs:

T. Cottrau Denza
   Santa Lucia.   Funiculi, Funicula.
Giardini
   Come, Thou Almighty King (Italian Hymn).

ENGLISH FOLK SONGS

English music shows very clearly Italian, French, and, later, Teutonic influences. Many of the English folk tunes have been copied from the Irish, Welch, and Scotch. The English, being a sturdy, vigorous people, have produced folk songs of straightforward melody, regular rhythm, simple lyricism, homely sentiment, and little ornamentation. Although both the people and the royal house have been much interested in, and always have had a great respect for, the art of music, they have achieved few masterpieces.

Of late, however, the English school of music has assumed greater importance. The younger composers have evinced a meritorious ardor and boldness in writing music in all forms, large and small, and their zeal shows good results. The country has encouraged music education; many royal schools and colleges of music have been founded and supported. The oratorio has been cultivated in England more than in any other country. In organ-building, the English show much skill, while many English organists have become noted performers. Special attention is now paid to the cultivation of boys' voices. Church music, as sung by the English boy choirs, is unsurpassed. Ballads and ballad-singing are popular in England.

On the whole, English folk songs are less tempestuous and introspective than those of Ireland, Scotland, or Wales. They have a *healthy jollity and sturdiness, directness and simplicity, reflecting the vigor and matter-of-fact attitude of the English people*. English folk songs are *lively in character* and are mostly in the major key. The music is free from excessive ornament and eccentricities of rhythm. The subjects of the songs are usually based on agriculture, hunting, love-making, which last is expressed with tenderness rather than passion.

(See: *100 English Folk Songs*, edited by C. J. Sharp; *Fitzwilliam Virginal Book;* Playford's *Dancing Master;* and The Beggars' Opera.)

Some old English folk-dances are Sellinger's Round (St Leger's Round, or, The Beginning of the World); Bean Setting; Black Nag; Bobbing Joe; Chelsea Reach; Green Sleeves; Gathering Peascods; Hewitt's Fancy; Jenny Pluck Pears; Parson's Farewell; etc.

Examples of old English Airs:

Barbara Allen.	Oh, No, John.
Polly Oliver.	The Cuckoo.
Nancy Lee.	Now Is the Month of May.
Sing We and Chant It.	It's a Rosebud in June.
A Sailor for the Sea.	Hard By a Crystal Fountain.
Blow, Ye Winds, Heigh-Ho.	The Flight of the Earls.
My Bounty Boy.	To the Maypole Haste Away

Tobacco's but an Indian Weed.
A Wet Sheet and a Flowing Sea.
Down Among the Dead Men (old drinking song).
The Wind Blows Out of the West Countries.
Drink To Me Only With Thine Eyes.

Composed folk songs:

DR. ARNE
    Rule Britania; The Lass With the Delicate Air.

BISHOP
    Home, Sweet Home.

CAREY
    Sally in Our Alley.

H. PURCELL
    Fairest Isle; Mad Bess; Ye twice; Ten Hundred Deities.

B. TREHARNE (ARR.)
    Come, Lasses and Lads; Down, Derry, Down; The Three Ravens.

SCOTCH FOLK SONGS

Like all folk music, Scotch music shows the influence of such instruments as the harp, crwth, violin, and pipe, all of which were used by the people. These instruments were all popular during medieval days, but the national instrument of Scotland is still the bagpipe. The origin of the bagpipe dates back to antiquity. Although found in Asia, Africa, and Europe, it reached its perfection in Scotland. The charm of the bagpipe can only be appreciated when heard out of doors. The fact that most Scotch melodies are based on the pantatonic, or five-tone scale, shows that much of Scotch music is probably due to the use of the tonally restricted bagpipe. The "Scotch snap," a rhythmic peculiarity in which the first tone has but 1/4 of the duration of the second tone, is also due to the bagpipe.

Scotch folk songs have an unusual charm in rhythm and melody; and those of the Scottish Highlands are wild and irregular. The songs *reflect the love of home and country and the sturdy independence and pathos of its people. They tell* of the warlike spirit of the clansman, his fierce love for, and loyalty to, his native hills, his stern sense of duty. Many of the tunes are older than the words now sung to them. Besides numerous love songs and those which reflect the customs of the people, songs were composed which com-

memorated almost every historical event. Of course, there are
a number of songs that belong to both Scotland and England
—Jack O'Hazeldean is an example of a borderland ballad.

Numerous poems by Robert Burns have been adapted to
old Scotch tunes, and others have been set to original music.
There are but few outstanding composers from Scotland itself. Very likely, the Puritanical opposition of the church
retarded the musical growth of the Scotch. Many noted
composers have made use of Scotch folk tunes in their
works; Mendelssohn's Scotch Symphony is an example.
(See *Seventy Scottish Songs,* edited by Helen Hopekirk.)
Old Scotch folk songs:

Allister MacAllister.	And We're All Nodding.
Get Up and Bar the Door.	Sky Boat Song.
John Anderson.	Scots Wha' Hae' Wi'.
Jock O'Hazeldean.	The Strathspey Reel.
The Campbells Are Coming.	The Smiling Spring.
The Keel Row.	The Piper of Dundee.
Turn Ye To Me.	Wi' a Hundred Pipers.

Wallace Bled (Hey Tuttie Taitie).

Coming Through the Rye (old dance tune).

Auld Lang Syne (This song is built on the five-tone scale,
in which the 4th and the 7th tones of our major scale
are absent. It is the melody of an old song: I Fee'd
a Lass at Martinmass.)

Loch Lomond (It dates back to the days of the Jacobites
(early 18th century), and it based on the old six-tone
scale. Lomond Lake is the largest in Scotland; Ben
Lomond, the highest of the Scottish highlands, towers
at the head of the lake. The words of the song have
been differently explained.)

Composed Scotch folk songs:

LADY SCOTT	MILLER
Annie Laurie.	Bonnie Doon.

J. E. SPILMAN

Flow Gently, Sweet Afton; The Bonnets of Bonnie
Dundee (The Band at a Distance).

Representatively Scotch folk dances are the Highland
Fling and the Highland Schottishe.

WELCH FOLK SONGS

Wales was the last stronghold of the original inhabitants of Britain. It is a small but very mountainous country. Musical culture was decidedly advanced in Wales; it dates back earlier than that of Scotland or England. There is absolute proof of this assertion, for most of the Welch folk songs we know today have been sung in England for so long that they are frequently classified as English folk tunes. The *Welch Eisteddfod* is a song festival that originated at the time of the bards in the 6th century at Conway. This congress was held yearly to foster national music and literature; there were competitions for musical and poetic compositions and performances, all to maintain Welch national feeling and stimulate interest in the language, songs, and customs. Surely, the Welch are a singing people.

Welch folk music is of a somewhat wild character, and, on the whole, rather rugged and strong. *It is noted for its simplicity, regularity of structure, and freedom from outside influence.* Welch music is often serious, telling of the deep religious fervor of its people; some is even martial in character, but it lacks the element of humor in Irish folk music. Many of the Welch folk songs are stirring vocal marches which evidently were used as songs in days gone by.

Some old Welch airs by unknown composers are Deck the Hall; The Ash Grove; Men of Harlech; The Dove; etc.

Owen's All Through the Night is the most famous composed folk song.

IRISH FOLK SONGS

To tell about Irish music would take more time and space than is at our disposal. Only the barest outline can be given.

The Egyptian historian Hecatarus writes in 500 B.C. about harpers in Ireland. Before the coming of St. Patrick to Ireland in A.D. 432, the Druids made use of music in their services and had a system of musical notation carved on their sacred stones. The earliest of harpers dates from the 6th century, when these annual gatherings at Tara's Hall were first instituted.

The earliest use of the diatonic scale is attributed to the Irish; and they were also the first to make use of counterpoint. It is said that Europe received its earliest teachers of music from the abbeys of Ireland.

During the wars of the 16th, 17th, and 18th centuries, the art of music declined in Ireland, and many Irish melodies were rewritten in the English style. However, Ireland has produced some of the most beautiful and varied folk music in the world. The Irish retained their love for music throughout centuries of oppression and amid their constant striving for independence. In fact, their songs are a strange mixture of joy and sorrow which is characteristic of the Celt. Many of their folk songs are old, and they often have odd but fine harmonies. The best Irish tunes are *very melodious, plaintive and pathetic; strong in human appeal;* or filled with a heroic quality which cannot die. Even the songs in lighter moods have an irresistible appeal; and none ever lose their sweetness. Practically every occupation of the Irish people has its own individual tune, sometimes sung merely to describe it. Love and sorrow are the most popular subjects of the Irish folk song. Of course, the Irish jig, reel, and hornpipe are known the world over. Note especially Miss McLeod's Reel, a most popular dance tune of great antiquity, which reflects the lighter yet poetic spirit of the people.

For about 150 years the music of Ireland has had no existence apart from that of Ireland.

(See *Sixty Irish Songs,* edited by W. A. Fisher; also the songs collected by Thomas Moore.)

Old anonymous Irish Airs:

Bendemeer's Stream.   Father O'Flynn.
My Love's an Arbutus.   The Fairies' Dance.
Wearing of the Green.   Robin Adair.
The Harp That Once (Gramachree—Love of My Heart).
Believe Me If All Those (My Lodging Is in the Cold, Cold Ground).
The Meeting of the Waters (The Old Head of Dennis)—written in a scale of but six tones, the seventh, or leading tone, being absent.

Farewell to Cucullain.
Londonderry Air (Time Marches On).
Last Rose of Summer (The Groves of Blarney).
The Minstrel Boy (The Moreen).   Oh, the Shamrock.

Composed folk songs:

BALFE
Killarney.
F. N. CROUCH
Kathleen Mavourneen (a splendid ballad).
LOVER
The Low-Backed Car; The Girl I Left Behind Me.

Some old Irish folk dances are the hornpipes; reels; Miss
McLeod's reel; rakes of mallow; white cockade; wind-that-
shakes-the-barley; etc.

RUSSIAN FOLK SONGS

Geographically, culturally, ethnographically, Russia is
partly Asiatic, and the influence of the East is a potent one
on Russian music. Climate forms the temperament and the
characteristics of a people, and the music is influenced by
that temperament and those characteristics. Hence, Russian
music is extremely variegated and interesting, as it is very
typical of that nation. It contains strains of Slav, Tartar,
Gypsy, Mongolian; melancholy tunes, rhythmic and vigorous Cossack dance songs, and Ukrainian peasant airs. This
music brings to light the characteristics of a peculiar race.
A great variety of local color is given to Russian songs by
the enormous size of the country, its endless steppes, and
the many points of difference among the various parts of the
land. The monotonous scenery of Siberia, with its inter-
minable stretches of gloomy forest, produces a people who
are silent and sad; in the same way, the intense cold and the
bitter struggle for existence have left their mark; and in his
music, the Russian pours forth his innermost thoughts.

The impetuosity of the Russian is curiously demonstrated
in his music. The listener is brought under the influence of
its visions, its eternal longings. Russian music puts us under
the spell of a land far beyond our ken. The exotic and unfamiliar rhythms and the frequent displacement of the
accent seem to be very pointed examples of this, not to

mention the unusual and different harmonies. However, the music gives way at times to moments of unutterable gloom. Perhaps this is the cry from the heart of a people who have never yet known or enjoyed real freedom. If the Russian gives vent at times to moments of unspeakable grief, he is not devoid of a true love of gaiety and fun.

The folk song appeals to the true Russian. It consoles him in his sorrows; it accompanies his merrymaking; it is the friend of his youth; and, when old, he plays the same strain on his balalaika that he knew and loved as a boy. We are constantly finding folk melodies used with splendid effect by Russian composers. Yet are we to look for the distinctly Russian note in Tschaikowsky's works? Here and there is a reminiscence of the people's song, as in that marvel of lightness and floating beauty, the 5/4 waltz in his 5th Symphony. No doubt, there are various traces in Tschaikowsky common to Russian folk songs, but the Russian element is more in the national temperament, the grinding pessimism of his openings, the barbaric contrasts and the tremendous emotionality of his music. These are Russian in the extreme. While these masterworks are perhaps not entirely original, yet through the use of folk melodies they are given to the world and thus saved from oblivion.

Russian folk songs include songs of labor, marriage, prison, death, superstition and play. Many of them show the influence of the Jewish orthodox service, the ancient system of the Hebrews, and the influences of the Greek Catholic Church. Some of them are strange and exotic and show a frequent use of uneven measure (five beats to a measure), a feature conditioned by the peculiarities of the language, which inevitably has a great influence upon the folk songs of any country. The best songs of Russia are *sad and favor the minor mode*, but they are *beautiful and poignant;* and in the *eastern part of the country, they are strongly affected by Oriental influences; others are distinguished by a mad gaiety*.

Only a thorough knowledge of the life and character of this strange yet gifted people can help us to understand their music. It is really necessary to become acquainted with Russian literature and pictorial art—with the works of Go-

gol, Tolstoi, Dostoyevsky, Chekhov, and the paintings of Perov and Veretschagin. Modern Russian composers have said the first words of a semicivilized nation in the world of music. It would be surprising, with all this wealth of material, if their works did not contain innumerable beauties and much that is wonderful and new.

The Russians and Bohemians have many points in common in their use of melodic and harmonic songs.

Most Russian folk songs can be classified as:

1. *Melodic songs—dance songs:* They are in the major key, lively in character, and are sung in unison and used to accompany dancing.

2. *Harmonic songs—folk songs:* These are sung in harmony, are in a slower tempo, and mostly in the minor keys.

Perhaps the deepest basso voices are found in Russia. This, very likely, is due to the fact that in Russian churches no instruments are allowed. *A capella* singing is much fostered in Russia.

Lately, the Russian ballet has come into prominence. Free music schools have been organized, and some of the most gifted violinists, pianists, and cellists before the public today are Russians.

Glinka is considered the father of Russian orchestral music. Many fine composers have made the Russian folk song the central idea in their symphonic works. Before Glinka, during the entire 18th century, the development of music in Russia was practically in the hands of imported Italians. Russia probably ranks second to Germany in its wealth of folk tunes. The *balalaika*, somewhat like a guitar, is a very popular instrument.

Russian folk songs:

Dark Eyes.	Tempest.
Down by Mother Volga.	The Caged Bird.
Finnish Runs.	Harvest Moon.

Dancing in the Snow (Ukrainian).
Volga Boatman's Song. (It is the song of the Volga bargemen as they haul their heavy craft. The men sing and pull the ropes to the rhythm of the song.)

The Wild Rider.   The Troika Bells.
Vesper Hymn.   The Cossack's Farewell.

Composed folk songs:

A. TITOFF
The Red Sarafan. (The *sarafan,* or robe, is the national costume of female peasants.)

VON LWOFF
Russian National Anthem.

Listen to Glinka's Mazurka; Kamarinskaiya (Russian folk
dance); A. Rubinstein's Romance; Russkaya Trepac (Russian folk dance; Tschaikowsky's March Slav (written for a
concert of wounded soldiers in St. Petersburg, as a result of
the War of 1876 between Turkey and Serbia); Rachmaninoff's Prelude in C♯ minor; Hopac; Krassny Sarafan; Orien-
tale; Raspashol (Russian gypsy); Two Guitars; Black Eyes
(Russian gypsy); etc.

POLISH FOLK MUSIC

Poland has always produced musicians. From the 16th
to the 18th century, however, they were unable to express
themselves in a style typical of their native land. They
adopted in turn the Italian, French, and German styles. It
was reserved for Chopin (1810–1849) to express the soul of
all Poland in his striking works.

Polish folk music abounds in sad and mournful strains.
But this melancholy strain is of a poetic rather than a tragic
character, and *Polish songs are quite cheerful and sprightly.*
Some good songs have been written by Polish composers;
they are full of syncopated notes, intricate rhythm, and difficult melodic intervals.

Similar characteristics are found in the four great divisions of the music of the Slavic race: *Russian, Polish, Bohemian, and Hungarian. The Poles and the Hungarians are
more passionate and intense in their dances,* as well as in the
use of instrumental forms, than the Russians and Bohemians.
Poland has produced considerable orchestra music, but most
of their music is written for the piano.

The national dance of Poland is the charming *mazurka;* but the stately *polonaise* and the brilliant *waltz* also are extremely popular, Chopin has given the world the finest idealized waltzes, mazurkas, and polonaises.

Polish folk songs:

Farewell.   On the Water.
Rachu, Rachu, Ciachu (dance song).
Matthew Stopped. (It reflects the melancholy, sadly gay
    feeling native to the Slavic temperament.)
Star Lullaby.   Praise Ye the Lord.

Listen to the National Hymn, Boze Cós Polke; Jeszcze Polska Nie Zginela; Krakowiak; Obertas z Dukli; Noskowski's Polonaise; Mlynarski's Mazurka; Wieniawski's Kuajwiak; Chopin's Nocturne, Opus 15, #3, #1; Valse, Opus 64, #1 (Minute Waltz); Polonaise Militaire; Mazurka, B major; Mazurka, Opus #3; etc.

BOHEMIAN FOLK SONGS

The countryside of Bohemia is very picturesque, and the spirit of its woodlands, streams, and mountains is always plainly felt in Bohemian music. Bohemian music is quite similar to that of the other Slavic races, especially Poland's. Both countries assimilated much from their neighbors—Germany, Austria, and Russia. Bohemian folk songs and folk dances show but slight changes in character. On the other hand, Bohemia and Poland have retained their own individual languages and customs. In short, there was no definite Bohemian school of music until about 1850. It was originated and fostered by Smetana (1824–1884), an ardent follower of Liszt and Wagner. He incorporated Bohemian traits (*the polka and furiant*) into his music, just as Liszt had done with Hungarian folk music. Smetana's style is thoroughly original; his form is free, yet coherent; and he has a color sense and great powers of orchestral description.

Of all the Slavic countries, Bohemia has the most cheerful and lighthearted folk music. It is *striking in its melodic rhythmic and dynamic expression.* Many of the songs have a very graceful character; others a dancelike quality expressive of gay and healthy feeling. The polka, a very popular dance, originated in Bohemia.

Dvorak (1841–1904) is considered the representative Bohemian composer by reason of his greater breadth and more cosmopolitan style. He has wonderful ability in handling the orchestra, as can be seen in his symphonies, overtures, operas, etc. Surely, his New World Symphony is a masterpiece.

Other noted composers include Z. Fibich, J. B. Foerster, L. Janácek, V. Novák, J. Suk, B. Martinu. Among the outstanding violinists, we note Frederick Laub, F. Ondricek, J. Slavik, O. Sevcik, J. Kozian, J. Kubelik, etc.

There are excellent conservatories of music in Prague, Brno, Bratislavia, etc. The leading symphony orchestra is in Prague, and there are good orchestras in the radio stations of Pilsen, Ceske, Ostrava, etc.

Bohemian folk songs:

Fare Thee Well.	Good Night.
Yuletide Night.	Praise Him.
The Wedding.	The Wheat.
My Homeland.	

O'er Tatra's Mountains Flashed the Lightning.
Battle Hymn of the Hussites. (This patriotic song had its origin in the wars of the "Hussites," as the followers of John Huss—1369–1415—were called.)

The Cheerful Heart.	Come O'er the Sea.
Turn Around Me.	Hush-a-bye Angel.
The Wild Wind.	Maiden's Confession.

Representative composed folk songs are Smetana's Cradle Song; Dvorak's Humoreske; Songs My Mother Taught Me; etc.

HUNGARIAN FOLK MUSIC

Hungary, situated between the Balkans and Russia, is populated by Magyars (the real Hungarians), Gypsies, Jews, Slavs, and Greeks. What, then, is typically Hungarian music? In general, Hungarian music expresses a will rather than a sentiment. Like Russian music, it does not have in it melancholy or "crying laughter." Even Hungarian elegies have a resolute character. The rhythm of Hungarian folk

music is sharp, resolute, and varied; the melody moves freely and easily; the form is clear, short, well balanced, and
concise, not veiled as in French music. *Original Hungarian
music is vigorous in melody but devoid of ornament; it has
richness of ideas rather than a persistent and diligent development.* Obviously, this is the reason why no Hungarian
composer has been able to produce such monumental and
dynamic works as Bruckner and the like. The lively nature
of the Hungarian is suggested in *erratic rhythms and fitful
tempos.* The cembalon is a very popular instrument; so is
the violin. The people have a special love for music and
dancing, which are closely associated, and they make extensive use of both at all their ceremonies. The most distinctive
type of Hungarian folk dance is found in Hungarian music,
where the gypsy musicians have for many years adorned all
the folk melodies with their own elaborate ornamentation
and have made use of surprisingly curious rhythmic changes.

The Hungarian minor scale is favored; it has a weird
effect, because of its augmented 4th: c d e♭ f♯ g a♭ b d. An
endless variety is possible when the scale is employed with
syncopated rhythmic and oriental effects. *Hungarian music
is not gypsy music. Hungarian music uses the pentatonic
scale and the repetition of the first part of the melody in the
lower 5th.*

The *czardas* is a dance form of two parts; the slow *lassan,*
generally in minor, and of melancholy character, is by turns
sober and sentimental; and the rapid *friska* is wild, impassioned, and jubilant. Other popular Hungarian dances are
the *szolo,* in which the men whirl the women around in the
air; and the *verbunkea,* a military dance for men, in which
some patriotic air is sung while the dancers swing wine bot-
tles over their heads as they dance.

Frank Erkel, who lived at about the time of Glinka, was
the first to express authentically Hungarian nationalism in
music. He was the first to propagate Hungarianism in his
music (operas such as Bathory Maria; Hunjadi Laszlo; Bank
Ban, 1861; Dosza Gyorgy; Nameless Heroes, 1880; also, the
Hungarian National Anthem).

Liszt (1811–1886) was the first composer to use the wonderful contrasts of rhythms and syncopation characteristic of Hungarian music. He was the creator of the *rhapsody,* writing fifteen of them. They are based on the tunes of the Hungarian gypsies who for years imposed their special type of melodic and harmonic ornamentation on the old Hungarian melodies. The result is music that features contrasting moods of the deepest melancholy and the most frenetic joy. The rhapsody is an elaborate composition, wild and disconnected, and made up of fragments of melodies. Its ~~...~~ folk dance (czardas); and it has three kinds of melodies—a slow, mournful song, a playful dance, and a furious, whirling sort of dance. It is distinctly national in character.

Bela Bartok (1881–1945) must be credited as the founder of the national Hungarian school of music. He and Zoltan Kodaly prepared the settings for modern Hungarian folk songs based on Magyar music.

Listen to Ablakom, Muskatlis Ablakom; A Ven Cigany; Itthagyom a Falutokat; Tudad-e Babam Nepdal; Ritka Buza (Golden Wheat); Tis par Csokot; Lavotta; One Kitten, Two Kittens.

Also:

BERLIOZ
Rakoczy March (National Air).

BRAHMS
Hungarian Dances (idealized expressions of these unique and remarkable dances of Hungary).

HAUSER
Czardas; Hungarian Rhapsody; etc.

J. HUBAY
Hejre Kati (from Scenes de la Czardas).

M. KASEMAYER   KELER-BELA
Hungarian Dance.   Hungarian Lustspiel Overture.

KODALY   F. LISZT
Psalmus Hungaricus.   Hungarian Rhapsodies.

GYPSY MUSIC

Gypsy music, whose origin is perhaps Asiatic, is spontaneous, impulsive, without inhibition, natural, emotional, and frank. The best gypsy music is heard in Russia, Rumania, Hungary, and Spain. Spanish gypsy music is perhaps influenced by the music of the nomad Arabs of Morocco. The gypsy music of Russia is often melancholy and nostalgic. The *Hungarian gypsy music is highly emotional, capricious, erotic, with sudden changes of mood, from sparkling gaiety to deep pathos*. Even the smallest Hungarian villages have always maintained their own gypsy orchestras. The violin leads, by playing an improvisation of some old gypsy dance, and the other players follow the leader, guided only by their own instinctive love for harmony. The cembalon accents the rhythm, the tune usually beginning on the downbeat and in duple time. Many musicians of Hungary are gypsies of oriental descent, and they are well known for their taste for finery and ornamentation; their Hungarian music has become highly ornamental. The musical ornaments imply singular dexterity of execution and a special aptitude for purely superficial invention in decoration. *Hungarian gypsies always adorn their melodies with curious runs, twists, and turns, as well as chromatic tones—very rhapsodical in nature;* they use no printed music. Roumanian gypsies often imitate the sound of birds in their music. Its performance demands great mastery of the violin, but in a free and unschooled style. Incidentally, Roumanian folk music and dance music is vivid in phraseology, full of little trills and jerks, as well as quaint and somewhat plaintive intervals.

Listen to Deep Sorrow; Don't Leave Me; Stars in the Sky; Wind, Tell My Sweetheart; Gypsy Air (Kurt Steiner). (See *The Gypsy Violin,* Belwin Edition, N. Y.)

DANISH FOLK SONGS

Denmark, not as large as West Virginia, is the smallest kingdom in Europe. One third of the country consists of hundreds of islands, many uninhabited. It is the land of scientific farming; the land where extreme poverty is unknown; the land of Shakespeare's *Hamlet* and of Andersen's *Tales.* It is the birthplace of Thorwaldsen, Holberg, Bering, Jacob Riis, Drachmann, Nexo, and Rasmussen. No wonder, it is much loved by tourists, who roam from the sights of Copenhagen and Odense to the dunes of Skagen.

Danish folk songs have regular rhythm and usually are in the major key. They *are perfect in formal outline* and are as polished as the works of a great master. There are many lovely Christmas carols and legendary songs relating to the sea and the bold deeds of the Vikings, besides some of the most remarkably composed folk songs to be found among any people.

The Danes have ever been partial to reels, which, by the way, are similar to those of Scotland. Like other Scandinavian people, the Danes also enjoy those dances which tell or act out a story; and many of their dances are descriptive of the trades or occupations of the workers. There is a curious influence of French mimicry in their descriptions of their own folk industries which makes their folk dances quite unusual and charming.

Denmark has produced no composers of great distinction, save Gade, Lassen, Schytte, and Enna. Danish musicians have written songs and instrumental music, but few operas.

Danish folk songs are the Danish Folk Dance (Dansk Folkvise); Jutland Dance Song; etc.

Composed folk songs:

N. Gade
    The Birch Tree.

C. A. Nielsen
    The Eagle.

H. Rung
    Denmark National Air (In Denmark I am Born).

Lange-Muller
    Shine Bright and Clear.

Danish folk music includes the Ace of Diamonds; Crested Hen; Dance of Greeting; The Hatter; Little Man in a Fix; Seven Jumps; Shoemakers' Dance; etc.

Also listen to such piano music as J. Bachgraad's Sonnet; R. Nordraak's Vale Caprice; A. Winding's Nocturne; N. Gade's two excellent sonatas for violin and piano.

SWEDISH FOLK SONGS

Sweden is the land of old castles, forest-fringed lakes, the midnight sun, and the aurora borealis. It is a thousand miles from the flower-decked meadows of tourist-haunted Skane to wild, romantic Abiske in the north. The Gothenburg Canal is the world's finest inland voyage; and Stockholm, the imposing capital, is girded by seas and forests. Sweden is the land of Nobel, Ericson, and Linnaeus; it is also the land of many firsts—Swedes were first to arrive in America, 500 years before Columbus; first to recognize the United States; first to penetrate "the northeast passage"; etc. Its copper company at Falun is the oldest business on earth, established in 1225.

Swedish music, including folk songs, has been influenced by foreign political conditions such as the Thirty Years' War (1618–1648); the establishment of the French court in Stockholm during the reign of Charles XII; and the proximity of Germany. Perhaps their folk dances have remained more truly characteristic than their folk songs.

Swedish folk songs are generally in a happy vein; and in some the Tyrolean yodel is suggested. At any rate, they are less tragic and melancholy than those of Norway and Finland. Some of the *older songs were founded on the Gregorian scales*, and *many of the tunes begin on the unaccented beat*. However, the *majority of the folk songs are based on the regular scales*.

The *lute,* especially imported from Italy, has become one of the national instruments of Sweden. Male choruses are also very popular throughout the land.

Swedish folk dances include the Bleking; Carrousel; Gustaf's Skal; Hop Mor Annika; I See You; Nigarepolska; Tantoli; etc.

Traditional folk songs:

A Vermeland thou Lovely (a fine and much beloved song).

Fresh Spring Breezes.
Hush, O Hush Thee.
When I Was Seventeen.

Peter Swineherd.
I See You.
Swedish Mountain Polka.

Composed folk songs:

PETERSON-BERGER
  Klock-Ringing.

SÖDERMAN
  Swedish Wedding March.

E. SJOGREN
  In the Sultan's Garden.

RINGSTRÖM
  Star Eyes.

W. STENHAMMER
  On St. John's Eve.
  Swedish National hymn.

NORWEGIAN FOLK SONGS

Norway is the majestic land of the north, the land of twelve thousand miles of fjords unequaled anywhere else in the world; the land of rugged mountain masses, glaciers, and snowfields; the paradise for winter sports and the land where the ski was born. It is warmed by the Gulf Stream and thus is never too cold. Like its neighbors, Finland and Sweden, it is a glorious country for the midnight sun. It is the land of Ibsen, B. Bjornson, Knute Hamsun, Amundsen, Hansen, and Grieg. It has more potential water power than any land in Europe, and its prehistoric remains go back 8,000 years.

Norway always retained her independence in art, although joined to Sweden for many years. Ole Bull, Sinding, Swendson, etc., are well-known names. Norwegians like to sing; and the male chorus, especially, is very popular.

Norwegian folk songs are distinctly individual. Their *melodic contours show an erratic disregard for form and conventions. The drop from the 7th to the 5th of the scale is frequent—c b g. The harmony is rugged. The rhythm suggests the weird antics of the mysterious elves and gnomes of the underworld, as well as the rough and boisterous peasant enjoying the dance.* There are two classes of Norwegian folk songs: one bold and vigorous, the other tender and plaintive. Most of the songs deal with simple events of life; some are hunting songs; some are humorous; and others have a direct and simple poetical appeal.

Grieg (1843–1907), a born lyric poet, was the one Scandinavian composer able to draw from the folk songs of his native land the material for works of great charm. His fame rests upon his fine songs and descriptive piano pieces; though his suites, his piano concerto, and his wonderful violin sonatas proved that he was not lacking in the power of color and description thoroughly his own.

Old folk-songs:

Gamale Norge.	Ole, Ole.
Astri, mi Astri.	Home from the Saeter.
Down the Valley Goes the Herd.	

Composed folk songs:

H. KJERULF
   Last Night the Nightingale Woke Me; Twilight Musing.

R. NORDRAAK	OLE OLSON	SINDING
National Hymn.	Sunset.	Sylvelin.

Norwegian folk tunes include Jeg Elsker Dit Smil; Row to the Fishing Ground; Sangerhilsen Nor De Foreuede.

Also listen to Grieg's Peer Gynt Suite; Norwegian Wedding March; Violin Sonatas; and Swendson's (1840–1911) Romance for Violin and Piano.

FINNISH FOLK MUSIC

Finland, a country of virgin forests and meadows, many splendid lakes, and much wild moorland, is a land of majestic beauty, but great sadness. Life is harsh, because the climate is so severe and cold. The people, although living for centuries under Swedish rule and for some time under the Russian yoke, have preserved their individuality. Both the beauty and melancholy of Northern nature and the stern conditions under which the Finnish people live have contributed to the depth and sincerity of their art. Since about 1835, they have made much progress in the development of a national art. A number of important and significant composers have come to the fore, and much is expected of them in the future. *Finnish folk music is eloquent; it is tinged with deep melancholy, and usually is in the minor mode.* It is rugged and filled with the strain of life in that land of snow and ice. Then, too, in the art of

Finnish composers there is melancholy and despair, expressing the feeling of an exiled and oppressed people.

J. Sibelius (1865–1957) was Finland's greatest composer; in fact, he also ranks among the noted composers of the world. Some time ago he was pensioned by the government in order to be able to devote himself entirely to composing. He has contributed to his country a great wealth of new folk music, thus enriching greatly Finnish culture. Much of his music, although original, is at the same time folk music as well as art music. It expresses his love for his native land and for all nature.

Finnish folk music includes the Karjapihassa; Kevälaulu; Majani Kanssa-Sottüsi; Turun Polkka; etc.

Songs of Finland:

O. MUSIKANTO
Melancholy.

E. MELARTIN
Farewell.

S. PALMGREN
In the Willows.

J. SIBELIUS
A Flowret by the Wayside.

Also listen to A. Järnefelt's Berceuse; Preludium; S. Palmgren's Finnish Rhythms (Sketches); J. Sibelius' tone poem, Finlandia; Romance, Opus 24, #9; nine symphonies; etc.

SPANISH FOLK MUSIC

Spain has a very fascinating and individual type of folk music. Practically all this music, however, is derived from the Moors who invaded the country in the 8th century and spread their dominions rapidly. The Moors brought with them much science and art, which they had learned from the Greeks and Byzantines. They made Cordova the finest city in Europe at the time; and the great mosque at Cordova is still one of the best examples of Moorish architecture in the world. The greatest stronghold of the Moors was Granada; and here was the magnificent Moorish palace. The Moors were not driven out of Spain until about the time of Columbus; and Spain then became one of the greatest and richest of European powers. However, her progress in music was not in keeping with her achievement in many other fields.

The Moors left their influence on Spanish music, introducing the guitar, which became the most important Spanish instrument, and bestowing an oriental character to many of the folk songs. Another influence on Spanish music was brought from central Europe by the troubadours, who came to Spain with their poetic romances and their lutes, which were introduced into Europe by the returning Crusaders.

Spanish composers imitated the formulas of other nations, and it was left to the people to preserve the native musical expression. Many years have not altered this condition greatly. What has contributed much to the individuality of Spanish music is the extreme poverty of the people as well as the geography of the country. Spain is very mountainous and wild, almost inaccessible to the transportation of the modern age. In other parts of the country there is a certain overpowering monotony in the landscapes and sunlight. Its life moves slowly and languidly, with a *dolce far niente.* Poor peasants do not travel far, nor do they come into contact with other people with different traditions. Thus, very ancient folk songs still are sung, especially in the north of Spain. These songs are probably of Asiatic origin, and are very rhapsodic and florid. There is also a diversity, brilliance, and a flaunting of color in buildings and costumes, a hint of passion and intensity in the swish of skirts, the swagger of *caballeros* and the little boys playing *el toro.*

The *guitar* is the most popular instrument and is used not only to accompany the voice but also as a solo instrument. Another instrument used both to accompany the voice and to play solos is the Spanish *gaitos,* a shrill-voiced species of oboe.

Very fine folk songs are heard in Spain, such as the Cancion Andaluza; Linda Mia; Free as a Bird; La Cachucha; Meus Amores (My Beloved); Song of Asturias (Praviana); Farruca; Spanish Gypsy; etc. Of the composed folk songs, we may mention J. Vaverde's Pinks (Clavelitos); and Alvarez's Song of the Prisoner (El canto del Presidario), Juanita, and La Paloma (The Dove)—an incomparable tune, truly characteristic of the music of southern Spain. It reflects tropical grace and tenderness in its melody and its remarkable combinations of rhythms. In the bass is felt the swaying of the habañera, while the melody it accompanies has a rhythmical irregularity and caprice seldom found in the music of countries other than Spain and certain parts of the Orient.

Surely, the temperament of the Spanish people is reflected in their graceful, charming folk songs, their glorified dance tunes and descriptive music—all embodied in vivacious and glowing rhythms and attractive melodies. Much of the appeal of Spanish music arises from this. The *alborada* is a morning serenade, a folk-song; and the *seguidilla* is one of the most famous of Spanish dances.

Spain is still somewhat medieval in character. She is just beginning to realize her importance politically; and science, literature, and art are more and more cultivated. Spain has been the setting for several operas not by Spanish composers, but which have a certain Spanish flavor. For instance, there is Don Giovanni, by Mozart; the Barber of Seville, by Rossini; Il Trovatore, by Verdi; and Carmen, by Bizet. R. Strauss has written a tone poem on the unique character of Don Quixote.

García, the famous Spanish vocal teacher, was successful in producing more noted singers than any other teacher of his time. Sarasate (1844–1908), the great Spanish violinist, became known the world over for his marvelous playing and composing. P. Casals, the eminent Spanish cellist, also is known everywhere.

It is true that Spain never has had any great composers; but now a talented school of young composers is on hand, full of nationalistic spirit and ideas, which undoubtedly will excel the past in output, content, and individuality. These musicians realize the value of their own folk music and write frequently and characteristically in their style. Albeniz, de Falla, Granados, and others have incorporated in their works the peculiar rhythms of Spanish folk songs and dances. Note the graceful and sensuous Spanish Dance, by Granados; Romanza Andaluza (Spanish Dance #3) by Sarasate; Fete Dieu a Seville (cello solo) by Albeniz; Jota (a Spanish dance), and Nights in the Garden of Spain, by de Falla; and the opera Goyescos, by Granada; etc.

Also listen to La Borrachito; La Cancion de la Escola; Grana y Oro—Paso Doble; Maleguena; Los Rumberos; La Sevillana; Spanish Dance (by de Falla—Kreisler); Vals Español (by Giron); La Zagalina; etc.

AMERICAN MUSIC—INDIAN MUSIC—NEGRO MUSIC—ARMY SONGS
RAILROAD SONGS—COWBOY SONGS—JAZZ AND SWING MUSIC

In the study of folk music we find that the climatic and economic conditions of a country, which are expressed in the people's struggles and sorrows, triumphs, and joys, all have a strong influence on music and the other fine arts.

American music, in its beginning, was altogether European. At first—up to about 1700—American music was entirely under the influence of the Puritans, who looked upon music with disfavor and discouraged its use in the church service. The *Bay Psalm Book*, published in 1640, contained many old tunes previously brought from Holland. (Notice Old Hundred, Dundee, etc.) Then, gradually, songs and dances of Ireland, Scotland, Wales, England, Germany, and France became popular in various settlements of America during the 18th century. However, our economic status gave little opportunity for leisure and the cultivation of the fine arts.

We can hardly expect to have a folk music of our own. The American people trace their origins from the various nations of Europe and Asia. True, we have found folk tunes among the Indians. But up to the present, America, whose entire culture, musical and otherwise, has been derived from European sources, has not as yet perfected the development of a musical school. Lately, musical activities have increased considerably. Annual music festivals and conventions in many cities, and individual concerts and recitals of every kind, are given throughout the country. They have become commonplace in our social existence. New symphony orchestras are being organized in almost every city of importance. A good deal is also being done by the Women's National Federation of Music Clubs. Enthusiasm for music is constantly increasing, and the spread of musical culture promises well for the future.

The two races most closely identified with early civilization in America are the Indian and the Negro.

It is very natural that *Indian songs and dance tunes* have been of considerable influence in the shaping of American musical expression. Note the striking examples of Indian themes used in American music: Cadman's From the Land of the Sky Blue Water and At Dawning. Lieurance's By the Waters of Minnatonka, Sad Moon of Falling Leaf; MacDowell's Indian Suite for Orchestra, based on real Indian melodies; Skilton's Two Indian Dances (Deer Dance; War Dance); V. Herbert's Dagger Dance from Natoma, which shows pronounced rhythm, the repetition of the short phrase, and the five-tone scale; and so on.

Likewise, the *songs of the plantation Negroes*, born in slavery and oppression, have *considerably influenced the character of American musical expression.*

The real *Negro folk music* was seldom heard in the past outside the camp meetings of the colored people; but these old spirituals are now becoming more widely known through records, the radio, and TV. These songs express an individual folk character which is original and distinct. They reveal the sorrow, joy, the spiritual longings, and the superstitions of the race.

The Reverend C. D. Pike, of the American Missionary Association, brought out the first book of Negro songs ever published, in 1872. His collection of Negro spirituals, which were then called "*jubilee songs,*" was little more than a crude source book. All the striking and peculiar harmonies of the colored singer were lost. Pike had apparently entrusted the arrangement of his songs to some manufacturer of Methodist hymns.

It was not until 1914 that the Negro song was intelligently examined by the late H. E. Krehbiel, the noted music critic of the New York *Tribune.* He published his *Afro-American Folk Songs.* Krehbiel was a German scholar of the conscientious type, with much knowledge of music, and so his study was a valuable one.

The gaps in his work are now admirably filled by J. W. Johnson in his book, *American Negro Spirituals*. Mr. Johnson, a colored man, has gathered all his materials from original sources. He grew up in the south and was interested in music from his earliest years. With his brother, J. R. Johnson, he was mainly responsible for the rise of *jazz music*. However, the Johnsons are no mere jazz promoters. They are both educated musicians, and their book is one of dignity and value. J. W. Johnson discusses in a long preface the origin and nature of Negro spirituals; and J. R. Johnson presents scores of them in his own arrangements.

The spirituals probably are mulatto rather than Negro. All the original slaves brought in was a series of unusual, extraordinary rhythms, but few of them were accompanied by what we would recognize as melody. The Africans had tunes, but they were tunes of a vague, wandering sort. They lacked what we call "form." They could not convey that sense of design, that feeling of unity and coherence, which characterize civilized melody.

But, as said before, the rhythms of the Negro were splendid; all that was needed to make good songs was a fine melodic pattern. Now it is probable that melody came from the camp meeting, and at some time not earlier than the end of the 18th century. The whites of the South made no effort to teach the slaves the fine arts. The slaves were only interested in saving their souls, especially after the first tours of Francis Wesley. Salvation was attempted *en masse*. Camp meetings arose; and the camp meeting was a place of sturdy and even vociferous song. The Negroes memorized what they heard and then adapted it to their native rhythms. Thus, the spirituals came into being.

This purely Negro contribution—good *rhythm*—was most important. To this day some Methodist hymns seem banal to musicians because they lack variety of rhythm. But the spirituals are full of various rhythms, and when they are sung properly by colored singers from the south, they give immense pleasure to lovers of music.

The Negroes, having started with Methodist hymns and improved them by joining the text to lively rhythms, next improved them as melodies. That is, they displaced their obvious cadences with cadences of a great piquancy, and relieved their monotony with bold modulations. Some of these modulations, as Mr. Krehbiel demonstrated in his book, were derived from Africa. Savages know nothing of the modes or keys that trained musicians use. They see nothing wrong about inserting a C natural or a $D\sharp$ into the key of D major. The American Negroes did this in some of the spirituals, and the effect was very brilliant and thrilling. In addition, they improved the harmonies of the hymns; and the result was lovely, indeed. During the last generation, music has adopted much of this striking harmony. When white musicians began to put such unusual harmony into their own music there were bitter protests from all the pedants; but now many of their innovations have become quite orthodox. Indeed, music that does not contain such modern harmony seems monotonous and insipid. But it was satisfactory to the African ear long before we learned to tolerate it.

As both Johnsons show, *the Negro is a harmonist* far more than he is a melodist. *He is, first of all, interested in harmonies and rhythms.* His sense of harmony is quite unequaled among primitive people. Whenever a crowd of colored fellows begin to sing any current song, however banal, they will presently give it new interest by introducing strange and often entrancing harmonies. In such part-singing, even among those ignorant of musical notation, the natural blending of voices is extraordinary. Negro songs contain frequent repetitions of short phrases, a necessity where there is no written music. Their rendition is often antiphonal, a leader singing a phrase which, in turn, is repeated by a chorus. They seem to have a natural talent for that sort of thing. Quite often, in the midst of harsh discords, they produce effects of beauty.

Imitations of Negro songs the so-called "American folk songs"—like Dixie, Old Black Joe, Swanee River, etc.—are not in any strict sense Negro folk music; they were composed by white men who were highly gifted in their capacity for writing simple, appealing melody. Folk songs, like all other songs, are written by individuals. The people choose the ones that are to survive. Sometimes, of course, repetition introduces changes, but those changes are not important. The basic song belongs to one bard, unknown though he may be, and to him alone.

Johnson tells of such a bard whom he knew as a boy, one called "Singing Johnson," but no relative of his. These singers usually traveled about, singing for their keep. When they struck a new neighborhood, they would make up songs about what was going on—the advent of a new and powerful preacher, the conversion of a notorious sinner, a great fire or flood, the hanging of the local daredevil, etc. Naturally, most of these songs were soon forgotten, but a few always survived. The best of these songs are the spirituals we know today.

It would be nice if we could discover the authors of some of them and give credit where credit is due. Whoever wrote Swing Low, Sweet Chariot; Deep River; Roll, Jordan, Roll; etc., left a heritage to his country that few white men have surpassed. He, or they, surely were great poets.

How fine was the impression made by the great tour of Dett's Negro Choir of spiritual singers, which held European music centers spellbound. To have heard this choir sing, Were You There When They Crucified My Lord? or, Listen to the Lambs, was an unforgettable emotional experience. Hall Johnson's choir and the singers of Fisk University also have made splendid impressions.

Negro music is based on the five-tone scale; contains frequent repetitions of phrase; and is rhythmically smoother than Indian music. "For most of his spirituals the Negro resorted to religious texts, perfectly or imperfectly remembered, and altered in accordance with the needs and temperament. By this means he expressed in a manner crude and elementary, yet with an eloquence that carried conviction, his feelings and his dreams." The Negro has also striking ability for ensemble performance. A solo voice leads; the other voices may respond in the regular manner to supply the full harmony, or the different singers will sing apparently at random and improvise, with the greatest confidence and facility, parts of their own.

Examples of Negro music:

Go Down, Moses.
Swing Low, Sweet Chariot.
Couldn't Hear Nobody Pray.
Mammy's Song.
Nobody Knows de Trouble I've Seen.
Shout All Over God's Creation.
Sometimes I Feel Like a Moanin' Love.

Golden Slippers.
Roll, Jordan, Roll.
Good News.
Deep River.

Steal Away.
Live A-Humble.

American folk songs:

Good Night, Ladies.
There's Music in the Air.
When Johnie Comes Marching Home (P. Gilmore).
Down in the Valley (Kentucky Mountains).
Yankee Doodle (old air).

Jingle Bells.
Ten Little Indians.

The Quilting Party.

Composed American folk songs:

CARRIE J. BOND
A Perfect Day; I Love You Truly; Just a Wearyin' for You.

JULIA W. HOWE
Battle Hymn of the Republic.

J. STAFFORD SMITH
The Star Spangled Banner (composed in London, about 1775, to the words of Anacreon in Heaven).

GEO. ROOT
Battle Cry of Freedom; Just Before the Battle; Tramp, Tramp, Tramp; Vacant Chair.

O. SPEAKS
On the Road to Mandalay.

S. A. WARD
America, the Beautiful.

LILI STRICKLAND
Mah Lindy Lou.

FOSTER
Indian Times; My Old Kentucky Home; Old Black Joe; Uncle Ned; Nelly Was a Lady; Swanee River (Old Folks at Home); Massa's In the Cold, Cold Ground.

A popular folk dance is The Arkansas Traveler.

Army songs sprang into existence during the Civil War;

and although some of them lacked the requirements of good composition, they enjoyed a great popularity during that period.

G. F. ROOT
Tramp, Tramp, Tramp; Battle Cry of Freedom (Rally 'Round the Flag); Rosalie, the Prairie Flower; etc.

H. C. WORK
Marching Through Georgia; Kingdom Comin'; Babylon is Fallen; Nicodemus the Slave; My Grandfather's Clock; Lily Dale; Father, Dear Father.

D. EMMET
In Dixie Land (1859); Old Dan Tucker (Emmet was a principal member of Bryant's Minstrels).

CH. HALL
John Brown's Body Lies Moldering in the Grave.

W. KITTREDGE
Tenting on the Old Camp Ground.

H. McCARTHY
The Bonnie Blue Flag (written 1862 to words by Mrs. A. Ketcham to an old Irish melody by McCarthy).

Lumberjack tunes are The Logger's Boast; Driving Saw Logs; etc. A famous work song is John Henry. Railroad songs and ballads include Casey Jones; The Train that Never Pulled In; Mama, Have You Heard the News? Cowboy songs include The Old Chisholm Trail; Git Along, Little Dogie; Bury Me Not on the Lone Prairie; Goodbye; Old Paint; etc.

CONCERNING JAZZ AND SWING MUSIC

It is reasonable to suppose that music which is universally accepted must have a universal appeal. Jazz music has been heard the world over. Obviously, it has something strangely universal, something compellingly human and all-inclusive in its make-up. Jazz and Swing music bear about the same relation to classic music that *slang* does to standard literature. No doubt, slang is "language in the making." Now it does happen that sometimes a word or phrase with a certain cleverness or fitness become permanent parts of the language. But such instances are rare. Sometimes a colloquial slang phrase gains international acceptance. (The term "all right" is used in Europe and Asia, because Americans are heard to say it so often.) So, there are several influences contributing to American music, and jazz and swing are the melting pot into which poured the blues, the hillbilly tunes, the work songs, cowboy songs, and ultramodern dance tunes.

For a century and a half we have imitated the European style, and we really have never had any genuine American music. Whether we like the classical or not, at least we have pretended to do so. Swing music is a form of jazz. It is native, and like the folk music of other countries, will evidently some day form a vital part of American symphonic literature. As mentioned before, American music to some extent rests on the use of either Indian or Negro melodies, perhaps both, as well as on certain distinctly American musical ideals. All these tend to become traditional; and with increasing spread of appreciation, they will supply the foundation for a representative national art.

Jazz and swing music borrow their rhythmical beat from the jungles of Africa, imported to America by Negro slaves and preserved in plantation ditties, barn-dance songs, and spirituals.

The best of jazz and swing is the finest popular music known; such music contains a musical refinement and sophistication, and there is a vast number of well-trained cosmopolitan musicians who play it. Ravel has said that jazz is a living source of inspiration for all modern composers. Our modern music world would be strange, indeed, if it did not show an interest in the markedly influential jazz and swing. If jazz and swing had done nothing more than to break down certain old orchestral tendencies, they would be justified. It is in the instrumentation of modern jazz orchestras that the musician is mainly interested. It represents an advance in orchestration similar in extent to that made by Beethoven and Wagner. Jazz has opened up wonderful instrumental possibilities, and jazz orchestration has become a real art and developed rapidly. Indeed, the lessons to be learned from it will not be forgotten by composers of serious music.

It appears that Gerschwin's Rhapsody in Blue and his Piano Concerto are the pieces upon which the jazz and swing futurists pin their hopes. These works are a direct encouragement for a more ambitious attempt to employ jazz in the legitimate artistic forms of concert music. Gerschwin's Piano Concerto is made up in the main of rhythms and tunes in the popular vein. In this way, the first movement is based upon a "Charleston" motive, introduced by bassoon, horns, clarinets and violas; while the second theme is announced by the piano. The second movement is in the form of a nocturne; and the final movement is "an orgy of rhythm, starting violently and keeping to the same pace throughout."

Now there are others who claim that jazz has an extremely limited chance to raise itself above the level of the dance hall and the musical-comedy stage; and, so long as it is written by people who only have the most commonplace ideas and the most rudimentary technique, no one will be able to take it seriously. But should a composer with ideas and a technique take it up, the form will be found too small, too infantile for him. At any rate, the question of jazz in connection with music of serious character, of developing it in accordance with the stricter rules of form and composition, and of using it in works of symphonic proportions, is receiving considerable attention from serious-minded composers.

Composers like Stravinsky, Milhaud, E. Satie, Ravel, G. Auric, Hindemith, Carpenter, Copeland, Harris, and others, have written ragtime, jazz, and swing music. They have taken the new rhythms from dance music and have added them enthusiastically to their ballets, orchestral and chamber music. Because of this, they surely have not lowered our occidental standards of music. Carpenter's ballet, Skyscrapers, reflects some of the many rhythmic movements and sounds of modern American life. It has no story, in the usually accepted sense, but proceeds on the simple fact that American life reduces itself essentially to violent alternations of work and play, each with its own peculiar and distinctive rhythmic character. The action of the ballet is merely a series of moving decorations reflecting the obvious external features of this life. This fine work represents the first attempt in a ballet of serious dimensions to bring into being a purely American choreography as an art form.

Irving Berlin has written Alexander's Ragtime Band, Memphis Blues, All Bound 'Round with the Mason-Dixon Line, and many other jazz tunes; there are striking jazz pieces by L. Gruenberg, such as Daniel in the Lion's Den, which uses Vachel Lindsay's poem from the standpoint of a Negro preacher; then there is a Synconata, or syncopated sonata, as well as a Jazetta, for violin and piano. W. C. Handy and Duke Wellington, both Negro composers, are well-known writers of "blues" dances. These dances are somewhat slower than ordinary jazz. Duke Ellington has written Black, Brown, and Beige, the New World a'Comin' (after the book by R. Ottley), and other works.

Jazz music has three distinct principal traditions: the *New Orleans,* the *Memphis,* and the *Chicago tradition.* It began in New Orleans, St. Louis, Memphis, Chicago, and New York.

New Orleans jazz is the "traditional" or "classic" jazz from which every other type derives. Its style was evolved by Negro bandmen before World War I, and was based upon the folk music of the Negro, work songs, spirituals, and blues, the French and Spanish strains of cosmopolitan New Orleans, as well as military marches. This "hot" jazz music was in the strong, syncopated rhythms of Afro-America, involving a great deal of improvisation by the players who divised spontaneous parts around a given theme. The American Negro, who had little or no formal musical training, used his instrument for personal expression. In New Orleans a colored barber "Buddy" (King) Bolden was the first to employ some sort of jazz with his band in 1886. It was the first attempt at "improvising." But the first real jazz orchestra was the "Original Dixieland Band" of 1912 in New Orleans. In New Orleans, likewise, the word "jazz," as well as other words such as "break," "straight," etc., were invented at about the same time.

Dixieland is the name usually given to music by white

players stimulated by the colored New Orleans style. Often the white players tend to be less ardent though more polished than the Negro performers.

The *Chicago tradition* of jazz is probably of the greatest importance, since it was in Chicago that the fine colored musicians of the South received their first national recognition and began exerting powerful influence upon popular music. In short, the disciples of New Orleans developed the Chicago style. This was during the Prohibition era. As against the languid airs of New Orleans, the Windy-City jazz of Chicago was hard-boiled. The night clubs were full of liquor and excitement, so Chicago jazz reflected this atmosphere. Somewhat less lyrical than New Orleans music, it took on punch and honky-tonk strenuousness; in addition, Chicago players began to make much of individual solos along with their group improvisations. (See records of Eddie Condon, "Wild Bill" Davison, and others.)

Swing music: Around 1925, the public applied the word "jazz" to anything from the real hot article to sugary dance orchestra renditions. To distinguish their own music, the musicians began to call jazz "swing." About this time there developed a marked jazz style for so-called "big bands" (14 to 16 men). It alternated hot solo improvising with arranged, strongly rhythmic passages for the brass and reed sections. This music, excellent for dancing, became a public sensation within a short time. The bands became known as "swing bands" and their music as "swing music." (See records of Duke Ellington, Gene Krupa, Fletcher Henderson, Joe Jones.)

Bebop: Usually, musical forms of any sort go as far as there is a persistent impulse to explore and experiment. By 1935, the jazz field was full of good instrumental technicians. Naturally, some of them became discontented with traditional jazz forms and worked toward new ways. This happened especially in Harlem. The musicians followed their own jazz rhythms and the subtle trends of new harmony; they tried steadily to use augmented chords, extreme dissonances, polytonality (several keys at a time), and atonality (no definite key). They also tried eccentric rhythms

(Caribbean). All this was known as "bebop." (See records of Charles Parker, Dizzy Gillespie, Bill Harris.)

Modern Jazz: A great many younger players who have been influenced by jazzmen of former years now form the ranks of "modern" jazz. These musicians are responsible for the new heyday of jazz; they are not only crack players but students of musical theory; and they are devoted to good composition in the jazz idiom. They do not endorse cheap, clamorous imitations of the earlier styles. (See records of Lester Young, Gerry Mulligan, Milt Jackson, Oscar Peterson, Pee Wee Russel, etc.)

A *"break"* is something like a cadence; in the break all instruments stop except one which, in free form, varies the theme. "Straight" jazz is the music played as written; in "hot" jazz the themes are varied at each occurrence (improvised). The various dances—one-step, two-step, cakewalk, black-bottom, stomp, charleston, shimmy, foxtrot, etc. —vary more in the manner in which they are danced than in their musical structure or performance.

The well-known Tiger Rag is nothing but a "jazzing" of an old French quadrille. Note also the relationship between Tea for Two and Ravel's Pavane pour une Infante Défunte. Other sources for jazz and swing music are Puccini (Tosca; Avalon—Foxtrot); music by Tschaikowsky, Chopin, Bach, Mozart, Beethoven, etc.

Jazz music has three distinct features: *orchestration* (saxophones; muted cornets and trombones; wailing, squealing clarinets; noisy and novel percussion devices); *definite melodic and harmonic make-up* ("blue" tones; discordant chords, etc.); and *various involved rhythms based on syncopation.*

Through centuries the dance and its rhythms developed from the popular music to art. The dances in a suite by Vivaldi, Bach, Handel, etc., were originally simple folk dances before such types as the allemande, courante, sarabande, and gigue were artistically created by the great masters of the 17th century. The same is true of the minuet before Haydn and Mozart used it in idealized form in their sonatas and symphonies. In those times much was said and written concerning concessions made to the public taste by these noted composers. It is reported that the waltz, when it first appeared, was branded as a piece for sailors' girls played in the dens and saloons of harbor cities; just as, in our time, the tango has been similarly condemned. But this was at a time before Schubert and Beethoven, in the German dances (*Laendler*), and Chopin, Brahms, Reger, and the Viennese musicians had created their artful waltzes. Clearly, these outstanding composers have by no means put music on a lower level by their use of dance tunes.

It may be held that these tunes were European dances which, even before they were idealized in the works of the masters, were more advanced, more cultivated, than the music of the Negro. Well, let us see. Take, for instance, the sarabande. Originally, it was a Spanish dance which was considered as strange a form as a tune imported from South America at present. The sarabande also has syncopated notes. Often new forms, the exotic ideas of foreign countries, have put life into our own music. Oriental tunes came by way of ancient Jewish music of the temple into the Gregorian chant; and then the latter found a use in many a fine mass or motet by composers of the Middle Ages up to Palestrina and Lasso; others found uses for Turkish marches and *Janitschare* music, as in Mozart's and Beethoven's works. The influence of gypsy music upon the masters of the 19th century was extensive, not to speak of the musical folklore in the creations of the Romantic era and of the present day. Influenced by the tunes of the early American Indians, Busoni wrote his primitive but rhythmically effective Indian Fantasy. So we note that it is useless to speak against the use of jazz in serious music—jazz that has conquered the entire dancing world.

In times of changes of style, new primitive forms have superceded more developed ones. The at first rather simple homophonic forms displaced the artful polyphonic forms of the Middle Ages in 1600. The conservatives at that time condemned in the same vehement manner the *"nuovo musiche"* as primitive and artless, just as they condemned the change of style of the baroque to the early classic period when the contrapuntal masters were being replaced by composers of, at first, rather simple folklike serenades, and the like. Matters are not different today. Since the coming to the fore of music for entertainment—the popular dance tunes—the technique of jazz, its rhythms, its elemental vitality, its possibilities of improvisation, its melodic and harmonic contact, have all been more or less adopted by many composers.

Much information may be obtained by perusing *American Jazz Music*, by Wilder Hobson. It not only traces this music from New Orleans through its transitions, but tells its story in terms of jazz itself and of the noted jazz musicians who developed it and still are developing it. Even the concert musicians are told how they may learn to understand the basics, at least, of swing music. The book closes with a list of thirty phonograph records that are the unadulterated article and are still available, though some are over twenty years old. The men who recorded them are named and their solo parts identified.

Another interesting book, *Jazz—Hot and Hybrid*, by Winthrop Sargeant, goes much deeper into jazz origins than most studies of that kind. It examines jazz beyond the New Orleans era; in addition, it takes swing apart and examines the separate pieces. The book is a scholarly study, not a mere collection of stories about jazz musicians.

The exaggerated rhythm and freedom from all conventional forms in music, as emphasized by jazz and swing, is really the manifestation of people's love for unrestrained moods and fancies. No doubt, it was jaded taste which required the thumping of tin cans, the ringing of bells, the scraping of sandpaper, and all manner of musical noises. It was nerves craving stimulation. Music, at its best, is soothing, inspiring, restful—not this thing suddenly turned slave-driver, whipping on our overactive nervous system. But this sort of musical noise is demanded by some people, and so it is continued. Yet there are some who hold that jazz and swing will eventually take the road to oblivion, just like any other art development which is not fundamentally sound.

The strength of the jazz band lies in the novelty of its

technique. From the viewpoint of rhythm, the continued use of syncopation permits this music to be performed, without resorting to rich and varied orchestration. Unusual expression has been made possible by the methods employed for scoring jazz in its more ambitious forms and, also, the use of the various instruments. After the first onslaught of sound effects came a noticeable emphasis on melody; then came the period of the "blues," the melody of which was merely supported by a clear, stereotyped rhythmic outline. The percussion instruments were scarcely in evidence and grew more and more emotional. Thus, in the jazz band, we have found a form of artistic expression which is absolutely our own. Some of our leading jazz bands have attained a high degree of perfection in their performances. But there really are few possibilities to make use of them. So far, the possibilities have been exploited mostly in dance music, such as, ragtimes, fox trots, shimmies, etc. Of course, it is distinctly bad taste to use and transcribe famous compositions for jazz orchestra. Jazz and swing arrangements of classic themes are utterly uncalled for at any time and place. Such products are designed to appeal to people who prefer to wriggle to any kind of jangling rhythm. People with any sense of the beautiful cannot really like these perversions of lovely and noble music. All in all, it is a bad commentary on the endurance of undiscriminating hearers in a mad age. Some of the best melodies of Schubert, Schumann, Chopin, Tschaikowsky, Johann Strauss, Wagner, etc.—such as the Peer Gynt Suite, Tosca's Prayer, Prelude in C♯ minor by Rachmaninov, Rubinstein's Melody in F—have been put into a new dress by Tin Pan Alley to provide dance themes.

It is evident that noisy jazz, which requires but limited musicianship, will not endure; but the better class of jazz, which demands artistry, will do so to a limited extent. The ingratiating syncopations, the novel harmonies and bizarre tone-colors of good popular compositions are much above the ordinary jazz level. The chord sequences of dominant 7ths and 9ths, which as late as 1900 caused such wonderment, have become quite common in the latest fashionable dances. No doubt, in a very short time the polytonal and atonal harmonies will become rather frequent in the dance music of the future. Zez Confrey has used the pure major and minor chord simultaneously in his striking Kitten on the Keys, and Gerschwin has gone even further in his Rhapsody in Blue.

The discouraging thing about jazz is the fact that it has been viewed in such false perspective—either condemned completely or inordinately exalted. Those who condemn it say that jazz might even incite murder, for it is the music of hysterics, of jangled nerves, of an overwrought and neurotic generation. They also say that jazz and swing alike are made of the most temporary fabrics, and nothing is really worth while except that which lasts. Jazz is an art that undermines the restraint and intellectual poise upon which civilizations are built. It offers us only a temporary escape into the realm of forgetfulness; it does not encourage us to strive after anything; it does not offer us ideals, induce us to sacrifice ourselves for great causes, nor instill in us a sense of human dignity. The symphonies of Haydn, Mozart, Schubert, Beethoven, and Brahms, the tone poems of Strauss, or the music dramas of Wagner inspire us; they provoke aspiration for human perfectability. Jazz and swing, of course, do not do this.

The encouraging thing about jazz is that in its orchestrations *it uses sound and novel principles of harmony and counterpoint,* and thus *definitely raises the average level of musical intelligence.* Furthermore, jazz orchestration *uses unusual and novel combinations of instruments to produce new, striking tone colors.* Despite its limitations, jazz possesses the indefinable, elusive quality which is the earmark of real musical expression. Jazz has vitality. It does not try to sound the depths of human devotion, but it vibrates in sympathy with our lesser impulses. Jazz shows an impelling purpose, and it has a legitimate function in music. To the mind of a tolerant and reasonably sensitive music enthusiast, *good jazz is an interesting and highly stimulating type of music.*

The style and technique of jazz music are musical factors which we have to consider. Of course, there is good and bad jazz—and, indeed, too much bad jazz. But today we can see that the good jazz outlives the bad. The good jazz will not, by any means, lower the quality of serious music. Outstanding composers may—as was done long ago—raise the dance forms of the present day to a higher level. Already we have proof of this, as may be seen in representative works by our best American composers. Clearly, one does not have to be a proponent of jazz and swing music to note its cultural and historic influence upon the new music.

8

THE PERFORMANCE OF MUSIC

1. STANDARDS FOR LISTENERS

THE purpose of the chapters on piano, violin, solo singing, orchestra, etc., is to tell the reader, or listener, what he has a right to expect from a good performer—namely, a good performance. Certain standards of interpretation as well as of composition need be established so that the listener may really judge the musical value of what he hears, quite aside from personal and other considerations.

To begin with, it must be noticed that there is no analogy in any other art to the executant, or performer, in music. No other art, not even the dramatic, is so dependent upon a mediator as music. Music not performed is dead. On the staff the notes are stationary; they imply motion, but they do not move. The rapidity of the succession of sounds, their grouping and shading, are determined to a large extent by interpretation. Incidentally, our musical education would be more sound if the true nature of performance—re-creation —were sufficiently stressed. *Self-expression, based on the qualities, temperaments, intuitions, and feelings of the performers, is important.* Expressiveness is more important than intellect. Much must be felt, even though it is not indicated in the score.

The music-lover, therefore, must know something about the ways of performance, as well as the laws of composition. To listen intelligently, he must clearly understand not only his own part but also that of the composer and the interpreter and what each contributes to the complete musical experience. The composer, the creative artist, gives us the experience of his feeling for beauty, his own personality, his fullest and deepest expression of himself as a man and as a fellow being. When we speak of the style of a composer, we mean by it the total result of an individual character and the particular period of time in which he lived.

What is good playing and singing? What are we to look for in playing and singing? What does the performer add out of his own taste, knowledge, and genius? What is the distinction between good, bad, and mediocre in musical performance? Of course, strictly speaking, people have to be educated up to a recognition of excellence in musical ideas only if they have been educated down to something else. In other words, *people who have been brought up on jazz, swing, and similar popular music have to be educated up to the music of the great masters.*

The music-lover is called upon not so much to bestow awards of praise or censure as to observe, understand, and enjoy. But before he can understand music, he must actually live it. He must take seriously his task as a listener. Taste and sensibility may both be considerably developed by intelligent practice. That means listening to music of all schools and all periods, old and new. And, in order to further the art of music, it means to listen intentionally, consciously, and with intelligence. The appraisal of values, leading to judgments, will follow enlightenment; but inquiry comes first. An increase in appreciation of music will result in a decrease in the toleration of the poor performer. The best is the enemy of the merely good, and a still greater enemy of the mediocre, or poor.

Good performers, singers, and players have been judged according to their fulfillment of two requirements, the first being wholly technical, and the second being wholly in the nature of responding to, or interpreting, the work performed. *They are artists if they do not merely depend on the technic necessary* to capture an audience, *but show also an expressive power* that is well used in the interpretation of great works. If they depend too much on technic and mechanical ability, and actually lack the expressive qualities, they are called "virtuosos." However, some good singers and players have sufficient musical feeling and are called "virtuosos" only because they have such remarkable technic that it attracts more notice than their expressive qualities. But in so far as technic means lack of expressive power, the term "virtuoso" is a reproach.

Now, the interpreter exists to serve the composer—to re-create the message of the composer. As listeners, we must be able to recognize what the interpreter is doing to the composition at the time he re-creates it. We must note the interpreter's part in the performance we are hearing. We ought to have a more or less ideal conception of the style that is proper to the composer whose work is being performed; and ideally, we ought to be able to observe to what degree the interpreter is reproducing the style within the make-up of his own personality. We may fall short from attaining this ideal in listening, but it is well to keep it in mind as an objective.

A general remark as to *technic:* A good singer or player has practiced the physical details of the art until there is no uncertainty as to his ability to reach a certain tone, to stay on the pitch, to keep time, to perform rapid passages with sufficient flexibility, and to emit pure tones without rasping interference. In short, his technic must be automatic—a habitual response to the sense of touch and feeling. Good technic puts the listener at his ease, instead of putting him on edge every moment, worrying over possible disaster. Otherwise, instead of relaxing and enjoying himself, he becomes weary, as though from the strain of actual effort.

A general remark as to *interpretation:* The performer who interprets the composer's music must have sufficient artistic intuition to enable him to enter into the spirit of the music. He must sense the music's appeal and endeavor to make others also feel it. He must bring out "those characteristic marks of nationality, of form and style, of historic background, and of individual genius which are found in most great music." Of course, in his performance he expresses his own intuition while he re-creates the work and interprets it by his own individuality. The mastery and performance of a sonata, a violin concerto, or an opera aria involves the simultaneous co-ordination of every faculty—physical, mental, and spiritual. A successful performance means even more. It brings to the performer a poise and freedom of manner which can hardly be attained in like measure by any other form of activity. Surely, the performer puts life and meaning into the composition.

Of creative artists, the composer is the one who is most dependent upon a multitude of intermediate agents between the public and himself; intermediate agents, either intelligent or stupid, devoted or hostile, active or inert, are capable from the first to the last of contributing to the brilliance of his work or of disfiguring it, misrepresenting it, and even destroying it completely.

Concerning our craze for the "star system," we certainly agree with Sigmund Spaeth in his view concerning the "nothing-but-the-best" attitude toward music, out of which has grown an automatic monopoly of the concert field by a few artists with "name value." To be sure, the world is full of other worthy performers who are as much aglow as these artists with the passion of delivering the great message of music, yet who find it difficult, if not impossible, to get a hearing before they have established a "name value." If musical audiences considered their artists with as much intelligence as baseball fans consider their players, it would be much better for the art of music. It does not make the slightest difference to the baseball patron whether a new player comes from back of the yards or the sandlots of Kokomo. All he wants is to be shown some proficiency in the game, and he surely knows it when he sees it. "Until we stop eternally asking who is performing and begin to take an interest in what is to be sung or played, we cannot honestly consider ourselves a nation of true music-lovers." Of course, in voicing these views, we are not saying that there should not be standards of performance, or that it would be all right for an amateur to go into a professional career without sufficient preparation. We must put the performer where he belongs as an interpreter of a greater man's ideas. We place him often on too high a pedestal by our uncritical adulation. The performer is, after all, only the messenger; and if we exaggerate his importance, we may overlook entirely the significance of the message itself.

2. GENERAL REMARKS CONCERNING EXPRESSION

In language we convey our meaning by means of definite sounds and symbols, which stand for concrete objects, ideas, or actions. As we have pointed out again and again, the meaning of music is more complicated and subtle and, therefore, more difficult to convey. If a performer arouses no emotional response by his singing or playing—in other words, if he does not bring out the meaning of music—we say he lacks "expression."

Behind the elements or material of music—rhythm, melody, harmony, form, and tone-color—lies the personal message of the composer. This message is communicated to the listener through the performer. Music is more than a sensuous art; it is an art which has many moods to express, many emotions to convey, that affect each of us differently. Music is such a powerful influence in human life because it arouses in us these different feelings—feelings which are the main causes of our actions. But music on paper is meaningless as such. Likewise, the meaning or expression of music has no power to arouse moods without a performance—performers are necessary to sing or play it, to interpret it. Performers who perform the music as created by the composer are essential. It is a subtle and difficult, as well as fascinating, task to perform music in such a fashion that the significance of the personal message shall be conveyed and a sense of beauty aroused in us. *A sense of beauty must be aroused in us. Music must thrill us, it must exalt us!* Also, our emotions must be aroused to the point where we feel as the composer felt, but where each of us applies these feelings to our own subjective joys and sorrows and satisfactions, as only we know them. Failing to bring about suitable emotional states in the listener, and arousing in him a sense of the beauty of the music, the singer or player has very little left to show that his effort has been worth while—he has performed without expression. After all, uniformity of response in listening to music is perhaps not possible, nor desirable. Music is the most popular and the greatest of all the arts because of its wonderful power to arouse this universal emotion. Yet it does not necessarily follow that this power should make us respond exactly in the same way. While the performer may legitimately add a message of his own (i.e., give his own interpretation) to that of the composer, the basis of all expression must be found in the music itself. The performer must convey the personal message to us in such a way that it is easily apprehended.

A statement has been made that, to listen to music no actual knowledge is necessary; that music is an art rather than a science; and that it makes its own direct appeal to the listener's sense of beauty. Without retreating one bit from this viewpoint, it is still possible to admit that the whole problem is not quite so simple. There is an important pleasure in music whose keenness is largely dependent on the amount of knowledge which the listener possesses. In a strict sense of the word, it is a nonmusical pleasure which heightens the musical pleasure. Technical knowledge adds to the enjoyment of music because it assures a realization of fine craftsmanship. Delight in fine workmanship, the satisfaction of watching a composer or a performer surmount his obstacles and achieve his end—this is the extra joy which music offers and which requires in anyone who is to experience it a fair amount of musical knowledge.

Something very similar to this delight exists in the other fine arts and crafts. In the art of architecture our admiration is aroused time and time again by the masterly way in which the great builders of the world have solved problems of stress and strain without spoiling the beauty of their designs. In fact, the problems are merged with the beauties to such a degree that the two become one, and an art of the highest type emerges.

The ingenuity of a composer is put constantly to the test. He must lead his voices gracefully and, at the same time, keep the total effect in mind. Again, the restrictions of the various instruments and of the several types of human voices limit him on all sides. He must bear in mind constantly the *need for variety* and *the underlying unity and balance of his work*. If his fear of a particular difficulty causes him to adopt some obvious protective device, merciless critics will call this a piece of poor workmanship. The device must be a part of the beauty of the music—the means must become an end. Thus, the vexed composer is called upon to solve many obstacles, yet his music must sound spontaneous, straightforward, and inevitable.

The performer has his troubles, too. He may not slacken his tempo as he approaches some atrocious technical difficulty. He is not even allowed to change his conception of a passage because the new conception of it might make things a bit easier for him. As far as his listeners are concerned, the performance flows directly from the performer's inner sense of what the music should be. In addition, he must work in absolute and complete harmony as to conception with his accompanying pianist, organist, or orchestra.

The listener who knows definitely that the difficulties of the composer and performer are real, and who further knows exactly what they are, may add this fascination for fine craftsmanship to the other, more strictly musical, satisfactions which a composition or a performance of it supplies. The possibility of gaining this extra gratification is the basis of the widespread belief that a person must "know" something about music before he can listen to it intelligently.

Let us return to our main subject of discussion, namely, general remarks concerning expression.

In order to bring out expression in music, the performer uses the following means: *tempo; dynamics; phrasing; and tone-color.*

Tempo: Tempo, or the rate of speed, is one of the most important means of expression. The tempo must be appropriate to convey moods; it must be steadily maintained, except where variation in speed is necessitated by means of changes in the character of the music. Tempo marks are indicated by words such as adagio; moderato; allegro; presto; vivace; etc. Changes of tempo are indicated by such words as accelerando; ritardando; etc. Sometimes the composer tells his wishes concerning tempo through metronome marks.

As tempo is a part of rhythm, it is advisable to discuss good rhythm briefly from the standpoint of performance. It involves:

1. Correct accentuation (strong and weak beats).
2. "Accurate performance of the various rhythmic figures, each tone being given its proper duration value"; that is, variety in tone length.

Dynamics: Dynamics, also known as "nuance," or "light and shade," refers to the loudness or softness of tones. Tones cannot exist without dynamic power. Tone is the first source of expression, and in its various gradations it has a range of esthetic value. Sudden and violent changes in the strength of tone have definite meaning. Slow and gradual gradations are still another source of expression. Musical enjoyment does not depend entirely upon quality of tone or upon rhythm or harmony but is greatly influenced by strength alone. Notice the bugle call, as well as the sonorous resonance so often heard in the scores of the great masters. Not less moving is the effect of a pianissimo phrase—it may convey deep and large feeling. Again, a dreary monotony may be produced by a repeating tone or chord which has no variation in power or no accent. Dynamics has much variety; it is capable of increasing or decreasing intensity, and the gradations are extremely subtle and flowing.

A composition meant to express tenderness and yearning, such as a lullaby or a meditation, may be utterly spoiled by being sung or played too loudly or too vigorously, and vice versa. The shading with which one performs has a great deal to do with the mood aroused in the listener. Dynamic marks are indicated by such words as forte; piano; morendo; expressivo; etc. Changes in dynamics are indicated by such words as crescendo; diminuendo; etc. It must be born in mind, however, that dynamic directions are always relative, never absolute. Every good singer or player knows that it is for himself to decide just how these directions shall be interpreted. At the best, composers can do no more than suggest the relative values of these changes in tone volume. The forte of a symphony orchestra playing tutti is quite a different thing from the forte of a solo violinist.

Phrasing: Phrasing is the grouping of tones or bits of melody. Phrasing is used in music very much as it is in language. Intelligent language requires that words be grouped, that groups be separated from one another, and that unimportant ones be passed over somewhat lightly. Punctuation marks are the mechanical means of indicating phrasing in language; while in music we use phrase marks—legato, staccato, rests, and accent marks. Phrasing of vocal music, being usually more complex, requires much experience for its application and discernment.

Tone-color: Tone-color, or *timbre,* is another means of expression. As in speaking lovingly to someone the quality of our voice is different from when we are angry, so, in music, feeling is conveyed by the different qualities of tone. The quality of the voice or tone of the instrument must be varied —that is, tinted—to bring out a certain mood or idea intended by the composer and which, in turn, will be aroused in the listener when hearing that particular tone quality. The various qualities of tone in a big orchestra form a very valuable means of illustrating musical ideas.

Through persistent ear-training and careful listening, tone-color may be recognized and appreciation and enjoyment of music increased.

The meaning of vocal music is comparatively simple to convey by the performer and to comprehend by the listener, for we have the text as a guide.

In listening to vocal music (or opera) we must make every effort to get at least the general significance of the text. If the song is sung in a foreign language, look up the meaning of the title, if nothing else. If possible, secure a translation of the words and try to visualize the picture represented in the poem or story. It will be easier to respond to its meaning, to the expression of the music—its mood— when the song is actually sung.

The essential requisites of good singing are:

1. *Pure and beautiful tone quality* (including flexibility of the voice, as well as accompaniment).
2. *Correct intonation and rhythm.*
3. *Intelligent phrasing.*
4. *Clear enunciation.*
5. *Conveying* somehow the meaning, *the mood* of the song.

In listening to instrumental music, we encounter even more difficulties than in listening to vocal music sung in a foreign language. Either the title is so vague as to have no connection with the music, and we have to depend largely on the performer to arouse in us appropriate feeling, or we do not even have a title which connects the music with the ideas, actions, and objects of ordinary life. Now, without a fitting performance, the personal message of the composer remains a sealed book and we do not get to know the wisdom contained in its pages. At any rate, expression, as considered by the composer, is the essential and integral part of the music. It is *the expression* which must be conveyed to the listener. A simple dance tune often means nothing more than the physical expression of rhythm by way of a pretty melody. In listening to simple rhythmic music, we need not seek for any hidden message. But a sonata, a symphony, or a tone poem has a hidden message. Music arouses a mood—of tenderness, exaltation, despair, depression, or courage, as the case may be; and this mood, together with the inherent beauty of the composition, is its real expression. The performer must, therefore, do everything he can to arouse in the listener an emotional response to the meaning and to the beauty of the music. He must not be content merely to have enabled him to enjoy tone quality or the digital dexterity of his own performance.

Surely, the ability to listen to fine instrumental works, with full appreciation of their beauty and meaning, cannot be acquired in a day nor in a year. If we are sufficiently ardent to search patiently for some time, and to remain consistently in the presence of the best, we will be rewarded by coming to understand and to feel the real spirit—the soul of music. Music, like great literature, takes maturity of thought and breadth of experience for its comprehension and appreciation.

While it is impossible to set up a definite standard by which we can declare compositions as good, bad, or mediocre, we can, however, indicate a few pointers which will assist in helping our decision.

The first criterion of a work of art is *sincerity*—it must not appear false or artificial. Every composition must make some appeal to the emotions or to the intellect. If there is no real feeling on the part of the composer, no feeling can be aroused in the listener. There must be a feeling for beauty and symmetry in the composition if it is a genuine work of art; and it must appeal to our higher, not our lower, nature.

The second criterion is that the *material should be used in the best possible way* and be presented according to the character of the work. Above all, the idea must be presented in such a manner as to convey the composer's meaning and be intelligible to the listener. Great ideas, placed in a wrong setting, will fail to make an appeal. Passages may be given instruments to which they are not at all suitable. Again, notes may occur which jar on the ear of the listener and thus weaken or destroy the impression to be made. Of course, a composer of genius will have ideas that are beyond his time; or he will use his material in new and unexpected ways which make it hard for his listeners to grasp. This explains why some composers have been neglected during their lifetimes, while others, though inferior, are acclaimed as wonderful musicians.

The third criterion is that the *instruments* by which the work is performed *must be used with reference to their particular functions*.

Listen to the masterpieces repeatedly, study them, live with them, and then beauty will be revealed. Obviously, an occasional visit to the concert hall to listen to some widely advertised artist can no more bring this about than a true appreciation of great paintings can come as a result of passing through an art gallery or two, nor appreciation of fine literature as the result of desultory, cursory reading.

Even though the listener does not fully understand the words of a song, or cannot grasp all the details of instrumental music, if in singing or playing we interpret the essential thing—the pathos, tragedy, or humor of the music —we have conveyed most of the personal message of the composer. If such an experience does not take place, if the listener is not made to respond to the essential meaning of the composition—its *mood*—then we have lost the spirit, the expression, the soul of the music. True, we have enjoyed the beautiful tones, their exquisite shading, the exact rhythmic figures, the flexibility of the voice, or the dexterity of the fingers, but we have only gotten its outer shell. The varied emotions which music can express so eloquently must come from inner feeling. This true inner feeling is something clear, definite, inevitable within the performer—it is his inner guide while making music; and only this deep inner feeling can make music spontaneous and eloquent, no matter how perfect the technic, the tone, or the intellectual mastery.

3. THE PIANO

It has been pointed out before that music is the one art which has no counterpart in nature, as painting and sculpture have, and that its printed symbols are as mysterious to the person of ordinary culture as the alphabet is to the illiterate. These printed notes must always await the mediation of the interpretative artist.

What qualities make for good solo piano-playing, and what critical principles should be applied to the work of any particular player? "The technics of piano-playing in their lowest sense are the mechanics, the operations of the machinery of fingers, wrists and arms. Let it be admitted at once that technics include ability to strike without error and at a given speed all the notes set down in a composition." The true aim of piano technic is the *production of a tone of beautiful quality and singing character* under all conditions—rapidity, force, and clarity in brilliant work. The secrets of modern tone may be traced to two principal factors: perfectly equal development of all the fingers, which leads to their absolute independence, and expert management of the pedals.

However, the singing tone would become tiresome were there no rhythm in the playing. Rhythm resolves itself into *correct timing and accentuation.* Every note must have its proper duration, or else the rhythm is disturbed. Every tone must be sounded with the correct dynamic relationship to those which precede and follow it, or else the rhythm disappears.

The *shading must be full of variety, balanced and distributed* like the lights and darks in a fine printing; crescendo and diminuendo must be clearly noticeable; there must be fulness without confusion, force without violence, delicacy without weakness; a fine touch—a crisp staccato and a sustained legato; a melodic and rhythmic line.

To master dynamic effects is, for the pianist, a task of a lifetime. He must constantly strive for variety and beauty of tone if he is eager to attain true artistry. No less must the music-lover appreciate its value and train his perceptions to detect and respond to the most delicate gradations in beautiful sound.

The scholarly pianists, those who are reflective and analytical, with a fine sense of form, are usually distinguished for their *clear-cut, scholarly phrasing;* they often sacrifice other means of expression to gain their end. Other pianists take delight in masses of sound and powerful contrasts of tone. They are the bold, impetuous, and impressionistic ones who emphasize the broader lights and shades rather than minute dissections; they do not take such extreme pains to make the rhythmic or melodic outline evident.

Of course, either tendency, carried to excess, leaves something to be desired.

To recapitulate, piano technic is properly used as a means to the end of artistic expression; and finger-and-wrist skill is by far the most noticeable aspect of the playing of a good pianist. If his rapid passages, trills, and other embellishments are clear, even, and well controlled; if his octave passages are played by a rapid, fluttering swing of the wrist; if his chords are played without a blur of noise—in short, if his artistic efforts are obtained by control and variation of power, not by abuse of it, and if he plays his piece in the tempo suited to the music and gives it expression by changes of speed as well as of power, and if he does not abuse the use of the pedal, then he has mastered the technical side of his art.

However, the good pianist is known by his all-around musicianship. He is to be judged by his own individual work. *He is a great artist if he plays with control and variety of speed and power; if he brings out his themes with expression; and if he properly balances section against section, obtaining thereby the best possible effects.* He must interpret a piece according to its inherent nature and according to the composer's meaning, evenly and quietly, or loudly and with passion, but not overdo things and become eccentric. In other words, he must not try mainly to display piano technic.

So much for the mechanical features of piano-playing. Behind the technic must be the soul of the artist. Temperament—the conveyor of musical emotion—is what we all want. Temperament is hard to define but easy to discern. It is the vital spark which lies in the soul of an artist. It is inspiration—for which hungry aspiration is often taken as the real thing. The true artist surely must be absorbed in the work of his hands. It is his nationality, character, and experience which give him the capacity to receive the emotional content of the music and the ability to transmit it to the minds of the listeners.

From what we have said, it follows that the pianist must possess three attributes: *mental grasp of his music and mental control of his playing; susceptibility to the peculiar beauty* and the peculiar emotion or *mood* of the pieces he performs; and *executive ability to bring his understanding and his feeling for them to clear and persuasive expression.*

(Note: There is a curious feature in the public attitude toward a great pianist, and that is that, once a person has been recognized as great, he is expected to remain so for the rest of his life. And this applies equally well to violinists, cellists, singers, and conductors.)

4.   THE ORGAN

Much has been said about piano-playing that applies also to the organ, the king of instruments.

The *organ* is a wind instrument. The tones are made by blowing through metal tubes or pipes ranging in size from the very small to huge ones about 16 feet high. These are manipulated by the organist by means of knobs or stops, which are placed above his *keyboard, or manual.* A large organ, by the way, will have a great number of pipes and up to five keyboards, or manuals. Each of the five manuals, as well as the pedals, will have many stops; and each stop represents a set of pipes, usually one for each key. The pedals tones provide the groundwork, somewhat like the basses and cellos in the orchestra. Some of the largest organs built have up to 10,000 pipes.

A modern organ actually consists of: the *great,* the *swell,* the *choir,* the *solo* and the *pedal.* Each has its separate keyboard; each has its separate function; also, the shape, size, and material of which the pipes are made are greatly varied to produce different kinds of tone. The *great organ* has the more powerful stops to bring out majestic and grand tones. The *swell organ* is used for enriching the great organ, giving it brilliance and color as well as dynamic shading. It has a number, a diapason, flute and string stops and a reed chorus producing compound overtones. The *choir organ* is used mainly for accompanying, although it has some solo stops, as well as harp and chimes. The *solo organ* has such stops as the flute, gamba, English horn, French horn, and the loud "reeds"—trumpet, trombone, and tuba.

The compass of the *pedal* is 32 tones; the compass of the *manuals* is 61 tones. The four kinds of tone on the organ are the *diapason, reed, flute, and string.* A geigen tone belongs to the family of diapason; a trumpet tone belongs to the family of reed; a bourdon tone belongs to the family of flute; and a salicional tone belongs to the family of string. The *celeste* is a percussion instrument.

Variations in power come chiefly from the performer's use of different stops, which are not all equally strong. The effects made are of infinite variety. Almost any instrument can be imitated and tones from the highest soprano to the deepest bass produced. The art of using the proper stops is called "registration." Here and there, a composer marks his registration pretty fully, but more often he leaves it to the decision of the organist. Of course, experience is the best guide for the combination of stops. Then, too, different organs may differ greatly in effect. However, certain main principles of combination are given in organ handbooks. "Thus, the softer bourdons and diapasons, perhaps stopped, form the basis of soft tones, with some smooth stop added to make them blend well. . . . An open diapason increases the tone, while the addition of other 8-foot and 4-foot stops brings fair power. For loud tones, the doubles are used to add the lower octave, while still more foundations, mutations, and mixtures are thrown in" (A. Elson, *The Book of Musical Knowledge*).

Through the medium of mechanical devices called "couplers," the organist can play on two or more keyboards at once and so sound two, three, or four organs. Each organ chamber has its own separate shutter to control *crescendo and decrescendo;* in addition, there is a general *crescendo pedal* which controls the entire organ.

As to the technique of producing a magnificent, unique tone, an organist requires a fine sense of tone-color and tonal balance, plus an innate good taste to guide him. For this reason, each composition rendered becomes a creation of the performer himself. In addition, an organist must have a special touch. An organ key, once pressed down, goes on sounding until it is relieved, and then just as suddenly stops sounding. So the organist must press a key only exactly as long as he wants it to sound. He must be able so to time this pressure and release in long passages that the intervals produce a perfect legato. He must be able to render staccato tones when staccato is wanted. Thus, a high sense of harmonic build-up and shading, agility with hand and foot, ability to think right hand, left hand, right foot, left foot, all at once, and in terms of hundreds of stops, keys, and foot pedals for every phrase—these make the good organist.

The listener will, first of all, observe the quality of tone when hearing the organ. If he can see the player manipulate the stops, very well; but, of course, he can hear changes of any importance in the tone. It really will not take him long to tell whether the deep 16-foot stops are used or not; and after a few trials he may even learn to detect the use and probable number of mutation stops. There is little to watch about finger technic. What is necessary for the organist is that *his touch be clear enough and quick enough* to force the wind into the pipes properly *while he plays the pedals* with the feet. So it is really a question of *handling his registration properly*. If he does this, he will obtain magnificent effects and work up to immense climaxes—in short, he will be a great organist.

5. THE VOICE

The *human voice* (German, *Stimme;* French, *voix;* Italian, *voce*) is produced by the organ of speech—the throat, windpipe (trachea), larynx, vocal cords, lungs, diaphragm, rib muscles, pharynx (nose and mouth), tongue—plus proper breathing, i.e., inhaling and exhaling.

The so-called *"chest quality"* (register) is obtained when the vocal cords vibrate at full length along their straight edges, which are thus held tightly to narrow the opening, known as the "glottis." Naturally, increased tones mean increased tension. Chest tones have fullness and chest quality.

The so-called *"head quality"* (register) is obtained when the throat is left lax and the nose open. Of course, the head tones (which may be developed by humming through the nose) require none of the fatiguing stiffening of the throat that is needed for chest tones. Head tones have a smooth, light quality. The *falsetto*, in reality, is simply a very high part of the head register.

A good singer will always blend head and chest tones skilfully, and, of course, have complete breath control.

Voices are classified as follows:

1. Basso profundo—full and deep.

2. Basso cantante—somewhat smoother and more fluent.

3. Baritone—ranging between bass and tenor in compass and quality.

4. Tenor robusto—heroic quality, vigorous, strong; the highest natural male voice.

5. Tenor lyrico (*tenor de gracia*)—smooth and sweet in quality, but not so strong as heroic tenor.

6. Contralto (alto)—broad and strong in quality; the lowest female voice.

7. Mezzo Soprano—practically the same range as the contralto, but more lyrical; ranging between the contralto and soprano.

8. Soprano, dramatic—vigorous in quality; the highest female voice.

9. Soprano, coloratura—somewhat more smooth and fluent than the dramatic soprano; can be handled with the most brilliant flexibility; well suited to sing the Bell Song from Delibes' Lakme, as well as other arias by Donizetti, Rossini, etc.

In order to succeed in vocal execution, the singer (like the great violinist, pianist, or cellist) must keep in constant practice. He or she must not only practice execution but develop tone quality as well. A good voice is partly a natural gift, but it really must be much improved by careful training.

Comparatively few persons have sung great songs, played an instrument superbly, or made good verses. Usually, such activity is a professional performance that is deliberate and cultivated, instead of spontaneous. Generally speaking, the public is quite ignorant of, and careless to, the critical questions of art.

The average person seems not to be able to grasp the antithesis between art and Nature. The statement that *art is art simply because it is not Nature* bewilders him. He sees no merit in a portrait or a landscape except that of superficial likeness. Likewise, poetry tells him nothing, because it is non-natural speech. In the drama his warmest approval is given to crude productions of plays of actual everyday life. In singing, he confines his attention to the more obvious and sensational qualities of the voice, such as brilliancy or power, together with the necessary means of personal appeal, such as the singer's physical charm, stage presence, and magnetism. He often does not appreciate fine singing, because the voice is used for a twofold purpose, and each of its functions is, to some extent, unfavorable to the full exercise of the other. That is to say, *the voice is a musical instrument capable of giving pleasure* by abstract sound; *and the voice is a medium for the conveyance of thought* by means of words.

Now, there are singers who stress too much either the voice as a musical instrument or as a medium for thought. Of course, beautiful singing is neither wholly poetic expression, nor is it wholly pure tone and finished technique. It is both—emotional expression and technical completeness. Both qualities must unite, and there is no inherent reason why they should not supplement and sustain one another.

Mr. Henderson, the former music critic of New York, surely was justified in saying that, of all the branches of musical performance, singing is the one which the great majority of music-lovers know the least. Surely, singing is difficult to judge calmly and dispassionately, because the personal influence of the artist, exercised almost without the intervention of a medium (such as a violin, a piano, etc.), reaches the listener with a direct force.

"Singing is the most clearly expressive form of music. Song has text which makes the emotional schedule plain; and the music, following the text, is vital with feeling. It is obvious that the higher type of song is that in which the music most accurately voices the emotional content of the words. It is equally obvious that the highest type of singing is that which is devoted to the interpretation of this kind of song, whether it be a mere song or a whole opera. . . . The great concert singer is one who excels in the delivery of the most artistic songs."

Now, there may be much difference of opinion as to the correct interpretation of a song; but as to the technical merits of its delivery, there should be none whatever. Whether a person sings well or badly is not a matter of opinion but a matter of fact. Let us state the fundamental principles of vocal technic.

Fate gives us voices; and men, by their intelligence, imagination, ambition, industry, and artistic conscience *train them* in the shaping and the transmission of the tone, in the molding and the adjustment of the musical phrase, in all the niceties and all the suggestions of diction. There are voices that thrill or charm of themselves; and there are voices that stir and allure by what they impart and by their manner of imparting. In this second category lies the truer and finer artistry of song.

The first principle of vocal technic is that *the upper and the lower registers shall be equalized.* This means that there should be no audible change of quality as the voice passes from one register to the other; that the upper and lower registers do not sound like two different voices.

The second principle of vocal technic is *good tone production.* The equalization of the registers belongs to the general department of tone reproduction, which is the foundation of all good singing. The secret of good tone production is management of the breath. A continual unsteadiness, a lazy sliding from tone to tone, does not show an expressive voice. Every tone sung should be absolutely pure, i.e., all the breath should be turned into tone and none should escape with a hissing sound. The tone should be clear, i.e., it should never sound as if there were some obstacle in the singer's mouth that prevented part of it from coming out and kept it muffled down the throat. The tone should be free, i.e., it should never sound as if it were sung through a squeezed-up throat (throaty tone). The tone should be sound and firm from the first instant. The beginning of a tone is called the "attack." With a good attack, the tone has no suggestion of timidity and uncertainty; it sounds as if it had been already formed perfectly and were only waiting to be set free. The tone should be capable of a gradual increase in dynamic force to its fullest capacity and its diminution to the faintest pianissimo. It is upon this power, known as *"mezza di voce,"* that the expression of emotion largely depends. Sensuously beautiful tones are immediately appreciated by people with a normal hearing capacity. People are thrilled with rapture upon hearing a flood of glorious tones produced by a great singer. Our whole frame seems to quiver in sympathetic vibration. This extraordinary effect is not merely physical, it is also psychological. A voice capable of producing such effect through its sensuous beauty alone is rare. It is acquired only after years of prolonged and intelligent labor under the direction of very able and experienced teachers. The greatest natural gifts of voice amount to nothing without this training to control the tone.

The third principle of vocal technic is a *perfect legato style*. It is the foundation of the singer's manner of delivery; it is the *sine qua non* of all pure, fluent melodies, such as the themes of songs and opera airs. *Legato* in Italian means "*bound*," and in the legato style the tones are bound together in a single current. Each tone is sustained until the very instant the next one is begun, yet the voice, at the conclusion of the first tone, must not gradually slide through the interval between that and the one which follows. Such an effect is called *portamento,* or "carrying the voice." It may be used occasionally with beauty; but its constant employment is a grave defect and leads to all kinds of bad singing, including singing out of tune. Correct intonation is a prime requisite—the voice must always be exactly on the pitch. This, of course, excludes tremolo. A confirmed tremolo is a nervous, debilitating thing. It is a mark of infirmity and often a forerunner of loss of voice, the result of physical weakness or false vocal method. A persistent "wobble" is as much out-of-tune singing as a persistent flatting. It is never to be approved, but sternly to be condemned or pitied. Of course, singing out of tune—being off pitch—may be due to the singer's inability to hear certain tones mentally.

The fourth principle of vocal technic is *good vocalization*. This means the pure emission of vocal sounds. Pronunciation of vocal sounds purely is an essential of good vocal technic. The singer must be able to produce a good tone on any of the vowels at any musical pitch within the range of the voice. This is one of the greatest difficulties of singing.

The fifth principle of vocal technic is *distinct articula-*

tion, or diction. This means distinct enunciation of the consonants. The singer's articulation must be so distinct that every person in the audience can follow every word of the text sung by the artist. Of course, we take it for granted that the hall is not too large and that the listeners have normal hearing. There is positively no reason why the words of a song should not be clearly enunciated. A singer who does not enunciate clearly simply does not know how to do so.

The sixth principle of vocal technic is *correct phrasing.* By "phrasing" is meant the division of the melody into connected groups of notes, each of which is to be sung in a single flow of breath. Breath control should never be inhaled at any point where the action is an interruption of the musical idea. A melody must not be broken into disjointed fragments to accommodate the breathing of the singer. The breathing must accommodate itself to the melody. Correct phrasing is an essential quality of artistic singing. Many singers would derive much benefit from the study of the laws of form or design in music, for good phrasing must obey the laws of form. The singer's execution should be very much like that of a good violinist. In fact, a singer, as well as a lover of music—and especially a lover of good singing—can learn much by listening to fine violin-playing.

The ornaments of singing, which are the "stock in trade," so to speak, of the coloratura singer, are showy and surprising, because they are difficult to perform with perfect flexibility and accuracy. However, they are more valuable as exercises in acquiring command over the vocal organs than as showpieces, because vocal or instrumental virtuosity is not the essence of true art. True, there was a time when trills, staccato, roulades, and cadences were regarded as indispensable to good singing, but we have outgrown such ideas. Centuries of experience in singing have proved that in the domain of true vocal art an equalized register, a good tone, perfect legato, good vocalization, distinct articulation, and correct phrasing are the main requirements. After all, the purpose of song is deep emotional expression, and for this ornaments are of little value.

The practice of coloratura song is indispensable even to

a singer who does not fully master it and never intends to display it in public, for it helps the vocalist in the attainment of abilities which all styles require. *We all must aim above the mark to hit the mark.* A singer must give the impression of ease and security at all times. No indication of effort should be noticeable, no matter how difficult the passage. In every phrase, each tone should be as distinct as it is in the playing of a Bauer, Horowitz, Spalding, Kreisler, or Gieseking. All music, of whatever type, should be sung with clear-cut delivery of every tone. Each chromatic scale should be a succession of plainly distinguishable half-steps, not a portamento slide; a trill should be a trill, not a flutter on one tone or a "gargle."

To summarize: The singer is a great artist if he or she has a good quality of tone; has good and easy breath control; is accurate in pitch; has good attack; and renders the music with due regard for balance, contrast, and unity of the whole, at all times conveying sympathetically the meaning of the words. A song is not meant to give advice nor to inculcate sound moral sentiments. It is a work of art designed to be beautiful in itself. One's approval of the moral of the song should not influence his judgment of it. The chief object of this chapter is to provide the listener with some standards for judging musical beauty; and these must, in addition, be established by means of an explanation of the song and song form in general, and the *Lied* in particular, plus a generous amount of listening to great art songs. The ear, like the eye, has to be cultivated to appreciate this beauty; and there is only one way of cultivating the ear—by listening carefully to really good singing. Also, if a few of the great songs of the world are heard as often as possible, it will be a simple matter to compare their beauty to others.

Requirements of a good song:

1. It should have good words.
2. It should have beauty of melody of its own, irrespective of the words.
3. It should reproduce perfectly the form of the poem—logical and satisfying.

4. The music should reflect absolutely the sense of the text and mood of the poem—the music must present an idea.

5. It should exhibit a lofty simplicity of style.

6. It should have a moderate compass.

7. It should have an accompaniment throughout in sympathy with the emotional character of the work, one that enhances and enriches the melody, not a mere background.

8. Any Lied that passes these requirements is likely to be a good one.

Among famous singers we need mention just a few, omitting details of their lives and careers, as these may be studied in many books on that subject, such as H. C. Lahes' *Famous Singers;* H. T. Finck's *Success in Music;* etc.

The great female singers are: Francesca Cuzzoni; Faustina Bordoni (the wife of the composer Hasse); Mrs. Billington (Elizabeth Weichesel); Lucrezia Agujary (one of the highest sopranos ever known); Angelina Catalani (noted coloratura singer); Henrietta Sontag; Mme. Tietjens (a dramatic type); Giulietta Grisi (born in Milan in 1815, died in Berlin in 1869, wife of the celebrated tenor Mario, both members of the Puritani Quartet in Paris); Giuditta Pasta (said to have been the first to introduce real acting into opera); Mme. Maria Malibran (who later married the great violinist DeBeriot), and her sister Paulina Viardot (both singers of the dramatic type, daughters of the elder Manual Garcia and sisters to Manual, the younger, all exceptional performers and teachers); Jenny Lind (a fine example of the value of hard work, she sang under the management of Barnum); Adelina Patti (a coloratura noted for the birdlike clearness and flexibility of her voice); Paulina Lucca (the great Viennese whose expressive voice and impassioned acting stirred everybody); Sophie Arnold (the fine singer of Gluck's works); Mme. Schroeder-Devrient (noted for her dramatic role in Beethoven's Fidelio and Wagner's operas); etc. Other dramatic Wagnerian singers were Amalie Materne; Schott; Niemann; Fischer; Brandt; Brema; Ternina;

Lilli Lehmann; Lillian Nordica; Schumann-Heink; Lott Lehmann (the noted Lieder singer); etc.

Among great men singers we find: Porpora; Farinel; Senesino; Caffarelli; Bernacchi; Rubini, the tenor; Lablache, the great basso; Braham; Sims Reeves; H. Wachtel, the former cab-driver; Brignoli; the De Reszke brothers; E. Caruso; P. Althouse; L. Melchior; R. Crooks; J. T. Marshall; Guiseppe Siboni (noted tenor, 1782–1839, who settled in 1819 in Copenhagen as director of the opera and conservatory); etc.

6. CHORUS SINGING

The *chorus is a large group of singers of different types of voices.* It is sometimes used as a part of a large orchestra work, as in oratorios, masses, cantatas, etc., but rarely in symphonies, as in Beethoven's glorious Ninth Symphony. More often, the chorus is the main thing, instruments being used merely as an accompaniment; or, less often, it may be heard unaccompanied—*a capella.* In church music, a choral group is often called a "choir."

The main types of voices are: *Female*—1. *Soprano,* the highest natural range, although sometimes boys sing it; 2. *Mezzo-soprano,* a slightly lower range; and 3. *Contralto,* the lowest female voice in range, but richer in color. Sometimes the contralto is incorrectly called "alto," although the term denotes the highest pitched male voice and is almost entirely *falsetto,* i.e., forcing the voice in such a way as to reach tones higher than the normal register. *Male*—1. *Tenor,* the highest usual adult voice; 2. *Baritone,* a lower range, and one which is not so much a low tenor as a high bass; and 3. *Bass,* the lowest male voice.

The requirements of good chorus singing are: *quality and balance of tone, correct intonation, attack, precision, unanimity, phrasing, and enunciation.* Most of these terms have already been explained in the chapter on the orchestra.

The quality of tone should be full, vibrant, and pure. The tone of a chorus should always be sweet and musical, no matter how powerful it is—mere noise is not musical. It should be a smooth and fluent tone, without harshness or uskiness. Balance of tone is absolutely essential to good chorus work. There should be no preponderance of any one section, or of any two sections—too many sopranos and not enough basses is a defect. All sections must be capable of precisely the same degree of power.

Correct intonation likewise is absolutely essential. Singing out of tune is not good singing. By "attack" is meant the onset of the vocal force at the beginning of a passage. This should be firm and sure. It should never be weak, timid, irregular, or uncertain.

"Phrasing" is the division of the melody into connected groups of notes, each of which is to be sung in a single flow of breath.

"Shading," or "nuancing," means attention to the manifold possibilities of light and shade. A good chorus is capable of the greatest niceties of shading; and these refinements must be practiced.

"Enunciation" refers to the clear delivery of the text. There is positively no reason why the text of a chorus should not be enunciated in such a manner that the audience can follow it: "It can be done; and, therefore, it ought to be done."

It is a great pity that there is so little interest in choral singing. After all, no amount of listening can take the place of personal participation in choral singing, which alone provides an opportunity to realize the full spiritual and emotional value of such music—not even listening to music produced by professional singers and players.

(Note: *"Antiphony"* is much like a question and answer in tone. Sometimes one person sings or plays a phrase, and another sings or plays an answering phrase. At other times, a single person is answered by a group. Usually, contrast is involved in antiphony; often the answering phrase is in some way different in timbre or texture from the first phrase. The principle of antiphony has existed for centuries.)

7. THE VIOLIN

The use of the violin as a solo instrument is widespread, and in the orchestra it is indispensable. Unlike many instruments which have only one or two distinctive tone-colors, the violin has many. It can express every shade of feeling, from the greatest sadness to the wildest joy or uncontrolled fury.

All that has been said in relation to technic, intellect, and emotion, with reference to good piano-playing, applies also to good (solo) violin-playing, and, indeed, to all musical performance. It remains, therefore, only to consider the special qualities of good technic in violin-playing.

As in piano-playing, the true aim of "technic is the production of a tone of beautiful quality and singing character under all conditions of force and speed"; so it is in violin-playing, with the addition (which is at once a new difficulty and a considerable advantage) that the performer creates the tone wholly by himself.

The first principle of violin technic is *"intonation,"* or accuracy in stopping. The creating or placing of the tone is known as "stopping," the fingers being said to stop the strings at certain points to get the correct pitch. When playing on two or more strings at a time, the violinist must do what is called "double stopping." And as this is more difficult than single stopping, it belongs to the more complicated technic of the violin. Without question, accuracy in stopping, or putting the fingers on the right spot, is the *sine qua non* of all violin-playing, because inaccuracy means playing out of tune. This, of course, cannot be tolerated. Intonation must prove alike the flawless ear and the unerring hand.

The second principle of violin technic is a *good tone*. The quality of tone in violin-playing is due to the excellence of the instrument, the character of the finger pressure in stopping, pure strings, and most of all, the manner in which the bow is drawn, or the "bowing," as it is called. It is the great variety in the motion and pressure of the elastic violin bow, responsive to the slightest gradations in the muscular action of the arm and wrist, that brings out the tone quality. This great delicacy of touch explains why every player's tone has individuality of character, and this individuality reflects very strongly the personality of the performer. Now, what is a "good" tone? A good tone is one that is always pure, mellow (sweet), expressive, and sonorous. The tone should always be pure, with that clarity of a crystal which comes from absolute freedom from scratching of the bow or twinging of the strings. The tone ought to seem to flow spontaneously from the violin, and the mechanical process of rubbing the bow back and forth should not be heard. The tone should always be mellow. It should not be squeaky, or metallic, or wooden. The tone should always be liquid. It should always be sonorous. It should be vibrant, not dead or hollow.

The third principle of violin technic is the *correct use of the vibrato*. Quivering of the fingers of the left hand is employed to produce the vibrato, which is very effective when not used too much, as it generally is.

The fourth principle of violin technic is *the mastery of bowing, good phrasing*, etc.—in short, *good general technic*. It means good legato, staccato, flying staccato (*arco saltando*), tremolo, spiccato, glissando, trills, and other kinds of bowing. Here we must not confound mere display of acrobatic skill with true artistic violin-playing. Technic should always be a means, never an end. Plain "virtuosity has always been a stumblingblock in the path of true art." Double stopping, harmonics, pizzicato passages, and other bits of technical display may be followed in part with the eye by watching the fingers of the player's left hand and his bowing of the right arm. But, after all, the artist should be judged by the ear. The player should never make a performance a mere medium for the exhibition of technical tricks; he should perform without the smallest hint of labor or display in the accomplishment of bravura passages, difficult transitions, or occult harmonies. He should use his skill in stopping and bowing to make the violin sing, no matter what be the nature of the music.

By way of explanation, we may mention that the attentive listener will note that some players have a large tone and others a small one. This difference is partly due to instruments of different make, or of different ages (new or old).

To summarize: The good artist has impeccable technic, faultless intonation, an absolutely pure tone, and a dis-

criminating vibrato. He also has insight and high musicianship, plus a transmitting and transfiguring force. He plays
with exceeding opulence of tone, as resonant as it is rich, as
sensitive as it is full-bodied and songful. This tone, we repeat, is the product of a fine and ready mastery of the technic of the violin; also, a refined musical intelligence; and,
finally, of that instinct and affection for the instrument that
gives it confidence to whisper its secrets into his ears, and
through him, to the listener. Furthermore, he is not merely
faithful to his composer; he idealizes his work by true expressive power, real delicacy of feeling, and emotional
warmth that is not exaggerated but which is free from every
technical and temperamental infirmity. Thus, he is pursuing
an ideal perfection.

8.   THE ORCHESTRA DESCRIBED

No doubt, the most complex and the most difficult kind
of music to which we may listen is orchestral music. The
reason for its richness is that, in addition to the elements or
materials of all music—*rhythm, melody, harmony,* and *form*
—there is the further element of *tone-color,* obtained by virtue of the employment of many different kinds of instruments.

Besides the radio and TV, there are excellent machines
on the market that make it possible to obtain quite good
impressions of the actual tone-color of the symphony orchestra and band. We can now study the orchestra and many
compositions written for it on records; hence, it can exert
much influence. The tone quality of each instrument may be
learned, as well as the marvelous tone-color effects of various
combinations of instruments.

Obviously, the *ability to recognize the individual character and tone-color of each instrument is* one of the first
things *necessary to the appreciation of orchestral music.*
The study of scores, allied to attentive listening, is clearly a
ready means to this end. To take a few examples from well-
known works: horn solo of slow movement—Tschaikowsky's
5th Symphony; English horn solo of slow movement—
Franck's Symphony; clarinet solo near the end—Sibelius'

En Saga; flute solo—Rossini's Overture to William Tell; oboe solo—slow movement of Brahms' Violin Concerto; bassoon solo—Dukas' L'Apprenti Sorcier; trumpet solo—Beethoven's Overture to Leonore, #3; three trombones in unison—Wagner's Overture to Tannhäuser; etc. Such passages are made impressive in their tone-color by the co-operation of ear and eye whenever the music is read as well as heard.

In learning to listen to an orchestra, note first of all passages played by the string instruments alone, by the woodwind instruments alone, and by the brasses alone; then get the effect well into your mind. Notice which instrument it is that is playing a solo passage in contrast to another, which theme is given to a flute, to an oboe, then to a clarinet, and so on. Try to hear what is being done, and always notice who is doing it. Try to find out what combination of instruments can make some particularly fascinating and novel effect. At first, use your eyes to help your ears. It is surprising how quickly discrimination is developed. It will be obvious that there can be no complete appreciation of orchestral music unless one can detect such things. Remember, what we expect has a good deal to do with what we hear.

The modern symphony orchestra, so delicately balanced and interrelated in soft passages, so overwhelming in sonorous parts when the whole body of from 90 to 110 men play together, is the outcome of some 300 years of development. Around 1600, the small group of instruments put together to support the first operas and oratorios were not only defective in mechanical construction but had parts written for them really better suited to voices. In fact, vocal music was the only style that had then been developed. The place of violins was taken by the clumsier viols. Flutes, oboes, and bassoons had defective systems of fingering and were apt to be out of tune. Sometimes their tones were bad, had to be coaxed, or were avoided altogether. Trumpets and horns were without valves. They could produce only a few tones, separated by large intervals. Of course, clarinets were unknown. Composers were learning constantly about new and more effective ways of writing for the existing orchestra, and they were demanding from time to time that other instruments should be added. Such men as Meyerbeer, Mendelssohn, Berlioz, Wagner, and R. Strauss included in the orchestra the tuba, the English horn, various kinds of clarinets, as well as other brass, wood-wind, and percussion instruments. Naturally, the size of the orchestra increased also. Beethoven asked for no fewer than eight violins for his Seventh and Eighth Symphonies. His request indicated that even this figure was unusual in the Vienna of his time; but in Germany the major orchestras boasted as many as 24 violins. The orchestra of the Paris Conservatoire had 31 violins. By the end of the 19th century the standard orchestras closely resembled those of our own day both in size and in make-up.

No doubt, the invention, development, and use of musical instruments has, to a large extent, shaped the course which the art of music has followed. Thus, to explain the development of harmony as the result of the work of vocal composers alone is to ignore one factor of great importance.

The symphony orchestra consists of *four sections,* or group of instruments:

1. The *string section* includes *the violin, viola, cello, and double bass.*
2. The *wood wind section* includes *the flute, piccolo, oboe, English horn, bassoon, contra bassoon, clarinet, and bass clarinet.*
3. The *brass section* includes *the French horns, trumpets, bass trumpet, trombones, bass trombone, and tuba.*
4. The *percussion section* includes *tympanies, bass drum, snare drum, bells, cymbals, triangle, tambourine, xylophone, chimes, celesta, castanets, etc.*

In addition there are: one or two *harps* and a *pipe organ.* A full symphony orchestra comprises from 80 to 110 men. By combining two or more different instruments (i.e., sometimes only one from one section, with another instrument from another section), the modern composer brings about extraordinarily colorful effects. A large modern symphony orchestra has from 50 to 60 string players. Of course, there is no reason to believe that the 20th-century orchestra is a stable unit. Composers still seek new colorings, and instrument-makers as well as performers still attempt to satisfy them. Sometimes the tables are turned, and an instrument maker (as has happened so often in the past) will develop a new medium and dare composer and performer to use it. There is no predicting what the orchestra of 2050 will be like.

Nothing is more the product and, at the same time, a triumph of the human mind than the orchestra, with its polyphonic sounds of life. Not more than about 100 years have passed since the orchestra, in its present organic form and combination, was brought into existence. All times and all nations, however, which make up human culture, have helped along. The older Orient gave us the string instruments—especially the Arabs, whose *rebek,* out of which came the violin, is the king of instruments. Gladstone once said, "To perfect that wonder of travel has perhaps not required the expenditure of more mental strength and application than to perfect the wonder of music—the violin." The older Celtic-Germanic North formed with the rebek the bulk of the orchestra, whose energetic body was colored deeper and enriched through the invention of the violincello and the double bass by the Italians. Finally, to all of these was added the genuine viola—alto—which completed the string quartet, or string section, of the orchestra.

The various wooden and metal, stiff or fantastic-looking instruments, and the many complex motions of the performers, taken as a whole, appear rather curious to the outer eye; but they create through the medium of the ear a picture in our consciousness incomparably full of life, a portrait of our own inexpressible thoughts and feelings.

What is it that moves us when we listen to a full orchestra playing a symphony? It shakes our spirit with great might and guides it with a surety against which we have no resistance and no will of our own. Has eternal nature become self-expressive? Do her latest wonders manifest themselves? Nature, that like a Sphinx rests forever deaf and puts before us in her plain appearance the deepest riddles of life, suddenly solves all these questions and reveals herself in a language which has nothing to do with words or pictures. In music she speaks so clearly and forcibly that not to understand is impossible.

9. THE STRING INSTRUMENTS

The *violin* is known to everybody. It is very versatile; for it is not only the dominating soprano instrument of the symphony orchestra but one of the most popular in solo use on the concert stage. It is unique in being capable of very rapid, agile motion and also of long sustained tones. The upper register is often used for highly emotional melody, and the lower to express solemnity and dignity. The four strings are five tones apart and are tuned G.D.A.E.

(Note: The *violin piccolo* was a small violin, usually tuned a minor 3rd higher than the violin. It was much used in open-air serenades, with a flute, harp, and other similar instruments. Concertos were written for these little violins. J. S. Bach often used the instrument, generally making it play in octaves with violins. In his cantata, Herr Christ, der Ein'ge Gottes Sohn, the violin piccolo has an important obligato part in conjunction with the piccolo.)

A violinist can put more individuality into his playing than any other musician, for he controls the tone quality with both the left and the right hand. The left hand "stops" the strings and determines the exact pitch of the tone to be produced. The fact that both the speed and the pressure of the bow can be absolutely controlled by the performer gives to violin-playing its real character. Indeed, it takes unusual talent, or even genius, to handle the bow arm (right hand).

"Double stopping" is the playing of the strings simultaneously. "Harmonics" are high, piercing tones, above the normal reach of the instrument, produced by lightly touching a vibrating string at various points. "*Pizzicato,*" an effect often used, consists of plucking the strings instead of using the bow (see Brahms' Sonata in A major for Violin & Piano). Sometimes, to dampen the tone and produce a low, sweet effect, a "mute," or "sordino," is inserted between the strings above the bridge. Another effect is to play *"col legno dell arco,"* i.e., striking the strings with the back of the bow.

When listening to a violinist, notice the luscious bass of the G string, the clear, honeyed treble of the E, the almost human tone of the D, and the brilliant A string.

Listen to these beautiful violin solos:

BACH	ELGAR
Air on the G String.	Salut d'Amour.
GODARD	
Adagio Pathetique; Berceuse (Jocelyn).	
HANDEL	MASCAGNI
Largo.	Intermezzo, Cavalleria Rusticana.
MASSENET	
Meditation, from Thais.	
RAFF	SCHUBERT
Cavatina.	Ave Maria.
SCHUMANN	SAINT-SAENS
Träumerei.	Havanaise.

The *viola* (German, *Bratsche;* French, *alto;* Italian *viola*) is shaped like the violin and is about 1/7 larger. Its strings, *C G D A*, are five tones apart. The viola is one of the oldest instruments of the orchestra. Originally, it was the "arm-fiddle," or *viol da braccio*, of the 17th century. The strings are thicker and heavier than those of the violin. The viola is the most helpful of the instruments, for it can serve either as the alto or the tenor of the string choir; it can double the first or second violins; and it can provide the bass part in soft passages where the lower strings are not used. Its function is to provide support, to augment, to enrich, to fit in.

The compass of the viola is from C, octave below middle C, to A, octave above it. Its music is written in the alto, or C clef, which places C on the third line of the staff. It is its beautiful quality of tone that makes the viola so valuable. Gloomy, elegiac, brooding, sombre, melancholy, dark, and even forboding in the lower register, in its upper range it becomes mellow, tender, pathetic, and inexpressively winning. Its dramatic power is now recognized by all composers.

(Note: The viola family comprised several branches:

viola da braccio [*arm-fiddle*]; *viola da gamba* [*knee-fiddle*] much in use in the 18th century, but which gradually came into disuse about 150 years ago; *viola d'amore,* [*viola d'amour*], a modern viola-like instrument which was very popular and melodious. Meyerbeer used it in his Les Huguenots.)

Mozart used the viola in passages where he needed a tender, sad, or melancholy voice. Berlioz was one of the first to use it as a solo or obligato instrument in his Harold in Italy, to represent the melancholy wanderer of Byron's verse. Beethoven used the violas and cellos to play in unison the beautiful melody of the slow movement of the Fifth Symphony. Mendelssohn used the viola beautifully in the slow movement of his Italian Symphony. Wagner gave the viola a fine solo passage in his Overture to Tannhäuser. Brahms gave the violas special prominence at the beginning of his great Requiem. There is also a fine solo passage for viola in Ippolitoff-Ivanoff's Caucasian Sketches.

(Also, note viola concertos by M. Gould, R. R. Bennet, D. Milhaud, A. Tansman, etc. Outstanding violists are Maurice Vieux of France, Wm. Primrose, a native of Scotland, etc.)

The *cello* (French, *violoncelle;* Italian, *violoncello*) is bigger than the viola and lower in its tones. Its wonderful, velvety, deep, rich tones are more similar to the human voice than any other instrument. As a solo instrument, the tone of the cello is of great beauty. The cello was developed from the early *viola da gambe, or knee-fiddle,* of the 17th century. It is tuned in 5ths, as is the viola, but it is an octave lower in pitch. Because of the depths of its voice and the thickness of its strings, it is not capable of playing passages as rapidly or of as great difficulty as the violin or viola. *Tremolo, vibrato, glissando, saltando,* and other devices of bowing, are easily obtained; the *pizzicato* effect is excellent, and so are *double stopping;* also, *harmonics* of good quality may be played. The *mute* can also be used with ease.

The cello can provide an adequate, sonorous bass part to the strings, but the unusual and beautiful quality of this instrument has caused it to be used in the orchestra as the baritone of the string choir—even as the tenor voice. In the string quartet it takes the fourth part. The first string of the cello is tuned on A, below middle C; the second string on D; the third on G; and the fourth on C.

Listen to this cello music:

BEETHOVEN
Sonata, Opus 69, Cello & Piano.

MASSENET
Elegie.

ROSSINI
Overture to William Tell.

SAINT-SAENS
The Swan.

WEBER
Overture to Freischütz (soft passage in The Prayer).

The *string bass, or double-bass* (German, *Kontrabass*), produces the lowest tones in the orchestra. Its strings are tuned *E A D G* in the bass clef, but sound an octave lower than they are written in order to avoid the use of many extra lines below the staff. It is the largest of the *viol* family and has to be played standing up. The thickness of the strings requires much strength to stop them; and double stopping is almost impossible, unless one of the tones comes from an open string.

The double-bass is an important instrument; no large orchestra could be without one. It takes the bass part in the orchestra, but it may be used in solo passages with telling significance. Its tone-color is heavy, gruff, ponderous, portentous, or it can be grotesque and comical. The mute produces no change in quality; harmonics are of little value; but the tremolo, glissando, and pizzicato are very effective. The double-bass is often used to burlesque effects of the lighter instruments. Beethoven was the first to bring out most wonderfully the possibilities of the double-bass; and he also was the first to make it important in the orchestra. In practically all of his symphonies, he wrote passages for the bass part that are not only wonderfully impressive but also of the utmost importance and significance.

Listen to these double-bass passages:

J. S. BACH
Ye Lightnings, Ye Thunders (St. Matthew Passion).

BERLIOZ
Symphonie Fantastique.

Rossini
    Overture to William Tell.
Beethoven
    Ninth Symphony (first part of finale).
Gluck
    Orpheus, 2nd act.
Saint-Saens
    The Elephants, from Carnival of the Animals.
Weber
    Overture to Freischütz.

The *harp* (German, *Harfe;* French, *harpe;* Italian, *arpa*)
is a descendant of the ancient lyre. It has been thoroughly
modernized. The modern concert harp, which has double-
action pedals, is the work of S. Erard, who perfected it in
1810; while a further improvement in construction was made
in 1872 by Cousineau. Since then the harp has undergone
little change, except better workmanship and beauty of
design. The harp has a range of 6½ octaves and may be
played in any key by means of seven pedals which shift the
pitch of the entire set of strings. To aid the performer, the
C strings of the harp are colored red, and the F strings
blue. Flat keys sound better, because then most of the
strings are open. The harp is tuned in the scale of C-flat
when its strings are open. The harp pedals, unlike those of
the piano, are used simply to regulate pitch. Harp music
is written for two hands on the staffs used for piano music,
bass and treble.

It is an important instrument, even though composers
use it sparingly. The wonderful tones do not sing for long,
but sustained effects are possible through *tremolo, glissando*
(sliding up and down the scale and touching every tone on
the way), and *arpeggio* (literally, "harplike"), in which
the fingers leap rapidly over a widespread chord, playing the
tones in progression, instead of simultaneously.

Spohr wrote many sonatas for violin and harp. Wagner
makes use of the harp to introduce the Prize Song in the
Meistersinger; he also uses it in Lohengrin to accompany
Elsa's recital of her dream; in Tannhäuser, in the lovely
Evening Star song; also, in Das Rheingold, in the Entrance

of the Gods into Valhalla (finale); and in the Fire Music
from the Walküre. Note also Mozart's Concerto for Flute
& Harp; and Beethoven's Overture to Prometheus.

10. THE WOOD-WIND INSTRUMENTS

The *flute* (German, *Flöte;* French, *flute;* Italian, *flauto*)
is really a simple tube, once made of wood but now usually
of metal, with a hole to blow into and a number of other
holes to produce the different tones. The flute was perfected
in 1832, with the mechanism still used today, and invented
by Bohm (1794–1881). Formerly, it was impossible to cover
all the holes of the flute by the fingers if they were cut an
equal distance apart; that is why the flute was often out of
tune. But now the flute, with its marvelous agility and clear
limpid voice, is a most useful instrument in the orchestra.

The flute and the piccolo (which is a half-sized flute)
are the only instruments which the player blows across,
instead of into. The lips of the player act as the reeds against
the sharp edge of the hole, or embouchure, which is on the
side of the instrument.

The flute has a clear, smooth sound that expresses a melancholy sweetness. The tone-color varies according to the
register, or pitch; the lowest octave is dull and soft; the middle register sweet and full; and the highest tones are brilliant and piercing.

The flute is best used as the brilliant coloratura soprano
of the wood-wind choir, and it is often combined with the
soprano voice as an obligato instrument in cadences expressing operatic madness, surprise, or ecstasy. One of the
loveliest entractes of Bizet's Carmen is for two flutes and
harp; Tschaikowsky has written a superlative trio for flutes
in his Danse des Mirlitons (pipes) in the Nutcracker Suite;
and Van Vactor has written a fine Concerto Grosso for
Flutes.

(Note all sorts of rapid runs, trills, etc., in the aria for
voice and flute, Sweet Bird that Shun'st the Noise of Folly,
from Handel's Il Penseroso. Note also the Concerto for Harp
and Flute by Mozart, and his fine opera, The Magic Flute.)

The *piccolo, or octave flute* (German, *kleine Flöte;*

French, *petite flute;* Italian, *ottavina*), which has a penetrating high voice, is much louder than its size would suggest—exactly half the length of the regular flute. It is akin to the military fife and is often heard in military music. The piccolo sounds an octave higher than the written part; and its compass is nearly three octaves. Occasionally, this high voice is also used to give a sparkling, brilliant effect, especially in picturing wild, frenzied merriment or infernal revelry. The shrill, sharp, piercing tone may be heard above all the other instruments. The piccolo fills an important place in the orchestra. The high tones may also give a martial effect, as in the cadence of Beethoven's Egmont Overture. Wagner uses it effectively in his Ride of the Valkyries; Magic Fire Scene; and the Flying Dutchman Overture. Berlioz uses three piccolos in the third part of his Damnation of Faust. Note its softer use in the aria, Ye pretty warbling choirs, from Handel's Acis and Galatea; also the Infernal Waltz in Meyerbeer's Robert, and the drinking song of Weber's Freischütz.

The *oboe* is a double-reed instrument. It is the old English "hautboy," called *"hautbois"* by the French (literally, "high wood"), and descended from the *shawn (chalumeau)* of antiquity and the German *Schalmei*. The sound is made by two pieces of thin wood, or cane, placed together much like two pieces of a leaf to make a squeaking noise. The tone is astringent, rather harsh and nasal in quality in the lowest register; ready and penetrating, though somewhat nasal, in the middle register; and thin and more piercing in the upper register. The oboe gives the pitch to all the other instruments with its *A*. To play an oboe demands great skill and considerable lung-power.

The oboe is admirably suited to portray effects of pastoral simplicity and rustic merriment, as in Beethoven's 6th Symphony; also, note the effect of simplicity in the movement In the Fields of Berlioz's Symphony Fantastique. Still another effect is that of pathos and grief, as in the funeral march of the Eroica Symphony by Beethoven. Handel wrote six oboe concertos; and there is another concerto by Kalliwoda. Beethoven wrote a Trio for Two Oboes and English

Horn; and A. Foote composed a set of three pieces for oboe and piano. The oboe is also effectively used in the Scotch Idyl from Henry VIII, by Saint-Saens; in the slow movement of Tschaikowsky's 4th Symphony, where it announces the opening theme; also, in the beginning measures of Gounod's Faust.

The *English horn, or alto oboe,* is a double-reed instrument. Its reeds project in a curve. The English horn is m ch like its soprano sister, the oboe; and while it usually plays in a lower register, its range is nearly the same. *"Cor anglais"* is its French name; and in German it is called *"Englisches Horn."* The English horn has a full, rich, and rather melancholy tone; and it is the favorite representative of pastoral moods among the great composers, suggesting the shepherd's pipe.

It is heard to great advantage in the slow theme of Dvorak's New World Symphony. It plays the Alpine Shepherds' Music in Schumann's Overture to Manfred; Wagner uses it beautifully for the shepherds' melody, offstage, in the last act of Tristan and Isolde. Also, note the Minuet for Two Oboes and English horn by Beethoven. Sibelius uses it beautifully in the Swan of Tuonela, representing the swan that sings mournfully while floating on the river of Death. Rossini's William Tell Overture, Wagner's Tannhäuser Overture, Berlioz's Symphony Fantastique, and other works present passages for the English horn.

The *bassoon* (German, *Fagott;* French, *basson;* Italian, *fagotto*) is a double-reed instrument. The present bassoon was constructed by Alfrenio, a canon in Ferrara, in 1540. It has a tube so long that it would be inconvenient if it were not doubled in itself. The bassoon is longer than the other wood-wind instruments. The mouthpiece is curved, and it protrudes from the middle like a budding twig. The tone-color of the bassoon is impressively earnest, rough, sombre. The lower register forms a good bass to the wood-wind instruments; the middle register is dull and hollow; while the upper tones have a penetrating power that is as striking as a cry of pain, agony, distress. The bassoon can croak like a frog; hence, it is used for grotesque and comical effects. It has been called the "clown of the orchestra." Usually, three bassoons are used in the symphony orchestra.

Grieg uses the bassoon for the Kobold Music, and In the Hall of the Mountain King of his Peer Gynt Suite. Wagner lets the bassoons burlesque the stately march of the Meister-singers in the Prelude to that opera. It is also used to advantage in Mendelssohn's Intermezzo from A Midsummer Night's Dream; Bizet's Carmen Suite #1, and Dragoons from Alcala; Berlioz's Symphony Fantastique; Meyerbeer's opera Robert le Diable; P. Dukas' Apprenti Sorcier; Beethoven's opera Fidelio (grave-digging scene); etc.

The *contra bassoon* (German, *Kontra-Fagott*) is the largest instrument of the oboe family. It has a tapering tube about sixteen feet long. Very similar to the bassoon in tone quality, it sounds an octave lower than it is written, giving a deep bass for the wood-wind section of the orchestra. Its tone is deep and impressive, similar to an organ pipe.

Haydn used the contra bassoon in The Creation; Beethoven used it in his 9th Symphony and in the grave-digging scene of his opera Fidelio. It is much used in modern large orchestra works.

The *clarinet* (German, *Klarinette;* French, *clarinette;* Italian, *clarino*) is a single reed instrument. It was perfected in 1690 by Johann Denner of Nuremberg, later by Stadler of Vienna, and by Sax of Paris. One of its medieval proto-types, the *chalumeau,* persisted in use till the time of Gluck. The sound of the clarinet is made by a single thin piece of wood or cane placed against a sort of chisel-shaped mouth-piece. As the tube is two feet long, the instrument has a compass of over three octaves and possesses four distinct registers of tone. The middle register is the best; and the highest register has about the same tone quality as of the flute, but is less brilliant in quality. All in all, the tone of the clarinet is weird and sombre, as well as very liquid and full, eloquent and tender.

The fingering of the clarinet is very different from other wood-wind instruments. It is impossible to play in certain keys; therefore, three instruments are used. They are in the keys of C, B♭, and A. The C clarinet plays what is written; while the others are transposing instruments, sounding a different key from the rest of the orchestra. In order that they may sound the same key with the other instruments, their parts are written on the score in a different key. The clarinet in B♭ is used for flat keys. As signature, use 2♭ less than writing for violins, i.e., one whole tone higher (C minor, write D minor; E♭ major, write F major; etc.). The clarinet in A is used for sharp keys. As signature, use 3♯ less than writing for violins, i.e., a minor third higher (E major, write G major; B major, write D major; etc.).

The clarinet is the only wood-wind instrument which can increase and diminish its tone. The clarinet in a military band takes the place of the violin in the orchestra. A good clarinet player can produce rapid runs, trills, and lively tricks of all kinds, in serious or comic mood.

The clarinet did not come into prominence in the orchestra until the end of the 18th century. Neither Bach nor Handel employed it. But it was in use in military bands about 1760. Mozart was the first composer to use the clarinet in important works for orchestra and chamber music. There are no clarinets employed in symphonies by C. Ph. Emanuel Bach, who began writing them in 1741, but the clarinet is used in the works of Johann Christian Bach, brother of Emanuel. (Notice Mozart's use of the clarinet in his famous E flat Symphony 1788.) The clarinets now used in Handel's Messiah were introduced into the score by Mozart. Beethoven used the clarinet in his Pastoral Symphony. Every great composer since Mozart has used the clarinet in important runs. Rossini charmingly lets it play a calm, pastoral melody after the storm in his famous Overture to William Tell. Wagner gives it a beautiful passage in the first act of Götterdämmerung. Note also the Second Rhapsody by Liszt; and the second movement of Scheherezade by Rimski-Korsakov, as well as the Prelude to his opera Coq d'Or. Spohr wrote a Concerto for Clarinet and Orchestra; so did Mozart (Koechel, 622).

The *bass-clarinet* (German, *Bass-klarinette*) is pitched an octave lower than the regular clarinet. The tube is larger and is bent, turning up at the bottom, pipe-fashion, with a bell of brass. The upper end is of metal, bent to make it more convenient for the player. The range of the bass-clarinet is the same as that of the clarinet, but an octave lower. The bass-clarinet, like the clarinet, originally was made in three keys; but the instrument in E flat is the only one used.

The bass clarinet has the ability to increase and diminish its tone. The pianissimo of the instrument is especially impressive. The quality of the tone is sombre, rich, and clear, similar to the low register of the clarinet. Although the bass-clarinet does not possess the agility of the bassoon, its deep voice is often used as the bass of the wood-wind choir when the bassoon is otherwise busy. Its exquisite middle voice is often given solo passages, as may be noted in Liszt's tone poem, Tasso, and Les Preludes. Berlioz used it to picture the gloom of descending night in his Damnation of Faust. Meyerbeer used it in his Les Huguenots, and it even takes the melody for a time in the Coronation March from his The Prophet. Occasionally, the bass-clarinet is also used for grotesque effects.

The *saxophone,* constructed in 1840, is named after its inventor, A. Sax; and, although made of metal, is classed with the wood-wind instruments, because it has a reed like a clarinet. The alto, the tenor, and the baritone saxophone are used mostly. It has become the outstanding instrument of modern popular music; and it is also used more and more in serious compositions. A good player produces a tone of incredible beauty, with amazing . . . . Saxophones are much used in the French military bands.

Meyerbeer used saxophones in the Coronation March of The Prophet; and R. Strauss used it in the final movement of his Sinfonia Domestica. Bizet wrote a charming melody for the alto saxophone in his L'Arlésienne Suite.

The *Heckelphone,* named after the German inventor Wm. Heckel, is practically a baritone oboe, nearly an octave lower than the ordinary oboe. The size of its double reed is between that of the English horn and the bassoon. Its tone is more luscious than the bassoon's, more powerful than the English horn's, and more saturated and darker in color than the oboe's, which it resembles in structure.

Nickisch, Weingärtner, Steinbach, H. Richter, and other conductors have welcomed the heckelphone as a valuable addition to orchestral instruments. Strauss made use of it in his opera Salome.

11. THE BRASS INSTRUMENTS

The *French horn* (German, *Waldhorn;* French, *cor;* Italian, *corno*) has a curled tube of brass so long that, if it were straight, it would stick out from the player's mouth for about fourteen feet. It is a descendant of the medieval hunting horn carried by men on horseback, who, for ease in carrying, wound the long tube about their necks as they rode along. The mouthpiece of the French horn (as well as of all the brass instruments) is a metal cup, against which the lips are pressed to produce a tone. The French horn has three valves, or ventils; the first valve puts into use enough extra tubing to lower the pitch a tone; the second will lower the pitch a semitone; and the third, a tone and a half. The French horn is a transposing instrument. The horn in F is used the most, because it has the best quality of tone. If the horn part written in C sounds an F on the F horn, then a part for the F horn must be written in E in order to sound in the key of A. The tone is soft, tender, and mellow; then again bold and loud, suggesting forest scenes and hunting calls. When muted it sounds foreboding; and once heard in its full sweetness and purity, it is not easily forgotten.

Von Weber uses four horns beautifully in his Freischütz Overture, and so does Mendelssohn in the third movement of his Italian Symphony. Tschaikowsky gives French horns an amusing chromatic passage in the first movement of his Fourth Symphony. R. Strauss makes a comically realistic use of muted horns in Don Quixote. Wagner employs the horn in the third act of Tannhäuser; and in the second act of Tristan and Isolde, where the nocturnal hunters unexpectedly and tragically return; and when Siegfried is killed in the second act of his Götterdämmerung. Also, note Massenet's use for muted horns in the Angeles Movement of his Scènes Pittoresque. Thomas uses it in his Overture to Mignon; and observe the horns in Schubert's C major Symphony, closing theme of the finale.

The *trumpet* (German, *Trompete;* French, *trompette;* Italian, *tromba*) represents the soprano voice of the brass choir. The trumpet had its origin in ancient times in blowing through the horns of animals. This was followed by the use of military trumpets made of metal by the early Greeks and Romans. As the instrument had a very long tube, the Romans found it very convenient to carry if the tube were folded; and this idea has been followed in the manufacture of trumpets ever since. In Monteverde's time two kinds of trumpets were used—the *clarino* (*clarion*), a small, high-voiced instrument, and the *tromba,* a larger and deeper-toned one.

The tube of the trumpet in C is eight feet long—about half as long as that of the French horn—and it is one octave higher in pitch. This tube is narrow and cylindrical, opening out into a small conical bell. The mouthpiece is cup-shaped, the lips of the player acting as the reeds. The trumpet is provided with crooks and valves similar to those employed on all brass instruments. Trumpets are made in several different keys, but those in general use are in B and A, as they possess the most brilliant tones. The tone is clear and noble, martial, strong, and bracing. It is penetrating in fortissimo passages, and the clearest and most powerful in piano passages. The range of the trumpet is from the G below middle C up to 2½ octaves.

The individual voice of the trumpet was rarely heard until the time of Beethoven; an outstanding exception being the use of the instrument by Handel in The Messiah, where the brilliant tone-color of the trumpet is heard as an obligato to the aria, And the Trumpet Shall Sound. An example of a fine pianissimo passage is found in Schubert's Andante of the G major Symphony, where the trumpet and the oboe are heard in the same theme. The military association of the trumpet has caused its use in many works of that type, such as the 1812 Overture by Tschaikowsky. Listen also to Suppé's Light Cavalry Overture; Verdi's March from Aida;

Beethoven's Leonore Overture; Wagner's The Herald's Calls, from Lohengrin, and the Walküre, the Rheingold, and Sword motives.

The *bass-trumpet* (German, *Bass-Trompete*) is a valve instrument constructed to sound an octave deeper than the usual trumpet, but whose tone is similar. Invented by R. Wagner, it was used in his Nibelungen music; also, in much of recent orchestral music.

The *cornet* is a development of the old-style post-horn, used in the days of the stagecoach, and somewhat similar to the modern auto horn. The cornet (in B or A) is similar to the trumpet and a very important member of the brass band or military band; but it has really never been accepted in the symphony orchestra. It is more flexible in its effects than the trumpet; also, more commonplace in tone—rather blatant and vulgar. It has a tube only half as long as that of the trumpet and thus plays an octave higher. In the upper register it produces tones much more easily.

The *trombone* (German, *Posaune;* Italian, *trombone,* from *tromba,* a large trumpet) is a sort of trumpet with a U-shaped sliding dodge for making it longer or shorter, so making lower or higher tones. That is why it is also called "slide trombone." It has a very long history. The trombone, like the trumpet, is of ancient origin. The principle of the slide, or elongation of tubes, has been ascribed to Tyrtaeus, in 685 B.C. At the close of the Middle Ages, trombones were well known in Germany. Formerly, the trombone was known as the "*sackbut.*" In some towns in Germany, and probably elsewhere, four trombone players form a quartet to play *chorales* (hymns) from high church towers at special seasons of the year. This custom has recently been imported into the United States, especially in Bethlehem, Pennsylvania, and Winston-Salem, North Carolina.

The trombone plays the tenor part in a brass quartet. In its serious moments, the trombone is especially sonorous and capable of intoning thrillingly broad and sustained melodies. Its tones are very solemn, grand, and noble, or menacing. It may portray almost every broad emotion, from sacred calm to the wildest strains of martial glory. In addition, its sombre tones are well fitted for tragic effects, having a portentous and threatening quality. The use of the slide makes fairly rapid passages possible, thus enabling a soloist to dazzle an audience; but in orchestral work the trombone is treated more slowly. The trombone parts are written as they sound.

The trombone is used by Mozart with fine effects in Don Giovanni and The Magic Flute; by Beethoven in the 5th, 6th, and 9th Symphonies; by Schubert in his great C major Symphony; by Berlioz in his Requiem (Day of Judgment); and by Brahms in his symphonies. Liszt employs it thrillingly in Les Préludes and in Tasso; and Wagner uses it with great effect in The Flying Dutchman (3rd act, sailor's scene) and in Tannhäuser, especially for the climax of the Pilgrims' Chorus; etc.

The *bass-trombone* (German, *Bass-Posaune*) is very similar in appearance, construction, and tone to the trombone. It is used only for its lowest tones. The brass-trombone demands much breath from the performer and is therefore harder to play. R. Wagner, R. Strauss, Tschaikowsky, Stravinsky, and practically all recent modernistic composers wrote for it.

The big *Tuba, or bass,* belongs to the family of brasses. It has been improved by the modern valve system (the *ophicleide,* its predecessor, was really a bass bugle). The tuba was invented by a German bandmaster named Wieprecht. Its tube, if spread out in a single length, is about 18 feet long. Its voice is very powerful; and its penetrating, deep, rumbling, gruff tones reinforce those of the string bass.

The straight tubas are called *"upright basses"* and the curled ones are called *"helicon basses."* There are two sizes of either shape, one in E for bass tones, and the other in a low B for very, very deep tones. The bigger tuba is sometimes called the *"bombardon."* The smaller tubas are not found in the orchestra but take part in military bands, especially in France, under the name of *"saxhorns."* The tenor tuba and a small-bored baritone instrument are called *"alt-horns."*

Wagner gives the tuba a characteristic theme in his Faust Overture and in Siegfried (dragon music); also, in the first act of Die Walküre, to picture the character of Hunding. Bruckner used the tuba in his 7th Symphony; Berlioz, R. Strauss, and many recent modern composers have used it often.

The *baritone* is a small, straight tuba also known as the "*althorn.*" It has a deep-throated, sonorous tone of great flexibility. This instrument resembles the euphonium, and they both play the same part, which is rather high bass. Some bands use one, and some use the other; large bands use both.

The *Euphonium* is a form of tenor tuba and sounds a 5th higher, in the key of B. Its tone somewhat resembles the trombone's in quality; but they are weaker than those of the bombardon. The euphonium and the baritone look much the same, and they play the same part. Both are used in bands.

The *serpent*, said to have been invented in 1590 by E. Guillaume, a canon of Auxerre, is really a type of the old cornetti, or *zinken* (as the Germans called them). At first, the serpent was a wooden tube curled up within itself, somewhat resembling a snake in form. It was played by stopping holes which had been bored into the tube; but toward the end of the 18th century two keys were added. George II, King of England, was attracted to the instrument and introduced it into the bands of the army. The serpent had long been used in French churches; and in England it was used in little bands which played the accompaniment to psalms, hymns, etc. The tone of the instrument is raucous and unpleasant—"frigid and abominable blaring." In the 19th century the serpent was supplanted in orchestras by the *ophicleide*, which, in its turn, was succeeded by the *bass tuba*.

Handel used the serpent in his Fireworks Musick; Beethoven used it in a march for military band; Auber used it in his Masaniello; and Rossini in his Siege of Corinth. There is a part for it in Mendelssohn's Calm Sea Overture and his Prosperous Voyage, as well as in his Oratorio St. Paul. Wagner used it in his Rienzi and in his Liebesmahl der Apostel; and Verdi employed it in Vespri Siciliano.

12. THE PERCUSSIONS

The *kettledrums, or tympanies* (German, *Pauken;* French, *timbales;* Italian, *timpani*) are copper kettles covered with drum heads. Tympanies can be tuned to any particular kind of tune, necessitated by the key in which the music is written. Thus, in the key of D, usually, they are tuned in d and a; etc. They are played with two sticks (felt-covered heads). The different kind of sticks give different sorts of tones; and the performer can also vary the tone by striking at different places. A stroke near the side gives a sharp and bright tone; while one in the middle is rather dull. The drums may also be muffled; if covered with a cloth, it will deaden and shorten the tone. The tone runs from a velvety softness to thunderous rumbles. It is rhythmic and capable of suggesting anxiety and suspense. A trill on these drums consists of a roll produced by rapidly alternating the drumsticks. The notes of the kettledrums are now written as played.

Beethoven used kettledrums very effectively in the finale of his 4th Symphony; Tschaikowsky employed them beautifully in the first movement of his 4th Symphony; Berlioz, in his Symphony Fantastique, puts the tympanies to famous use, and in his Requiem he employs eight pairs of kettledrums; Meyerbeer, in the second act of Robert le Diable, introduced an entire march for kettledrums played by two pairs on the notes G D C E. Wagner used them most effectively in his Siegfried's Funeral March; also, in The Flying Dutchman, Lohengrin, Walküre, etc. At the start of Brahms' First Symphony, the kettledrummer relentlessly beats out the slow tripling time with marvelous effect. The Gershwin Piano Concerto, likewise, begins with a rhythmic motive for kettledrums alone.

The *bass drum, or big drum* (German, *grosse Trommel;* French, *grosse caisse;* Italian, *gran casse*) makes the same low, booming sound all the time. It is used in marking rhythm, and is practically indispensable.

The *nagara, or naqqara,* known in England as *kaker* and in France as *nacaire,* was originally an Arabic drum introduced into Europe during the Crusades of the 13th and 14th centuries.

The *snare drum, or side-drum* (German, *kleine Trommel;* French, *tambour;* Italian, *tamburo*) is a drum that has gut cords or snares stretched against the underhead, which snap against it and make the tone brisk, instead of hollow. It can give both single taps and long rolls, and can aid in working up great climaxes. A strange dull and rolling sound can be produced by playing with the drumhead somewhat loosened.

The *street drum* (German, *Strassen-Trommel*) makes a hollow sound. It is used in street parades, by drum and bugle corps, drum and fife corps; etc.

The *xylophone* (German, *Strohfiedel;* French, *claque-bois;* Italian, *gigelira*) consists of strings of wood graduated to produce the diatonic scale. They are supported on felt (formerly ropes of straw) and are struck by hammers held one in each hand. The *marimba* is another type of xylophone, much enlarged, improved, and often used by the people of South America.

Victor Herbert uses the xylophone in his Czardas from the Fortune Teller. It is skilfully used in Saint-Saens' Dance Macabre; also, in Renicek's Schlemihl, to picture revelry.

The *cymbals* (German, *Becken;* Italian, *piatti*); the *triangle; tambourine; castanets; sleighbells; rattle; chimes*, or *bells* (German, *Glocken;* Italian, *campana*); *Chinese gong* (*tom-tom*); *Glockenspiel, or carillon; celeste;* etc.—all are used to produce delicate, tinkling sounds of ethereal charm and other percussion effects.

Mozart, in his Turkish March, uses the bass drum, cymbals, and triangles very effectively. Wagner uses striking bell figures in his Parsifal and employs the Glockenspiel in the slumber scene of the Walküre, as well as at the Entrance of the Toymakers' Guild in the Meistersinger. The triangle is used effectively in Liszt's Piano Concerto in E. Wagner uses cymbals excellently in the Venus scene of Tannhäuser. Note the use of castanets in the dance scene of the second act in Bizet's Carmen. The tambourine is used by Berlioz in his Roman Carnival Overture and in his

Childe Harold Symphony. The celeste is employed with good effect by Tschaikowsky in his Nutcracker Suite. The Glockenspiel is used only in passages of extreme sweetness. (Note the Feuer-Zauber scene in Wagner's Walküre, as well as Mozart's opera, The Magic Flute.)

The *wind-machine* consists of a simple sheet of canvass held against a revolving cylinder. As the cylinder increases in speed, the sound becomes higher in pitch, and vice versa. Besides being used in the orchestra, it is also used in the theater. R. Strauss employs it in his Don Quixote.

The *bagpipe* is one of the most interesting folk instruments. It dates from ancient days. Early bagpipes have been found in Persia and Greece. The Romans were particularly fond of their bagpipes, Nero having been an enthusiastic performer. Although always associated with Scotch music because of its use by the highland regiments, the bagpipe is still the instrument used by the shepherds of many lands, including Poland, Italy, Southern France, Scotland, and Ireland.

It takes its name from the leather bag which acts as a tone chamber for air blown into it by the player, who operates small bellows under his arm. Connected with the bag are two, sometimes three, drone pipes, all playing the same tune; a chamber pipe plays the melody. In its best-known form it has four pipes. One, the "chanter," has a double reed and eight holes, which give it a musical range of slightly over one octave. The other pipes, the drones, possess single reeds which produce one continuous sound.

When pastoral life became popular among the aristocrats in the days of Marie Antoinette, the bagpipe, under the name of "musette," was introduced at the French court. The dance called the "musette" took its name from the instrument. The bagpipe has numerous forms, such as the old German *Sackpfeife;* the French *cornemuse;* the *bignon* of Brittany; and the Calabrian *zumpogna*—all blown by mouth.

The *cymbalum* is a Hungarian variety of the old-time dulcimer, whose ancestry can be traced back to the Assyrians. The instrument, resembling a large zither, is played with two hammers.

The 'balalaika, of ancient Slavonic origin, is common among the Russians and Tartars. It is a narrow, shallow guitar, with two to four strings.

13. WHAT CONSTITUTES GOOD ORCHESTRA-PLAYING?

The critic and the lover of music may often be in doubt as to the merit of a composition, but they need not be so in regard to the worth of a performance. The qualities that make excellence in performance are all well known. It is necessary only that the ear be able to detect them. Differences of judgment about the technical qualities of a musical performance should not exist. It is not a matter of opinion but a matter of fact whether a person plays the organ or violin well, or sings well or purely. The critic should be personally unbiased and acquainted with the technique of the art in order to pronounce judgment upon a performance.

Now, what are the requirements of a good orchestral performance?

The modern orchestra is the result of a long development. It is a body of instruments selected for their ability to perform the most complex music. A first-class orchestra must possess a wide range of timbre, a great compass, the greatest flexibility, and a solid sonority which can be maintained from the finest *pp* to the heaviest *ff*.

It is impossible to convey in writing any idea of the timbres of the various instruments. These can only be learned by hearing them.

The characteristics of good orchestration (i.e., the art of writing for the orchestra) are: *solidity, balance of tone, contrast,* and *variety.* Solidity is obtained by a proper disposal of the harmony so that certain tones in the chords do not stand out too prominently at the expense of others. Balance of tone is a proper adjustment of the forces of the wood winds, the basses, the strings, and the percussions, so that one group shall not overpower the other. Contrast thus also gives variety, but variety is widened by mixing tints. More variety of tone-color may be obtained by having a flute play with a clarinet than a flute with an oboe, and different combinations produce different tone-colors.

Everyone should learn to discern these changes in tone-color and, also, accustom his ear to hearing the voices of all the instruments at once. Many persons do not hear anything definitely except the principal melody; wonderful effects are lost to them because they have not learned how to follow different voices of the orchestra. Everyone should acquire the habit of careful listening. Our ears are not used half as much as our eyes, and for this reason much pleasure is lost in listening to music.

What constitutes good orchestra-playing? Simply this— *"balance, equality and solidity of tone, precision, unanimity, flexibility, nuancing,* revelation of the value of the middle voices."

Balance of tone requires that one part of the orchestra should not overpower the other. It is the result partly of good orchestration, partly of the make-up of the orchestra, and partly of the work of the conductor. The quality of the tone should be rich, smooth, and sweet.

Solidity is partly due to orchestration, partly to good playing. Solidity is easier to recognize than to describe, but one cannot fail to notice the difference between a full, substantial, resonant body of tone and one that is thin, hollow, or nasal. Lack of solidity comes sometimes from poor balance; sometimes from poor acoustics in the hall; at other times from a lack of unanimity in the orchestra or from a paucity of instruments.

Precision means accuracy in beginning and ending a tone. The attack "of every phrase should be so precise that the orchestra speaks as one voice, and the end of a tone should be reached by every instrument at the same moment."

Unanimity demands that all the instruments should play exactly together all the time; there must be no running ahead or lagging behind.

Flexibility requires that music should never sound rigid, but should seem to come in a constant stream of pushing sound. Absence of flexibility is due sometimes to bad playing but more often to bad conducting.

Nuance is attained by giving attention to the manifold

differences of light and shade of *p, f, crescendo, diminuendo, ritardando,* etc.

14. CHAMBER MUSIC

Chamber music, such as the trio, quartet, quintet, sextet, octet, etc., is music for a combination of instruments. It has appealed to the cultivated musical ear ever since the evolution of the violin. Surely, the playing of stringed instruments, such as the early viols, must have laid a firm foundation for the performing of chamber music. It contains fascinating rhythmic, melodic, and harmonic patterns, exquisite refinements of form, and definite tone-color, in addition to sufficiently complicated polyphony. All chamber music is absolute music. It is the purest and the most exacting of all forms of musical art, and it may be compared to the essay in literature or to etching in the plastic arts. Like them it appeals only to the intelligent minority. Chamber music is free from a vulgar virtuosity. It is also free from the specious appeals of sensationalism. Eminent classic and modern composers have given us an almost limitless repertoire to provide our music-lovers with the pure enjoyment such music-making affords alike to listeners as well as players. To write a truly fine string quartet, for instance, requires a very good musician; any poor workmanship is easily detected. In chamber music there is concentration, an economy of style, a resolute exclusion of everything irrelevant. All finely conceived art employs the method of concentration—the omission of the irrelevant. The creation of pure four-part harmony, because of its comparative simplicity, requires that no voice may be secondary. No doubt, it is in the intimate unity of the four parts which comprise the string quartet that we find the charm which captivates, which makes the amateur player so earnest an enthusiast, and which compels the professional to strive for greater perfection.

There is a widespread belief that string-quartet music is purely mental; that it is incapable of inducing genuine musical delight; and that it is fully satisfying only to certain individuals who derive a pale kind of joy from sound patterns as such. This misunderstanding is an outgrowth of the perfectly sound idea that chamber music is a comparatively austere form of art. After all, two violins, a viola, and a cello—played together—have neither wide color nor dynamic range. Also, the combination lacks the strong rhythmic pulse which the piano gives to some other forms of chamber music. But to think that the string quartet plays purely mental music is entirely unjustified. Purely mental music would be an abomination; and if this charge were true, the string quartet would deserve all the disregard that it gets. The fact is that the string quartet is capable of an infinite number of expressive gradations—of color, dynamics, and rhythm—within its limited range. The gradations are small, of course, but they are adequate and effective in their way. The string quartet can convey emotions as surely as the orchestra, although, of course, they are quite different in kind. They are usually subtler, which accounts for the greater concentration which this form of music requires.

The listener to chamber music should expect the same excellence of performance as from the orchestra, with something additional. While it is not possible to obtain from three, four, five, or six instruments that massive solidity of tone which is expected from an orchestra, we should have in chamber music a perfect homogeneity of tone, an absolutely even quality and force, which perhaps no orchestra can equal. Of course, balance and quality of tone are essential to a good chamber-music performance, and they are taken for granted. In chamber music something more than unity is required for a truly fine performance; it requires give and take, with the leadership for a moment with one instrument, then with another, and shifting in delicate adjustments which, in turn, make almost imperceptibly for new balances. Each player and instrument is independent yet works for their mutual benefit, implying an interdependence and close association for a common end. Neither self-expression nor self-exploitation has a place in chamber music. All four players are willing to subordinate themselves when another part, for the moment, is more important; all have a conception of the whole tonal design, not only the single part that each is playing. Each instrument has its individual ends to achieve, but always in relation to the other instruments. This is just the opposite of solo playing. Homogeneity is obtained partly from good work by the players and partly from the quality of excellence of the instruments.

The string quartet occupies a unique position among musical creations. Though invented by Boccherini, it was greatly improved by Haydn, Mozart, and Beethoven. Haydn wrote 34 string quartets. He devised a style that gave the four instruments of the string quartet their measure of independence. His quartets have freshness, charm, humor, clearness, and sweetness, as well as strength. Mozart, who also wrote 34 quartets, and Beethoven and Schubert, though each carried forward new ideas, showed plainly at the outset how much they were indebted to Haydn. Schumann remains, except for Schubert, the most important chamber-music composer before Brahms. Mendelssohn contributed some pleasant works in which the classic and romantic were blended. Other notable string-quartet writers are: Dvorak, Smetana, Borodin, Tschaikowsky, Franck, Fauré, Debussy, Ravel, F. Schmitt, B. Bartok, P. Hindemith, and A. Schönberg.

Without question, more scrupulous care has been bestowed on the selection and refinement of the proper themes for the string quartet, and more energy and zeal have been displayed in the working out of the whole, than in the construction of many an opera. The string quartet may be considered as the test of genius, musicianship, taste, feeling, and facility of the composer. Consummate skill is required in handling themes, and the purest and most sincere feeling, in order to suffuse the whole with that moderate yet sufficient warmth necessary to excite and maintain the listener's true interest.

The favorite instrumentation of string quartets has always been two violins, viola, and cello—the chief representatives, since the days of Monteverde, of soprano, alto, tenor, and bass in the orchestra. The string quartet is best suited for the expression of musical ideas of a certain delicacy and refinement; anything like boldness and complexity is not attempted, because the volume of tone produced is rather weak.

The success of the string quartet rests wholly upon the sympathy and teamwork among the composer, the players, and the audience—a teamwork favored by, and based upon, good taste, solid study, and an interchange of refined feeling and intelligence. It is a delightful unanimity produced by fine music, good execution, and an intelligent audience.

Surely, *precision, unanimity, flexibility, and nuance* can all be carried to a finer finish in the performance of a trio, or a quartet, than in an orchestra. Three, four, five, or six players, inspired by devotion to their art, animated by a common sympathy, which is the result of long association, and directed by a deep and serious study of the masterpieces of chamber music, can play with a finish, with a subtlety of expression, which no orchestra can equal. Listening to chamber music—and this applies whether or not a piano is one of the instruments—the listener should always remember that *none of the players are to stand out as soloists;* in short, *balance of tone must be demanded.*

Chamber music, perhaps, is never so inspiring or grandiose as the music of a symphony orchestra. Chamber music is the most intimate form of music; and it is heard to the very best advantage in a large room or small hall. It is a form of musical entertainment in which the sensuous element is kept in the background; the most direct appeal is made to the judgment, and, next, to the emotions. To love and to understand quartet-playing is a sure evidence of superior taste in music. Anyone who desires to comprehend the esthetic qualities of music should attend chamber-music concerts often.

Fine chamber music lives up to certain simple standards of excellence. When listening to chamber music, bear in mind:

1. *The form.* It should be clear in its general outlines, with details elaborate enough to avoid monotony.
2. *The melodies.* They should be striking, individ-

ual, and of sufficient interest rhythmically to make up for lack of volume or tone-color.

3.   *The instruments.* They should be used to show as much independence as possible in the group, yet they should reveal a sort of polyphony from their related parts.

There is no reason why chamber music, played by a string quartet, trio, quintet, etc., should be less popular to the average audience than, for example, a song recital by a singer. Naturally, it is utterly impossible for a singer to give as much variety of expression or present as many contrasting characteristics as with the three, four, five, or six different instruments used in the performance of chamber music. The limit of the musical compass alone is at least a partial argument in favor of the trio, quartet, etc. When the composer writes for voice, he must limit himself to the possibilities of the voice. Besides these limited possibilities of compass, it is easy to overtax the voice's endurance. Bow instruments and the piano—as well as their players—need very few "breathing spells." The composer can almost write what he likes, from the deepest tones on the piano and cello to the highest tones on the violin and piano. Trills, turns, rapid scale passages, and other ornament needed to give the desired character to music, may be used freely by the composer. The bow instruments can sustain tones almost indefinitely. Polyphonic passages or movements may be written—yes, even imitation is at home in chamber music. Motives and phrases, antecedents and consequences, are flitted from one instrument to another. When one instrument sings a ballade, another may dance a jig, and still another sing a counterpart, and so on. Indeed, chamber music is almost perfection in its variety.

If the average audience would hear string quartets as often as it hears solo performers, chamber music would be much more popular. As we all know (or ought to know), the appreciation of any fine art is a matter of experience. To use Thomas' expression, "Familiar music is popular music." Familiar chamber music *is* popular music. And, by listening often, it does not take so very much chamber music to learn to appreciate it.

15. THE LAYMAN MUSIC CRITIC

Perhaps the most dangerous enemy of any musical enterprise is the amateur critic—not the reasonably well-informed layman who has views of his own concerning what he hears, but the person who knows next to nothing about music, yet knows what he likes. This critic is as eager to spread his opinions as any expert; and although musicians may smile at his absurdities, other amateur critics are likely to accept these notions as fact.

Strangely enough, some of the beliefs of this amateur are:

> That singing today is not what it used to be in the days of Caruso.
>
> That playing died out with Liszt, Rubinstein, and Busoni.
>
> That Mendelssohn is an uninteresting composer.
>
> That any opera other than one by R. Wagner is not good.
>
> That opera in English is only for the uneducated.
>
> That modern and ultramodern music is just a jumble of unpleasant noises.
>
> That many American singers and conductors lack training and experience.
>
> That any artist who has appeared for a long time is *passé.*

Beware of this amateur critic! He usually ruins the pleasure which a listener may find in a good concert.

The important mission of the true musician is twofold: *He interprets the works of composers;* and *he teaches others to listen intelligently.* Listening is just an intelligent habit. *Listening means thinking of what we hear,* while hearing does not require such mental effort. *Listening is active;* hearing is passive. *Intelligent listening means concentration, discrimination, imagination, information, and exercise of feeling.* All things being equal, the difference between those who get a definite impression from music and those who do not lies in the degree of applied sympathetic mental activity.

Listening to music should be considered like listening to anything else. One should learn early in life that *music is something to think about,* something more than a mere pastime. When the listener hears music by the classic masters, he is sure to expect a clear form, logical development of themes, artistic effects of contrast, and perfect symmetry. When listening to modern music, he may expect impressionistic or program music—effects of blended tonal colors that are to be taken as a whole and not analyzed into the simple tonal colors that make up its material; also, considerable artistic contrast and balance, but in a freer form than that of classic music. Much of the listener's time in hearing music is taken up in looking at his program to watch for coming events in the orchestra. He will do well to learn the plot of the piece before he hears it and thus enjoy the feeling of having solved a puzzle successfully. Merely following a string of effects, with a view to seeing what they mean, will add to true musical enjoyment.

A lecture or a book without logical arrangement and concise expression has little or no value. The same is true of music; *music likewise must contain ideas which are as well developed* as those in spoken or written language. Listening should bring a delight that is sensuous and intellectual, as well as emotional.

In criticizing a composition as a whole, notice that it is or is not:

1. Sufficiently melodious.
2. Logical and clear in its design as to form.
3. Distinct and effective in its rhythmic structure.
4. Sufficiently charming and full in its content from the point of view of harmony and modulation.
5. Sufficient in its demand for contrast and climax.
6. Written conveniently and sensibly with reference to the possibilities of the instrument or instruments for which it was designed.

7. Provided with an appropriate title.
8. As good in sound as it looks on paper.

In criticizing a performance as a whole, notice the following points:

1. *Solo singer.* Tone quality—whether thin, harsh, metallic, full, mellow, mild, nasal, hollow, etc.; vocalization; legato; enunciation; phrasing, and general interpretation; musicianship and temperament; appearance of soloist and demeanor upon stage; and kind of program offered.

2. *Chorus, vocal quartet, etc.* Tone quality; intonation; balance of tone; phrasing; shading; general interpretation; and ensemble.

3. *Instrumental soloist.* Tone quality; intonation; touch; vibrato; general technic; musicianship and temperament; appearance of soloist; poise; and kind of program offered.

4. *Trio, quartet, orchestra (small or large).* Quality and solidity of tone; balance of tone; precision (attack); unanimity; flexibility; shading; general interpretation; appearance and demeanor upon stage; and program offered.

5. *Accompanist.* Too loud or too soft; proper shading; proper tempo; whether indifferent or in sympathy with the soloist; appearance and demeanor upon stage.

Obviously, man is more than a mere body listening to sound. What is it that gives the sounds their value? What is it that makes one group of sounds preferable to another? Evidently, not only their sensual, intellectual, and emotional expression, but their sum total and *plus*—a universal significance or beauty which these sounds must have and for which our instinct searches. We are satisfied only when the music has that significance or that beauty.

THE PROFESSIONAL MUSIC CRITIC

What is criticism? Criticism is a sort of service; it is judging a thing by a certain standard, i.e., it notes strength as well as weakness; it is specific; it is constructive—it judges a person's innate ability, technic, and the works he has produced; it is limited, in general, to matter specifically aimed at; and it is polite. Criticism is a judgment, or detailed examination and review, a careful analysis of any subject with respect to its value, beauty, truth, or goodness. Matthew Arnold said it is "a disinterested endeavor to learn and propagate the best that is known and thought in the world." All this implies that a critic should understand the principles upon which the art that he criticizes is founded. In ancient times Aristotle was considered the greatest of all critics, as well as the first; but no one ever accused him of being unjust. Also, Plato, Socrates, and Aristophanes were all critics of their own work as well as the works of others, but their criticism was constructive, not destructive, in design or intent.

To be a good professional critic is *to be well informed, to possess knowledge, a good supply of common sense and sympathy, and exquisite taste.* And yet, with all this, criticism (any criticism) is just one writer's opinion. One of the first laws of good conversation is that all parties sign in advance any disclaimer of infallibility. Otherwise the free play of opinion becomes a dull setting forth of convictions. Exactly the same sort of thing applies to criticism. The possibility that the writer may be mistaken, that he may be basing his conclusions on unsound premises, must always be present in his mind and the minds of his readers. "The use of criticism . . . is to sift, not stamp, a work," says Margaret Fuller. William Foster Abthorn tells us that "Criticism should be nothing but an expression of enlightened opinion, as enlightened as possible, but never dogmatic."

It is surely not necessary to be an artist in order to be a good music critic. This has often been proved. It is more important that a critic who gives judgment on musical matters of all sorts—compositions, books, performances, etc.—should have a wide range of knowledge of the art as a whole than that he should himself be a practicing expert in one branch of the art. But he must be an authority in matters of taste and knowledge. We do not think artists would necessarily be alike as critics any more than they are as artists. There would be tolerant and intolerant ones. Naturally, their wide knowledge would always be useful; but the question of tolerance and intolerance involves more than any technical knowledge. It involves a state of mind, a certain point of view, plus sincere feeling.

The thing which the public abhors is the general incompetence of music critics and the lack of standards in their profession, with a consequent unevenness of preparation and an indefinite aim. Errors of fact, or wrong judgments and misconceptions resulting from an imperfect background —most of them imaginary, but a great many of which are real—are the subjects of numerous letters and conversations of the "what-is-the-world-coming-to" variety. Of course, we concede the fact that no sane professional critic claims to be infallible, and we also hasten to point out the obvious truth that no youth in his right mind ever chooses musical criticism as a profession and sets out deliberately to acquire the education and experience which the ideal critic needs. As a consequence, the ideal music critic hardly exists.

There are two reasons why hardly anyone tries to acquire this background. First, the chances of ever securing a position as a music critic are fantastically small. Our nation of about 150 million people employs only about sixty music critics at fair or good pay. Second, the time and effort involved are enormous. Even the most gifted person could hardly become a thoroughly competent critic with less than twenty years of part-time study, practice, and observation. Consequently, the procedure has been: first, get the position; then fill in the more obvious gaps in background as rapidly as possible. Naturally, this cannot take the place of years of unhurried preparation.

Obviously, a good way to acquire the schooling an art critic needs is to start in the smallest center and advance by regular steps to bigger positions and audiences. Thus, he can learn the rudiments of his task, which are those of sound repertorial principle and a really practical and helpful analysis of performances, compositions, or other subjects timely and applicable to the situation in hand. The art of music criticism should be developed and systematized. There should be the step-by-step progress from apprenticeship to master. There should be a sure promotion in his work and increasing opportunities for creative expression on the really challenging issues of his art.

However, in spite of this, we have made a fine beginning. Such men as Abthorp, Finck, Hale, Gilman, Henderson, Krehbiehl, Olin Downes, and others of the old-guard eastern critics, who virtually founded the profession, were men of much learning and solid integrity.

Critical ability is rare because it requires, besides the critical faculty, a deep and broad knowledge. A really good critic must possess these three general requirements: 1. Absolute impartiality and fearless honesty; 2. A thorough education and rich experience; and 3. A responsive temperament that reacts with enthusiasm to a fine performance, but also knows the shortcomings of mediocre work.

Such qualities can hardly be found in a music critic who is young. Youth precludes the possibility of having heard all the music necessary for a good critic. It takes years to acquire a rich and varied experience.

The question: Is music criticism really of value to the world? comes up again and again. Let us hear the opinions of two eminent musicians. Vincent d'Indy writes: "I consider that criticism is useless. I would even say that it is harmful. . . . Criticism generally means the opinion some man or other holds about another person's work. How can that opinion help forward the growth of art?" On the other hand, F. Weingärtner asserts: "Criticism is a sort of daily bread to art; it is indeed, the life-elixir of art. Criticism excites attention and awakens the interest of the public. Without art, no criticism; but without criticism, there can be no art. To be sure, criticism sometimes destroys that which has been carefully built up, but in the majority of cases it builds up, helps along, shows new paths, and directs into new fields." It is worth noticing that d'Indy, the foresworn enemy of criticism, was himself a critic, while Weingärtner was not.

The artist who denies the necessity of criticism, unless he means merely bad criticism, is, of course, also evading the question; for he too is face to face with the very necessity he disclaims. The singer or player is a critic of the music he interprets; and confronted with a free choice of material, treatment, and style, the composer has to exercise a critical faculty undreamed of by the majority of those who light-heartedly criticize his work in the press. He starts a process that, after all, is carried on later by every listener. As Oscar Wilde puts it: "The true artist is a critic, and the true critic is an artist." Wagner even wrote about his theories before he put them into practice; it was his press works and the intelligence of his arguments that appealed to the King of Bavaria before he heard one tone of his music. A difference of opinion is quite another thing from having no opinion at all. When a critic declares with conviction that to him J. S. Bach is boring, or that Debussy is dull, we become interested, for we have found a new point of view. Diversity enriches criticism, as it does the arts to which criticism is applied. Without it, there can be no individuality.

In a charming lecture, "Criticism and Beauty," A. J. Balfour reminds us: "That is for every man most lovable which he most dearly loves. That is for every man most beautiful which he most deeply admires. Nor is this merely a reiteration of the old adage that there is no disputing about tastes It goes far deeper; for it implies that, in the most important cases of all, a dispute about either love or beauty would not merely be useless; it would be wholly unmeaning. Let us, then, be content, since we can do no better, that our admiration should be even as our loves."

Since the days of Quintilian and Cicero, we have been told that in the long run the public is neither a bad judge nor a good critic. Popular judgment is in the nature of things ill considered and fleeting. It is the product of momentary gratification or disappointment.

"A taste or judgment does not come ready formed with us into the world. Whatever principles or materials of the kind we may possibly bring with us, a legitimate and just taste can neither be begotten, made, conceived, or produced without the antecedent labor and pains of criticism," wrote Shaftesbury.

Musical criticism is in a far more backward state than literary criticism.

One of the hardest tasks of a professional music critic is to find something to say about an art which transcends language, an art whose claim to greatness is based on its power to start where language ends. Strictly speaking, there is little to say about a Beethoven or Brahms symphony, for language's most colorful words hardly express the indefinite beauty of music. It has already taken the raw material of life and brought it into a perfect form. However, something must be said about its performance.

The music critic faces two grave dangers in the practice of his calling. One is that he will hear too much really good music and gradually blunt his sensibilities. The other is that he will suffer the shattering effect great art is likely to have on human conceit. We believe our ideas and ways of doing things are just about right; then we behold the artist at work and realize that there is much to learn from him.

It is what we understand and enjoy that shows the standard of our taste, not what we fail to understand and enjoy. It is better to enjoy thoroughly, and to appreciate by our own efforts a little that is good, than to be led by popular acclamation to enjoy something that is almost as good if its appreciation did not require any effort or thought. In short, we must begin the development of our taste, and the study of interpretation, by using our own faculties.

After we have found that we like to sing, play, or listen to a certain piece of music, the next step is to decide why we like it and why we *ought* to like it. Is it because of the dignity of the rhythm, the force or the sweetness of the melody, the richness of the harmony, the obviousness of its form, the extraordinary tone-color, the beauty of its orchestration, the subtlety of its expression, or the wonderful climax? It is of great advantage to know the important requisites of musical composition. Here they are: a mastery of the principal details of relations and associations of tone, harmony, counterpoint, etc., which may be acquired; an active and fertile imagination and discrimination, which may be cultivated and developed to a large extent; a strong and well-balanced intellect; and, finally, emotional passion, which cannot be acquired but must be innately present in the make-up of the individual.

There are emotional as well as physical excesses. *Emotional excesses have their physiological effects, and physical excesses have their emotional effects*. Current opinion would seem to indicate that the difference between these excesses are more of degree than of kind. Evidently, too much music —as certainly too much of anything else—will one day bring us to the point where the strength of the stimulus has to be increased. In music, very likely, that increase in strength means more vivid harmonic coloring, stronger and odder rhythms, more striking instrumental tone-color, and the like.

Let us discuss now the duties of the professional music critic.

The first duty of the professional music critic should be to *guide public judgment; to give an educational introduction of a work of art and its production; and to create a healthy atmosphere for music*. He should notice only such faults which can be corrected. Criticism worth writing—or reading —should always illuminate the art. It should state the reason for liking the music and the performance. The musician should seek to raise the standard of his playing or singing by conceding the rights of the critic and by encouraging honesty, intelligence, fearlessness, impartiality, and sympathy wherever he finds them. The artist will find in constructive criticism an intelligent recognition of what he is trying to do, as well as overt and implied advice on how to do it better. Thus, the critic who can state sound reasons for his beliefs and for the conclusions he has reached concerning a work of art or its interpretation, even if he is not altogether right in his premises, will inevitably carry more weight than one who merely gives his opinion, however sensitive and discriminating his taste may happen to be. Perhaps too many critics for the press depend upon effrontery and a copious use of technical phrases to carry them through. Of course, it is difficult to write musical criticism at once intelligent and intelligible; and neither confined to

a dry discussion of the mechanics of form and of craftsmanship nor running into vaguely rhetorical phrases. This
difficulty arises from the fact that the special subject matter
of music is difficult to express in language. The meaning of a
Sousa march, a Waldteufel, or a Strauss waltz, requires extraordinary literary skill to express in words. A musical idea
is as definite and as indefinite as perfume—or even more so,
for most odors can be associated with their sources, while
music is most itself when conveying sheer feeling, without
reference to any concrete subject whatsoever.

Really, the music critic is a historian of the contemporary
musical scene. He ought to describe the music more than
its effect upon him; and he ought to describe just what was
heard so that even the reader who did not attend the concert can get at least some conception of it. Then, too, we
need a more careful, sober first judgment and a little more
maturity in evaluating our later judgments. Music is a steady
stream of progress. There have always been masterpieces in
every period—and, for example, Stravinsky's Le Sacre in our
own time is one of them.

Music should not be discussed by a mere pedant nor by
a sentimentalist. Who selects the music critic? This question
might be asked oftener, since the destinies of many musicians, notably beginners, are frequently swayed to success
or failure by judgments passed (sometimes lightly) on their
best efforts. If the music reporter, eager for a slapdash, jour-
nalistic style, says the singer "gulped the simple aria Celeste
Aida," the singer is apt to lose an engagement. Surely, the
verdict of a critic is of importance and influence.

The art and music critic should say something which is
comprehensive in scope. Merely to point out random details
about a work of art is to destroy a strong interest in art
rather than to foster a growing love. We expect the critic to
apply standards that are more or less comprehensive in
scope, not merely those suited only to the particular art
work at hand. After all, to qualify as a critic a person must
have more than sensitivity to the sensuous and structural nature of things of beauty; he must have knowledge and understanding of the relations of art to other things in life—to

science, to philosophy, to morality, to economics, to religion. His evaluations must not be limited to the relations among art works themselves.

The second duty of the professional music critic should be *to arouse curiosity as well as interest, paving the way for popular comprehension.* Especially should he have sympathy for, and encourage, talent as well as genius. It is the duty of a music critic, as pointed out by R. Schumann (no doubt the greatest critic of them all), to encourage the great artist and to facilitate an understanding between him and the public. It would be an advantage if the critic told in advance the important numbers on the program and why we should hear them. He should excite our curiosity, discriminate, and prepare us to enjoy the music. If the artist is still unknown, he might tell us why he should be heard. The critic is a person qualified to think and to feel. He must have a good ear and be able to determine correct intonation in a singer or player, balance of tone in an orchestra or chorus, good technic, etc. He must be very broad in his taste, outspoken in his judgment, unalterable in his allegiance to high ideals.

The safest plan for a critic is to mix common sense with his personal preferences. Naturally, the judgment of the music critic is based upon his own musical ability as well as on experience gained while listening intelligently to many recitals, concerts, and operas. This gives him good insight into the worth of many compositions and potentialities of performers.

However, the profession of art and music criticism suffers in the public mind, and so in its practice, from the widespread feeling that it is easier to tell a person how to do a thing than to do it oneself. This is true, of course; but there is another side to criticism than merely telling some artist how to play a concerto or sing an aria. His largest job, of course, is that of interpretation. The critic must attempt, by an alternate means, to do exactly what the composer has tried to do. The artist endeavors, by means of his art, to communicate an idea—or, rather, a feeling—to others. Some are not sensitive to this feeling of the work of art. Here is the true opportunity of criticism—to step in and, by means of interpretation, aid the composer in communicating his feeling. Criticism should aid the public to assimilate musical works.

The artist will find in true criticism intelligent recognition of what he is trying to do and overt or implied advice on how to do it better. The art and music critic should illuminate some aspect of a work of art not otherwise apparent. A work of art means something different to each age; and with a changing outlook, judgments upon art must inevitably be altered. Of course, this does not mean that any point of view may be acceptable. But what we need is worthwhile criticism to the new interpretations of art, in keeping with the changing patterns of culture. In many cases, no doubt, criticism has been, and still is capable of revealing something new in a work of art, something beyond the ordinary. Strong personalities continually arise, become active, and give expression to changes in criticism. Indeed, these personalities develop amid shifting patterns of culture in which new judgments are wanted concerning new issues. Art is sensitive to the demands and the interpretative needs of the age. Art must continually be reinterpreted and reassessed in the light of changing ideals and experiences.

A good music critic must exert himself continuously in all directions so as to avoid becoming a one-sided Bach enthusiast, a Debussy hater, or a Ravel, a Stravinsky, or a Roy Harris promoter. This is one of the trials of the craft, and a reputation for fairness and catholicity of taste is surely desirable. Although it is manifestly impossible to keep one's likes and dislikes a complete secret, every event to be reviewed should be approached with a completely open mind. But, of course, judgment on such intangible things as music and art are, of necessity, personal.

Constructive criticism—the ideal criticism—may condemn or blame by ignoring. A critic who neither teaches nor inspires an audience or artist does not write criticism but unprofitable praise or blame. It should be incumbent upon music critics not to compare the efforts of modern composers with the harmonic and rhythmic processes in use long ago with which they have become familiar; but, rather, they should study the ideas of innovators, taking into consideration the trend of the new spirit and analyzing the nature of the impulses and aspirations awakened by a new way of living. The public must not be afraid of getting to like ultra-modern music, thinking that it might corrupt its taste for the older music. The playing of music of the classic and romantic school will not be stopped by the performance of modern music. Such modern music does not alter our conception of the existing laws of melody, harmony, form, tone-color, etc. If music gives us pleasure, inspiration, and education, if it means anything to us, then we owe something to music. We ought to be willing to listen to what a new composer has to say and hear a new work several times. Critics find it a difficult task to discriminate between that which arises from a mere desire to astonish and that which is an inevitable result of the evolution of things in general, due to the driving force of events and the development of culture in a different environment. This difficulty, however, is bound to give renewed life to the critical spirit itself, so often in danger of getting into a rut. After all, it is very important for the development of the art of music that those who "comment should keep intellectually on the same level with those who create."

Unfortunately, some music critics do not interest themselves sufficiently in the state of mind of their contemporaries; they do not attempt to find out what is new in music and directly inspired by the aspirations and impulses of the people. Many of our art critics brand modern works as anarchic; yet if they are to remain equal to their task, they need to acquire a suppleness and elasticity of mind possessed by specialists in physical science. Scientists are accustomed to constant changes and find them an inspiration to future progress. Music critics, likewise, must become accustomed to all the successive modifications of established ideas by new musical experiments. As an example of what we mean, it is only necessary to listen to the harmonies of a fundamental fifth to understand that all tones placed side by side may be justified, even though they appear most complicated.

The music critic who cannot play any instrument or read notes must hear a work performed many times in order to understand it; though it must be admitted that there is such a gift as musical intuition. Some persons have the power of immediately grasping the musical contents of a new work, even at a single imperfect performance, that seems amazing to many a highly trained academic musician. This re-creative gift is closely related to the creative gift of the composer. To be sure, every great work of art requires for its full appreciation a sensibility as fine as that of its creator. The critic should always take the standpoint of the artist and appraise the work in accordance with the completeness with which it fulfills its author's intentions. Criticism should be an independent agent, an art in itself at least one step ahead of the art upon which it comments, a source of vitality to the working artist, and a source of ideas to the art-minded public.

The music critic applies his standard. He grasps details in their proper order and sees how they contribute to the fulfillment of the composer's structural design and emotional conception. He listens discriminatingly. Because of his experience and his knowledge of the principles of art, he knows what to look for and can grasp relationships as well as perceive details. His memory stores a number of masterpieces which he is able to compare with one another and use as standards for the appraisal of other works. He is well prepared to grasp the real significance of what he sees and hears. Out of this discipline comes judgment, and finally, taste and enjoyment. Surely, the true music critic is one who sees below the surface of things, who distinguishes the essentials from the accidents—the spirit within the form. When criticism is inspired by the highest purpose, in which duty blends with privilege, then it is at its very best.

As said before, the first duty of the professional music critic should be to guide public judgment. He must be dogmatic in this matter; for he can only declare something is beautiful after he has won the confidence of his readers. When he uses the word "beautiful" with reference to compositions or their interpretations, others, too, understand the full richness of its meaning. The development of critical judgment is largely accomplished by means of contact and intellectual experience with *the Beautiful, the True, and the Good,* as well as by comparison. The critic should show concretely how his judgments apply to the work of art. Theory is no substitute for keen perception, nor can it take the place of experience. A critic who fails to show superior knowledge of the subject of which he speaks simply lacks basic authority. To prove his criticism, the critic should have a wide background of experience in his art as well as strong sensitivity to, and keen perception of, the work of art under consideration. No one should undertake to write criticism who knows only a single type of art.

The third duty of the professional music critic should be *to do away with nonentities and to discourage mediocrities.* "Mediocre music-making is a sin against art," Liszt once wrote. As about 75% of all music-making is mediocre or worse, it is a big job for the music critic to do the weeding. Only a small minority are musically gifted. This raises the question: What should a critic's attitude be toward the study and practice of music? Naturally, he believes in a policy of unquestioning enthusiasm for the art as a whole. Yet do we realize the difficulties of maintaining such a policy?

We must not lose sight of the fact that too much enthusiasm may cause us to blur the distinction between the cultural and the economic aspect of music. The study of music is not an *open sesame* to an easy and lucrative life; on the other hand, the study of music has great value in promoting happiness. Of course, the music critic ought to tell the truth. In so doing, he can offend no honest teacher of music. In fact, he can probably help, for the fine arts need more attention than the industrial arts. Without question, nearly everybody nowadays hears too much music, and many persons perform too much. We would, to a much greater extent, enjoy what we hear and perform if we had less music, compositions carefully chosen and studied not necessarily from their technical aspects but from the point of view of understanding and consequent appreciation.

Every normal person should have the opportunity to study music early in life. This study should be continued to a point where his capabilities or lack of them become clearly noticeable. Above all, more attention should be given to training people for the enjoyment of music—in short, to intelligent listening. Where real talent is found, there is no question whether to encourage it. However, we must mention that even though a person has a grim determination to make music, either as a singer, player, or teacher, it simply should not be encouraged in the majority of cases. More often than not, the practice of a fine art will not free us from economic necessities. The number of persons who make a good living from music in any city is comparatively small. We must not assume that the economic law of supply and demand is going to change, out of deference to the supply. It is the duty of the music critic to encourage the study of music for its own sake, and to give a true account of the present status of the profession. Indeed, many are called, but few are chosen; creative genius is most rare, and great interpreters, the priests of art, are almost as rare. Unfortunately, interpretation almost invariably means obtruding the personal character of the performer into the performance. Thus, we get all sorts of readings of famous compositions—sentimental, erratic, intellectual, old cynic, young miss, feeling-intellectual, and so forth.

Composers and performers should be judged by their best achievements. Artists and works of genius should be helped along by dwelling on their merits and ignoring flaws, as long as the merits of the performer or the music make for good on the whole. Also, remember that a professional music critic who listens to the first group of pieces only may express keen disappointment; while another, who listens perhaps to the last group of pieces only, may depart feeling wildly enthusiastic. Not a few artists are apt to be nervous and need thawing out before they can do themselves justice. The *constructive criticism, the ideal kind, condemns or blames by ignoring*. The sooner a bad concert is forgotten, the better; if the concert was on the whole good, excepting one or two minor slips, the audience promptly forgets the slips in its total pleasure. The wise critic helps in forgetting—he does not mention the slips.

The main thing for the performer is *to feel something*. So much playing and singing is uninteresting because performers are not conscious of any emotion or feelings. They allow their minds to wander, instead of entering into the inspiration of the composer and touching a higher, finer part of themselves and their listeners. Truly, there is a mystic communion in music played by the *whole self* which satisfies and helps, but this kind of music is rarely heard. There must be accuracy in music. We must be true to ourselves in order to deliver the higher message. To sing or to play with expression means to be absorbed in the beauty and exaltation of the music; it means that we have forgotten ourselves and have entered into a higher realization of beauty and power.

From all this, it follows that music is only performed perfectly when it comes to us absolutely pure and universal, unconditioned by time or place. When the great artist speaks, whether in stone, cement, marble and steel, clay or bronze, colors, pencil or crayon, in words or in tones, he speaks to a world that is beyond time or place, beyond all ideas of good or evil, beyond today or yesterday. He speaks of that world because it is the world in which he dwells. How music is to be performed so as to have that universality, that freedom from time or place, that rare and final beauty, no man knows; but many of us know that quality when we hear it.